AF323118

INTER-KOREAN RELATIONS:
PROBLEMS AND PROSPECTS

In post–Cold War thinking, North Korea was expected to collapse and be absorbed into a single Korean state by the democratic regime in South Korea. Fifteen years later, this has not happened, and June 2000 saw a summit marking the warmest inter-Korean relations yet. Over that time period, the two Korean states found instead new mechanisms and methods for interacting with each other on the level of *de facto* if not yet completely *de jure* sovereign states and have begun to overcome some of the shadows cast by the partition and violent war that befell the peninsula following World War II. This book examines the origins, dynamics, and impacts of these multi-level relations between North and South Korea, situating them variously as two incomplete nation-states, as a single national entity, and within a larger international environment. The contributors demonstrate how inter-Korean relations have fostered new forms of conflict management and reconciliation on the peninsula.

Samuel S. Kim is Adjunct Professor of Political Science and Senior Research Scholar at the Weatherhead East Asian Institute, Columbia University. He is the author or editor of 21 books on Northeast Asia and published more than 150 articles in edited volumes and leading international relations journals.

Books Written Under the Auspices of the Center for Korean Research
The Weatherhead East Asian Institute
Columbia University 1998–2004

Samuel S. Kim, ed., *North Korean Foreign Relations in the Post-Cold War Era* (Hong Kong and New York: Oxford University Press, 1998).

Samuel S. Kim, ed., *Korea's Globalization* (New York: Cambridge University Press, 2000).

Laurel Kendall, ed., *Under Construction: The Gendering of Modernity, Class, and Consumption in the Republic of Korea* (Honolulu, Hawaii: University of Hawaii Press, 2001).

Samuel S. Kim, ed., *The North Korean System in the Post-Cold War Era* (New York: Palgrave, 2001).

Charles K. Armstrong, ed., *Korean Society: Civil Society Democracy, and the State* (London: Routledge, 2002).

Samuel S. Kim, ed., *Korea's Democratization* (New York: Cambridge University Press, 2003).

Samuel S. Kim, ed., *Inter-Korean Relations: Problems and Prospects* (New York: Palgrave, 2004).

Inter-Korean Relations: Problems and Prospects

Edited by
Samuel S. Kim

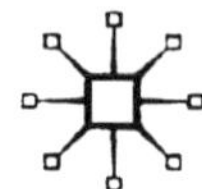

INTER-KOREAN RELATIONS
© Samuel S. Kim, 2004

First published 2004 by
PALGRAVE MACMILLAN™
175 Fifth Avenue, New York, N.Y. 10010 and
Houndmills, Basingstoke, Hampshire, England RG21 6XS
Companies and representatives throughout the world

PALGRAVE MACMILLAN is the global academic imprint of the Palgrave Macmillan division of St. Martin's Press, LLC and of Palgrave Macmillan Ltd. Macmillan® is a registered trademark in the United States, United Kingdom and other countries. Palgrave is a registered trademark in the European Union and other countries.

ISBN 1–4039–6477–7 hardback

Library of Congress Cataloging-in-Publication Data

Inter-Korean relations : problems and prospects / edited by Samuel S. Kim.
    p. cm.
  Includes bibliographical references and index.
  ISBN 1–4039–6477–7
    1. Korea (South)—Relations—Korea (North) 2. Korea (North)—Relations—Korea (South) 3. East Asia—Relations—Korea (North) 4. Korea (North)—Relations—East Asia. 5. East Asia—Relations—Korea (South) 6. Korea (South)—Relations—East Asia. 7. International organization. I. Kim, Samuel S., 1935–

DS910.2.K7157 2004
327.519305195—dc22   2004044255

A catalogue record for this book is available from the British Library.

Design by Newgen Imaging Systems (P) Ltd., Chennai, India.

First edition: September 2004
10 9 8 7 6 5 4 3 2 1

Printed in the United States of America.

Contents

List of tables and figures		vii
Contributors		ix
Preface		xiii
Chapter One	Introduction: Managing the Korean Conflict *Samuel S. Kim*	1
Chapter Two	Inter-Korean Relations: A South Korean Perspective *Scott Snyder*	21
Chapter Three	Inter-Korean Relations: A North Korean Perspective *Charles K. Armstrong*	39
Chapter Four	Inter-Korean Economic Relations *Samuel S. Kim and Matthew S. Winters*	57
Chapter Five	China and Inter-Korean Relations: Beijing as Balancer *Andrew Scobell*	81
Chapter Six	Japan in Inter-Korean Relations *C.S. Eliot Kang*	97
Chapter Seven	Russia in Inter-Korean Relations *Elizabeth Wishnick*	117
Chapter Eight	The U.S. Role in Inter-Korean Relations: Container, Facilitator, or Impeder? *Victor D. Cha*	139
Chapter Nine	The Legal and Institutional Approach to Inter-Korean Relations *Jeong-Ho Roh*	159
Chapter Ten	International Organizations and the Inter-Korean Peace Process: Traditional Security Versus Nontraditional Security *Shin-wha Lee*	175
Chapter Eleven	The Challenges of Peacefully Reunifying the Korean Peninsula *Abraham Kim*	197
Index		219

List of Tables and Figures

Tables

4.1 South Korean–North Korean trade (1989–2002) — 58

4.2 Inter-Korean trade for the year preceding and following the October 2002 nuclear revelation by the DPRK — 58

4.3 Comparison of major economic indexes of North and South Korea (2002) — 61

4.4 Chronology of Inter-Korean agreements, 1972–2003 — 69

8.1 U.S. role in Inter-Korean Relations (IKR) — 140

8.2 Images of the United States and North Korea — 147

8.3 Negative attitudes toward the United States and North Korea by age distribution — 148

8.4 South Korean attitudes toward the United States (June 2003) — 150

8.5 South Korean views of the Bush administration's policy toward North Korea — 150

8.6 Attitudes on the withdrawal of U.S. forces from Korea — 150

9.1 LWR construction status as of end of August 2003: Overall completion—32.85% — 171

10.1 Chronology of North Korea–UN Relations, 1947–91 — 177

10.2 South and North Korea's Membership in International Organizations (2001) — 179

Figures

4.1 South Korean–North Korean trade (1989–2002) — 64

4.2 South Korean–North Korean transactional trade (1989–2002) — 64

4.3 South Korean–North Korean commission-based processing trade (1989–2002) — 65

4.4 South Korean–North Korean non-transactional trade (1989–2002) — 66

4.5 Inter-Korean visits — 68

Contributors

Samuel S. Kim (M.I.A. and Ph.D., Columbia) is Adjunct Professor of Political Science and Senior Research Scholar, the Weatherhead East Asian Institute, Columbia University. He is the author or editor of 21 books on East Asian international relations and world order studies including, most recently, *Korea's Democratization* (ed., 2003); *The International Relations of Northeast Asia* (ed., 2004); and *The Two Koreas in the World Community* (forthcoming). He has published more than 150 articles in edited volumes and international relations journals, including *American Journal of International Law, Asian Perspective, China Quarterly, Harvard China Review, International Interactions, International Journal, International Organization, Journal of East Asian Studies, Journal of Peace Research, World Politics,* and *World Policy Journal.*

Charles Armstrong (Ph.D., Chicago) is Associate Professor of History and Acting Director of the Weatherhead East Asian Institute at Columbia University. He has published widely on Korean politics and modern history, including most recently *Korean Society: Civil Society, Democracy and the State* (ed., 2002) and *The North Korean Revolution, 1945–1950* (2003). A two-time Fulbright scholar, he is currently writing a book entitled *Tyranny of the Weak: North Korean and the International System.*

Victor cha (Ph.D., Columbia) is Associate Professor of Government in the Edmund Walsh School of Foreign Service and holds the D.S. Song-Korea Foundation Chair in Asian Studies at Georgetown University. He is the award-winning author of *Alignment Despite Antagonism: The United States–Japan–KoreaSecurity Triangle* (1999) (winner of the 2000 Ohira Book Prize) and Nuclear North Korea: A Debate on Engagement Strategies (2003) (with David Kang). Cha has written articles on international relations and East Asia in journals including *Survival, Foreign Affairs, International Security, International Studies Quarterly, Political Science Quarterly, Orbis, and Asian Survey.* He is a former John M. Olin National Security Fellow at Harvard University, two-time Fulbright Scholar, and Hoover National Fellow at Stanford. He is currently Director of the Project on American Alliances in Asia at Georgetown, and is writing a book manuscript entitled The Cradle or the Brass Ring: The United States–China Battle for Influence in Korea.

C. S. Eliot Kang is serving at the U.S. Department of State as a senior advisor in the office of Regional Security and CSBMs, Bureau of Political-Military Affairs. His contribution to this volume was written before he joined the U.S. Department of States and reflects solely his views. He is on leave as an associate professor of political science at Northern Illinois University. He received his Ph.D. from Yale. He also studied at Princeton and received his A.B., *summa cum laude*, from Cornell. He has taught at the University of Pennsylvania and was a research fellow in at The Brookings Institution. He was also an International Affairs Fellow of the Council on Foreign Relations and a visiting fellow at the Japan Institute of International Affairs. His professional background includes working for the investment banking firm of Dillon, Read, & Co., Inc. Specializing in security and economic issues of Northeast Asia, he has published numerous book chapters and articles in publications such as *International Organization*, *Comparative Strategy*, and *World Affairs*.

Abraham Kim (Ph.D. Candidate, Columbia) is a national security analyst for the Wargaming and Analytical Research Division at the Science Application International Corporation (SAIC). Currently, he is finishing his dissertation, entitled, "Healing Divided Nations: How and Why States Peacefully Reunify?" Mr. Kim formerly served as a policy analyst at the Center for Strategic and International Studies and has written extensively on Asian security issues. Some of his works have appeared in *The Asian Wall Street Journal*, *Washington Times*, *Journal of Korean Defense Analyses*, and *Journal of International Affairs*. Kim received his B.A. from Boston University and an M.A. from Harvard University.

Shin-wha Lee, Associate Professor at the Department of Political Science and International Relations, Korea University, received her Ph.D. (International Relations) from the University of Maryland at College Park and held a Postdoctoral Fellowship at the Center for International Affairs, Harvard University (1994–97). Among her previous positions were Researcher at the World Bank (1992); Special Advisor to "the Rwandan Independent Inquiry" appointed by UN Secretary General Kofi Annan (1999); Chair's Advisor of ASEAN+3 East Asian Vision Group (2000–01); and Coordinator of UNESCO Chair on Peace, Democracy and Human Rights (2000–present). She has published more than 40 articles (in English and Korean) covering the fields of environmental and human security and the role of the UN, international organizations, and NGOs. Her recent books include *Environment Matters: Conflicts, Refugees & International Relations* (Seoul and Tokyo: WHDI Press, 2001), a translated volume (2002) of Ted Robert Gurr's *People vs. States: Minorities at Risk in the New Century*, and a UNESCO report on *Ethical, Normative and Educational Frameworks for the Promotion of Human Security in East-Asia* (2004).

Jeong-Ho Roh (J.D., Columbia) is Director of the Center for Korean Legal Studies at Columbia Law School. Previously, he specialized in mergers and acquisition and international law at Skadden, Arps, Slate, Meagher & Flom (New York) and Bae, Kim & Lee (Seoul, Korea). He also served as a legal officer at the Korean Ministry of National Defense. He is currently serving as Legal Advisor to the Korean Ministry of National Unification on the North Korean light water reactor project and is a member of the Legal Assistance Council at the Korean Ministry of Justice. He is a coeditor and contributor of *Constitutional Handbook of Korean Unification* (2003).

Andrew Scobell is Associate Research Professor in the Strategic Studies Institute at the U.S. Army War College and Adjunct Professor of Political Science at Dickinson College. He earned a Ph.D. in political science from Columbia University. Scobell's research focuses on political and military affairs in the Asia Pacific Region. He is the author of *China's Use of Military Force: Beyond the Great Wall and the Long March* (Cambridge University Press, 2003).

Scott Snyder is a Senior Associate in the International Relations program of The Asia Foundation and Pacific Forum CSIS, and is based in Washington, DC. He spent four years in Seoul as Korea Representative of The Asia Foundation during 2000–03. Previously, he has served as a Program officer in the Research and Studies Program of the U.S. Institute of Peace, and as Acting Director of The Asia Society's Contemporary Affairs Program. He has recently edited with L. Gordon Flake a study entitled *Paved With Good Intentions: The NGO Experience in North Korea* (2003), and is author of *Negotiating on the Edge: North Korean Negotiating Behavior* (1999). Snyder received his B.A. from Rice University and an M.A. from the Regional Studies East Asia Program at Harvard University. He was the recipient of an Abe Fellowship, administered by the Social Sciences Research Council, in 1998–99, and was a Thomas G. Watson Fellow at Yonsei University in South Korea in 1987–88.

Matthew S. Winters is a graduate student in political science at Columbia University with international relations as a field of concentration. His research is focused on globalization and the changing political roles of international institutions. He received a B.A. in political science (*summa cum laude*) from Columbia University, composing two senior theses, one on globalization and one on the role of *Chosen Soren* in Japanese–Korean relations.

Elizabeth Wishnick is a research associate at the Weatherhead East Asian Institute at Columbia University and a visiting scholar in the Political Science Department of the Graduate Faculty of Political and Social Science at New School University. In 2002–03 she was a Fulbright Visiting Scholar at Lingnan University in Hong Kong. She is the author of *Mending Fences: The Evolution of Moscow's China Policy from Brezhnev to Yeltsin* (Seattle: University of Washington Press, 2001) and of numerous articles on great power relations and regional development in Northeast Asia, published in *Asian Survey, NBR Analysis, SAIS Review, Journal of East Asian Affairs, Issues and Studies*, and *Perspectives Chinoises*, as well as in several edited volumes. She received a Ph.D. in Political Science from Columbia University, an M.A. in Russian and East European Studies from Yale University, and a B.A. from Barnard College, and speaks both Russian and Chinese.

Preface

As if to compensate for their failures to predict the end of the Cold War, German reunification, and the collapse of the Soviet Union, many pundits in the 1990s were seen committing the opposite fallacy of prematurely optimistic predictions about the collapse of the Democratic People's Republic of Korea (DPRK) and the reunification of the Korean peninsula. In the first half of the 1990s, especially in the wake of Kim Il Sung's sudden death in July 1994, the predicted lifespan of the DPRK ranged from months to a few years, and it had to be updated as North Korea kept passing deadlines for its obituary. Speculation about the coming collapse of North Korea is still present, but it is no longer as widespread, as assured or, as popular as it once was. Few South Koreans expect—or even want—to see reunification in their lifetimes, even as Pyongyang remains alarmed by and armed against a German-style reunification by absorption.

Artificially divided by an accident of history, North and South Korea have long had mutual dreams of hegemonic reunification, of bringing the Korean people together under their own mantle. As a consequence, hostility and fear have prevailed on the Korean peninsula since its division in 1945 with the two Korean states battling against each other in the fratricidal politics of competitive legitimation and delegitimation. With the end of the Cold War, the situation on the peninsula has been altered in some ways but not others. On the surface, the harsh reality of Cold War relations still seems to prevail as two militaries stare at each other across the heavily armed DMZ (demilitarized zone). But in more subtle ways, the fundamental nature of inter-Korean relations has shifted, both impacted by and impacting upon domestic politics, regional politics, and the role of international institutions.

These changes were symbolized succinctly by the June 2000 inter-Korean summit that saw Kim Dae Jung, then-president of South Korean, travel to the North Korean capital of Pyongyang. Despite all the South's unification pomp that surrounded the historic summit, and despite the habit-driven claim in the North that these are "the greatest successes in the reunification movement since the country was divided into two parts over half a century back," the great paradox surfaced when President Kim Dae Jung and Chairman Kim Jong Il embraced each other before global television audiences, symbolically signaling their acceptance of each other's legitimacy. Even more remarkably, the front page of the June 15, 2000, issue of *Rodong Sinmun*, the official organ of the Korean Workers' Party, introduced the South Korean leader to the domestic audience for the first time as "Daehan Minkuk Daetongryong Kim Dae

Chung" (Republic of Korea President Kim Dae Jung) and as a co-signer of North–South Joint Declaration. The summit seemed to have brought the two Koreas down to earth from their respective dreams of hegemonic unification, to a position of peaceful coexistence as two *de facto* if not fully *de jure* sovereign states. And the fact that inter-Korean relations have continued in the face of provocations ranging from naval incursions to missile tests to nuclear weapons programs testifies to the depth of inter-Korean relations.

Looking at the history of interaction between North and South Korea over the past 15 years, one realizes that a set of variegated influences of variable intensity have effected the peculiar pattern of engagement in the face of continuing enmity—or perhaps of enmity in the face of incremental engagement. Looking for singular explanations at either the domestic or the international level yields more questions than answers about the jagged patterns of inter-Korean relations. No single mono-causal theory or variable provides much leverage in explaining the paradox of continuing economic, social, and cultural exchanges and cooperation in the midst of armed standoff on the divided peninsula.

The Korean conflict both influences and is influenced by the regional politics of Northeast Asia. During the Cold War, East–West conflict was dominant in the region, and today its shadow lingers over the two Korean states, albeit in attenuated form. The four major external powers—China, Russia, Japan, and the United States—in many ways continue to play out a great power game in Korea. At the same time, however, there is a need not to put all emphasis on the international setting. Domestic politics and dyadic interactions have a significant role to play in the shaping of inter-Korean relations. And new international actors—such as global and regional organizations—have new and innovative conflict-management roles to play in moderating the Korean conflict and fostering the inter-Korean peace process.

The asymmetries of inter-Korean relations, the geostrategic location, and the divided polity—to name a few of the geopolitical and geoeconomic attributes of the two Koreas—make examining the Korean conflict both interesting and challenging for theory, policy, and comparative analysis. The odd mix of stasis and innovation since the end of the Cold War, however, makes it imperative that both scholars and policy-makers track and explain such dynamics. Collapsist arguments about North Korea have too long been used as an excuse not to study inter-Korean relations. Today it is increasingly clear that engagement across the DMZ or around the DMZ via multiple channels and actors may be helping to avoid collapse in the North and may aid in averting the apocalypse on the Korean peninsula.

This volume is designed to parse inter-Korean relations from several vantage points in order to identify and explain the origins, dynamics, and implications of relations between the two divided and incomplete Korean states. The contributors look at the different arenas in which inter-Korean relations are played out and suggest pathways that have taken the relations between the two countries to the point at which they are today and that will determine their future direction and form. In contrast to accounts that keep the variables strictly at the domestic or at the international level, this book analyzes inter-Korean relations critically with all the relevant factors included. It is the interplay of these varied causal factors that helps explain why and how inter-Korean relations continue to be sustained and what possibilities and limitations are in store for the peace process on the divided Korean peninsula.

The introductory chapter presents a conflict management framework for examining status competition—even legitimacy war—between two highly competitive states still technically at war. Chapters two and three look at the domestic factors behind inter-Korean relations as well as the supporting logics, while chapter four posits a functional logic to explain growing inter-Korean economic, social, and cultural exchanges and cooperation despite the continuing military standoff at the DMZ. Chapters five through eight bring in the roles that the great powers of Northeast Asia—China, Japan, Russia, and the United States—have played and will continue to play in inter-Korean relations. Chapters nine and ten situate inter-Korean relations institutionally and in a broader international context, and chapter eleven offers some critical assessments of the outer possibilities and limitations of Korean reunification in the uncertain years ahead.

This project was born out of an international conference under the auspices of the Center for Korean Research of Columbia University's Weatherhead East Asian Institute. The event was held May 31–June 1, 2002, at Columbia University, where contributors and other participants engaged in a fruitful exchange of ideas and assessments about the progress and prospects of inter-Korean reconciliation. I would like to thank the chapter contributors for their originality, hard work, and collaborative spirit on meeting not only the high standards of scholarship but also for coping with a series of extended deadlines for the seemingly endless revision, as well as update requests racing against the rapidly changing headlines and moving targets on the turbulent trajectories of inter-Korean relations, especially since the October 2002 revelations of North Korea's highly enriched uranium (HEU) program. Moreover, this project, like many previous research endeavors sponsored by the Center for Korean Research, would not have been possible without a generous research grant from the Korea Foundation.

In addition, I would also like to express my gratitude to my colleagues at the Weatherhead East Asian Institute for their continuing support and encouragement. I am grateful to my graduate student research assistant, Emma Chanlet-Avery, for her characteristically skillful, efficient, and multitasking work in the library and on-line research, and for stage-managing the preparation of the book manuscript during the academic year of 2002–03.

Finally, it was a pleasure to work with Palgrave (formerly St. Martin's Press) in the production of this book. I am particularly grateful to Anthony Wahl for his unflagging support and encouragement and for his role as an invaluable collaborator and navigator throughout the publication process. Special thanks are due to Heather Van Dusen and Ian Steinberg for their efficient steering of the manuscript through the various stages of production. The usual disclaimer still applies: the editor and chapter authors alone are responsible for whatever local, inter-Korean, regional, and global errors in fact or interpretation that may still remain in the book.

Samuel S. Kim
New York, New York
December 2003

Chapter One

Introduction: Managing the Korean Conflict

Samuel S. Kim

No division of a nation in the present is so astonishing in its origin as the division of Korea; none is so unrelated to conditions or sentiment within the nation itself at the time the division was effected; none is to this day so unexplained; in none does blunder and planning oversight appear to have played so large a role. Finally, there is no division for which the U.S. government bears so heavy a share of the responsibility as it bears for the division of Korea.

—Gregory Henderson (1974)[1]

So—you must destroy a South Korean plane. That country, as you know, has been in considerable turmoil recently. The political climate is more volatile than any time since the War of Liberation. Their constitution is being revised, and there are elections to be held toward the end of this year. By destroying this plane we intend to increase this sense of chaos and ultimately to prevent the Olympic Games from taking place in Seoul. Other nations will not want to risk their athletes, for fear that either their planes will be destroyed or that once in Seoul their athletes will not be safe from terrorist attacks.

—The Director to Kim Hyun Hee (1987)[2]

It can be said that there exists on the Korean Peninsula at present only confrontation between the Koreans in the north and the south and the United States.

—Joint New Year (2003) Editorial[3]

In the early 1990s, for the first time since the Korean War (and particularly in the wake of German reunification), it became common to hear and even faddish to assert that the issue of Korean reunification by Southern absorption was no longer a question of "whether" but of "how and when." And yet to think about Korean reunification today is to encounter a paradox. At no time since the end of World War II, when Korea was liberated and divided, has the prospect of Korean reunification perhaps seemed closer, yet never has the time horizon been so uncertain or extended. Fifteen years after the end of the Cold War, reunification no longer seems imminent, but the aspiration retains an aura of inevitability.

The rapid succession of momentous changes in the international system from 1989 to 1991—the crumbling of the Berlin Wall, German reunification, the end of the Cold War, and the demise of the Soviet Union and international communism—created the first wave of euphoria that divided Korea too was heading inexorably toward reunification. Then, in the wake of the sudden death of North Korean

President Kim Il Sung in July 1994, there was a second wave of predictions by many that North Korea would either collapse within six months or experience a German-style reunification by absorption within three years. Even South Korean President Kim Young Sam (1993–97) embraced this "collapsist" view, seeing North Korea as a "broken airplane" that would be headed for a crash landing, ushering in reunification by absorption. At a summit meeting held on Cheju Island in April 1996, leaders of South Korea and the United States agreed to promote jointly a two-plus-two formula—the Four Party Peace Talks—even as they privately arrived at the conclusion that collapse in the North could come as soon as within two or three years.[4]

A third great wave of commotion about unification surrounded the historic inter-Korean summit of June 13–15, 2000 (this time more within the Korean peninsula than beyond it). Despite the official claim in the North that these events were "the greatest successes in the reunification movement since the country was divided into two parts over half a century back,"[5] a great paradox surfaced when President Kim Dae Jung and Chairman Kim Jong Il embraced each other before global television audiences, symbolically signaling their acceptance of each other's legitimacy. The summit seemed to have brought the two Koreas down to earth from their respective dreams of hegemonic unification to a position of peaceful coexistence as two separate states. While Pyongyang paid mandatory lip service to the supreme task of building "one nation, one state with two governments and two systems" without delay under the "federation system" (formerly described as the "confederation system"), in the wake of the summit it proclaimed publicly for the first time that "the issue of unifying the differing systems in the north and the south as one may be *left to posterity to settle slowly in the future*."[6] Throughout the months before and after the summit, Kim Dae Jung repeated his now familiar line that he did not expect Korean reunification on his watch or in his lifetime.

The paradox of survival in the North[7] in the midst of the continuing economic and nuclear crisis raises several key questions for scholars and policy-makers concerned about the future of the Korean peninsula. The central issue for this volume is to track and explain the dynamic interplay of domestic, inter-Korean, and external factors that shape and constrain inter-Korean relations. What is the nature of the Korean conflict in post–Cold War Northeast Asia? What really explains the enduring inter-Korean conflict in light of the post–Cold War global trend of rising ethnonational conflicts in many of the trouble spots of the world? These conflicts had been suppressed and overlain by the East–West conflict during the Cold War, but the inter-Korean conflict, in one of the oldest and most homogenous nations in the world, has nothing to do with ethnicity. Is inter-Korean cooperation more or less likely when the four major external powers—China, Russia, Japan, and the United States—are directly engaged in the resolution of the conflict? To what extent and in what specific ways can the major powers meet the post–Cold War challenge of preventing, controlling, restraining, or encapsulating the inter-Korean conflict in its various contentious manifestations? What mix of preventive diplomacy, peacekeeping, peacemaking, peacebuilding, and peace-enforcing measures are available or required to avert another war on the Korean peninsula? Will the future of inter-Korean relations resemble the recent past? What are the prospects for a peaceful and democratic reunification? The asymmetries of inter-Korean relations, the geostrategic location, and the divided polity—to name a few of the geopolitical and geoeconomic attributes of the two Koreas—make examining the Korean conflict both interesting and challenging for theory, policy, and comparative analysis.

In order to forward this inquiry, this introductory chapter proceeds in four sections. The first explores and depicts in broad strokes the paradoxes of the Korean conflict in the post–Cold War era. Drawing upon the literature of the field of international conflict studies, the second section employs a conflict management (CM) approach as a synthetic conceptual framework for assessing the promise and performance of inter-Korean relations, with a primary focus on the most recent developments. With this approach, we seek to avoid the pitfalls of any monocausal theory or single-factor and single-level explanation for the Korean conflict. The third section, working from the major findings and arguments of the contributors to this volume, examines the complex interplay of global, regional, and local forces that have influenced and shaped the patterns of conflict and cooperation in inter-Korean relations. The fourth and final section briefly addresses the vexing, double-edged question of how and whether the two Koreas can rise to the challenge of managing asymmetrical security interdependence without triggering war or a cataclysmic system collapse in the North.

The Paradoxes of the Korean Conflict

To examine the Korean conflict in its persistent and pervasive form is to be confronted with a great variety of puzzles of both theoretical and real-world significance. Despite the end of the Cold War and superpower rivalry and despite the historic inter-Korean summit of June 2000, the Korean peninsula remains a zone of fratricidal conflict and a potential flashpoint for renewed violence, with grave consequences for regional security in Northeast Asia and beyond. Even today, almost half a century after the Korean War "ended" with an armistice accord, the so-called demilitarized zone (DMZ) easily stands out as the most heavily fortified conflict zone in the post–Cold War world, where more than 1.8 million military personnel—including some 37,000 U.S. troops—confront each other, armed to the teeth with the latest weapons systems. Indeed, the Korean situation has acquired such security-deficit monikers as "powder keg," "the fuse on the nuclear powder keg in the Pacific," "the scariest place on earth," and "the last glacier of Cold War confrontation."

As divided Korea turns 59, exceeding the 35-year Japanese colonial rule by more than two decades, the Korean conflict is one of the most protracted and intense of its kind since the end of World War II. Yet no divided country (including China, Germany, and Vietnam) had been previously united as an independent political entity so continuously or so long as Korea. Unlike almost all of the 191 member states of the United Nations that include two or more ethnic communities of significant size, throughout two millennia of history Korea has been united ethnically and linguistically, and from A.D. 668 until 1945 it lived under the same rule with the same territory, language, race, customs, and history, and with the same strong and powerful neighbors to envy and resent. There is thus a substantial disparity between the primordial unity of the nation and people of Korea and its more recent divided status as two incomplete states, giving rise to continuing asymmetries between the growing expectations for Korean reunification and the limited integrative capabilities and compatibilities on the ground.

Over the course of the past decade the two Koreas have appeared on several occasions to be finally ready to move to the brink of a momentous peace process, only to end in disappointment each time. The 2000 Pyongyang summit was most remarkable historically because it was initiated and executed by Koreans themselves with no external shock or great power sponsorship, perhaps serving to remind some scholars that inter-Korean relations can indeed occur on the dyadic level. The previous inter-Korean accords had been responses to major structural changes external to the Korean peninsula. Suddenly, at least from June to November of 2000, the capital city of Pyongyang, the city of darkness, became a city of diplomatic light and a primary arena for diplomatic influence and competition among the Big Four of Northeast Asia (China, Russia, Japan, and the United States), as inter-Korean relations returned to a more international field. The notion that the Pyongyang summit had improved prospects for melting the remnant Cold War glacier on the Korean peninsula seemed to have intensified the needs and efforts of the four major powers to readjust their respective Korea policies to rapidly changing realities. In the end, however, Pyongyang's high hopes and expectations from the "Clinton in Pyongyang Shock" turned into the "Bush in Washington Shock," with low and ever-diminishing returns. Just beneath the surface there remain the seemingly unbridgeable political, economic, social, and psychological chasms that have been created over a half-century of legitimacy war.

Equally revealing is the fact that the Joint Declaration from the 2000 summit has nothing to say about military and security matters, not even in general terms about working together for tension-reduction and confidence-building measures (CBMs). The summit has made hardly a dent in the military power of South and North Korea, and the potential for renewed hostilities on the Korean peninsula persists and may now be intensified in the context of the North's nuclear revelations of October 2002. It is clear that Pyongyang wants to discuss security issues last, if at all, and then only with the United States. In contrast, the Basic Agreement (1991) stipulates that "the two sides shall endeavor together to transform the present state of armistice into a solid state of peace between the South and the North and shall abide by the present Military Armistice Agreement (of July 27, 1953) until such a state of peace has been realized" (Article 5). The Joint Declaration of the Denuclearization of the Korean Peninsula of 1992 also stipulates in peremptory language that "the South and the North shall not test, manufacture, produce, receive, possess, store, deploy or use nuclear weapons." These historic accords have been honored more in their breach than in their observance or implementation, as the Democratic People's Republic of Korea (DPRK) made clear with the revelations that sparked the standoff that began in late 2002.

The factors that impede movement toward conflict prevention, abatement, and resolution efforts on the Korean peninsula as well as a more normal post–Cold War regional security architecture in Northeast Asia are related primarily to Pyongyang's security or insecurity behavior in its multiple contentious manifestations. With the collapse of the socialist "Second World" and with Moscow–Seoul normalization came the notion that military power and threats are fungible strategic and economic assets for regime survival. The North Korean regime frames such saber-rattling as the last trump card, and there is as yet no evidence of any basic change in the "military-first" policy. On the contrary, the North Korean military continues to grow in both conventional and asymmetrical forces, with increasing emphasis on the latter. Abandoning such military power would leave Pyongyang without the single most important lever in its asymmetric conflicts and negotiations with South Korea, the United States, and Japan.

Seoul's responses and discourses on the Korean conflict have shifted from conflict suppression through deterrence to conflict regulation based on a wide range of CBMs and social and economic functional cooperation.[8] The Republic of Korea (ROK) has sought to move dialogue to non-security areas—and to support dialogue with concrete exchanges and interactions—as a means of alleviating the security dilemma and hostility that prevails at the thirty-eighth parallel. On the other hand, what has triggered fireworks in the domestic politics of both Koreas has been the designation of North Korea as the "main enemy" of South Korea in the annual defense white papers since 1995, including the post-summit *Defense White Paper 2000*. The Kim Dae Jung government considered removing the "main enemy" designation after Pyongyang demanded the change as a precondition for resuming dialogue, only to encounter strong military and conservative opposition at home. Against this backdrop, the Ministry of Defense first announced a delay, then changed the white paper from annual to biennial, and finally opted not to issue again the defense white paper during President Kim Dae Jung's term, which ended on February 25, 2003.

The Korean conflict continues in the transformed post–Cold War East Asian strategic environment, and inter-Korean relations today are not very different from those in the Cold War era, despite the dissipation of superpower rivalry. This suggests that the dynamics of conflict formation on the peninsula have been far more endogenous than exogenous. This reinforces the necessity of looking at inter-Korean relations in terms of the multiple playing fields on which they are fomented and played out. While the international level has long been discussed and understood, it is critical to consider both global and regional perspectives and to consider also the domestic origins and impacts of inter-Korean relations. And the dyadic level, of course, cannot be allowed to get lost as it sometimes has in light of seemingly larger global geopolitics.

There is no mistaking the extraordinary consequences of the Korean conflict on U.S. East Asia policy as well as on great power politics in Northeast Asia and beyond. By dint of Cold War alliance treaties, China and the United States remain *de jure* and *de facto* parties to the Korean conflict. If war breaks out, furthermore, the United States would be swiftly involved by virtue of its troop presence on the ground. More than once since the "end" of the Korean War, the United States has come close to war on the Korean peninsula, most recently in the heat of North Korea's nuclear brinkmanship in June 1994.[9] Even as this crisis unfolded, a new situation was developing with the continuing implosion of the command economy in the North and the politics of political and ideological fragmentation in the South.

As the situation on the ground continues to change in unpredictable ways, however, much of the scholarship on conflict analysis and management remains grounded in and structured by the realist legacies of the Korean War. There is a need for a more integrated road map that would help us better understand and explain the Korean conflict, which is riddled with contradictions. The fact that the euphoria of the inter-Korean summit of 2000 vanished so quickly has underscored the need for a deeper understanding of the dynamics of this conflict. One approach that might serve to explain why different levels of interstate and intra-state relations and different issue areas matter at different times is the CM approach.

Conflict Management Conceived

An argument for the relevance and utility of a CM approach[10]—both in general and in looking at inter-Korean relations—requires dispelling at the outset several heroic but misconceived assumptions standing in the way of our inquiry: (1) that all conflicts are inherently bad or dangerous and as such should be eliminated or resolved once and for all, (2) that there is a single-level or single-factor solution to all armed conflicts or security dilemmas, and (3) that diagnosis and prescription are always matched. All human relations may be seen as interlaced with the two closely related processes of conflict and cooperation; only a small percentage of conflicts escalate to violence or war.[11] Thus we are interested in analyzing and managing only those potentially violence-prone conflicts, along with various ways and means of coping with these conflicts in inter-Korean relations.

A synthetic multidimensional CM model provides an appropriate and promising yet relatively underappreciated guide for the study of conflict, including the Korean conflict. The progressive decay of the Westphalian sovereignty-bound world order combined with the twin pressures of globalization from without and localization from within makes it all the more important that we take a synthetic multidimensional approach to the study of international conflict. There is a consensus, at least in the United States, that IR theorizing and policy-making remain disconnected. Much of IR theorizing is (mis)perceived and dismissed as an endless "beauty contest" of, by, and for the chosen few theorists, who have little if any inclination to communicate with policy specialists, let alone area specialists. The synthetic CM approach directly tackles the important yet under-studied gaps between the different cultures of academe and government and between theory and practice in foreign policy.[12] To say that there is no single all-encompassing cause of conflict is to say that rarely does a single factor at any given level determine the way a country's foreign policy is conceived and implemented, and that there is therefore no single CM solution.[13]

For analytical purposes, conflict management may be defined narrowly as referring to the regulation, mitigation, and containment of full-blown conflicts—that is, crisis management[14]—or broadly as encompassing the wide spectrum of preventive diplomacy, peacekeeping, peacemaking, peace-enforcing, and post-conflict peace-building strategies in the life cycle of conflict.[15] The synthetic, multidimensional CM approach is and proceeds from the latter definition, which calls for a broad understanding of the sources of international conflict and the responses to it. Parts of each chapter in this book implicitly answer the question of how the issues of inter-Korean relations create opportunities for managing the possibility of military conflict through substantively different or militarily limited means.

Despite or perhaps because of the end of East–West conflict and superpower rivalry, managing armed conflict remains one of the most daunting challenges confronting the peoples and states of the post–Cold War world community, as well as scholars and policy-makers. In the first decade since the Cold War there have been important developments in the CM field and on the ground. A changing geopolitical landscape of post–Cold War armed conflicts has at least several characteristics; the two most relevant for the Korean case are:

1. Intra-state armed conflicts (wars within states) greatly outnumber interstate armed conflicts (wars between states) by a ratio of more than 9 : 1. Between 1989 and 2000, for example, there were 111 armed conflicts in 74 locations, and all but 7 of them (6.3 percent) were intra-state armed conflicts. Of the 33 armed conflicts recorded in 2000, only two were interstate. This is in marked contrast to most empirical studies of major armed conflict and war in the nineteenth and most of the twentieth centuries.[16]
2. Whereas only 5 percent of the casualties in World War I were civilians, the proportion had risen to 50 percent in World War II and to as high as 90 percent in post–Cold War armed conflicts. To this must be added the estimate of the United Nations High Commissioner for Refugees (UNHCR) of the primary role of vicious internal conflict in generating 26 million refugees and 24 million internally displaced people at the end of 1994. Another troubling feature of such conflicts is the collapse of state institutions, especially the police and judiciary, with resulting paralysis of governance, breakdown of law and order, and general banditry and chaos.[17]

A glance through the literature suggests how our perceptions of sources of international conflict and our responses to it have changed over the past decade.[18] The study of international conflict is adjusting, as it must, to the changing realities on the ground. Indeed, the rise of intra-state armed conflicts seems to have served as a kind of force-multiplier in catalyzing several important shifts—partial paradigm shifts—in the study of international conflict.

First, there has been a shift away from conventional concerns about great power wars and superpower rivalry toward a greater focus on intra-state conflicts and state-making identity wars. Given the unique condition of the Korean peninsula, work on each of these topics has relevance in examining the new developments in the Korean conflict. These new concerns have also brought a shift away from systemic-level analysis toward a focus on domestic and societal sources of international conflict, especially the "diversionary" use of force for domestic political purposes. The current position of domestic societal-level explanatory variables at center stage in the study of international conflict is a belated response to their long neglect in the literature, to the decline of systemic imperatives, and to the increasing salience of the "black hole" syndrome in many weak or failing states. Third World political leaders, including, it would seem, Kim Jong Il, tend to conceive of security primarily in terms of maintaining domestic stability, legitimacy, and their own political power.

Second, there has been a shift away from systemic-level variables toward dyadic-level interaction variables. In addition to long-standing research on dyadic power relationships and power transitions, new research projects at the dyadic level on enduring rivalries, strategic bargaining, territorial contiguity, and economic and security interdependence have generated much stronger and more policy-relevant empirical findings than those for systemic patterns or national-level behavior.[19] The impact of enduring rivalry and territorial contiguity as independent variables on dyadic war as the dependent variable is especially important and relevant for the study of the Korean conflict.

Third, there has been a shift toward a more dynamic and process-oriented conceptualization of international conflict. Conflict is now defined and operationalized as a series of steps from background conditions, to the occurrence and evolution of militarized disputes, to the outbreak of international war, steps that in turn affect background conditions.[20] In this view, it is possible to isolate moments in the chain of conflict where particular actions are appropriate. In regard to the Korean conflict, there is a diversity of views among the relevant actors as to what those chains look like and where they can and cannot be broken. This yields the need for multilevel and multicausal analysis.

Finally, there has been just such a shift from monocausal or single-factor explanations to a multifaceted and multidimensional approach to conflict analysis and management. Most armed conflicts have multiple issues or causes underlying them (e.g., state-creation, ethnicity or ethnonationalism, territorial disputes, ideology, or national unification). Indeed, any single, all-encompassing explanation can hardly be expected to handle empirically or theoretically "conflicts of different types with different starting points in 44 countries that have different histories and cultures and are at different stages of economic and political development."[21] No serious scholar in the field of CM studies still subscribes to structural realism and its preoccupation with parsimonious system-level explanation. Interaction effects among variables at different levels in the processes leading to violence and war are now considered key.

It follows from the above that evidence of effective CM is likely to include partnerships between and among the different types of actors at several levels in disparate cases. No single actor—the United Nations, regional organizations, great powers, or nongovernmental organizations (NGOs)—possesses all the necessary resources, skills, and strategies for the successful prevention, containment, or resolution of complex armed conflicts. More than one set of intervention strategies or response mechanisms may be necessary to address sources of conflict at different levels of analysis. For both scholars and policy-makers the main thrust of CM in the post–Cold War era requires a shift from "a culture of reaction to a culture of prevention."[22] There is general agreement that conflict prevention—"preventive diplomacy" in UN parlance—is all about moving the focus of attention and action to early "upstream" stages in the life cycle of conflict. This is seen as the most cost-effective way to prevent disputes from arising in the first place or, failing that, to prevent existing disputes from escalating into lethal armed conflicts.

Analysis of some of the recent developments on the Korean peninsula through a CM lens may show that a recognition of the worth of such preventative medicine is coming into being. Inter-Korean relations have become more diverse and more relevant since the end of the Cold War. As they grow in functional breadth and depth, inter-Korean relations will continue to increase their relevance at both domestic and international levels and will continue to involve domestic, regional, and global actors. The chapters of this book represent a number of attempts to capture this functional change in an analytical fashion.

The Korean Conflict: Sources and Responses

As noted earlier, the new development of CM theories has involved an expanded horizon of analytical variables. No longer is conflict seen as something that happens at the international level strictly because of international causes. The divided Korean nation is a particularly explicit case of conflict emerging at different levels and because of different logics. Conflict is also managed at these different levels. Therefore, it can be noted that four established or emerging dynamics characterize the setting for conflict analysis and management on the Korean peninsula: politics at the local level, inter-Korean dyadic relations, continued great power politics, and international organization. Interactions both within and between these arenas define the current state of inter-Korean relations.

The Local Level

The domestic politics of the two Korean states are formed in binary opposition to each other. Over the course of their mutually antagonistic existence, both the ROK and the DPRK have sought to claim legitimacy over the entire Korean peninsula and have necessarily had to deny the legitimacy of the other state and its strikingly similar claim. At the international level, this has led to competition for diplomatic recognition and for sole UN membership, in addition to the more obvious competition for military superiority. But the game of competitive legitimation has also had significant ramifications within the states and societies of the two Korean states, effects that produce positive feedback and then themselves impact the demeanor of both international relations and inter-Korean relations.

As Scott Snyder describes in chapter two, the impact of competitive legitimation politics is dynamic, and it has recently undergone major changes in South Korea. Whereas the government traditionally manipulated information about the DPRK, beginning with Roh Tae Woo's *Nordpolitik*, in which he made diplomatic forays toward China and the Soviet Union, information about the DPRK became freer and more truthful in the ROK. Combined with other aspects of liberalization that had the particular effect of highlighting voices that had been opposed to the South Korean authoritarian regimes, new discourses developed in South Korea, discourses that directly impacted the balance of inter-Korean relations.

Snyder picks up the story with Kim Dae Jung's presidency and his Sunshine Policy, using editorial content analysis and public opinion data to chart cycles of attitudes toward inter-Korean relations. For instance, a high level of initial skepticism toward the Sunshine Policy was overcome, but revelations in 2003 about the financial transfers undertaken by Hyundai to facilitate the inter-Korean summit of June 2000 caused a noticeable diminishment in enthusiasm for Sunshine-like policy initiatives toward the DPRK. Through his research, Snyder finds that overall South Koreans remain supportive of interaction with the North, although he also finds an interesting generational gap in which older South Koreans are more skeptical about the possibilities of engagement while the younger generations expect less benefits from reunification, should it come. In a democratic South Korea, it is these developing attitudes that will influence the ROK's policy toward the DPRK and consequently inter-Korean relations as a whole.

In North Korea as well, Charles Armstrong finds an evolution of attitudes toward inter-Korean relations, although because of the limitations on both scholarship and public discourse in North Korea, these are necessarily elite attitudes. Chapter three details the DPRK's three key principles for inter-Korean relations and the pursuit of reunification but notes that both Koreas have begun to treat each other in a manner befitting recognized sovereign states. Describing the "reunification theology" of the DPRK, Armstrong argues that the North's attitude toward reunification has not changed in terms of essentials but has become more liberal and less fundamentalist. In the new millennium, the DPRK has already undertaken several elements of "reform by stealth": local markets, overseas education, emphasis on science and technology, new taxation, new prices, truer exchange rate, and the Sinuiju special economic zone. Key to inter-Korean relations is the fact that North Korea needs cooperation with and support from the ROK to continue and consolidate these reforms.

This means that inter-Korean relations are instrumental in terms of any North Korean economic revitalization and therefore essential for Kim Jong Il's continued legitimation as the leader of the DPRK. Indeed the role of the Dear Leader, Kim Jong Il, is essential in inter-Korean relations as how the current temperature of inter-Korean relations feeds or undermines his legitimacy in large part determine the North Korean stance on inter-Korean relations. Kim—and probably the entire North Korean regime—has survival as its ultimate goal and, as Armstrong points out, therefore has an intuitive fear of an end like that which befell East Germany: regime demise and state absorption. Paradoxically then, inter-Korean relations entail a threat that is in fundamental contradiction with the DPRK's ideological belief in the superiority of its system.

South Korean leadership is also an interesting barometer of inter-Korean relations, especially of the degree of international character. Snyder points out that the main issue in Roh Moo Hyun's 2002 election was *not* North Korea, despite the nuclear revelations of October 2002 and the interactions consequent from the June 2000 summit. This reinforces the description of inter-Korean relations as becoming more normal, more like those between any pair of sovereign states.

The Inter-Korean Dyadic Level
The dyadic level is the most obvious framework in which to situate inter-Korean relations, particularly if the evolution toward more typical, Westphalian international relations is underway. In a series of accords and agreements reached over the years, the dyadic relationship between North and South Korea has come quite close to that of mutually recognized sovereign states. In 1972, the two countries signed the July 4 Communiqué, agreeing to improve relations and promote exchanges. The 1991 Basic Agreement (Agreement on Reconciliation, Non-aggression, Exchanges and Cooperation) and Joint

Declaration of the Denuclearization of the Korean Peninsula marked the start of inter-Korean relations in the post–Cold War era. At the 2000 joint summit both announced a new beginning in dyadic relations and created a foundation for a set of new agreements on economic engagement and social and cultural exchanges.

In chapter four, Samuel Kim and Matthew Winters look at developments in inter-Korean economic relations—a phenomenon with a 40-year gap in activity—to demonstrate that there have been absolutely remarkable changes in the relationship between North and South Korea since the end of the Cold War. Beginning with small exchanges of goods in the early 1990s, South Korea now is the North's second-largest trading partner. And this trade has continued despite nuclear revelations, naval provocations, and missile testing by the DPRK. One of the key components of this trade is processing-on-commission (POC) trade, in which South Korean companies export raw materials to the DPRK and then import finished or semifinished products. This type of trade involves the creation of new jobs in North Korea, some degree of technology transfer, a fair amount of investment in the North from the South, and, most importantly, direct contact between North and South Koreans. In addition, since the mid-1990s Seoul has increased its flows of "non-transactional" trade, which is the exchange of noncommercial goods, such as those used in the Korean Peninsular Energy Development Organization (KEDO) reactor projects or for humanitarian aid. Chapter four argues that these increased trading relations are part of a program led by the ROK but accepted by the DPRK to create functional linkages between North and South in the interests of CM, peace, and reunification. Because of this grand functional program, Seoul has overlooked Northern security threats in order to continue allowing and promoting trade and investment.

Nonetheless, there have been limitations to the amount of economic contact between North and South. While the DPRK has expanded the number of citizens that it sends abroad to study economics and business and has passed some important economic reform legislation, South Korean investors remain frightened about the security and profitability of their investments in the North. And while trade numbers may be growing and increasingly impressive, it is investment that will make the most difference in terms of the North Korean economy and, the authors argue, in terms of economic relations fostering peace on the peninsula. In addition, cultural and social exchanges—visits to Mt. Kumgang and family reunions—have not been as productive as some had hoped. While spectacular media events, they have not spawned the type of lasting connections between North Koreans and South Koreans that can be considered true functional linkages.

Many aspects of inter-Korean economic relations remain uncertain. The face of investment could change entirely if the new Kaesong Industrial Complex in North Korea were to take off; it has already attracted attention from a number of small and medium-sized companies in South Korea. The reconnection of roads and railways between the two countries—with the rail project being of particular interest to Russia—will reduce the transaction costs of trade and embed both countries in a larger trading system. Pyongyang has recognized the essential need to open itself to foreign economic agents and has undertaken legal reform to encourage investment and trade. South Korea is the most likely source of the funding that can revitalize or at least stabilize the DPRK's economy.

Jeong-Ho Roh, however, in chapter nine, describes the situation differently and with less optimism. He finds that the absence of reliable enforcement mechanisms between the two Koreas means that inter-Korean agreements lack legal effect. In Roh's opinion, "inter-Korean agreements and bilateral relations rest on an illusory—or fictional—legal foundation," which he sees as a result of the fact that a permanent peace treaty never has been completed and that the 1953 Military Armistice Agreement remains the prevailing legal arrangement for inter-Korean relations. Because of this, the Basic Agreement describes the inter-Korean relationship as "not being a relationship as between states," but rather "a special one constituted temporarily in the process of unification."

While some of the recent dyadic interactions may have seemed like those between sovereign states, Roh denies that there is any recognition of mutual sovereignty and says that all of the agreements between the two states have carefully sidestepped this issue. In this view, dyadic-level inter-Korean relations remain something apart from normal international relations and make bilateral relations more complex and opaque than they might otherwise be. For Roh, violation of inter-Korean agreements can result only in symbolic protest, since there is no meaningful legal enforcement mechanism. Such breaches have been frequent. As an example, he suggests that North Korea's withdrawal from the Nuclear Non-Proliferation Treaty (NPT) in January 2003 and the ensuing nuclear standoff constitute a direct violation of the Joint Declaration of the Denuclearization of the Korean Peninsula, but one in which the legal significance and possible punitive outcome are uncertain.

In his chapter, Roh also captures the dynamic of brinkmanship and retreat that characterizes the DPRK's direct interactions with the South. In September 1996, a North Korean submarine carrying commandos undertook an incursion into South Korean waters and beached itself, resulting in 37 deaths. In response, the ROK stopped work on the KEDO-sponsored nuclear reactors in North Korea, leading the DPRK to threaten to resume its nuclear program. Before allowing talks to begin, South Korea demanded an apology over the submarine, and the DPRK, in turn, demanded that the ROK apologize for not having expressed condolences regarding Kim Il Sung's death in July 1994. Sadly this pattern of aggressive advance and then sudden retrenchment is characteristic of inter-Korean relations, and Roh's description of the absence of legal norms and standards may elucidate one of the reasons for this.

Ultimately the most significant area of inter-Korean relations is the military/security level. Whatever other interaction North and South Korea are undertaking or engaging in, they continue to support two massive and well-armed militaries staring at each other across the DMZ. Abraham Kim, in chapter eleven, draws on the lessons of the literature on civil war termination to make some predictions about the future of inter-Korean relations. Intra-state wars are ended in a three-part process of negotiation, settlement, and implementation. In his chapter, Kim discovers a trajectory that could lead the two Korean states through this pattern.

In contrast to liberal views asserting that making the DPRK secure will lead to reunification, Abraham Kim proposes that it is a hurting stalemate that drives states to negotiate, and that stabilizing the DPRK with aid prolongs the status quo with its set of costs, such that progress toward reunification remains further off. Even in the event of negotiation, he is uncertain of the prospects of reaching a settlement, however, since settlement requires divisible stakes. But North Korea at the moment is inclined to be greatly fearful of superior South Korean power and of a South Korean desire to impose a liberal, capitalist democracy on the North. For the North to think otherwise will require a "heroic perceptual transformation." Should a settlement be negotiated, Kim asserts, the implementation will not be successful if it is undertaken only at the dyadic level; rather a third-party guarantor, most likely the United States, must be secured. The chapter concludes that the status quo division seems the most likely scenario for the future; in the event of a true crisis, reunification by force is a likely outcome.

The Role of the Big Four and Great Power Politics in Northeast Asia

Northeast Asian politics have long been defined by the conflicting—and less frequently, compatible—interests of four great powers: the United States, Russia, China, and Japan. The Cold War confrontation was played out in particular in Northeast Asia because of the geopolitical proximity of the United States, the Soviet Union, and their allies. China, after some years of relative isolationism, is recognizing its growing status as an international power and has decided to act the role of responsible great power. Japan, meanwhile, remains an economic powerhouse and a major, if sometimes reluctant, player in the geopolitics of a wider East Asia. All four powers have had, and continue to have, a marked influence on inter-Korean relations, and it is likely that future inter-Korean relations will be determined to no small degree by the international relations in which each of the two Korean states engages with these powers.

Andrew Scobell, in chapter five, points out the central position of China in inter-Korean relations. Of the four great powers, China is the only one to maintain good relations with both North and South Korea, and it does so by using low-key, conservative tactics. For instance, China supported the formation of KEDO as a part of the settlement of the 1994 nuclear crisis but opted not to participate in the organization. Scobell believes that Beijing has served a constructive role in reducing tensions and facilitating reconciliation between Seoul and Pyongyang, particularly since the advent of Roh's *Nordpolitik* in the late 1980s. China was then one of the first countries to move to a two-Korea policy, doing so in a *de facto* manner in the 1980s and then giving the policy *de jure* status with the 1992 establishment of diplomatic relations with the ROK. This is an ironic position for China, given its hostility to any suggestion of a multiple-China policy by states in the international system, but the position is effective and probably necessary.

China is also in a paradoxical bind because it stands to gain much more from economic interaction with the ROK than it does from any interaction with the DPRK, yet it fears the loss of another Leninist party state should the DPRK dissolve. More to the point, China fears a domestic crisis that could result from the implosion of North Korea, which would entail a massive influx of refugees into China. This drives China to manage as much as possible the DPRK's international situation. Scobell asserts that China deserves much of the credit for the April 2003 three-party talks in response to the 2002–03 nuclear crisis. Seeing China as a balancer against crisis on the Korean peninsula, Scobell notes that China ultimately has mixed motives in pursuing reform in North Korea and is mostly content with the status quo in the face of any "bold transformational initiatives."

Elizabeth Wishnick's research, which comprises chapter seven, indicates that Russia is seeking to play a greater role on the Korean peninsula than it did during the decade after the fall of the Soviet Union. This originates in part from a Russian desire to reassert great power status. Wishnick asserts that Russian policy-makers in the late 1990s, and especially with the coming of Vladimir Putin to the presidency, saw recovering Russia's lost influence in Pyongyang as a way to reenter the great power talks on inter-Korean relations and as a way to guarantee a Russian role in any Korean settlement. Like China, Russia is in a position to play a central role because it maintains relations with both North and South Korea; in fact Kim Dae Jung encouraged such a role during a 1999 visit to Moscow.

In addition, Russia has a serious economic interest in Korea. Russia could build oil and natural gas pipelines through North Korea to supply South Korea and Japan, and Moscow has been a big promoter of rebuilding an inter-Korean railroad; a connection to the Trans-Siberian Railway would increase shipping by tenfold. Russia is also a participant in the United Nations Development Programme's Tumen River Area Development Programme (TRADP) because, as Wishnick notes, it sees the TRADP as a means of shipping cargo to South Korea. At the moment, Russia has also found markets in both Seoul and Pyongyang at which it can sell some of the Soviet military hardware that it has on hand. Wishnick lists abundant reasons why Moscow will be motivated to pursue a relationship with Pyongyang as a means of maintaining its influence on the Korean peninsula. Perhaps Russia will come to play a larger role in Korea in the years to come, an interesting proposition, given its unequivocal support for reunification, as was outlined by Putin in a 2001 speech to the ROK National Assembly.

The attitude of Japan toward the Korean peninsula has likewise undergone a significant shift since the end of the Cold War. As C.S. Eliot Kang points out in chapter six, a combination of Japanese guilt and Korean ire related to Japan's colonization of Korea has led Japan to take a relatively quiescent and passive position on inter-Korean relations. But trepidation regarding Korean reunification and the nuclear weapons and missile threats from the North have caused Japan to stand up and take notice of the tides of inter-Korean relations. Kang describes significant Japanese surprise at the strength and degree of South Korean economic development, which, when combined with the perceived warming relationship between Seoul and Moscow, makes a reunited Korea appear to be a real economic threat. Indeed some in the ROK have accused Japan of taking interest in inter-Korean relations and making overtures to the North in the 1990s for the sake of keeping Korea divided. Despite these perceptions, Kang points out that Japan has played a positive role in inter-Korean relations in terms of making generous contributions to KEDO and working for the formation of the ASEAN Regional Forum (ARF)—functional linkages that matter to both Korean states.

As Kang points out, even if the great powers of East Asia claim to prefer passivity, they do have a real role to play in inter-Korean relations. For example, the Trilateral Coordination and Oversight Group (TCOG) works to integrate U.S., South Korean, and Japanese policy toward the DPRK: policy coordination that was successful in preventing a second missile launching by the DPRK, planned for 1999.

Using a defensive realist view of international relations adapted from the work of Stephen Brooks, Kang argues that Japan will continue to bandwagon with South Korea rather than balance against Korean power because of probabilistic assessments as to the real threats emanating from the Korean peninsula. If this is indeed true, it bodes well for Japan having a positive impact on inter-Korean relations and being able to play an increasingly functional and productive role.

When it comes to a discussion of the role of the United States in inter-Korean relations, there exists a wide range of impacts, perceptions, and realities. Because the United States is so deeply entangled in the Korean conflict, in the region, and in the global economic system, its policy toward and influence in inter-Korean relations is certainly variable and, depending on the administration in power, could be said to border on the fickle. Victor Cha, in chapter eight, therefore provides a threefold typology of the roles that the United States has played and might play again in inter-Korean relations. He traces the perception of the U.S. role to four factors: structural and relative capabilities-based explanations, alliance management explanations, domestic-politics explanations, and perceptual explanations.

During the Cold War, the United States served as a "co-container," explicitly containing the DPRK from making an attempt to forcibly reunify Korea but also implicitly restraining the ROK, particularly under Syngman Rhee and Park Chung Hee, from its own ambitions to reunify the peninsula through military force. South Korea disliked any deviation from this role, such as that perceived during the opening of relations with China and détente with the Soviet Union. At other times, the United States has played the role of facilitator, bringing the ROK and DPRK to the negotiating table, ostensibly for the purpose of reducing tensions on the peninsula but often because of alliance management needs, due to a South Korean fear that U.S.–DPRK dialogue was moving too far, too fast. The height of this role was during the 1994 nuclear crisis. Most recently, South Korean perception of the United States has been as an "impeder," a perception that resulted from the success of the Sunshine Policy and the decoupling of U.S.–ROK interests, such that the latter is interested in peninsular defense while the former is concerned with weapons proliferation issues.

Cha suggests that the perception of the United States as an impeder is not permanent. Although 2002 and 2003 saw a number of anti-U.S. protests and the election of Roh Moo Hyun due, in part, to anti-U.S. sentiment, South Korea's democratic norms, strategy of allying with great powers because of its geostrategic position, and perception of negative economic effects due to provocations from the DPRK will yield a lessening of the impeder label. It is likely that the United States will then return to a position in which it can be viewed as a facilitator of inter-Korean relations. Cha's research leads to a questioning of the connection between South Korean perceptions of the United States and South Korean policy toward North Korea. He usefully points out a path in which U.S. policy toward the Korean peninsula results in South Korean perceptions of the United States that, in turn, yield South Korean policy toward North Korea.

International Organizations

In a situation such as that on the Korean peninsula, where realist security norms seem to hold court with a vengeance, developments in international relations must sometimes come from nontraditional sources. There is a potential, therefore, that international organizations (IOs) might provide a mechanism by which breakthroughs can occur in inter-Korean relations. Shin-wha Lee captures this in chapter 10, in which she describes the role of international organizations in pushing nontraditional security views. While the ROK has been more active in joining international organizations than the DPRK, Lee notes the major success of incorporating the DPRK into the ARF, described as the "beginning of the end of North Korea's isolation." In addition, North Korea was building relations with the International Monetary Fund (IMF), World Bank, and Asian Development Bank before eruption of the 2002–04 nuclear standoff, and the DPRK has been involved with a set of international organizations and NGOs providing food aid for the past ten years. The work on the Tumen River Area Development Programme (TRADP) is providing a test case for the effects and limits of international development aid.

But the result of this involvement with international organizations is unclear. As Lee points out, the United Nations and other international organizations have played a limited role—and often an indirect one—in the inter-Korean peace process. Yet IOs certainly can play a role in maintaining peace and enhancing security on the Korean peninsula. They offer forums in which the two Korean states can meet, interact, and create functional linkages. This can reinforce advances made in inter-Korean relations and present opportunities for new initiatives.

Until it was effectively torpedoed in connection with the 2002–03 nuclear crisis, KEDO was serving a role in building connections between North and South Korea. As noted earlier, Jeong-Ho Roh's analysis of KEDO was ambivalent because of its ambiguous legal nature, although he was encouraged by Kim Dae Jung's attempt to delink KEDO from other aspects of inter-Korean relations in a two-track approach. As KEDO becomes a moribund institution, the chances of it further promoting functional linkages or serving as a test case for the viability of similar regimes fades away.

The Future of Inter-Korean Relations

As it is easy to say with Korea—and particularly with anything involving North Korea—the future of inter-Korean relations looks unclear. Indeed it seems more unclear now than it did in the early to mid-1990s when a broad swath of academics and policy analysts were predicting the imminent collapse of the North Korean regime and the reunification of Korea. Since this has not happened—and less people are now willing to predict that it will in the near future—the study of inter-Korean relations *per se* has revived itself. Once again, it is deemed important to look at the types of diplomatic, economic, functional, and military relations that exist between the ROK and the DPRK.

The contributors to this book have highlighted a very large range of factors that are impacting and will continue to influence inter-Korean relations and the CM options connected with them. These factors operate at four different levels in the strategic calculus of North and South Korea: domestically, dyadically, in the realm of Northeast Asian great power politics, and vis-à-vis international organizations. The significance of the different levels will vary depending on the issue being examined and the historical moment.

Several broad conclusions can be stated. The first is that the domestic causes of inter-Korean relations are not divorced from the international. Taking the analyses of Scott Snyder and Victor Cha together, one can note the way that external factors, particularly the role played by the United States, impact South Korean public opinion and inter-Korean relations, and consequently impact policy. Likewise, Charles Armstrong points out that the Pyongyang's policy toward Seoul in many ways has the United States as its target; the international weighs heavy in the minds of North Korea's leadership.

Likewise at the dyadic level, much of what can be anticipated about inter-Korean relations depends on the role of external guarantors or audiences. Jeong-Ho Roh's point that the several agreements and memoranda signed by North and South Korea have faltered because of the lack of a clear legal relationship between the two states is tempered a bit by the role that external actors can play in inter-Korean agreements. For instance, while it now finds itself in a state of limbo, KEDO emerged because of an agreement between the United States and the DPRK, yet facilitated functional relationships between the ROK and the DPRK. Abraham Kim's argument that the implementation of any settlement in the reunification game will require an external guarantor both reinforces this point and begs the question as to the role of external actors in inter-Korean relations at a point before negotiations on reunification.

As stated earlier, the four great powers in Northeast Asia matter deeply for inter-Korean politics. Japan and Russia are the supporting actors to the leading roles played by the United States and China, but each has recently taken more interest in inter-Korean relations. Russia hopes to reap economic benefit by developing its relations with both Korean states and through the possibilities of realizing increased trade with the South by establishing ports, railroads, and pipelines through the North. Japan's concern with the economic might of a reunified Korea combines with its angst over DPRK development of missiles and weapons of mass destruction to insure that it keeps a watchful eye on the peninsula.

The U.S. role, as Victor Cha describes it, is not as crystal clear as many might like to believe. Inter-Korean relations will be influenced heavily by perceptions in both the North and the South as to the role that the United States can and is likely to play. The DPRK has had a pattern of desiring to negotiate with the United States directly instead of with the ROK or in a multilateral setting; U.S. acquiescence or resistance to this will decrease or increase the quantity and salience of inter-Korean contact. Presumably, the reversion of the United States to the role of facilitator would be an aid to increased and improved inter-Korean relations, although its current perceived role as an impeder may very well encourage the South Koreans to strive for better contact with the North on their own, particularly if South Koreans view the United States as purposely trying to keep them divided from their national brethren across the DMZ.

While the United States receives the majority of the attention given its role as the world's only superpower, China is emerging as a key actor in the future prospects of inter-Korean relations—indeed in the future prospects of all East Asian relations. Like Russia, China has relations with both the ROK and the DPRK and can therefore serve a vital role in facilitating dialogue and functional connections and cooperation. The possibility of China serving as a guarantor of Korean reunification is underrecognized and certainly understudied. As Andrew Scobell describes, China supported the Sunshine Policy and has played a large role in both the four-party talks working toward a permanent armistice and the 2003 talks on the nuclear situation. But China's preference for working behind the scenes and for eschewing major initiatives in favor of CM and status quo maintenance would seem not to fit the pattern of greatpower politics by which major developments in inter-Korean relations might occur. Nonetheless, if China hews to its course of playing the role of responsible great power, it certainly could challenge the United States in some of the roles traditionally reserved for it in the space of inter-Korean relations. China's relationship with the DPRK in fact gives it somewhat of an advantage.

At this time, international organizations are unlikely to play a major role in inter-Korean relations. While KEDO served a function for a short time, it was helpless in the face of the October 2002 nuclear revelations by North Korea, and the United States shunted it aside. Neither large international organizations like the United Nations or the World Bank nor regional organizations like the ARF or the ASEAN-Plus-Three (APT) forum have had much to say vis-à-vis the future of the Korean peninsula. The issues facing the two Koreas are consistently judged by nearly all actors involved as best seen as part of and addressed through the means of traditional international politics and, indeed, traditional great power politics. The role of the security dilemma at the DMZ cannot be doubted, and the persistence of Cold War alliances throughout East Asia reinforces a zero–sum, relative gains atmosphere. This status quo makes it difficult for international organizations to gain influence or to perform functional tasks related to inter-Korean relations.

While this is descriptively true, the prescriptive viewpoint is almost certainly the reverse. That is to say, international organizations can undoubtedly serve a positive function in inter-Korean relations, creating linkages between the two countries and giving them space where they can interact that is in effect outside the Korean peninsula. Certainly in some cases the two governments will resort to the old game of competitive legitimation, but in other venues functional, diplomatic, and discursive connections can grow and lead to progress in inter-Korean relations away from the dominant Cold War, security dilemma standard. Newly minted East Asian regional organizations seem particularly suited for this task, again in connection with a Chinese aim to play the role of responsible great power.

Fifteen years into the post–Cold War world, inter-Korean relations remain mired in an anachronistic Cold War framework. Component to this are the continued relevance of the United States, the fact that domestic forces driving each Korean state's policy toward the other are internationally motivated, and the seeming dominance of zero–sum power politics. But by looking at the four different analytical levels, one can find glimmers of difference and hints of breakthrough. At the domestic level within the ROK, people are open to the DPRK and less willing to allow the United States to prolong the Cold War era status quo. In Northeast Asian neighborhood, Russia and Japan have heightened the attention they are paying to inter-Korean politics, and China is posed to play an increasingly larger role and perhaps, in the future, to challenge the United States as the trendsetter on the Korean peninsula. And international and regional organizations are coming alive in East Asia in a meaningful way so that North and South Korea might make functional use of them in relating to each other. The direct dyadic level remains the most traditional. Because of the lack of legal recognition of each other's sovereign status and because of the difficulties of finding a plan for reunification that actually relies on compromise and collaboration and not subsumption and absorption, the direct state-to-state approach to inter-Korean relations seems to provide little room for maneuver. But in the context of the other levels, this too may be overcome. In sum, inter-Korean relations are developing in multiple contexts and in association with different sets of actors, and only a multivalent perspective can capture the full range of future prospects.

Notes

1. Gregory Henderson, "Korea," in *Divided Nations in a Divided World*, ed. Gregory Henderson, Richard Ned Lebow and John G. Stoessinger (New York: David Mckay, 1974), p. 43.
2. Kim Hyun Hee, *The Tears of My Soul* (New York: William Morrow and Co., 1993), p. 84.
3. Joint New Year Editorial of *Rodong Sinmun, Joson Inmingun, Chongnyong Jonwi*, "Let Us Fully Demonstrate the Dignity and Might of the DPRK Under the Great Banner of Army-based Policy," January 1, 2003 at http://www.kcna.comjp/item2003/200301/news01/01.htm.
4. See Michael Green, "A North Korean Regime Crisis: US Perspectives and Responses," *Korean Journal of Defense Analysis* 9: 2 (Winter 1997): 7.
5. KCNA, November 18, 2000.
6. *Rodong Sinmun*, June 25, 2000, p. 6; emphasis added.
7. The new consensus in the South Korean and U.S. intelligence communities in early 2000 was that North Korea would survive at least until 2015.
8. Chung-in Moon, *Arms Control on the Korean Peninsula: Domestic Perceptions, Regional Dynamics, International Penetrations* (Seoul: Yonsei University Press, 1996), 9.
9. See Don Oberdorfer, *The Two Koreas: A Contemporary History* (Reading, Mass.: Addison-Wesley, 1997), chap. 13 and Leon V. Sigal, *Disarming Strangers: Nuclear Diplomacy with North Korea* (Princeton: Princeton University Press, 1998), pp. 113–127.
10. For a more detailed analysis of the CM approach, see Samuel S. Kim and Abraham Kim, "Conflict Management," in *Encyclopedia of Government and Politics*, ed. Mary Hawkesworth and Maurice Kogan, 2nd ed. (London and New York: Routledge, 2003), pp. 980–993.
11. It should not be assumed that all deadly conflicts are inevitable or necessarily escalate from one step to the next. Of the 827 conflicts for the period 1815–1976, there was less than a 10% probability of conflict escalation. See Zeev Maoz, *Paths to Conflict: International Dispute Initiation, 1818–1976* (Boulder, Colo.: Westview Press, 1982), pp. 62, 68.
12. The single best volume addressing the gap between theory and practice in foreign policy is Alexander L. George, *Bridging the Gap: Theory and Practice in Foreign Policy* (Washington, DC: U.S. Institute of Peace Press, 1993).
13. See Chester Crocker et al., eds., *Turbulent Peace: The Challenges of Managing International Conflict* (Washington, D.C.: U.S. Institute of Peace Press, 2001); Hugh Miall, Oliver Ramsbotham, and Tom Woodhouse, *Contemporary Conflict Resolution: The Prevention, Management and Transformation of Deadly Conflict* (Cambridge, UK: Polity Press, 1999); Jack Levy, "The Causes of War and the Conditions of Peace," *Annual Review of Political Science* 1 (1998): 139–165.
14. Miall et al., *Contemporary Conflict Resolution*, pp. 20–21; Peck 2001.
15. Boutros Boutros-Ghali, *An Agenda for Peace: Preventive Diplomacy, Peacemaking and Peace-Keeping* (UN Doc. A/47/277 – S/24111, June 17, 1992); *Supplement to an Agenda for Peace: Position Paper of the Secretary-General on the Occasion of the Fiftieth Anniversary of the United Nations* (UN Doc. A/50/60 – A/1995/1, January 3, 1995); Roger E. Kanet

and Edward A. Kolodziej, eds., *Coping with Conflict after the Cold War* (Baltimore, Md.: Johns Hopkins University Press, 1996).

16. Peter Wallensteen and Margaretta Sollenberg, "Armed Conflict, 1989–2000," *Journal of Peace Research* 38: 5 (2001): 629–644 and K.J. Holsti, *The State, War, and the State of War* (New York: Cambridge University Press, 1996).

17. Miall et al., *Contemporary Conflict Resolution*, p. 32; Boutros-Ghali, *Supplement to an Agenda for Peace*, paras. 12–13.

18. Levy, "The Causes of War and the Conditions of Peace"; Crocker et al., *Turbulent Peace*; Kolodjiez and Kanet, *Coping with Conflict after the Cold War*; Connie Peck, *Sustainable Peace: The Role of the United Nations and Regional Organizations in Preventing Conflict* (Lanham, Md.: Rowman & Littlefield, 1998).

19. Miall et al., *Contemporary Conflict Resolution*; John Vasquez, "Distinguishing Rivals That Go to War from Those That Do Not: A Quantitative Comparative Case Study of the Two Paths to War," *International Studies Quarterly* 40 (1996): 531–558; Levy, "The Causes of War and the Conditions of Peace."

20. John Vasquez, *The War Puzzle* (New York: Cambridge University Press, 1993).

21. Miall et al., *Contemporary Conflict Resolution*, p. 66.

22. Kofi Annan, *Prevention of Armed Conflict: Report of the Secretary General*, UN Doc. A/55/985-S/2001/574, June 7, 2001.

Chapter Two

Inter-Korean Relations: A South Korean Perspective

Scott Snyder[1]

South Korea's President Kim Dae Jung made a historic visit to Pyongyang for a summit meeting between the leaders of the two Koreas in June 2000. The summit was greeted at the time with great public euphoria, although the summit achievement has subsequently been tarnished within South Korea and abroad by revelations that the meeting was conditional upon the secret payment of almost US$500 million via the Hyundai Group. Kim Dae Jung confidently returned to Seoul after his three days of talks with Kim Jong Il and declared that there would be "no more war on the Korean peninsula." By achieving the unprecedented meeting between the two heads of state, Kim Dae Jung and Kim Jong Il reawakened previously unthinkable hopes and possibilities that came into direct conflict with long-held South Korean conceptions of an identity formed partially in opposition to the North. The prospect of inter-Korean rapprochement had potentially revolutionary and deeply contested implications for South Korean politics and society. South Korea's democratic liberalization led in directions that opened new possibilities and challenged the status quo, with profound implications for vested interests both inside South Korea and for the two Koreas.

Although the summit appeared to be a watershed that would bring about the end of inter-Korean confrontation, it has spawned the rise of a deep ideological division in Korean politics (a "South-South" divide) that had been hidden under the surface for many years as a result of South Korea's anticommunist ideology and authoritarian historical legacy. In fact, one effect of the summit was to infuse Korean factional politics with an ideological edge. Supporters and critics of the Sunshine Policy faced off against each other on policy toward North Korea and the future of Korea's democracy. This debate has deepened ideological cleavages within South Korean society.

The debate over the future of inter-Korean relations is made more complex by the fact that it is not only about the merits of accommodation with the North, but is also being driven by profound social changes that are occurring in the South Korean body politic as the space for democratic debate and free expression of ideas that were once deemed heretical has expanded within South Korea's own political spectrum. The "normalization" of Korean politics is changing the lens through which South Koreans consider their relationship with North Korea, in contradictory, confusing, and sharply ironic ways. The language of political debate between the traditional conservatives and progressive reformists is derived from Korea's traditional "anticommunist" foundations, and is only beginning to be updated to accommodate a broader spectrum of liberal discourse that is a normal part of the political discourse in mature liberal democracies elsewhere in the world. What has traditionally been described as "socialist" and thus beyond the bounds of acceptability in the constrained political discourse of Korea's authoritarian, conservative, traditional political order is now simply "liberal" or "progressive," and is a legitimate part of "normal" democratic discourse. Although the debate itself may be confusing and self-contradictory, it may be the evidence of the power that Korea's democratization is having as an ongoing trend that is fundamentally and decisively tilting the balance in inter-Korean relations.

Current ambiguity on this point remains a fundamental source of ideological debate and conflict between the conservative and progressive wings of South Korean society. The irony of this political debate is sharpened by the fact that many conservative hard-liners who are concerned about compromises with North Korea's totalitarian system are individuals who were also associated with past Korean authoritarian governments. Progressives, who grew up in opposition to South Korean authoritarianism, seem willing to accommodate a more severe North Korean variety of oppression without expressing concern over whether such compromises could lead to a backward step for freedom or democracy on the Korean peninsula. The success or failure of the next phase of South Korean policy toward the North may hinge on how the South Korean government is able to gain broad consensus on the fundamental purposes and quid pro quos envisaged as part of the engagement plan with the North, and how the North perceives and responds to such efforts.

This chapter reviews developments in the debate on inter-Korean relations during the Kim Dae Jung administration through editorial content analysis and public opinion polling regarding inter-Korean relationship. Special consideration will be given to the rise of ideology and South Korea's democratization process as fundamental influences on public perceptions of North Korea in the context of political change in South Korea. I examine the historic and recent role of North Korea as an issue in South Korea's democratic transformation and the South Korean public response to the historic inter-Korean summit and its implications for the sustainability of an inter-Korean reconciliation process.

North Korea as Viewed Through the Lens of South Korea's Cold War Authoritarianism

The issue of Korea's national division and relationship with the "other" Korea has always been an intense political issue that has influenced almost every aspect of Korean society. This is in part because even the development of the separate states in the North and South was driven by the need to build rival systems and national identities in opposition to the other. Just as the Charter of the Korean Workers' Party continues to hold out a revolutionary ideal that includes the overturning of the South's democratic system, the constitution of the ROK, Article IV of which states that, "The Republic of Korea shall seek national unification, and shall formulate and carry out peaceful unification policy based on the free and democratic basic order."[2] The acceptable ideological spectrum of debate within South Korean politics has as a result, consistently been limited to conservative or "anticommunist" positions.

A favorite way of attacking opposition candidates has been to label them as left-leaning or overly sympathetic to North Korea. This tactic was a well-worn method that had been used for decades by the establishment to attack popular outsiders from entering the ruling clique. Former president, Kim Dae Jung, who had been a longtime opposition leader, is an example.

The manipulation of policy toward North Korea in order to achieve domestic political gains can be traced back to the authoritarian leadership in South Korea under Park Chung Hee and Chun Doo Hwan. Although concerns about national security were at the fore in the 1960s, 1970s, and 1980s, these South Korean military leaders also found proposals for new dialogue with the North to be a politically useful tool for distracting the South Korean public from domestic problems or political tensions that threatened to boil over from time to time. Park Chung Hee is alleged to have imposed harsh penalties on "anticommunist" rivals to enhance his authority and public support. Some scholars cite the execution of the so-called members of the "People's Revolutionary Party" in 1964 and the so-called East German Spy Ring or the Dongbaeklim incident in 1968 where a large number (around two hundred) of Korean students, professors, musicians, and artists in Germany were "kidnapped" back to South Korea on charges of espionage as evidence of this assertion.

Under the government of Chun Doo Hwan, Minister of Construction Lee Kyu Hyo shocked the nation on October 30, 1986 by warning that North's construction of the Kumgang Dam was posing a great threat to the lives of the South Koreans. He stated that should the Kumgang Dam collapse, the 20-billion ton of water held by the dam would submerge the Kangwon and Kyonggi area, including Seoul. This caused widespread panic and fostered a public movement to build the Peace Dam. This warning by the construction minister was later proven to be groundless (in 1993). It was viewed as a ploy to divert away attention from the rising public demand for the direct election of the president. The bombing of KAL on November 29, 1987, ten days before the presidential election of Chun's designated successor Roh Tae Woo and the arrest of the bomber Kim Hyun Hee on the day before the election, are also seen as efforts to manipulate Korean public opinion in South Korea's first democratic election following the authoritarian period. Since the authoritarian government routinely restricted information about North Korea from the public on national security grounds, reunification proposals were a convenient vehicle for distracting the South Korean public from focusing on their own social or political grievances by trying to show that they were moving the nation forward in its aspirations for Korean reunification.[3]

The Evolution of Public Views Toward North Korea

South Korea's democratization and the collapse of communism in the Soviet Union and Eastern Europe were important turning points that affected South Korean public perceptions of North Korea. Although the North Korean threat remained a political "card" subject to manipulation in order to build support for Chun Doo Hwan's chosen successor in the 1987 election of President Roh Tae Woo, Roh himself initiated a change in North Korean policy from confrontation to limited engagement with the announcement of his *Nordpolitik* policy on July 7, 1988.

Rapprochement with Eastern European countries and the Soviet Union were initially carried out in conjunction with the 1988 Seoul Olympics. The normalization of relations between South Korea and the Soviet Union was made possible by meetings with Mikhail Gorbachev in San Francisco and Cheju Island in 1990. Then came the exchange of trading offices and the eventual establishment of diplomatic relations with the PRC in 1992. Inter-Korean exchanges and trade opportunities were expanded at that time, and the Roh administration forged the inter-Korean Basic Agreement at a prime ministerial meeting in Seoul in December of 1991. During this period the first course on North Korean communism was taught at Seoul National University, and materials on North Korea that were once restricted to specialists became available to the broader public. The South Korean public view of North Korea became more three-dimensional as the North was no longer viewed solely through the prism of ideology as an enemy and potential aggressor, but as a society and a people. North Korea's economic and food crises began to become better known in Seoul. Church-based humanitarian efforts to provide rice to North Korea date from the early 1990s under the Roh administration.

The effects of greater availability of information about North Korea continued under former president Kim Young Sam. Despite intermittent periods of tension and crisis that characterized the North–South relationship during Kim Young Sam's administration, the South Korean government formally initiated food assistance to the North in 1995 (even this effort was motivated primarily by domestic politics and the mistaken impression on the part of Kim Young Sam that such a "breakthrough" might assist his party's performance in local elections) and was indirectly criticized for failing to maintain adequate back-channel dialogue with the leadership in Pyongyang.[4] Public images of North Korea gradually focused on not only the North's continued efforts at confrontation, but also on the deprivation and need of the North Korean people in the context of the failure of the North's economic system. In the minds of most South Koreans, the North has come to occupy the dual identities of "main enemy" and dialogue partner—a formidable, persistent, and potentially deadly military threat and at the same time a people in desperate need of assistance from the outside world.

The Changing South Korean Views of North Korea

With the election of Kim Dae Jung as president, it was inevitable that relations with North Korea would come to the forefront of political discussion in South Korea. Even prior to his election, Kim Dae Jung issued public appeals for dialogue with North Korea, signaling a major reversal from the policy of his predecessor, Kim Young Sam. Kim Dae Jung made dialogue with North Korea his primary preoccupation, and in his inaugural speech, laid out three principles that were to form the basis for his new Sunshine Policy of engagement with North Korea. He asserted that South Korea would "never tolerate armed provocation of any kind," that the South had no intention of [undermining and] absorbing the North, and that his administration would "actively pursue reconciliation and cooperation between the South and North."[5]

South Korea's democratization has contributed to the gradual transformation of the position and role of North Korea in South Korean politics. However, the hierarchical institutional structures and legacy of old-style partisan tactics and ossified tactical and political maneuvering hewn during the authoritarian period have continued to serve as structural obstacles that have prevented meeting Korean public expectations under democracy. South Korean dissatisfaction with politics as usual, has gradually built itself up in the form of populist support for "new faces" in Korean politics; that is, Park Chan Jong and to a certain extent Chung Ju Young in the early 1990s, Rhee In-je in 1997, and finally the wave of reformist sentiment grew large enough for Roh Moo Hyun to ride it to victory in 2002.

The transition from being the litmus test that negatively defines the limits of acceptable political dialogue to being an object of maneuver and potential vehicle by which South Korean parties seek to gain tactical advantage, might arguably be seen as a step toward Korean reunification in the sense that North Korea's role in South Korean domestic politics is now an active rather than a passive one. North Korea's KCNA even issued a statement warning against an independent prosecution to trace the money trail involving over $US500 million in cash that was passed from Hyundai to North Korea on the eve of the inter-Korean summit, with the foreknowledge and approval of the Kim Dae Jung administration. On the other hand, according to exit polls announced by KBS on the evening of the 2002 presidential election, only 9.7 percent of Koreans considered policy toward North Korea to be a decisive issue in the campaign, compared to around 30 percent each for the purely "domestic" issues of clean government and anticorruption, respectively.[6] This trend held up despite the backdrop of North Korea's crisis escalation tactics in the confrontation with the United States and the interdiction of North Korean efforts to deliver SCUD missiles to Yemen in the days before the election, a good example of the extent to which voters no longer consider policy toward North Korea or the dangers of a North Korean threat as decisive influences on South Korean voting behavior.

Ideology and the Sunshine Policy—Rocky Road from Kim Dae Jung's Inauguration to the Summit

In overturning past policies of confrontation with the North and seeking an expanded opening with North Korea, Kim Dae Jung was not in a position to play the role of U.S. President Richard Nixon, whose conservatism gave him the domestic credibility in the United States to meet with Chinese communists without significant opposition. Rather, Kim Dae Jung's eagerness to reconcile with the North made him vulnerable to charges that he was overeager or naïve in his pursuit of reconciliation with North Korea. Given this background in the public terms of debate, it is notable that public opinion at the time of Kim Dae Jung's inauguration was cautiously supportive of the resumption of exchanges and cooperation.[7] In a survey conducted by the Ministry of Unification at the time, 71.3 percent of the public supported pursuing an exchange of special envoys depending on the circumstances, while 23.5 percent supported the active pursuit of such an exchange; 72.6 percent cautiously supported the possibility of an inter-Korean summit, and 82.6 percent supported the provision of food aid in a rational and prudent manner.[8]

The political attack against Kim Dae Jung's approach as it unfolded in the Korean media focused on two core areas following Kim Dae Jung's inauguration speech: (1) What is the appropriate price South Korea should pay for the active pursuit of reconciliation and cooperation with North Korea? (2) Did the Sunshine Policy compromise national defen.e and national security in any way? To the extent that Kim Dae Jung appeared overeager or overly dependent on North Korean good will in his relentless pursuit of reconciliation, he would be vulnerable to attack by his political opponents.

Although cautiously willing to experiment with the Sunshine Policy, most opinion in the early stages of the Kim Dae Jung administration showed cautious skepticism, as demonstrated in the following commentary from the *Korea Times* prior to the first intergovernmental dialogue under the Kim Dae Jung administration: "First of all, the government must proceed with the coming bilateral talks following a principle of reciprocity. It should refrain from giving undue concessions to the North's excessive demands. It goes without saying that the North must change itself to build a new relationship of mutual trust and reconciliation with Seoul."[9]

A series of North Korean submarine incursions into the South during summer 1998 highlighted the second concern as a central feature of debate over the policy. These incursions set the tone for public debate and provided an opening for a round of criticism of the Sunshine Policy as too lenient or failing to ensure South Korea's national security. The *Chosun Ilbo* warned, "This new submarine incursion is a test of the new 'Sunshine Policy' as, no matter how much the government wants to distance politics and business, a passive approach will be unacceptable to the people. If the government is seen to be too passive, there is nothing to stop North Korea from repeating its actions as past history shows us. The South Korean government must not blindly stick to its 'sunshine policy,' but should be seen to act firmly in questions concerning national security."[10] A Ministry of Unification poll conducted following the incident showed that the incursion dampened public support for the Sunshine Policy, with 52.6 percent arguing to keep the current policy framework, while 33.3 percent argued that there was a need for a complete readjustment of the policy. However, by mid-August, 42.2 percent of the public supported a tougher and more decisive approach to North Korea, while 37.1 percent advocated a milder approach to the North.[11]

With the launching of a North Korean Taepodong missile in August 1998 and continuous sporadic incursions into South Korean territory to the end of 1998, the international mood and that of the South Korean public remained cautiously skeptical about whether or not the Sunshine Policy could be successful. By fall 1998, the Kim Dae Jung administration began to set aside the term "Sunshine Policy" in its engagement policy in response to rising criticisms and lack of progress. However, the successful initiation by Hyundai of the Mount Kumgang tours was able to breathe life into public support for such expanded exchanges and cooperation, even under controlled circumstances, as a step forward over having no exchange at all. As shown in the following *Chosun Ilbo* comment: "Rather than improving South-North relations, the government's policy has served only to increase the number of provocations by the North, and if the government sent fails to make a decisive move, this vicious cycle of incursions will continue. When this kind of provocation happens, the government needs to observe the situation coolly, listen to the opinions and concerns of the people and then make a decision, rather than rushing to defend its policy. The majority of the public is behind the Mount Kumgang tour project, but it is becoming increasingly concerned with the easy attitude the government has been adopting in light of the series of recent provocations."[12] This assessment is borne out in the Ministry of Unification polling from December 21, 1998, which shows that 56.3 percent of those surveyed were favorable to engagement with North Korea, but the majority also criticized the policy for being inconsistent, unrealistic, or not timely.[13]

Despite the hard-won symbolic progress represented by the establishment of the Hyundai tours to Mount Kumgang, the promise and expectations for a balanced and reciprocal process of exchange and dialogue with the North remained a source of frustration in many commentaries on inter-Korean affairs. There was also much criticism that the inter-Korean dialogue process itself was not transparent, a frustration that probably reflected broader public frustrations regarding the pace of democratic consolidation and lack of transparency in South Korea's domestic governance. The *Chungang Ilbo* observed on the first anniversary of Kim Dae Jung's inauguration in February of 1999 that "we have now reached a point where dialogue between authorities, which we have repeatedly called for, cannot be delayed any further. . . . It can be said that almost all of the taboos about North Korea have been removed, something that could not have been imagined a few years ago. In such a situation, if the North does not come forward for dialogue, we will have no choice but to despair that the reconciliation policy toward the North is no longer effective."[14]

The mixture of frustration with the North's begrudging response and urgency to achieve a breakthrough that might succeed in transforming public opinion and consolidating support for the Sunshine Policy became increasingly apparent through the course of 1999 and early 2000. The international environment eased with the appointment of the Clinton administration's Special Coordinator for Policy toward North Korea, former defense secretary, William Perry, who proceeded with a lengthy and cautious assessment of North Korea's intentions, including a May 1999 visit to Pyongyang. President Kim Dae Jung persistently sought new channels for expanded exchanges with North Korea, promising to facilitate North Korea's access to the international community and continuing to provide humanitarian assistance in a steady stream to meet the needs of the North Korean population. *Dong-A Ilbo* wrote a prescient comment on the Kim Dae Jung administration's accomplishment, attitude, and strategic aims as it pursued a summit with North Korea:

> The government is proud of what it has achieved so far by accepting the North's policy of ignoring the South Korean government, in the name of the engagement policy. However, the people's sentiment is not necessarily compatible with this . . . If an inter-Korean summit is held, it will indeed be a "great event" that may change the course of the destiny for the Korean Peninsula. Accordingly, one should not be too hasty in arranging a meeting between the two heads of state.[15]

Momentum in favor of a more constructive relationship with the North, however, quickly dissipated as a result of a series of increasingly severe clashes and physical confrontations between naval forces and fishing vessels in the West Sea. These clashes and incursions across the disputed Northern Limit Line gradually escalated as South Korean ships attempted to physically block North Korean vessels from coming south. These clashes over the course of several weeks finally escalated into a military conflict, the most significant inter-Korean naval clash in decades. Naturally, the increased tensions cast doubt on the effectiveness of the Sunshine Policy, leading *Chosun Ilbo* to make the following comment about the Sunshine Policy and its implementation: "What conservatives oppose is the sunshine only policy. As clearly demonstrated in several surveys, people want a careful balance of sunshine and wind, carrot and stick. They want to be consulted and not have the president determine North Korean policy on his own without aides, ministers or the National Assembly. On this issue, he should not disregard the people's wishes, as it is important for the future of the country. To argue over the policy for too long a time, is also not beneficial, particularly when North Korea is closely watching."[16]

A September 1999 survey of Kim Dae Jung's handling of foreign policy shows support by over 65 percent of respondents, boosted partly by North Korea's missile moratorium and the apparent improvement in North Korea's relationship with the United States.[17] This support was sustained in the run-up to the April 10 summit announcement and was heightened by the anticipation of a summit that developed during May and early June 2000.

Assessing the Summit and its Impact on South Korean Politics

The summit and its immediate aftermath posed the greatest challenge for the leadership of the opposition Grand National Party, which despite its electoral victory of April had very real worries that the influence of the inter-Korean summit would remake the South Korean political landscape in unpredictable ways. Indeed, the weeks following the summit were dominated by a nationwide debate over every aspect of the summit and the South–North declaration, the terms of which generally reflected the themes of price, implications for South Korean national security, and implications for domestic political structure and politics outlined in the previous section. It is worth closely examining the tactical and strategic counterarguments of the opposition as they have unfolded, as a means of better understanding how the parties have interpreted trends in South Korean public opinion that will have a critical impact on the pace and direction of the inter-Korean reconciliation process.

Reflecting the strong public support generated in the immediate aftermath of Kim Dae Jung's visit to Pyongyang and the signing of the Inter-Korean Joint Declaration, opposition party leader Lee Hoi Chang offered restrained congratulations upon Kim Dae Jung's return to Seoul, while also attempting to lay down a number of important markers and guidelines for pursuing inter-Korean reconciliation in the future. The markers that most clearly defined the opposition's position and offered indirect criticism of the summit outcome, were as follows: (1) failure of the Joint Declaration to explicitly address tension reduction and establishment of peace, (2) the need to transparently pursue reunification policy based on principles of democracy and market economy, (3) failure to discuss South Korean prisoners of war remaining in the North, while conceding the return of long-term political prisoners in South Korea, (4) the need for reciprocity and transparency in economic dealings with the North, (5) the need for consultation and deliberation in the National Assembly. While pointing out additional areas not addressed by the Joint Declaration, Lee emphasized the opposition's passively skeptical attitude toward the

North's capacity to fulfill promises made as part of the Joint Declaration ("actions speak louder than words").[18]

Recognizing the achievement of the summit, family reunions and other cultural exchanges, Lee Hoi Chang consistently singled out the failure of the Kim Dae Jung administration to clearly define the objectives of the Sunshine Policy, the failure of the summit to address the conventional security situation, the need to strategically use economic assistance as a tool for inducing reforms in North Korea's system, and the need to pursue inter-Korean relations with a spirit of reciprocity. Lee also criticized euphoria and empty symbolism as by-products of the summit. "We must not put emphasis on a cozy South–North relationship for its own sake; rather we seek a relationship that is productive in solving substantive problems of interest to both our countries. Nor do we seek reunification at any cost; rather we pursue a just society for all Koreans."[19]

The inter-Korean summit stimulated a nationwide debate in South Korea over the potential impact of reconciliation with the North on institutions and society within South Korea. The prospect of institutional and social change is contentious within South Korean society because it could threaten long-standing vested interests on both the elite and institutional level and because of the difficulties of calibrating necessary institutional changes with the pace of rapprochement with the North. In fact, the prospect of rapprochement with North Korea under Kim Jong Il is truly revolutionary if one considers that, strictly speaking, President Kim Dae Jung's visit to Pyongyang was a violation of the National Security Law. Kim Dae Jung's statement upon his return from Pyongyang that there now "will be no more war" on the Korean peninsula elicited strong reactions within Korean society and stimulated heated debate on controversial domestic issues related to defense spending, policy, and the question of whether North Korea should be categorized as the "main enemy" in its Defense White Paper.

The primary South Korean interlocutor in preparations for the summit was the chief of the National Intelligence Service (NIS), Lim Dong-won, who appeared publicly with Kim Dae Jung and Kim Jong Il in Pyongyang, a fact that has stimulated a debate over the future of NIS intelligence collection activities directed toward North Korea. The role and purposes of the NIS became a matter of controversy, as the NIS assumed the dual roles of primary interlocutor in North Korean monitoring and the chief institution devoted to counterintelligence efforts against North Korea.

The issue of how North Korea should be portrayed in South Korean textbooks has also been raised in the aftermath of the summit with the change in the overall image of the North as a potential partner standing in uneasy coexistence with North Korea's image as an enemy. Surveys of South Koreans show a generational gap in attitudes toward North Korea and prospects for national unification, with older Koreans more skeptical of North Korea but more desirous of reunification, while younger Koreans recognize the North as a dialogue partner but are apathetic about prospects for reunification.[20] How and whether South Korean media should report critical remarks about North Korea became a contentious issue in Seoul, leading to the dismissal of the president of the South Korean Red Cross in December 2000 for remarks that were critical of North Korea. Some journalists have even voiced suspicions that the tax office probe of media companies launched in early 2001 represented an attempt to "tame" the media so as to squelch public opposition or criticism in anticipation of a return visit to Seoul by Chairman Kim Jong Il. An opinion column by *Chungang Ilbo* chief editorial writer Kwon Youngbin in October 2000 highlighted some of the key divisions that had been thrown into relief through continuous debate over the implications and impact of the June summit: "We believe, perhaps somewhat innocently, that inter-Korean issues could be resolved by the two Koreas embracing each other. This leaves no room for calculated negotiations to safeguard national interests. Advocates of the emotion-laden "embrace" approach are called pro-reunification while the negotiation supporters are branded anti-reunification forces."[21]

Prior to the summit, over 34 percent of Koreans surveyed viewed Kim Jong Il as a dictator, compared to less than 10 percent polled immediately following the summit, and over 97 percent indicated that they would welcome a visit by Kim Jong Il to Seoul.[22] Korean expectations for reunification also rose as a result of the summit, with over 71 percent of Korean students expressing optimism about the possibility of unification polled in July 2001 compared to only 59 percent a year earlier.[23] Public opinion polls from the end of 2000 show that almost 80 percent of the public supported a policy of cooperation and reconciliation with North Korea; however, the public gradually turned skeptical of Kim Dae Jung's generous approach to the North once again.[24]

Although South Korean public support remained strong through the symbolic and euphoric events following the summit until mid-September, public opinion toward the Sunshine Policy began to decline as the North continued to avoid substantive progress in conjunction with the symbolic exchanges that had come one after another and in each case—from divided families to combined symphony and operatic performances—had revealed their own stark differences between North and South Korean societies. A *Kyonghyang Sinmun* poll from early October 2000 shows that 57.1 percent of respondents supported the Sunshine Policy compared to 39 percent who opposed to the policy. While 59.3 percent of respondents regarded North Korea's actions as reflecting a "temporary change in attitude without renouncing the strategy of reunification by force," 29.3 percent regarded it as a "fundamental shift in policy, favoring South-North reconciliation."[25]

One factor that influenced a decline in public support for the Sunshine Policy was South Korea's own economic slowdown. The public perception was that domestic issues, including labor–management issues, public health care, anticorruption efforts within the government bureaucracy, and so on, were neglected or poorly handled by the Kim Dae Jung administration. In addition, the Kim Dae Jung administration consistently failed to respond to deepening domestic ideological divisions by reaching out and building a national consensus in favor of his policy toward the North. *Munhwa Ilbo* columnist Yun Ch'ang-chung wrote, "even if we assume anti-reunification forces really exist in the South, those in power have to demonstrate the leadership of even embracing such forces and winning their support. It is also their responsibility to do so. If the government gives the impression of neglecting the economy again, its North Korea policy will fail."[26]

The ideological division over the intent of engagement is clearly revealed in rationales that have been put forward for pursuing Kim Dae Jung's Sunshine Policy.

President Kim Dae Jung himself almost always presented a "liberal" rationale for pursuing engagement with North Korea, arguing that the leadership in Pyongyang has finally recognized the "true intentions" of the Sunshine Policy and has decided that it is possible to trust South Korea. According to this rationale, unconditional giving to North Korea is an essential vehicle for showing good faith, and eventually North Korea will also respond in good faith as trust has been built between the two sides. However, there is also a "realist" rationale for opening a political dialogue as a vehicle for inducing economic dependency and thereby defanging the North. This line of argumentation appeals to most South Korean conservatives, but is almost never used by the ROK government, partially because in recognition that such a rationale will only intensify North Korean mistrust and hesitancy to engage with South Korea.

Rapid diplomatic developments between the United States and North Korea during fall 2000 served to temporarily divert the energy of the North Koreans away from its interactions with the South and toward the prospects of a breakthrough with Washington. One of North Korea's top military leaders, Jo Myung Rok, visited Washington in early October, followed by a visit to Pyongyang by U.S. Secretary of State Madeleine Albright in late October 2000. The focus of this exchange was on improved U.S.–DPRK relations and a deal to end North Korea's missile exports. However, time ran out on that particular diplomatic effort, which might have led to a visit to Pyongyang by U.S. President Bill Clinton. The prospect of a U.S. presidential visit itself was enormously controversial, and helped to deepen ideological divisions in the debate over the policy toward North Korea, both in Washington and Seoul. Bush campaign advisors and the future senior policy staff viewed the Clinton administration's effort as premature and not close to the kind of deal that would justify the legitimacy Kim Jong Il would derive from a presidential visit.

Discussions about the prospect of such a visit led to a more aggressive Grand National Party stance, which publicly took the side of the Bush camp against a visit to Pyongyang in the waning days of the Clinton presidency. The ideological divisions over North Korea in Washington reinforced political divisions in Seoul between conservatives and progressives and helped set the stage for a failed summit meeting in early March 2001 in Washington between President Bush and President Kim Dae Jung. There were attempts to cover the extent of the disagreement over policy, but "ABC" (Anything But Clinton) attitudes, counterproductive public lobbying for continuity in policy among top Clinton aides, and the Kim Dae Jung government's endorsement with Russian President Putin only a week earlier of the Anti-Ballistic Missile Treaty (the overturning of which was a core policy of the new Bush team) effectively served to stall U.S.–ROK cooperation. The failed summit in March 2001 effectively ended momentum for Kim Dae Jung's Sunshine Policy for the remainder of his term in office and deepened internal ideological divisions in South Korea's domestic politics.

Despite the dramatic changes between Washington and Seoul, South Korean public opinion toward Kim Dae Jung's Sunshine Policy eroded relatively slowly. The South Korean public's eye was fixed not on Washington, but rather on the extent to which Kim Jong Il appeared to be cooperating in allowing exchange and cooperation efforts to move forward. As inter-Korean cooperation waned, so would South Korean public support. However, renewed cooperation efforts would help improve South Korean public opinion regarding the Sunshine Policy.

One year following the summit on June 11, 2001, a *Chosun Ilbo* survey showed that 50.1 percent of those surveyed believed that North Korea has not changed much and that 43.9 percent think that the Kim Dae Jung government is not managing policy toward the North well, compared to 33.9 percent who believed that the government is doing well.[27] The *Chosun Ilbo* provided clear evidence of the depth of the domestic cleavage between liberals and conservatives over the policy toward North Korea in a reflective first anniversary editorial that demonstrated the perceived threats accompanying reconciliation on the conservative side, the difficulties and failures of the Kim Dae Jung administration in achieving national consensus and support for reconciliation with the North, and the extent to which the cleavage itself revived historical political divisions between Right and Left reminiscent of the immediate postliberation political environment of the late 1940s:

> If you exclude the South's conservative camp when looking at the South as a partner in exchange, cooperation, and unification, then the question becomes: Who is unification for? How could that kind of reunification ever be true unification and not another division? The South's "conservatives" have been exactly the ones who have wanted to see the status quo maintained under peaceful coexistence instead of abolishing the old norms of division on the Korean peninsula.[28]

The seriousness of the ideological divisions within South Korea over the policy toward the North came to a head in late August 2001, following a controversial visit to the North for joint Liberation Day festivities by representatives from progressive South Korean NGOs. The North Koreans included as part of the itinerary some events that were designed to require specific demonstrations of support for and fealty to the North Korean government and Kim Jong Il. The issue of whether or not to participate in those activities divided South Korean NGOs and became a controversial issue in South Korea. The ROK government was forced to consider whether or not those who participated in the ceremonies honoring the North Korean state and its leader should be tried under the National Security Law. However, the biggest casualty of this event was Minister of Unification Lim Dong Won, who faced and lost a vote of confidence in the opposition-dominated National Assembly in late August. This was a severe setback and loss of face for Kim Dae Jung, although Lim Dong Won continued to direct North Korean engagement efforts as a private advisor to Kim Dae Jung inside the Blue House. The vote demonstrated the limits of public support for the administration and revealed the depth of opposition in the National Assembly to an approach to Korean unification increasingly viewed as "one-sided." Interestingly enough, however, polls conducted following this event suggested that the Korean public distinguished between the importance of continuing to engage with North Korea and the management of that process under the stewardship of the Kim Dae Jung administration. A *Kyonghyang Sinmun* poll showed an increase in public support for the Sunshine Policy to 64 percent compared with 57 percent in a survey conducted one year earlier, but public confidence in the Kim Dae Jung administration had dropped during that time to below 40 percent.[29]

A survey conducted by the Ministry of Unification only a week following the renewal of inter-Korean ministerial meetings at which new cooperation and exchanges were announced, also showed continuing public support for inter-Korean engagement policies. According to this poll, 76.8 percent of respondents fully or partially supported the Sunshine Policy, while 19 percent fully or partially opposed the policy. Over 60 percent of respondents supported continued provision of food aid to North Korea, while 38.4 percent did not support continued food aid.[30]

Two sets of statements at the end of January 2002 served to crystallize a growing gap between conservatives and progressives in South Korea. These statements linked South Korea's divided perceptions to differences in perception and approach between the U.S. and South Korean governments. First, President George Bush's State of the Union address at the end of January 2002, referring to North Korea as a charter member of the "axis of evil," galvanized public opinion and threw into relief the perception gap in Washington and Seoul. At about the same time, the newly appointed Minister of Unification Chung Se Hyon, said, "North Korea's atomic, biological and chemical weapons are not for the purpose of attacking the South, but to serve as a bargaining chip when negotiating with powerful countries." These two statements crystallized differences in approach and perception that have paralyzed inter-governmental coordination toward the North and have further contributed to perceptions that the choice for South Korea is between Washington and Pyongyang.[31] By February 2002, a Gallup Korea poll showed that 52.3 percent of respondents agreed with the opinion that aid should be given on a more give-and-take basis while engaging the North, while only 29 percent agreed with the statement that the Sunshine Policy was "contributing to peace on the Korean penin-sula so the policy needs to be continued," and 16.3 percent of respondents agreed that the Sunshine Policy "should be stopped since North Korea is not changing."[32]

Following the second clash in the West Sea in June 2002 that resulted in the sink-ing of a South Korean naval vessel and the deaths of four South Korean navy person-nel, support for the Sunshine Policy once again abated. In response to the question, "What policy direction should the government take toward North Korea in the future?" 59.1 percent of respondents agreed that "a strong policy stance should be taken in tandem with the Sunshine Policy depending on the North's attitude," 15.8 percent argued that "the Sunshine Policy should be abandoned and a strong policy stance should be pursued," 16.2 percent agreed with the opinion that the "Sunshine Policy should continue as it is," and 8.9 percent agreed with the opinion that the "Sunshine Policy needs to be strengthened."[33] However, public support for the Sunshine Policy returned after the North renewed exchanges and cooperation in the summer 2002, although increasing frustrations with the way in which they were implemented have been exacerbated by persistent rumors during the fall 2002 pres-idential campaign. Subsequently, the rumors were confirmed following the end of the campaign, that the ROK government used the Hyundai corporation as a conduit for hundreds of millions of dollars as payment for the summit. This was a rumor and allegation that had persisted in conservative circles from the announcement of the summit itself. The revelations resulted in widespread indignation and disappointment, despite the election of Roh Moo Hyun and the acquisition of general public support for continuing reconciliation with North Korea, there are strong public demands for a complete investigation and assignment of responsibility of the cash-for-summit charges that were not disclosed at the time of the summit announcement. A poll conducted by *Choson Ilbo* and *Gallup Korea* in January 2003 showed that

55.9 percent of respondents favored an independent prosecutor over a "political resolution" (34.9 percent). There was overwhelming support (81.9 percent of respondents) for the proposition that "assistance toward North Korea should be made in a transparent manner even if the progress in South–North relations will be rather slow," and 68.9 percent of respondents agreed that "the Sunshine Policy should be accompanied by a hard-line policy depending on North Korea's attitude."[34] Allegations of malfeasance and personal enrichment by officials involved, in addition to concerns about transparency in the implementation of the policy, eventually forced newly elected President Roh Moo Hyun to recognize the passage of an independent counsel to dig into the allegations and lay bare a more full account of the story while also attempting to protect the continuation of engagement with North Korea.

Conclusion

The inter-Korean summit was the most visible and bold effort between the two Koreas to achieve peaceful coexistence since the end of the Cold War. As has been noted in the introductory chapter, unlike other inter-Korean peace efforts, this initiative was unmediated by outside parties and indigenous to the two Koreas. Although the summit has now been tarnished by allegations that it was bought—and the Sunshine Policy has been subject to criticism for its failure to change North Korea—it is undeniable that the implementation of the Sunshine Policy during the Kim Dae Jung administration has revolutionized South Korean attitudes toward the North. The policy and the summit engendered a bitter ideological debate within South Korea on the merits, implementation, and end objectives of the policy. This debate coincided with South Korea's democratization, which in part made possible such a bitter debate, even while it brought to the surface and heightened conflicts internal to South Korea.

It is ironic that a main effect of the inter-Korean summit would be the deepening of ideological divisions between conservatives and progressives. Although many aspects of the summit were debated, the most divisive and fundamental question was whether it would be possible to compromise South Korea's democratic principles for the sake of building a better relationship with the North. We have shown earlier that despite reservations, South Koreans as a whole are fundamentally supportive of an engagement process with North Korea for a variety of reasons: it may be the only viable option, it could lead to change in North Korea, or it could help to heal national division and bring about reconciliation and North Korea's rehabilitation. However, there are fundamental differences between South Korean conservatives and progressives over how they see a potential union with North Korea. Conservatives expect that North Korea will adapt and join South Korea's vibrant democracy, while progressives appear to uphold Korean unification as a higher ideal than the preservation of democratic forms. Or perhaps progressives see the triumph of Korean democracy as so inevitable that there is little need to worry about the forms of unification; in the end the only choice for the two Koreas will be to pursue a unified democratic social and political system.

The transformation of terms of discourse in the South Korean political and social sphere resulting from South Korea's democratization has sharpened some fundamental, unresolved contradictions in policy toward North Korea. North Korea's future is a critical issue to be addressed as South Korea continues to search for an effective policy toward the North. How these issues are described and interpreted in the context of Korea's developing political discourse is a leading factor in determining the breadth of domestic political support for the Roh Moo Hyun administration's policies toward North Korea.

While the debate is ongoing, the new administration of President Roh Moo Hyun has signaled its eagerness to move forward in reforms and this might further enhance South Korea's democratization process. These reforms in many respects threaten the old guard and constitute an overarching battle between South Korea's traditional organizational hierarchy and structure for interaction based on seniority and tradition versus a more modern, complex, and egalitarian democratic approach to governance and policy-making. Roh has tried to take leadership out of the hands of the traditional elite and put it into the hands of a younger, more technocratic, and hopefully, more meritocratic set of leaders. One implicit assumption underlying such an approach is that Korea itself has progressed sufficiently that there is sufficient depth within the society so that ordinary professionals and scholars can make valid public policy proposals—without necessarily going to the blue-blood institutions or past leaders who have sat on top of and benefitted from hierarchies and a form of meritocracy that rewarded outstanding seniors from top schools at the expense of "ordinary" people who may be more in touch with their own needs and desires, and may be considerably more sophisticated in reading the North and its own political leadership than many in the elite would like to think. The question is whether the institutions within the society (media, business, civil society, military) have sufficiently matured in their respective spheres to be willing to pursue their respective policy objectives on the basis of the national consensus that President Roh called for in his inaugural address. How and whether that national consensus may be achieved is a fundamental challenge that the new government will face, and the management of South Korea's internal conflict over policy toward North Korea may be one of the most difficult prerequisites for the successful conceptualization and implementation of a South Korean policy toward the North that can truly bridge the gap in overcoming inter-Korean conflict and finally achieving reconciliation.

Notes

1. The opinions expressed in this chapter are personal views and do not necessarily represent the views of The Asia Foundation. This chapter is a revised and expanded version of an article entitled, "The End of History, the Rise of Ideology, and the Future of Democracy on the Korean Peninsula," originally published in the *Journal of East Asian Studies* 3:2 (May–August 2003): 199–223. I wish to acknowledge with gratitude the permission of Lynn Rienner Publishers to republish this article in revised form. I would also like to thank Eun Jung Cahill Che and Seon Yong Ban for providing research assistance in the preparation of this chapter.
2. The Constitution of the Republic of Korea may be found at http://www.moleg.go.kr/ mlawinfo/english/htms/html/law01.html.
3. Chong Chong-Wook, "Has North Korea Really Changed?" *Korea Focus* 9: 3 (March–April 2001), p. 53.
4. The November 1996 edition of *Wolgan Chosun* included a series of articles describing the history of secret inter-Korean contacts. The theme of the issue may be seen as a not-so-subtle hint to then-President Kim Young Sam that such contacts have traditionally been

regarded as an important means by which to enhance and assure security and avoid over-heating in the inter-Korean relationship.

5. Nicholas D. Kristof, "South Korea's New President Appeals to (the?) North to End Decades of Division," *New York Times*, February 25, 1998, p. 8.

6. KBS Survey results broadcast as part of election coverage on the evening of December 18, 2002.

7. Available public opinion polling used in this article come from a variety of sources, and questions may be intended to elicit differing responses, depending on the relative positions reflected by the polls' sponsors. Generally speaking, the Ministry of National Unification has sought to put a positive spin on public support for the Sunshine Policy, while other sources may be regarded as more critical. For this reason, the author has tried to provide detailed information on the questions that were asked in the polls as part of reporting on the variety of public polling data that he was able to uncover. To the extent possible, the same polling sources have been used over time to demonstrate fluctuations in public response. The analysis of the polls is designed more to discern trends, in combination with editorial content analysis, also designed to reveal opinions across the political spectrum.

8. *Chosun Ilbo* (Digital Chosun), February 27, 1998.

9. "S-N Governmental Meeting," *Korea Times* (April 7), 1998: 6.

10. "Another Submarine," *Chosun Ilbo* (Internet edition) in English, June 23, 1998. As reported in FBIS, document ID: FTS19989623001346.

11. Digital Chosun, June 29, 1998, August 19, 1998.

12. "Sunshine Policy, Again," *Chosun Ilbo* (Internet edition) in English, December 18, 1998. As reported in FBIS: SK1812134798.

13. Digital Chosun, December 21, 1998.

14. "Inter-Korean Dialogue Cannot Be Delayed Further," *Chungang Ilbo* (Internet version) in Korean, February 24, 1999. From FBIS Doc No.: SK2702122199.

15. "Preconditions for Summit," *Donga Ilbo* (Internet version) in Korean, May 6, 1999. From FBIS Doc No.: SK0705093999.

16. "The Sunshine Argument," *Choson Ilbo* (Internet version) in English, June 18, 1999. From FBIS Doc No.: SK1806135899.

17. *Source: Union Research—1,000 people surveyed from 13:30 to 21:30 on September 18.* http://www.union.re.kr/board/view.php?id=news&page=2&sn1=&divpage=1&sn=off&ss=on&sc=on&select_arrange=headnum&desc=asc&no=20).

18. Grand National Party President Lee Hoi Chang, "Remarks made by Grand National Party President Lee Hoi Chang at a press conference in Seoul, June 19, 2000," on the outcome of the recent summit meeting between South and North Korea (as posted on the GNP website: www.hannaradang.or.kr).

19. Lee Hoi Chang, "Toward Peace and Unification of the Korean Peninsula," *Korea Times*, November 1, 2000.

20. Han Mann Gil, "Role of Education in National Unification," *Korea Focus* 9: 2 (March–April 2001), pp. 133–146.

21. Kwon Young-bin, "Rational Policy on North Korea Desired: Transform Emotional North Korea Policies to Sustainable Cool-headed Approach," *Chungang Ilbo* (Internet version) in English, October 28, 2000. FBIS Doc. No.: KPP200001028000027.

22. *Donga Ilbo*, May 31; June 15, as cited in Lee Geun, "Political and Economic Consequences of the Inter-Korean Summit," presented at the 2001 KAIS International Conference, June 22–23, 2001, p. 11.

23. Han, "Role of Education in National Unification," p. 134.

24. Yi Tong-hyon, "Reporter's note: North Korea Policy Should Stick to Principles," JoongAng Ilbo (Internet version in Korean), January 2, 2001, FBIS Document No. KPP20010102000094. Gallup Poll Survey on Political Support, December 26, 2000.

25. Yi Chung-kun, "57% Support 'Sunshine Policy'...[Support] on Slow Decline," *Kyonghyang Sinmun* (Internet Version) in Korean, October 5, 2000. FBIS Document No.: Kpp200001006000004.

26. Yun Cha'ng-chung, "Kim Chong-il's Visit to South Korea Should be Realized in the New Year," *Munhwa Ilbo* (in Korean), December 29, 2000. FBIS Document No: KPP20001229000047.

27. Lee Geun, op. cit., p. 11.

28. "One Year On," *Chosun Ilbo* (Internet version-WWW) in English, June 14, 2001. FBIS Doc. No.: KPP20010615000009.

29. Pak Yong-nae, "50 Percent of Respondents Say 'President Kim is Not Doing a Good Job,'" *Kyonghyang Sinmun* (Internet version-WWW) in Korean, October 7, 2001. FBIS Doc. No.: KPP20011008000020.

30. Poll conducted by the Korea Research Center and Ministry of Unification "Public Opinion Poll Regarding Engagement Policy toward North Korea," September 24, 2001.

31. "Don't Worry, Be Happy," *Chungang Ilbo* (Internet Version-WWW) in English, February 3, 2002. FBIS Doc. No. KPP200203000053.

32. Gallup Korea—http://panel.gallup.co.kr/svcdb/recent_content.asp?objSN =20020203009.

33. *Chosun Ilbo* and Gallup Korea. Random sample of 1,011 adults over age 20 surveyed over the phone on July 6. http://www.gallup.co.kr/News/2002/release076.html.

34. Hong Yong-nim, "Chosun Ilbo-Gallup Public Opinion Survey—63 percent Believe 'Funds Transferred to North Korea Were Compensation for [North-South] Summit,'" *Chosun Ilbo* (Internet version), in Korean February 6, 2003. FBIS Doc. No. KPP20030205000022.

CHAPTER THREE

INTER-KOREAN RELATIONS: A NORTH KOREAN PERSPECTIVE

Charles K. Armstrong

Introduction

Despite the continued hostility and competition for legitimacy between the two Koreas, inter-Korean relations have slowly but steadily increased and diversified in recent years. From a North Korean perspective, this expanding interaction with Seoul embodies a fundamental contradiction in Pyongyang's worldview: the DPRK's long-standing "theological" belief in the superiority of the North Korean system and ultimate unification on North Korean terms on the one hand, and on the other a practical understanding that not only is the DPRK extremely disadvantaged economically—and in some ways even militarily—vis-à-vis the South, but that sustained and expanding contacts could pose a grave danger to the stability and viability of the North Korean political system. Yet Pyongyang seems willing to take that risk in order to rescue what remains of its economy and prevent even further decline and deterioration. Despite the inevitable talk of unification, inter-Korean relations are less important for Pyongyang as an end in themselves than as a means for economic revitalization, which is in turn an important part of Kim Jong Il's own legitimation. As long as inter-Korean relations offer these benefits without appearing to threaten the security and stability of the DPRK regime, Pyongyang will likely continue dealing with Seoul in a contained and limited fashion.

The crisis that emerged between the United States and the DPRK over North Korea's nuclear program in October 2002, quickly overshadowed some remarkable developments in inter-Korean relations and the first major signs of economic opening in North Korea in decades. In the first nine months of 2002 alone, North Korea agreed to cabinet-level talks with the South, the reestablishment of road and rail links between the two Koreas, and de-mining areas of the DMZ around these links; sent the first-ever delegation of North Korean athletes to South Korea, for the Asian Games in Pusan; hosted Japanese Prime Minister Koizumi in Pyongyang, where Kim Jong Il made the stunning admission that North Korea had abducted Japanese citizens in the 1970s and 1980s; and launched a series of economic changes that seemed to move North Korea definitively in the direction of market-oriented reform.[1]

Yet despite the "October Surprise" of North Korea's apparent admission to a secret highly enriched uranium (HEU) program in violation of international agreements, the subsequent collapse of the 1994 Agreed Framework that had frozen the DPRK's plutonium program for eight years, and the escalating crisis with the United States, North–South contacts continued and grew. Inter-Korean talks took place as scheduled in late January 2003, land routes on the east and west coasts were reopened, South Korean tour buses made the first overland tours to Mt. Kumgang in North Korea in over 50 years, the South Korean conglomerate Hyundai continued work on an industrial plant in Kaesong, and the two Koreas held a sixth round of family reunions. With the election of South Korean President Roh Moo Hyun in December 2002, the DPRK found its most cooperative South Korean government ever. While both outgoing president Kim Dae Jung and president-elect Roh condemned North Korea's moves toward nuclear weapons production, they also made it clear that— unlike the United States—South Korea would condone neither the use of force nor economic isolation and sanctions to compel Pyongyang's compliance. Rather, Roh emphasized even more strongly than his predecessor that inter-Korean economic cooperation would continue and that dialogue and economic inducements were the best means to bring about positive change in North Korea's behavior.

Seoul's gamble is that the United States and the DPRK would resolve the nuclear issue peacefully, while growing inter-Korean contacts would draw Pyongyang out and help establish a more stable and cooperative environment on the Korean peninsula. North Korea, for its part, demonstrated through its actions of the previous year that it was prepared to take important steps—small steps perhaps, but unprecedented and risky moves by North Korean standards—toward reform and cooperation. More than ever, the DPRK leadership seemed to understand that its interests were best served by working together with South; indeed, the U.S.–DPRK confrontation and anti-U.S. sentiment in the South seemed to be pushing the two Koreas together as never before. Of course, a military clash between the United States and North Korea or a new war on the Korean peninsula could change the equation entirely, and possibly lead to a disappearance of the DPRK. But few in South Korea, particularly in the government, seemed to take this is to be a real possibility. Assuming that the nuclear stand-off will not lead to a catastrophic war and that the DPRK will remain in existence for some time to come—the assumptions that underlay current South Korean (not to mention North Korean) behavior—then Pyongyang will continue to move toward incremental change domestically and greater interaction with South Korea externally. Increasingly, both Pyongyang and Seoul have treated each other as legitimate states rather than hostile non-state entities, and this mutual recognition is an important and necessary step toward any peaceful form of unification.

Pyongyang's Policy Toward Seoul to 2000

Despite considerable evolution in North Korea's Southern policy since the two states were founded in 1948, there are certain underlying principles that—in theory at least—have remained consistent. It is debatable how much these general principles really drive policy. They can rather be considered ideological boundaries within which a reasonably flexible policy can be constructed, sets of beliefs rather than concrete policy formulae; we might consider them part of the "theology" of the

DPRK.[2] These principles may be summarized as follows.

- Principle 1: The DPRK is the true representative of the Korean people, and the regime in the South is a grave threat to the very existence of the DPRK, backed by a ceaselessly hostile United States. Therefore the DPRK must have a *strong defense* at all costs against American and South Korean hostility. This defense is not just military, but also ideological: the people of North Korea must be protected from any ideological infection of South Korean or Western capitalism, which would only confuse the people and undermine unity and morale. Related to this is Principle 2.
- Principle 2: The people, as opposed to the government, of South Korea would warmly welcome unity with their Northern brethren and would be much more sympathetic toward the DPRK and its leadership, were they not restrained and indoctrinated by their government and U.S. propaganda. Therefore, the DPRK government should pursue *united front tactics* with sympathetic elements in South Korea (and abroad) whenever possible, dividing the people from their unrepresentative government.
- Finally, Principle 3: Ultimately the North's position will win because it is morally correct and will gain the support of the people of North and South. Therefore, at times *dealing directly with ROK leadership* has been considered a feasible tactic for unification. It is possible to negotiate with the ROK and even establish a "Confederation" bringing the two systems together under a single state, provided outside powers (meaning primarily the United States) do not interfere and the systems are left as they are for the time being. This is because, if left to themselves, Koreans (North and South) will eventually see the superiority of the North Korean system and voluntarily choose to be governed by it.[3]

Unification remains the stated goal of the North Korean regime and there is no reason to doubt that the population as a whole feels a strong emotional commitment to unification in the abstract. On the other hand, knowledge of real conditions in the South is virtually nonexistent for the populace at large and even for most of the DPRK leadership. But without altering these fundamental, "theological" principles of unification outlined earlier, North Korean policy toward the South has changed considerably over time. Increasingly, both Pyongyang and Seoul have treated each other as legitimate states rather then as hostile non-state entities.

Waiting for the Revolution, 1948–1972
Seoul–Pyongyang relations have evolved through three successive stages: the first two culminated in inter-Korean agreements in 1972 (the July 4 Communiqué) and 1991 (the Basic Agreement on Reconciliation, Non-Aggression, Exchanges and Cooperation), each of which raised great expectations of reconciliation and reunification on the Korean peninsula but were soon overtaken by renewed distrust and mutual hostility. The third stage has seen the emergence of the DPRK from a decade of internal and external crises—including the collapse of Pyongyang's communist

allies, the death of Kim Il Sung, the 1993–94 nuclear standoff with the United States, and the famine of the mid-1990s—and culminated in the June 2000 summit and resulting June 15 Declaration. While few concrete results of the 2000 summit have emerged to date, Pyongyang seems to have moved closer than ever to a policy of peaceful coexistence toward the South.

In theory, North Korea has never given up on the idea that South Korea would one day undergo a socialist revolution and join the North under a single revolutionary government. This idea was first expressed in 1946 with the concept of North Korea as a "democratic base" (*minju kiji*):

> In a country undergoing revolution, one area succeeds in revolution before another, establishing a revolutionary regime and accomplishing democratic reforms, and is a base for carrying out the revolutionary process through the whole country. The northern half of the Republic is such a base for anti-imperialist, anti-feudal democratic revolution in the whole country.[4]

While waiting for revolution to erupt "in the whole country," the revolutionary regime should unite with sympathetic elements in the nonrevolutionary part of the country. This is the origin of Pyongyang's United Front policy, and North Korea still attempts to cultivate the support of anti-government critics in South Korea. But since the democratization of the late 1980s, there has been little sign of sympathy for the DPRK among the shrinking group of South Korean radicals. It seems unlikely that the Pyongyang leadership puts much hope in a pro-DPRK cadre in South Korea, at least in the short run.

Initially, this United Front strategy was combined with a proactive military strategy, and in June 1950 North Korea decided to invade the South, a decision that was bold but by no means irrational under the circumstances. Indeed, the war would have quickly ended in the North's favor had it not been for the U.S.-led coalition's defense of the ROK. North Korean Foreign Minister Pak Hon-yong's prediction that a huge pro-Pyongyang uprising would erupt in the South in support of the Korean People's Army turned out to be wrong, and Pak paid with his life for his failure of prognostication; he was executed for treason in 1955. Nevertheless, the fact that the Rhee regime was saved by the U.S. and UN forces during the Korean War could be used to support the notion that the ROK was an artificial entity propped up by the Americans, and that a combination of North Korean fortitude and subtle subversion would undermine and ultimately destroy the Southern regime. This might be called North Korea's "Vietnam strategy," except that in contrast to the National Liberation Front in South Vietnam, there was no viable pro-Northern guerilla movement in South Korea after the Korean War. Pyongyang's approach seems to have been that since the ROK would collapse due to its own contradictions sooner rather than later, the North should bide its time and be prepared to move in and reunify the country when the opportunity presented itself. But a June 25–style invasion was never again attempted, for two reasons: the clear U.S. commitment toward the defense of South Korea, and the unwillingness of the USSR and China to support such a venture.[5]

Thus, when the "Student Revolution" of April 1960 arose and led to the removal of Syngman Rhee, the DPRK leadership hoped for a collapse of the Southern system that would lead to unification on North Korean terms. In order to achieve this end, the DPRK softened its rhetoric toward the interim Chang Myon government, which the North Koreans perceived as weak. Although this was couched in terms of "peaceful coexistence," the DPRK leadership seems to have felt that the South would soon come under communist control, and stepped up training of southern-born cadres for that end.[6] But after the military coup and the emergence of the Park Chung Hee government in 1961, this window of opportunity for unification on North Korean terms appeared to have closed.

Nevertheless, Pyongyang did not give up on a potential military solution to the problem of Korean division. In the 1960s, the DPRK focused on preparing for a military confrontation with the Americans and their "Fascist" lackeys that would end in a decisive North Korean victory. Beginning in 1962 North Korea embarked on a renewed program of military build-up under the slogan *chonmin mujanghwa* (arming the entire people), diverting precious economic resources into the military at precisely the moment when East bloc–assistance for postwar reconstruction was discontinued.[7] This proved to be a turning point for the DPRK economy; after an impressive period of postwar development in the 1950s and early 1960s, North Korea would never regain its economic advantage over the South, and the North's GNP growth would slow down, erode, and by the 1990s go into reverse.

In the area of inter-Korean relations, both Koreas at this time practiced their version of West Germany's Hallstein Doctrine or China's policy toward the Republic of China on Taiwan: refusal to recognize the rival state's existence or to maintain diplomatic ties with any foreign country that recognized it. Both Koreas were entrenched in their respective Cold War blocs, which reinforced the North–South Korean confrontation and inhibited North–South contact. This external environment changed dramatically in the early 1970s, when the Nixon administration made secret, and then public, overtures toward normalization with the People's Republic of China, North Korea's closest supporter. To preempt abandonment by their respective patrons, the two Koreas took matters into their own hands and began direct negotiations with each other, first through their respective Red Cross committees and then through a series of meetings between North and South Korean intelligence officers.[8] Just under a year after Henry Kissinger's secret visit to Beijing on July 9, 1971, Seoul and Pyongyang issued a Joint Communiqué on July 4, 1972, outlining their principles for peaceful unification.

Slouching Toward Coexistence, 1972–92
By the 1970s the DPRK had put aside, or at least moderated, its Southern Revolution strategy.[9] This does not mean that North Korea had given up altogether on the notion that the South Korean regime might collapse. Attempts to destabilize the ROK government through direct action reached a peak in 1968, with the infiltration of North Korean commandoes onto the grounds of the South Korean presidential compound, or Blue House. The commandoes came within a few hundred yards of their target, President Park Chung Hee, before they were apprehended by ROK security forces. This was followed by the North Korean capture of the American intelligence ship the *USS Pueblo*, whose crew was held captive for a year and was released following an American apology (swiftly rescinded) for spying on the DPRK.

Thereafter, direct action gave way to terrorist tactics by North Korean agents. In 1974 an ethnic Korean from Japan attempted to assassinate Park Chung Hee but failed, shooting and killing Park's wife instead. In October 1983, North Korean agents set off a bomb that killed a dozen members of ROK President Chun Doo Hwan's cabinet in Rangoon, Burma, although they missed killing Chun himself. While deplorable, the DPRK's assassination tactics were not the same as the kind of terrorism practiced by the Irish Republican Army in Britain or Islamic terrorist groups in the Middle East. The DPRK did not engage in random violence toward civilians, attempting to terrorize the population at large, but rather targeted political leaders for assassination.[10] This is consistent with the North Korean belief that the people and government in South Korea can be separated, and that eliminating unpopular South Korean leaders will create a favorable image of North Korea among the oppressed South Korean civilian population. One major exception to this tactic was the bombing of a Korean Airlines passenger plane in November 1987, which was apparently intended to create a climate of fear that would disrupt the 1988 Seoul Olympics. This turned out to be unsuccessful, and since 1987 there have not been any further DPRK-backed terrorist attacks on ROK citizens, as far as is publicly known. Indeed, Kim Jong Il's surprising admission in September 2002 to North Korea's kidnapping of Japanese citizens, explicitly denounced such terror tactics as a "regrettable" relic of the past and promised that North Korea "will prevent such things from happening in the future."[11]

The latter half of the 1970s was probably the last point at which the DPRK held any serious hope of a military solution that would unify Korea in the North's favor. The North Vietnamese conquest of the South in April 1975 might have suggested that Korean unification would follow suit, an idea reinforced by U.S. presidential candidate Jimmy Carter's campaign promise later that year to pull American troops out of Korea, signaling a reduced American military commitment to the ROK.[12] The confusion in South Korea following the assassination of Park Chung Hee in October 1979 seemed, like the aftermath of the April 19 Uprising almost twenty years earlier, to be another window of opportunity for the North to take charge of Korean unification. But the Carter administration reversed itself on the troop withdrawal, and Park's assassination (by his own chief of intelligence) was followed within two months by another military coup under General Chun Doo Hwan.[13] If there had been any chance that chaos in the ROK would invite a North Korean intervention at that critical moment, the establishment of Chun's iron-fisted rule and Reagan's unqualified commitment to the ROK's defense soon closed that window of opportunity. Thereafter, even the conventional military balance shifted away from the North, the economic gap grew increasingly in the South's favor, and the DPRK and the ROK experienced a "diplomatic reversal" with more and more countries recognizing the South at the expense of the North.[14]

The new movement in inter-Korean relations inaugurated by the July 4 Communiqué of 1972, a breakthrough moment that raised tremendous expectations in both the North and the South, ground to a halt in a little over a year. After a half-dozen meetings of the newly created South–North Coordinating Committee, the two sides reached an impasse and the North cut off talks in mid-1973.[15]

North–South Red Cross dialogue was revived in the mid-1980s and there was a brief flurry of cultural exchanges and visits of separated families in 1985, but this too quickly fizzled out. The next breakthrough in official inter-Korean relations would not come until the beginning of the 1990s, by which time the international environment had changed drastically, to the North's disadvantage.

The main DPRK proposal for the form of unification, to which it has returned consistently for more than two decades, is a "Confederation" of the two existing political systems on the Korean peninsula. Although Pyongyang did not outline in detail its proposed "Confederal Republic of Koryo" until 1980, North Korea first suggested such a confederation in August 1960 during the turbulent Chang Myon government in South Korea.[16] Seoul's initial response was, to say the least, not very enthusiastic. Over time, however, the North has shown more flexibility in its confederation proposal, a willingness to see confederation not as the end-goal of unification but a transitory institution and giving more rights to the two "regional governments." By 1991, in fact, North Korean officials including Kim Il Sung were suggesting that there was plenty of room for negotiation with the South on the form of confederation and that both sides within a confederated Korean system could have considerable autonomy even in its foreign relations, under the general rubric of military and diplomatic unity.[17] The "Confederal Republic" was in fact not dissimilar to the "Korean National Community" proposed as a unification strategy by ROK President Roh Tae Woo in the late 1980s.[18]

As the 1990s dawned, high-level North–South talks began again. After a setback caused by DPRK protests over the ROK–U.S. "Team Spirit" joint military exercises, the fifth in this series of high-level talks in December 1991 resulted in an agreement on reconciliation, nonaggression, and exchanges and cooperation.[19] The "Basic Agreement" was the most important declaration of North–South cooperation and coexistence since the 1972 Joint Communiqué, and was far more detailed than the 1972 agreement had been. It was followed in February 1992 by a joint "Declaration of the Denuclearization of the Korean Peninsula." Once again, hopes were high for a major change in North–South relations and for a new momentum toward reconciliation and eventual unification. But once again such hopes would be unfulfilled. Regional and global circumstances had shifted dramatically, to the detriment of the DPRK's position. The collapse of every communist state in Eastern Europe between 1989 and 1991, including the USSR itself, came as a deep shock to North Korea and deprived Pyongyang of most of its important trade partners, political supporters and allies. Even before the communist collapse, East European countries had begun to normalize relations with the ROK; by 1992, Russia and even North Korea's allegedly staunch ally China had established diplomatic relations with Seoul. It would take almost a decade for a reciprocal movement of Western countries normalizing ties with Pyongyang. Economically, South Korea had long since leapt almost unimaginably beyond the level of the DPRK. Far from the Basic Agreement ushering in a new age of equality between the two Koreas, the times seemed to call into question the very ability of the DPRK to survive as a socialist state. And then, the collapse of the DPRK economy and the nuclear standoff with the United States appeared to suggest that North Korea's days were indeed numbered. Movement in inter-Korean relations, much less unification in the North's favor, was a moot point.

The Politics of Survival, 1992–2000

At the beginning of the 1990s, the North Korean economy, which had encountered mounting problems since the 1960s, tipped over from difficulty to disaster. Indeed, the entirety of the 1990s was a decade of disaster for the DPRK, beginning with the collapse of every communist state in Eastern Europe, proceeding to a crisis over international inspections of DPRK nuclear energy facilities that nearly led to war with the United States in June 1994, the death of Kim Il Sung in July, and finally a series of natural calamities that pushed the North Korean food situation—never abundant to begin with—into full-scale famine.[20] North Korea spent most of the decade simply trying to cope with this megacrisis, and its leadership seemed unsure of where to take the country. Meanwhile, many in the outside world expected an inevitable collapse of the DPRK.

The threat to the DPRK's very existence in the 1990s was greater than at any time since the Korean War. North Korea's response was to batten down the hatches and proclaim its continued adherence to "socialism."[21] Pyongyang for the most part played a waiting game, maintaining the system while hoping for the "correlation of forces" to become more favorable toward the DPRK. As Paul Bracken has explained, the North Korean nuclear program was a way for the DPRK to "buy time for the regime to adapt to new international circumstances."[22] It is perhaps more accurate to say that the DPRK leadership wanted the world to go away until it changed more to Pyongyang's liking, but I would agree with Bracken's point that the DPRK nuclear program was a defensive, even desperate attempt at ensuring state survival in an environment suddenly much more hostile. In this case the gamble almost backfired, as the United States and North Korea came to the brink of war in June 1994, averted at the eleventh hour by the visit of former U.S. President Carter to Pyongyang and discussions with Kim Il Sung that led, finally, to the U.S.–DPRK Agreed Framework of October 1994.

By the late 1990s the domestic situation, though hardly rosy, had improved. After a three-year "mourning period" following the death of his father, Kim Jong Il emerged as general secretary of the KWP in 1997, and in the following year was reappointed chairman of the National Defense Committee, his main post and clearly the most powerful position in the DPRK. The younger Kim, presumably after a power struggle that can only be guessed at by outsiders, had consolidated his authority. The old-guard Manchuria guerilla fighters who dominated the centers of power under Kim Il Sung were disappearing from the scene through death or retirement; Kim Jong Il's generation was increasingly taking charge. By 1998 the "Arduous March" through hunger and distress was declared over, and the new slogans of the DPRK were *Kangsong Taeguk* ("Rich and Powerful Great Country," or simply "Powerful Nation") and *Songun chongch'i* (Military-first Politics).[23] By the end of the decade, economic decline had been arrested, at least temporarily; according to ROK Bank of Korea estimates, the DPRK economy grew 6.2 percent in 1999, its first increase in a decade, followed by a more modest 1.3 percent growth in 2000, 3.7 percent in 2001, and 1.2 percent in 2002.[24]

A New North Korea?

The new millennium began with the third major symbolic breakthrough in inter-Korean relations, the Kim Jong Il–Kim Dae Jung summit in Pyongyang in June

2000. This was preceded by a flurry of diplomatic activities toward Western countries, beginning with the normalization of ties with Italy in January 2000. Within two years, Pyongyang had established diplomatic relations with all but two of the European Union (EU) member states, the EU itself, Canada, Australia, the Philippines, Brazil, and New Zealand; in July 2000, with Seoul's encouragement, North Korea joined the ARF for East Asian security dialogue. Unlike in the past, these new and re-invigorated external relations were encouraged, rather than inhibited, by South Korea.[25] North Korea also attempted to mend fences with Russia, and Kim Jong Il visited both China and Russia in 2001, his first official visits abroad as North Korean leader. It appeared that the DPRK was suddenly emerging from its years of inward-looking crisis management and confusion and rejoining the world.

Whether North Korea was also changing internally is a matter of some dispute, but there have been some indications of change, if not anything officially and publicly called "reform," in both the rhetoric and the observable reality of DPRK life. Since the early 1990s, there have been signs of liberalization and the growth of local markets in the North Korean economy, what one American observer calls "reform by stealth."[26] In January 2001 the *Rodong Sinmun* announced a policy of "New Thinking" (*Saeroun kwanjom*), which called for scrapping outmoded habits and mentalities and putting all efforts into the technological reconstruction of North Korea, with special emphasis on information technology.[27] The sixtieth birthday celebration of Kim Jong Il in February 2002 and the ninetieth anniversary of Kim Il Sung's birth in April were further occasions for the DPRK media to exhort the people to work harder and focus on the development of science and technology. In order to accomplish these goals, the famously isolated DPRK has demonstrated a new willingness to learn from the outside world: in 2001, North Korea sent nearly 500 government officials and students abroad to study technical subjects, economics and business, almost triple the number Pyongyang sent in 2000.[28]

A year after "New Thinking" was officially launched in January 2001, the 2002 New Year's Joint Editorial published in the Korean Workers' Party newspaper *Rodong Sinmun*, the Korean People's Army daily *Choson Inmingun*, and the Kim Il Sung Socialist Youth League publication *Ch'ongnyonwi* celebrated the "successes" of the previous year and renewed the call for "radical change" in the economy.[29] The editorial outlined four "viewpoints" for what it called "Kim Il Sung's nation": (1) the Leadership (i.e., the spiritual leadership of the departed Great Leader), (2) the Juche idea, (3) the military, and (4) the socialist system. The last point was the most fully elaborated one and implied further reforms to take place in the North Korean economy. The editorial claimed that "priority will be given to goods supply to the popular masses and to the solution of the problems arising in improving people's daily life." Again without breathing the word "reform," the editorial stated,

> The changing situation and our revolution have an urgent need to improve and perfect economic management on revolutionary lines. To ensure the highest profitability while adhering to socialist principles—this is the main orientation to be adhered to in completing the socialist economic management, which our Party has set.

In March 2002, the DPRK Supreme People's Assembly approved a state budget for fiscal year 2002, which emphasized technical innovation and economic modernization.[30] Finally, the second half of 2002 saw the boldest steps yet toward real reform in the DPRK. At the beginning of July 2002 North Korea began to institute some of the most far-reaching economic changes since the regime was founded in 1948. The food distribution system on which much of the population had depended (at least until the famine of the 1990s) was reduced and modified; the price of rice was raised to near-market levels, and wages have been correspondingly increased as much as thirtyfold; the official exchange rate for the North Korean won was reduced from 2.2 to the dollar to nearly 200 won, approaching the black market rate; the taxation system, abolished in 1974, has reportedly been revived.[31]

The results of this economic restructuring a year later were mixed. On the one hand, anecdotal reports of runaway inflation and popular discontent have filtered into the Western media. On the other hand, the DPRK government has not retracted these reforms and seems committed to them.[32] The New Year joint editorial of 2003, for example, was much more militant than that of the previous year, reflecting the growing conflict with the United States. The editorial emphasized North Korea's "Military-Based Policy" (*Songun kichi*) and the need for a strong defense against the imperialists.[33] Yet it also stressed the need for "new change in economic and cultural construction," and repeated the earlier slogan of "ensuring the greatest profitability while firmly adhering to socialist principles." It may be that the question of economic reform versus "adhering to socialist principles" reflected a difference between the civilian leadership and the military, but by trying to have it both ways, the Pyongyang leadership appeared to see North Korea's *Perestroika* as irreversible, despite the increased security threat.

Apparently, the centerpiece of Pyongyang's economic "New Thinking" was to be a new special economic zone (SEZ) in the northwestern city of Sinuiju, across the Yalu River from China. Announced in September 2002, the Sinuiju SEZ was to have its own legal and economic system, and even issue its own passports, distinct from the rest of the DPRK. The man chosen to run the SEZ was a Chinese native of Dutch citizenship, Yang Bin, allegedly the second-richest man in China.[34] Unfortunately for North Korea's reform efforts, this attempt to build "Hong Kong North" had not even begun when it experienced a major setback: Yang Bin was arrested in the northeast Chinese city of Shenyang and subsequently deported, ostensibly on charges of corruption, but perhaps as a means for the Chinese authorities to show their displeasure at North Korea taking such an initiative without consulting China.

Even if North Korea's economic experiments were allowed to go forward unimpeded, it is questionable whether the DPRK could make its economy both "revolutionary" and "profitable"—a pairing that seems to suggest limited market-oriented reform while maintaining the rule of the Workers' Party and the Kim Jong Il leadership. But clearly the DPRK leadership, and presumably Kim Jong Il personally, have staked a great deal on improving North Korea's economy through such reforms. Even if it may not say so directly, Pyongyang cannot achieve this goal without improved relations with Seoul and Washington. Yet in the area of inter-Korean relations, much less U.S.–DPRK relations, the promise of the June 2000 Summit remains largely unfulfilled. Kim Jong Il never made his reciprocal visit to South Korea, which caused no small embarrassment and opposition criticism for Kim Dae Jung.[35] The reconstruction of the Seoul–Sinuiju railway connecting South Korea through North Korea to the border with China, a central goal of Kim Dae Jung's North Korea policy, had made little progress. The South Korean tours to the Kumgang Mountains in eastern North Korea, sponsored by the Hyundai conglomerate, turned out to be a major money-losing venture. But, above all, the improvement of ties with the United States, which Pyongyang had pursued in close connection to its policy toward the South, and which had built considerable momentum in the Clinton administration, ground almost to a halt with the beginning of the Bush presidency in 2001 and the new U.S. administration's more conservative approach to engagement. Then came the Axis of Evil speech.

The DPRK responded harshly to George W. Bush's condemnation of North Korea as part of the "Axis of Evil" along with Iran and Iraq in the president's State of the Union address in January 2002. A Foreign Ministry spokesman called the Bush speech "little short of declaring war against the DPRK" and accused the U.S. administration of "political immaturity and moral leprosy."[36] In contrast to the condemnation of terrorism and de facto sympathy for the United States right after September 11,[37] the DPRK spokesman suggested that the United States had only itself to blame: "Herein lie answers to questions as to why the modern terrorism is focused on the U.S. alone and why it has become serious while Bush is in office."[38] North–South relations, having already lost a great deal of momentum since summer 2000, were dampened considerably by the Bush administration's statements. It took a visit to Pyongyang by Kim Dae Jung's special envoy Lim Dong Won in early April to get inter-Korean dialogue restarted. On April 28, Pyongyang agreed to resume reunion meetings of separated family members and to move forward with high-level contacts and economic cooperation. Even a naval skirmish between the two Koreas in the Yellow Sea (or West Sea, as the North Koreans call it) on June 29, 2002, did not fundamentally deter North–South talks.[39] On August 11–14 the first ministerial-level North–South meetings in nearly a year took place in Seoul. At the same time, the two sides marked the fifty-seventh anniversary of liberation from Japanese colonial rule on August 15 with an unprecedented joint celebration, including the visit of more than 100 North Korean delegates to Seoul.[40]

Washington–Pyongyang relations also showed signs of thaw in late July and early August 2002, when Secretary of State Colin Powell met briefly with North Korea's foreign minister at an Asean meeting in Brunei, and the Bush administration sent Jack L. Pritchard as its first official envoy to the DPRK. Pritchard, who had met with Pyongyang's ambassador to the United Nations several weeks earlier in New York, went to North Korea in early August for the ceremony marking the start of construction on the first light-water nuclear reactor to be built by KEDO, the U.S.–South Korean–Japanese consortium formed under the auspices of the 1994 Agreed Framework.[41] And on the DPRK–Japan side, Prime Minister Koizumi's unprecedented summit meeting with Kim Jong Il in Pyongyang in September, where Kim made his extraordinary admission that North Korea had abducted over a dozen Japanese citizens in the 1970s and 1980s, seemed at first to open up a new era in Japan–North Korea relations and start the two countries on the road to normalization.[42] It turned out, however, that the Japanese media and public response to these revelations would illicit such feelings of hostility toward North Korea that normal relations appeared to be farther away than ever in subsequent months. Then came the "October Surprise."

The belated and tentative moves toward restarting U.S.–DPRK dialogue in late summer and early fall 2002 were dramatically derailed by the "Kelly revelations" of October. On October 16, the U.S. State Department announced that, some 11 days earlier, Assistant Secretary of State James A. Kelly had confronted his counterparts in Pyongyang with evidence that North Korea had "a program to enrich uranium for nuclear weapons, in violation of the Agreed Framework and other agreements."[43] According to U.S. accounts (North Korea publicly neither confirmed nor denied the accusation), the DPRK officials acknowledged the existence of this program and declared the Agreed Framework "nullified." But North Korea insisted that the United States was to blame for the failure of the Agreed Framework, and offered to enter a new set of talks to resolve the crisis. The United States repeatedly refused to negotiate with North Korea before Pyongyang ceased all of its nuclear-related activities, and in November Washington suspended deliveries of fuel oil to North Korea required under the Agreed Framework. This was followed by a rapidly escalating set of moves on the part of North Korea toward restarting its plutonium program, frozen by the 1994 Agreement: Pyongyang announced its intention to reopen its nuclear power plant at Yongbyon, expelled International Atomic Energy Agency (IAEA) inspectors at the end of December 2002, announced its withdrawal from the NPT in January 2003, and began to remove spent nuclear fuel rods from storage in February—the latter an act that had brought the United States and North Korea to the brink of war in 1994.

While the crisis in U.S.–DPRK relations deepened in 2003, North–South relations continued to move forward. Indeed, a distinctive aspect of the 2002–03 crisis was the common ground Pyongyang could find with the Seoul government in criticizing the American approach to Korea. This was the reverse of the 1993–94 crisis, in which the ROK government of Kim Young Sam deeply feared U.S.–DPRK "collusion" at the expense of South Korea's national interest. This is not to say that Seoul–Pyongyang relations became cordial or that Seoul suddenly broke its ties with Washington; Seoul decried North Korea's development of nuclear weapons, for example, and Pyongyang attacked the Roh Moo Hyun government for agreeing to send South Korean troops to Iraq.[44] Roh visited Washington in May, and he and President Bush tried to put a unified face on their policy toward North Korea; Pyongyang condemned the Roh–Bush joint statement as "a perfidious act which runs counter to the basic spirit of the June 15 North-South Declaration."[45] But various agreements and meetings between the ROK and DPRK went ahead despite the new nuclear crisis, including a seven-point agreement on inter-Korean economic relations, signed by the representatives of North and South Korea in Pyongyang in late May. The two sides agreed on the establishment of a special Industrial Zone in the North Korean city of Kaesong, reconnection of east and west coast railway lines, and other joint projects. The agreement was presented positively and in detail in the DPRK media, although it was uncertain whether much could come of it until the conflict between Pyongyang and Washington was resolved.[46]

Pyongyang's South Korea policy has always been closely linked to its policy toward the United States. Originally, this was because Pyongyang refused to recognize the legitimacy of the ROK and saw it as a "puppet" of Washington. Since the beginning of inter-Korean contacts in the early 1970s this attitude has softened, but whether or not North Korean policy-makers still view South Korea as a "client state" of the United States, they clearly see Washington as having significant influence over Seoul, a fact few would dispute. Thus, an important motive behind Pyongyang's policy toward Washington is North Korea's attempt to influence Seoul indirectly.[47]

Over the last decade or so Pyongyang has also sought improved ties with the United States for the direct political, security, and economic benefits they may bring to North Korea. Perhaps the most important motive is economic. Pyongyang seeks to get off the U.S. State Department's list of countries that sponsor terrorism not only to normalize relations with the United States, but also in order to qualify for loans and support from the World Bank, the Asian Development Bank, the International Monetary Fund, and other international financial institutions that are critical for rebuilding North Korea's shattered economy.[48] In order to achieve this, Pyongyang must walk a fine line between rhetorically condemning the United States as an enemy and impediment to Korean peace and unification, and making gestures of rapprochement and accommodation—for example, by sending Vice-Marshall Jo Myong Rok to meet with President Clinton in Washington in Late 2000. These two priorities—achieving the (especially economic) benefits of improved relations with the United States while maintaining its defense against the perceived hostility of the United States—are obviously acutely difficult for North Korea to reconcile, and Pyongyang has not always handled relations with Washington very adroitly, to say the least. Washington, for its part, has long insisted that improved in U.S.–North Korea relations be contingent on positive development in inter-Korean relations.

This Seoul–Washington–Pyongyang triangle is thus an inescapable reality behind North Korea's bilateral relations with South Korea and the United States. Even if one of these relationships is going well, a crisis or stumbling block in either U.S.–North Korean relations or North–South relations will impede the other. Seoul and Washington's policies toward Pyongyang had shown considerable convergence in the second Clinton administration, but had begun to diverge markedly under George W. Bush. After the October 2002 crisis, the rift between Seoul and Washington grew critical. In a way, this fulfilled one of Pyongyang's long-standing dreams: driving a wedge between Washington and Seoul, winning the sympathy of the South Korean people and government against a hostile United States. But for Pyongyang today, the problem with alienating the United States is twofold: first, North Korea still perceives the United States as the greatest threat to the existence of the DPRK, and therefore needs assurances of its security against the United States, as Pyongyang has repeatedly stated after the October 2002 revelations; and second, all the goodwill and even cash from South Korea will not make up for the continued U.S.-led economic embargo and the need for Western investment to rescue North Korea's moribund economy. Thus, North Korean officials have repeatedly stressed that what the DPRK wants from Washington is a "nonaggression treaty" with the United States, American recognition of North Korea's sovereignty, and American support for North Korea's economic reform and development.[49] Continued improvement in relations with South Korea, while an important goal of current North Korean policy, is meaningless without a normalization of relations with the United States.

The Future of Two Koreas

More than a decade after the end of the Cold War and the unification of Germany, Korea remains the last country still divided as a result of the post–World War II Allied settlement. The two Koreas have not even reached the degree of mutual communication and contact achieved by the two Germanies in the early 1970s, much less anything approaching unification. There is a certain irony that East and West Germany had such considerable contact while agreeing to postpone talk of unification to the indefinite future, whereas North and South Korea speak constantly of unification yet have very little contact.[50] It may be in fact that Seoul and Pyongyang are quietly and gradually moving toward a (pre-1989) German-style approach: de facto acceptance of each other as legitimate states and a policy of peaceful coexistence. The last East German ambassador to Pyongyang, Dr. Hans Maretzki, has suggested that the two Koreas simply recognize the status quo and accept each other as sovereign states with all the corresponding legal and diplomatic procedures this entails. In this way, Maretzki argues, rather than attempt to reconcile two systems that are ultimately irreconcilable, Pyongyang and Seoul could move forward in their bilateral relationship without threatening each other's existence as sovereign entities.[51] The problem of course is that this solution, as sensible as it may appear to outsiders, directly contradicts the long-standing principle officially upheld by both sides, that Korea is in reality one nation and that division can never be accepted as a permanent or indefinite condition. Of more direct concern for Pyongyang, the North Koreans know exactly how inter-German relations ended—with the collapse of East Germany and unification on West German terms—and want to avoid the fate of East Germany at all costs. This is the dilemma of inter-Korean relations for the DPRK: contact and improved relations with Seoul could bring substantial economic, political, and security benefits but could also threaten the North Korean regime's very existence.

For some time now, the number-one priority of the North Korean regime has been its own survival. In the face of what the DPRK perceived (and still perceives) as an extremely hostile security environment, especially after the collapse of communist states in the late 1980s and early 1990s, this has meant above all a strong military posture, including an enormous standing army and the potential threat of nuclear weapons. Since both domestic economic development and foreign relations are secondary to regime survival, the former two have suffered when DPRK regime survival was seriously threatened in the 1990s. In this sense, North Korea's military and security policy has been described by one Western observer as "essentially defensive and realist," not aggressive or irrational.[52] As far as the DPRK leadership is concerned, the Korean War proved that the United States has both the capability and intention to destroy North Korea; South Korea, from Pyongyang's perspective, has had the same intention and in recent decades also the capability. Logically, then, two factors will soften North Korea's position toward Seoul: deterrence of South Korea's (and America's) destructive capacity toward the DPRK, if necessary by playing the nuclear card; and/or a perceived change of intention. Arguably, it is only a combination of these two—a greater sense of security through deterrence, and a change of perceived destructive intention toward the DPRK—that allowed North Korea to respond positively to Kim Dae Jung's "Sunshine Policy" at the turn of the millennium. This also explains North Korea's dealings with the United States in the late 1990s, after the October 1994 agreement established a framework for U.S.–DPRK contact within which the United States would deal with the DPRK as a legitimate state entity. North Korea wants more from the United States, including the lifting of economic sanctions, diplomatic normalization, and a promise of "no first use" of nuclear weapons against the North.

From Pyongyang's perspective, a guarantee of survival from the United States would give a considerable boost to North Korea's ability to improve relations with Seoul. Such a guarantee, apparently almost within reach at the end of the Clinton administration, receded from Pyongyang's grasp after the more hawkish Bush administration appeared on the scene. Seoul's ability to engage North Korea is limited so long as Washington–Pyongyang relations are stalled. Even in the best of circumstances, North Korea remains cautious and defensive in its dealings with both Seoul and Washington. The crisis between the United States and the DPRK that began in the late fall of 2002 could push North Korea farther into a corner, and set back or even reverse the processes of internal reform in the DPRK and relaxation of North–South tensions. In the worst-case scenario, the conflict between the United States and North Korea could precipitate a war that would eliminate the DPRK altogether, as well as sow destruction and instability in South Korea, Japan, and China. By the middle of 2003, the Bush administration was preparing for such a contingency.[53]

The logic of DPRK foreign policy may appear idiosyncratic to outside observers, but it is generally consistent. Policy toward South Korea has shown an overall continuity in its fundamental principles while evolving tactically since the early 1970s. Pyongyang and Seoul have gradually shifted from uncompromising competitive legitimacy toward peaceful coexistence. Both sides seem to agree that, in the near term, inter-Korean relations are moving toward rapprochement rather than reunification. Perhaps its basic principle of ultimate unification has not changed, but North Korea's unification theology has clearly become less fundamentalist and more liberal as time has gone by. For all Pyongyang's talk of imminent unification, its actions and those of Seoul reflect rather a recognition of the status quo and the need for mutual trust and cooperation.

Emerging from a long decade of profound internal crisis, effecting economic change while maintaining political stability will be an enormous challenge for the Pyongyang regime. Recent signs of reform within the DPRK may finally allow North Korea to overcome this crisis, or they may signal the beginning of the endgame for divided Korea. The North Korean leadership has taken a great gamble in moving forward with economic reform and expanding contacts with the outside world, and with South Korean in particular. Deeper economic and political engagement with Seoul may be North Korea's best hope of rescuing its economy and avoiding a devastating conflict with the United States. Yet such a deepening of North–South ties may make the North little more than an economic dependency of the South, and undermine the North's own legitimacy.[54] Even the possession of nuclear weapons, should North Korea choose that path, will at best only postpone the inevitable and irreversible transformation of the North Korean regime.

Notes

1. James T. Laney and Jason T. Shaplen, "How to Deal with North Korea," *Foreign Affairs* (March/April 2003): 17.
2. For North Korean ideology as theology, see Han S. Park, *North Korea: The Politics of Unconventional Wisdom* (Boulder, CO: Lynne Reinner, 2002).
3. For an elaboration of this view, which claims to represent official DPRK thinking on the matter, see Kim Myong-chol, *Kim Chong-il ui T'ongil chollak* [Kim Jong Il's Unification Strategy], trans. Yun Yong-mu (Seoul: Sallimt'o, 2000). This book, originally written in Japanese by an ethnic Korean resident of Japan, had the rare distinction in Kim Dae Jung's South Korea of being banned, and its Korean American publisher jailed, for violating the National Security Law.
4. Cited in Kim Sun-gyu, "North Korea's Initial Unification Policy: The Democratic Base Line," in Kyongnam University Institute of Far Eastern Affairs, *Puk Han ch'eje ui surip kwajong* [The Process of Constructing the North Korean System] (Seoul: Kyungnam University Press, 1991), p. 220.
5. The United States was equally unwilling to support Syngman Rhee in attacking the North, a contingency that American military planners were taking seriously until the very end of the Rhee regime.
6. Balasz Solantai, " 'You Have No Political Line of You Own:' Kim Il Sung and the Soviets, 1953–1964," paper presented at the Woodrow Wilson International Center for Scholars, Washington, DC, May 28, 2002, pp. 27–28.
7. Karoly Fendler, "Economic Assistance and Loans from Socialist Countries to North Korea in the Postwar Years 1953–1963," *Asien* 42 (January 1992): 39–51; Ruediger Frank, *Die DDR und Nordkorea: Der Wiederaufbau der Stadt Hamhung von 1954–1962* (Aachen: Shaker, 1996).
8. In fact, some of the Red Cross delegates *were* intelligence officers, and began the process of dialogue under cover of the Red Cross meetings. Don Oberdorfer, *The Two Koreas: A Contemporary History* (Reading, MA: Addison-Wesley, 1997), pp. 14–15.
9. Yi Chong-sok, *Hyondae Puk Hanui ihae* [Understanding Contemporary North Korea] (Seoul: Yoksa pip'yongsa, 2000), p. 381.
10. David Kang, "North Korea's Military and Security Strategy," in *North Korean Foreign Relations in the Post-Cold War Era*, ed. Samuel S. Kim (Hong Kong: Oxford University Press, 1998), pp. 177–179.
11. Howard W. French, "North Koreans Sign Agreement with Japanese," *New York Times* September 18, 2002, p. A16.
12. Nicholas Eberstadt, "North Korea's Unification Policy, 1948–1996," in *North Korean Foreign Relations*, ed. Kim, p. 242; Oberdorfer, *The Two Koreas*, p. 84.
13. For an evaluation of the U.S. role—or lack thereof—in this process by Carter's ambassador to the ROK, see William H. Gleysteen, *Massive Entanglement, Marginal Influence: Carter and Korea in Crisis* (Washington, DC: Brookings Institution Press, 1999).
14. Barry K. Gills, *Korea versus Korea: The Political Economy of Diplomacy* (London: Routledge, 1996), p. 190.
15. Chuck Downs, "Discerning North Korea's Intentions," in *Korea's Future and the Great Powers*, ed. Nicholas Eberstadt and Richard J. Ellings (Seattle: The National Bureau of Asian Research, 2001), p. 96.
16. Yi Chong-sok, *Hyondae Puk Hanui ihae*, p. 382.
17. Selig S. Harrison, *Korean Endgame: A Strategy for Reunification and U.S. Disengagement* (Princeton: Princeton University Press, 2002), p. 76.
18. B.C. Koh, "A Comparison of Unification Policies," in *Korea and the World: Beyond the Cold War*, ed. Young Whan Kihl (Boulder: Westview Press, 1994), p. 156.
19. "The Politics of Inter-Korean Relations: Coexistence or Reunification," in *Korea and the World*, ed. Kihl, p. 135.

20. The DPRK never acknowledged the existence of a famine, referring instead to a (temporary) "food shortage" caused by natural disasters. Most outside observers believe that North Korea did undergo a famine between approximately 1995 and 1998; Andrew Natsios, vice president of the humanitarian agency World Vision during this period, argues that hundreds of thousands if not millions of North Koreans died as a result of a famine exacerbated by natural disasters, but rooted in economic mismanagement. See Andrew Natsios, *The Great North Korean Famine: Famine, Politics, and Foreign Policy* (Washington, DC: United States Institute of Peace, 2001).

21. Charles K. Armstrong, "A Socialism of Our Style: North Korean Ideology in a Post-Communist Era," in *North Korean Foreign Policy in the Post-Cold War Era*, ed. Samuel S. Kim (Oxford: Oxford University Press, 1998).

22. Paul Bracken, "The North Korean Nuclear Program as a Problem of State Survival," in *Asian Flashpoint: Security and the Korean Peninsula*, ed. Andrew Mack (New York: Allen & Unwin, 1993), p. 86.

23. These two "guiding principles" have been elaborated at length in, respectively, *Sahoejuui kangsong taeguk konsol sasang* [The Ideology of Constructing a Powerful Socialist Nation] (Pyongyang: Sahoe Kwahak Ch'ulp'ansa, 2000) and *Kim Chong-il Changgunui songun chongch'i* [General Kim Jong Il's Military-First Politics] (Pyongyang: Pyongyang Ch'ulp'ansa, 2000).

24. Bank of Korea, *GDP of North Korea in 2002* (Seoul: Bank of Korea, 2003). Admittedly the Bank of Korea figures must be viewed with some skepticism, but it is evident that by the end of the 1990s North Korea's downward spiral had at least been arrested.

25. Samuel S. Kim, "North Korea in 2000," *Asian Survey* 41:1 (January/February 2001): 20.

26. Harrison, *Korean Endgame*, p. 25.

27. *Rodong Sinmun*, January 9, 2002, p. 1; Yinhay Ahn, "North Korea in 2001," *Asian Survey* 42: 1 (January/February 2002): 47.

28. Nam Kwang-sik, "One Year of a 'New Way of Thinking,' "*Vantage Point* 24: 2 (February 2002): 10.

29. *Rodong Sinmun*, January 1, 2002, p. 1; *People's Korea*, January 12, 2002, p. 2. These editorials can be considered the DPRK's national "New Year's Resolution," announcing official priorities for the year, and have replaced Kim Il Sung's annual New Year address since the Great Leader's death in 1994.

30. "SPA Approves New State Budget Featuring Technical Innovation and Modernization of Economy," *People's Korea*, March 30, 2002, p. 1.

31. "North Korea Undergoing Economic Reform," *Choson Ilbo* (July 26, 2002); "Stitch by Stitch to a Different World," *The Economist*, July 27, 2002, pp. 24–26.

32. Western economists have only just begun to look into the impact of the July 2002 changes on North Korean economy and society. See Ruediger Frank, "A Socialist Market Economy in North Korea? Systemic Restrictions and a Quantitative Analysis," paper presented at Columbia University, March 13, 2003, and Marcus Noland, "Famine and Reform in North Korea," unpublished manuscript, July 2003.

33. "Let us Fully Demonstrate the Dignity and Power of the Republic under the Great Banner of Military-Based Policy," *Rodong Sinmun*, January 1, 2003, p. 1; *People's Korea*, January 11, 2003, p. 2.

34. Howard W. French, "North Korea to Let Capitalism Loose in Investment Zone," *The New York Times*, September 25, 2002, p. A3.

35. "A Ray or Two of Light in the Gloom," *The Economist*, August 17, 2002, pp. 33–34.

36. "DPRK Denounces Bush's Charges: Statement of FM Spokesman on Bush's State of the Union Address," *People's Korea*, February 9, 2002, p. 1. The response is also available online as "Spokesman for DPRK Foreign Ministry Slams Bush's Accusations," *Korean Central News Agency*, January 31, 2002; http://www.kcna.co.jp/calendar/january.

37. A DPRK Foreign Ministry spokesman stated on September 12 that "The very regretful and tragic incident reminds us once again of the gravity of terrorism. As a UN member the DPRK is opposed to all forms of terrorism and whatever support to it and this stance will remain unchanged." *Korean Central News Agency*, "DPRK Stance Towards Terrorist Attacks on U.S.," http://www.kcna.co.jp/calendar/september, 2001.

38. "Spokesman for DPRK Foreign Ministry Slams Bush's Accusations," *Korean Central News Agency*, January 31, 2002; http://www.kcna.co.jp/calendar/january.

39. In a most unusual gesture, Pyongyang responded shortly after the West Sea clash with a statement of "regret for the unfortunate incident," and urged that the two sides resume high-level talks "in order to put on the right track the North-South dialogue for reconciliation, unity and cooperation based on the spirit of the June 15, 2000 joint declaration." "North is Ready for Resumed Ministerial Talks," *People's Korea*, July 27, 2002, p. 1.

40. "Inter-Korean Festival Kicks Off in Seoul," *Korea Times*, August 14, 2002, p. 1.

41. "Work Starts on North Korea's U.S.-Backed Nuclear Plant," *The New York Times*, August 8, 2002, p. A14.

42. Howard W. French, "North Koreans Sign Agreement with Japanese," *The New York Times*, September 18, 2002, p. A1.

43. U.S. State Department Press Statement, "North Korean Nuclear Program," October 16, 2002; http://www.state.gov/r/pa/prs/ps/2002/14423pf/htm.

44. "Pyongyang Hits Seoul's Decision to Dispatch Troops to Iraq," *People's Korea,* April 22, 2003, p. 1.

45. "North, South Conclude 7-Point Agreement in Inter-Korean Economic Talks," *People's Korea*, May 31, 2003, p. 1.

46. "Fifth Meeting of North-South Committee for Promotion of Economic Cooperation Concludes," *Choson t'ongsin* (*Korea Central News Agency*), May 24, 2003; http://www.kcna.co.jp/index-k.htm.

47. The route to influence could also work the other way around. Selig Harrison argues that the main motivation for Kim Jong Il agreeing to a North–South summit in 2000 was to push Washington toward moving ahead with U.S.–DPRK normalization. Harrison, *Korea Endgame*, p. 88.

48. James Miles, "Waiting Out North Korea," *Survival* 44: 2 (Summer 2002): 42.

49. *Korean Central News Agency*, "Conclusion of Non-Aggression Treaty between DPRK and US Called For," October 25, 2002; http://www.kcna.co.jp.

50. I am indebted to Dr. Hans Maretzki, former East German ambassador to Pyongyang, for this insight. Author's interview with Ambassador Maretzki, Potsdam, Germany, July 29, 2002.

51. Hans Maretzki, "Korean Dilemma: Normalisation or Unification and Nothing," *Northeast Asia Peace and Security Network Special Report*, Nautilus Institute; http://www./pub/ftp/napsnet/special_reports/maretzki_unification.txt.

52. Kang, "North Korea's Military and Security Strategy," p. 182.

53. Bruce B. Auster and Kevin Whitelaw, "Upping the Ante for Kim Jong Il: Pentagon Plan 5030, a New Blueprint for Facing Down North Korea," *US News and World Report*, July 21, 2003; http://www.usnews.com/usnews/issue/030721/usnews/21korea.htm#top.

54. For an analysis suggesting that North Korea may become a "protectorate" of South Korea, see Alexandre Mansourov, "North Korea Goes Nuclear, Washington Readies for War, South Korea Holds Key," Nautilus Institute Policy Forum Online; http://www.nautilus.org/fora/security/0213A_Mansourov.html.

CHAPTER FOUR

INTER-KOREAN ECONOMIC RELATIONS

Samuel S. Kim and Matthew S. Winters

For more than four decades, there were no inter-Korean economic relations of any kind. Then on November 21, 1988, 40 kilograms of North Korean clams arrived in Pusan, the first realization of economic exchange between the two Koreas. The terms had been announced by South Korean President Roh Tae Woo in his "Special Declaration in the Interest of National Self-Esteem, Unification and Prosperity" and in the ROK's "Basic Guide for Cooperation and Exchange between South and North Korea." In January 1989, South Korea imported paintings, pottery, woodworking, and industrial art from the North, beginning a trade that totaled $18.7 million for that year. The following year saw the Doosung Industrial Company (Seoul) sign a direct barter contract with the DPRK, and in 1991 Samsung and Hyundai followed suit. Since those meager beginnings, inter-Korean trade has continued to grow and diversify, so that 2002 saw $343 million worth of commercial trade and an additional $298 million of non-transactional trade (i.e., border-crossing goods related to humanitarian and development projects). In 2002 the ROK became the DPRK's second largest trading partner after China.

What is rather striking about this growth in trade 40 forty years of strict noninteraction is its persistence and expansion in the presence of the so-called DMZ, which remains one of the most heavily fortified and sensitive conflict zones in the post–Cold War world, where more than 1.8 million military personnel, including 37,000 Americans, confront each other, armed to the teeth with the latest weapons systems. As shown in table 4.1, the 1994 nuclear crisis had no dampening effect as inter-Korean trade continued to grow in 1995 before receding slightly in 1996. While trade numbers fell in 1998 because of the Asian Financial Crisis, even the Taepodong missile crisis in August of that year could not derail the recovery. And despite the North's nuclear revelations in October 2002, the year 2003 was the most substantial trading year yet between the two Koreas. The month-by-month comparison of trade before and after October 2002 (table 4.2) reveals that trading has been substantially higher in each corresponding month except two.

This resilience of inter-Korean trade in the face of continuing military standoff is the key puzzle of both theoretical and real-world significance addressed in this chapter. Beginning with a review of international relations theoretical literature on the pacific benefits of trade and the role of economic interdependence in preventing or mitigating armed conflict, we argue that inter-Korean economic interaction defies

Table 4.1 South Korean–North Korean trade (1989–2002) (Unit: US$1,000)

Year	Import from North Korea	% change	Export to North Korea	% change	Total trade	% change
1989	18,655		69		18,724	
1990	12,278	−34.2	1,188	1,621.7	13,466	−28.1
1991	105,719	761.0	5,547	366.9	111,266	726.3
1992	162,863	54.1	10,563	90.4	173,426	55.9
1993	178,167	9.4	8,425	−20.2	186,592	7.6
1994	176,298	−1.0	18,249	116.6	194,547	4.3
1995	222,855	26.4	64,436	253.1	287,291	47.7
1996	182,400	−18.2	69,639	8.1	252,039	−12.3
1997	193,069	5.8	115,270	65.5	308,339	22.3
1998	92,264	−52.2	129,679	12.5	221,943	−28.0
1999	121,604	31.8	211,832	63.4	333,437	50.2
2000	152,373	25.3	272,775	28.8	425,148	27.5
2001	176,170	15.6	226,787	−16.9	402,957	−5.2
2002	271,575	54.2	370,155	63.2	641,730	59.3

Note: These figures include both transactional and non-transactional (i.e., noncommercial) trade.

Source: KOTRA at http://www.kotra.go.kr.

Table 4.2 Inter-Korean trade for the year preceding and following the October 2002 nuclear revelation by the DPRK (Unit: US$ million)

	2001–02	2002–03
October	38.621	97.944
November	32.954	126.655
December	40.276	74.060
January	27.400	47.397
February	28.737	41.351
March	31.881	39.431
April	41.971	37.985
May	56.280	42.415
June	28.668	59.655
July	26.402	71.962
August	39.478	65.618
September	62.255	98.901

Source: Ministry of Unification, Republic of Korea at: http://www.unikorea.go.kr.

standard commercial liberal explanations because of the *sui generis* character of the relationship between the ROK and the DPRK—at once a little more and a little less than two separate but fully sovereign states. Rather, a more synthetic and eclectic theory of inter-Korean economic relations is needed, one that can be specified by looking at developments in inter-Korean relations through the lenses of conflict management and functional cooperation, with nods also to traditional liberal and realist theories. We conclude with an assessment of the future prospects of inter-Korean economic cooperation and a cautionary note on the relevance of investment versus trade and the functional significance of inter-Korean social and cultural exchanges.

Competing Theoretical Perspectives and Explanations

The starting point for understanding inter-state economic relations has long been the classical liberal view that expanded trade is a remedy for war. "Commerce cures destructive prejudices," Montesquieu wrote. "It polishes and softens barbarous mores. The natural effect of commerce is to lead to peace."[1] Most often cited is Immanuel Kant's proposition that "the *spirit of commerce* sooner or later takes hold of every people, and it cannot exist side by side with war."[2] Economic interdependence, democracy, and international organizations constitute Kant's three-cornered construct of the structure of "perpetual peace." Frequent reference is also made to Norman Angell's sadly ironic prediction in 1912's *The Great Illusion* that war was conceivable under high economic interdependence only as an act of collective irrationality, a theory quickly tested by the outbreak of World War I.[3] Most recently, Bruce Russett and John Oneal and others have folded the economic interdependence argument into the theory of the democratic peace to suggest the appropriateness of Kant's formulation of perpetual peace in contemporary world politics.[4]

These liberal theories rely on an assumption that states are deterred from conflict by fear of losing the welfare gains that come with expanded trade and economic interdependence. The premise is that higher levels of trade will make conflict increasingly costly.[5] While the liberal analysis is usually intended for the systemic level, it can be applied at the dyadic level on the Korean peninsula. As the DPRK becomes increasingly reliant on trade with the ROK, it becomes increasingly costly for the North Korean government to undertake any actions that would damage this trade (and the aid coming from the South that is subsumed under "trade"). A whopping 77.2 percent of the DPRK's export trade in 2002 consisted of interaction with just three countries: Japan (23.3 percent), China (26.9 percent), and the ROK (27.0 percent). Likewise over half of its imports come from China, the ROK, and India. Badly in need of trading partners, the benefits to military action would need to be perceived as substantial in order for North Korea to undertake an endeavor that might interrupt these flows.

The liberal argument gives insight into why North Korea would not act so as to hinder or dissuade the growing level of trade with South Korea. However, given that trade with North Korea made up but the most meager amount of the ROK's $314 billion of international trade in 2002 and that, in terms of quantifiable economic benefits, the ROK gains little from this trade, the liberal argument does not provide sufficient explanation as to why South Korea continues to engage in trade with the North. Nor does it explain the origins of the trading relationship after 40 years of prohibition of economic interaction.

To begin answering these questions, it is important to remember that with trade comes *influence*. In his classic work *National Power and Foreign Trade*, Albert Hirschman demonstrates the "influence effect" of trade—as one country becomes dependent on trade with another country, the latter state has increasing influence in the policy design of the former state. Of course, with increased gains from trade comes increased vulnerability to this effect, and a state can avoid these vulnerabilities only if it is has alternate markets at its disposal.[6] The DPRK therefore finds itself in a position that, because it needs the economic benefits of South Korean trade and aid, it must bend in some ways to Southern suggestions for policy changes and economic reforms. The ROK recognizes this as well and understands the leverage that comes with trade. However, as explained later, South Korea is not using this leverage in a manifestly *realpolitik* way but rather in a more constructive, engaging manner.

Contemporary realist theories of international political economy draw some of their conclusions from Hirschman's understanding of trade but end up in a seemingly more reductionist position. For realists, states as security maximizers have a fear of inequality that can result from trading gains; realist theorists propose, that is, that relative gains matter.[7] From the southern side of the DMZ, however, the absolute gains in the North are simply not large enough to matter in the way that realists propose, as amply shown in table 4.3. By a similar logic, the DPRK cannot believe that it is improving the South Korean position through inter-Korean trade, given that it represents such a tiny fraction of total South Korean trade. Because the ROK holds such a superior economic and geopolitical position to the DPRK, Seoul has no reason to be worried that trade with the North will result in a military or economic advantage for Pyongyang. The realist economic analysis does not apply to the dyadic relations on the Korean peninsula, and relative-gains concerns can be disregarded in favor of absolute economic gains for the DPRK, something that is regarded as desirable in both Pyongyang, for reasons of regime survival, and Seoul, for reasons of peninsular stability. By the absence of the dynamic it proposes, the realist framework of relative gains, like its liberal counterpart, provides some intuition as to why trade continues on the Korean peninsula, but neither of the two mainstream international relations theories demonstrates why the ROK is involved in such trade in the first place or why it is willing to ignore Northern military-first policy posturing. Whether rejected or accepted, each describes a logic as to why there is an environment in which trade can persist but does not provide a logic as to why it actually does.

The problem with both the liberal and the realist relative-gains views of international trade in looking at Korea is that they reflect upon the impact of trade without considering the larger questions of its origins and the possibility of its non-*realpolitik* strategic use. Not surprisingly, theories that incorporate economic relations into a broader perspective provide more leverage in explaining why inter-Korean trade emerged 15 years ago and why it continues in the face of mutual security concerns. The dyadic trade being witnessed between North and South Korea can be reconceptualized by looking at it through the lenses of functionalism and conflict management.

Despite variations in usage, classical functionalism as formulated by its leading exponent, David Mitrany, is in essence a prescription for a welfare-oriented approach

Table 4.3 Comparison of major economic indexes of North and South Korea (2002)

Sector/category	Unit	North Korea (A)	South Korea (B)	A : B
Population	1 million	22.4	47.6	1 : 2
Nominal GNI	$ billion	17	477	1 : 28
Per capita GNI	$	762	10,013	1 : 13
Rate of economic growth (2002)	%	1.2	6.3	1 : 5
Total foreign trade volume	$ million	2,270	314,600	1 : 139
Exports		735	162,470	1 : 221
Imports		1,535	152,130	1 : 99
Trade balance	$ million	−800	10,340	
Trade as % of GNI	%	13	67	1 : 5
Scale of assessments for UN budget	%	0.009	1.728	1 : 192
Industrial structure	%			
Service		31.8	54.1	1 : 1.7
Mining and manufacturing		26.0	30.3	1 : 1.2
Construction		7.0	8.2	1 : 1.2
Agriculture, forestry, and fishing		30.4	4.4	1 : 0.14
Electricity, gas, and water		4.8	2.9	1 : 0.6
Coal production	1 million tons	23.1	3.8	1 : 0.2
Power generation capacity	1 million kw	7.6	50.9	1 : 7
Power generation	100 million kwh	202	2,852	1 : 14
Petroleum import	10,000 tons	58	11,724	1 : 202
Grains production	10,000 tons	394.8	620.0	1 : 1.6
Rice production	10,000 tons	168.0	551.5	1 : 3.3
Fishery products production	10,000 tons	74.6	266.5	1 : 3.6
Iron ore production	10,000 tons	420.8	22.7	1 : 0.05
Nonferrous metals production	10,000 tons	9.2	114.0	1 : 12
Cars production	10,000	0.57	294.6	1 : 517
Steel production	10,000 tons	106.2	4,385.2	1 : 41
Cement production	10,000 tons	516.0	5,201.2	1 : 10
Fertilizer production	10,000 tons	54.6	350.0	1 : 6.4
Synthetic fiber production	10,000 tons	2.7	234.0	1 : 87
Total length of railroad	Km	5,224	3,125	1 : 0.6
Total length of road	Km	23,963	91,396	1 : 3.8
Capacity of harbor loading/ unleading	10,000 tons	3,550	46,960	1 : 13
Shipping possession	10,000 tons	85.0	659.3	1 : 7.8

Sources: ROK Ministry of Unification and UN Docs. A/Res/55/5B (December 23, 2000) and ST/ADM/SER.B/568 (December 26, 2000).

to world order. Functionalism looks at that domain of international life that is assumed to be intrinsically more cooperative than conflictual: the domain of global "low politics." Concerned with finding openings within civil societies as well as between states and civil societies for a different sort of world order—one capable of sustaining peace over time—this approach envisions an inexorable move of the state system from a model of territorial conflict to one of transnational (non-territorial) cooperative networks of socio-functional interdependence. In essence, functionalism sees the territorial state system as incapable of resolving borderless social and economic problems and seeks to build functional institutions upon social interests rather than upon state interests. "Peace will not be secured," Mitrany argued,

> if we organize the world by what divides it. But in the measure in which such peace-building activities develop and succeed, one might hope that the mere prevention of conflict, crucial as that may be, would in time fall to a subordinate place in the scheme of international things, while we would turn to what are the real tasks of our common society—the conquest of poverty and of disease and of ignorance.[8]

In Mitrany's vision, the nation-state would be subverted indirectly and made irrelevant through intricate networks of trans-territorial social and economic interdependence. While committed to world peace as the ultimate end, functionalism attacks social and economic causes of war through an incremental "peace by pieces" approach. The logic of functionalism is that the promotion of welfare leads to the prevention of warfare by eliminating the long-term underlying causes of war.

While Mitrany and his followers spoke of functionalism as being built at the international level, the ideas certainly have applicability at the dyadic level. Viewed in a functionalist manner, inter-Korean economic relations can better be seen as part of a conscious plan—clearly on the part of the ROK and conceivably on the part of the DPRK—to develop ties between the North and the South, to promote contacts and interaction, and to bridge the social and cultural gap that has grown between two halves of a divided people over five decades of hostile separation. Inter-Korean economic relations are in many ways not at all about economics but about reconciliation and the reduction of political and military tensions. As Hirschman describes, broader influence comes from trading relations. The influence inherent in inter-Korean economic relations, while in some ways threatening to the weaker North Korea, also contributes to confidence-building measures that are a part of dealing with the larger security issue.[9] The functionalist solution seems particularly appropriate to Korea because of Mitrany's belief that the growth of functional linkages would lead to a change in popular attitude regarding the "us versus them" dynamic, such that people would be willing to look beyond the boundaries of the state.[10] On the Korean peninsula, looking beyond the boundaries of the two extant states in a contained sense means looking toward the reunification of the peninsula and of the Korean nation.

Coherent with a broad functionalist scheme is a conflict management approach.[11] Conflict management allows for dyadic interactions at multiple levels. Therefore, whereas the liberal and realist frameworks seem to suggest a direct causality between economics and security, keeping an eye on conflict management lets economic relations continue in the face of contrasting developments in the traditional security realm. The ROK, if operating under a conflict management perspective, can make a conscious decision to continue economic interaction in the face of the DPRK's surprise announcements about its nuclear program and in the face of naval incursions into ROK waters. These seemingly very negative occurrences are in part mitigated by more positive occurrences elsewhere in inter-Korean relations, such as on the economic front. Conflict management dissects an all-or-nothing security environment and creates varied pathways of engagement and response.

An odd pattern emerges from looking at these theoretical considerations. In the communist state that should be driven by ideology, economics would seem to be playing the driving role in inter-Korean economic relations, while in the capitalist state that should be driven by economics, a functionalist ideology and a pragmatic conflict management approach hold sway. The traditional liberal mechanism by which trade prevents conflict because of a rational cost–benefit assessment does well to explain why the DPRK cannot risk provoking Seoul to the point where it might cut off burgeoning economic relations, implying that there are limits to the patterns of its current hostility and that Pyongyang may just be testing the boundaries of cooperation. On the other side of the coin, inter-Korean trade arises as an exceptional case in realist theory in which the states are not dissuaded from engaging each other because of relative-gains concerns. Functionalist and conflict management ideas explain why the ROK is willing to continue to pursue inter-Korean relations in the face of various military provocations by the DPRK.

In a more strictly economic vein, Nicholas Eberstadt argued in 1994 that South Korea can choose to pursue a strategy of "rapprochement through trade" because the North Korean economic system objectively needs inputs that the South can provide, because the DPRK recognizes its deep economic difficulties, because the ROK has a growing need for a low-wage labor force, and because of the success of *Nordpolitik* in the early 1990s in using economics to broker rapprochement with communist states. He also noted, however, that the possibility of trade and investment relationships that are mutually beneficial from a strictly economic standpoint is constrained.[12] But in the past ten years, trade has more than tripled; clearly the constraints imposed by economic benefit concerns are being ignored or surmounted. The functionalist explanation fills in the missing pieces, although ultimately it is unclear how far market interaction between North and South Korea might go or where it might hit a roadblock. The fact that inter-Korean economic relations have been largely state-driven and state-moderated, for instance, implies that an entirely different dynamic might result under a more *laissez faire* environment. As discussed later vis-à-vis inter-Korean investment, issues in the security realm could have a larger impact if not for the current close control and cross-issue coordination by the central government in the North or in the South. Even with these caveats, however, the development of inter-Korean relations since the end of the Cold War has been remarkable, and the role of inter-Korean economic relations—and in the face of military provocations by the DPRK—is quite notable. As the evidence shows here, trade between North and South Korea serves a function in furthering relations and crafting peace.

Inter-Korean Trade

The first trade between the ROK and the DPRK, as noted earlier, was purely symbolic: it was accomplished because it could be and because it was impressive that it could be. South Korean President Chun Doo Hwan had raised the idea of trade in August 1984, leading to talks that collapsed two years later. Only with the cross-border shipment of artistic products in 1989 was inter-Korean trade truly inaugurated. But as trade developed over the 1990s, it began to have some economic meaning in addition to its continued symbolic importance. Gold, zinc, and iron were the first major trade products, imports from the North. After the mid-1990s, agricultural, forest, and textile products came to top the list. In 2002, animal products—mainly seafood—were the largest North Korean export on a value basis. As figures 4.1 and 4.2 show, inter-Korean trade was very strong during the years just before the

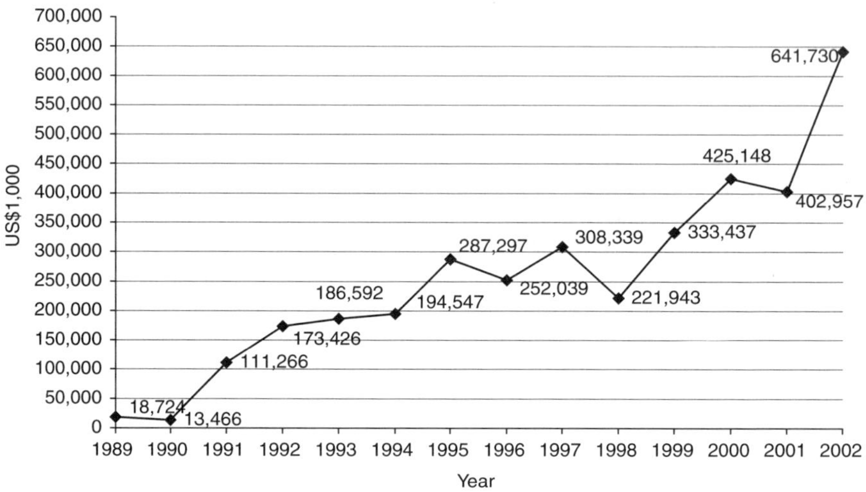

Figure 4.1   South Korean–North Korean trade (1989–2002).

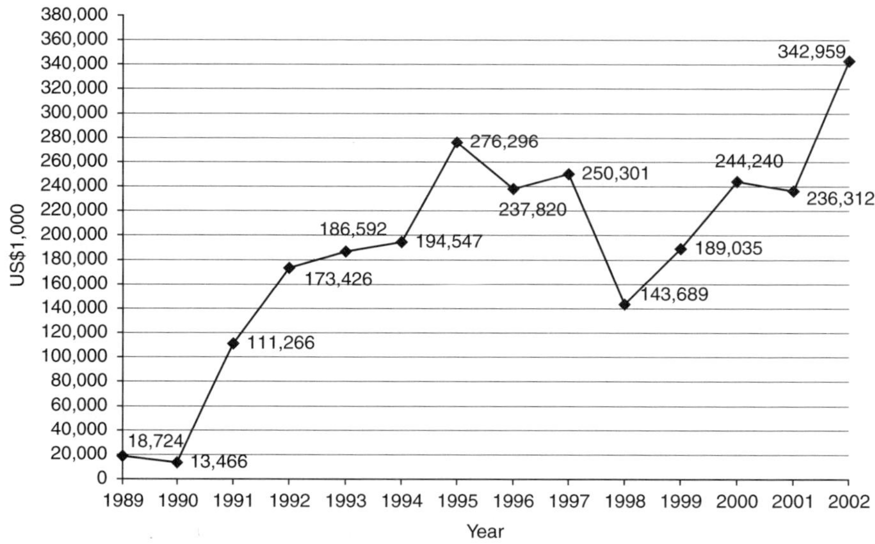

Figure 4.2   South Korean–North Korean transactional trade (1989–2002).

Asian Financial Crisis of late 1997. Trade fell substantially because of the crisis but then saw a terrific rebound in 2000 that was associated with the inter-Korean summit of June of that year. The Joint Declaration produced by that summit was conspicuously silent on security and military issues, in effect anointing economic relations as the practical pathway for the development of inter-Korean relations.

The most important development has been the quick growth of processing-on-commission (POC) trade, which involves South Korean companies sending raw materials north and then reimporting finished or semifinished products. This allows South Korean companies to take advantage of cheaper labor in the North, since rising wages in the ROK have made production less profitable there. As indicated in figure 4.3, POC trade began modestly in 1992 and rocketed to one-half of all transactional trade in 2002.

POC trade is comparable to Mexican *maquiladoras*—border factories that export directly to the United States. *Maquiladoras* are responsible for nearly one million jobs in Mexico and account for $40 billion in exports, one-half of Mexico's total, indicating the possibilities that might lie in store for North Korea in the future.[13] For South Korean companies, POC trade offers the greatest economic benefit. Besides the benefit of cheaper labor than in the ROK or even China, the ROK government classifies trade with the DPRK as *intra*-Korean trade, and therefore duties and rules that would apply under World Trade Organization statutes can be avoided.[14] POC trade also implies technology and information transfer. Many of the POC plants that have been established use South Korean machinery and supervisors. By 2003, South Korean companies were making shoes, beds, television sets, and men's suits in the North.[15]

POC trade alone is a remarkable development in inter-Korean relations given that it requires more and deeper communication than would mere exchanges of finished products across a border. It allows, referring to the framework above, more functional linkages between the two countries. The willingness of the North Korean

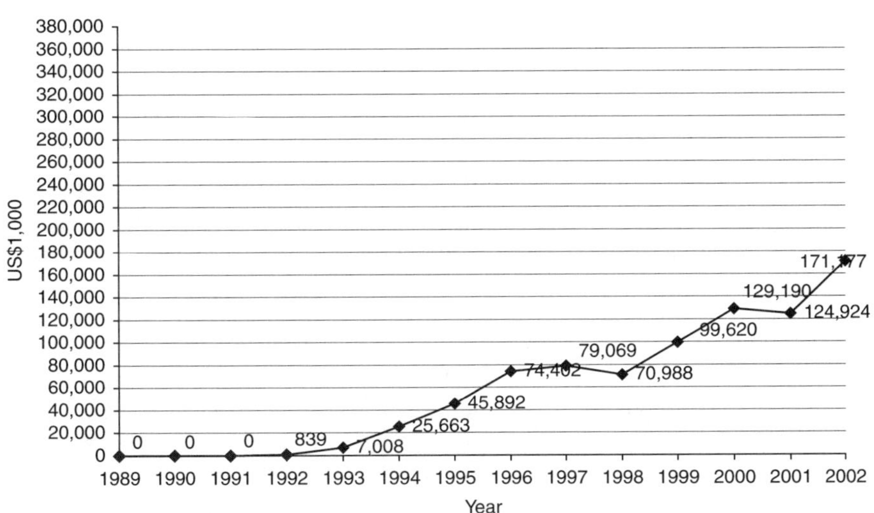

Figure 4.3 South Korean–North Korean commission-based processing trade (1989–2002).

government to allow South Korean supervisors and South Korean factory organization within its territory indicates a slackening of its fears of cultural pollution and of attacks on its political system. Indeed, in April 2001 the DPRK passed the Processing Trade Law, representing its deep interest in POC, and in 2003 the new DPRK prime minister, Pak Pong Ju, led a group of North Koreans on a tour of semiconductor plants in the South.[16] North Korea has found itself in a position such that it must engage in the contradictory pursuit of economic revitalization through the ROK as a mechanism for legitimating Kim Jong Il's regime and insuring its continued existence.[17] A note of skepticism might be sounded, however, given the unpredictability of Pyongyang. In November 2000, for instance, the DPRK denied Hansung Shipping vessels entry to the port of Nampo, even though that was the shipping line that carried 90 percent of all North–South POC trade at the time.[18]

In addition to classifying all trade with North Korea as intra-Korean trade, the ROK also includes in its trade statistics a category of "non-transactional trade." This is actually an accounting of aid sent to the DPRK, including goods related to the now-moribund KEDO nuclear reactor projects, the Mt. Kumgang tourist project, and humanitarian aid. The fact that the ROK statistically ties together commercial trade and aid is indicative of its perspective on inter-Korean trade: like aid, it is a component of a functional project of expanding interactions and relations with the DPRK in pursuit of a more peaceful and harmonious coexistence or reunified existence. Non-transactional trade began in 1995 and has increased to such a degree that it is almost as great as transactional trade. Figure 4.4 shows the massive growth in non-transactional trade since 1996. In comparison with the commercial trade

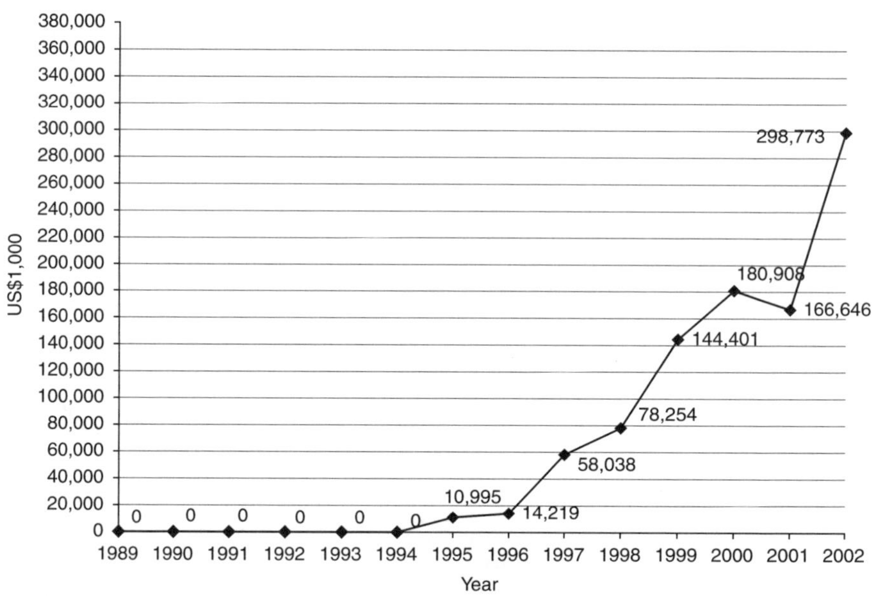

Figure 4.4 South Korean–North Korean non-transactional trade (1989–2002).

depicted in figure 4.2, non-transactional trade has seen greater and steadier growth, although growth in both categories has been concurrent, pointing toward the existence of a broader project of interlocking relations and flows.

To a certain extent, even the transactional trade is a form of aid. Because of a lack of hard currency, the DPRK cannot import South Korean goods to the extent that it might like, and so the ROK maintains a trade deficit with the DPRK in terms of transactional trade, although if non-transactional trade is included, trade since 1998 has technically yielded a surplus for the ROK. Clearly, given the proportion of the ROK's total trade that consists of inter-Korean trade, this trade deficit is not fiscally significant. With the DPRK's 2002 adjustment of its exchange rate from 2.1 DPRK won to the dollar to about 900 won per dollar, the balance of payments is likely to be more reflective of actual value and world market currency rates.[19] Nonetheless, the fact that South Korea is importing more than it exports implies a bolstering of the North's foreign exchange reserves, and South Korea has become the largest provider of hard currency to the DPRK, which it uses to purchase indispensable imports from other countries. In November 2003, the Inter-Korean Economic Promotion Committee agreed to begin conducting more efficient settlement clearance transactions on a trial basis in 2004 (see #38 in table 4.4).[20]

As Marcus Noland notes in regard to the Sunshine Policy of former ROK President Kim Dae Jung, the ROK's willingness to push trade forward and to provide aid under the guise of trade is part of an understanding that the South lacks the economic, social, and political capacity to handle a collapse of the North, making peaceful coexistence a preferable state. In addition, while the ROK's traditional reunification policy put an almost exclusive emphasis on high-level government-to-government talks, the Sunshine Policy sought to encourage nonofficial contacts. As Noland observes, the Sunshine Policy aimed to create "a set of interdependencies that in the long run would discourage the North from external aggression and perhaps even promote the internal transformation of the regime."[21] The threefold increase in trade over the term of Kim Dae Jung's presidency—from $221 million in 1998 to $641 million in 2002—is indicative of the success of the Sunshine Policy in this regard.

Within a functionalist framework, it is not increased trade alone that makes the difference. Nor is it just the increase of aid with trade that is notable. Key to both the functionalist scheme and the Kantian vision, and implicit in the use of trade as a tool of conflict management, is the idea that trade brings with it cultural, social, and ideological flows and changes. At a purely technical and pragmatic level, the growth in trade and the recognition of possible trade benefits has led to a degree of economic reform in the DPRK. A September 1998 constitutional revision mentions "private property," "material incentives," and "cost, price and profit" in a document that otherwise reads like an orthodox manifestation of the DPRK's *juche* philosophy.[22] Further, Pyongyang has been sending partisans abroad—430 in 2001—to study economics and business administration, and in 2003, three fact-finding missions went to Vietnam to study its economic reforms.[23] As figure 4.5 indicates, with visits from the North to the South beginning in 1999, the number of DPRK citizens who have been to the ROK has grown to a level that while still small is nonetheless quite remarkable. In July 2002, the North Korean regime announced major changes in its economic policy, including price changes, which in large part

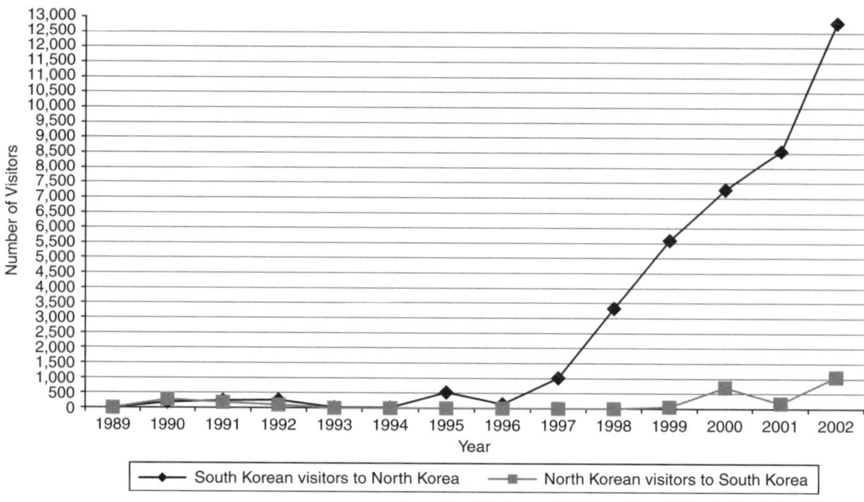

Figure 4.5 Inter-Korean visits.

were a response to the fact that food was being distributed through markets rather than through the state-run public distribution system.[24] These changes are significantly linked to inter-Korean economic relations.

For Kim Dae Jung, this trade-off in which the ROK supplied economic goods in exchange for—or at least expectation of—noneconomic goods from the DPRK is part of "comprehensive reciprocity." In a speech in the United States, Kim contextualized economic exchanges as part of a "larger framework within which there are certain things that we can give to North Korea and certain things that we must take from North Korea."[25] If economic reforms can be taken as evidence of this reciprocity, then they are indeed evidence of the success of the functionalist approach inherent in Kim's Sunshine Policy. However, as Charles Armstrong points out, it will take continued South Korean engagement and effort to insure that the DPRK consolidates these reforms; the functionalist project cannot be stopped short except at the risk of North Korea reverting to traditional mechanisms of survival and isolation.[26]

The extent of the ongoing project is captured in a phrase found in the declaration produced from the June 2000 Summit meeting. The fourth Article stipulates that the South and the North have agreed to "consolidate mutual trust by promoting balanced development of the national economy through economic cooperation and by stimulating cooperation and exchanges in civic, cultural, sports, public health, environmental and all other fields." In previous inter-Korean agreements, such as the 1972 Joint Communiqué and the 1991 Basic Agreement, economic exchanges and cooperation were regarded as goals per se, while the 2000 Joint Declaration treats them as a means to promote balanced development of the national economy. The use of the term "national economy" assumes an eventual integration of North and South Korean economies.[27]

Since the 2000 Summit meeting, over two dozen agreements have been signed between the two Koreas, as listed in table 4.4. These agreements can be grouped into three post-summit phases. From the date of the summit through the end of 2000, there was a flurry of cross-border activity with numerous delegations traveling in both directions, culminating in the four agreements of December 16, 2000, on the resolution of commercial disputes, the prevention of double taxation, transactions clearing settlement, and the protection of investments. An 18-month hiatus ensued, coinciding with the first year and a half of the George W. Bush presidency in the United States. In this second phase inter-Korean dialogue stalled and inter-Korean trade dropped, as seen in figure 4.1. The third phase began in August 2002 with a flurry of agreements, many having to do with cross-border road and rail connections.

Table 4.4 Chronology of Inter-Korean agreements, 1972–2003 (as of November 2003)[a]

#	Date[b]	Place	Agreement
1	07/04/72		South–North Joint Communiqué of July 4, 1972
2	12/13/91		Agreement on Reconciliation, Non-aggression, and Exchanges and Cooperation Between South and North Korea (The Basic Agreement)
3	01/20/92		Joint Declaration of the Denuclearization of the Korean Peninsula
4	02/19/92		Agreement on the Composition and Operation of Subcommittees from South–North High-Level Negotiations
5	03/19/92		Agreement on the Establishment and Operation of a South–North Joint Nuclear Control Commission
6	05/07/92		Agreement Regarding the Establishment and Operation of a South–North Joint Military Commission
7	05/07/92		Agreement Concerning the Establishment and Operation of South–North Liaison Offices
8	05/07/92		Agreement on the Establishment and Operation of a South–North Joint Commission for Exchanges and Cooperation
9	09/17/92		Agreement on the Composition and Operation of a South–North Joint Reconciliation Commission
10	09/17/92		Protocol on the Implementation and Observance of chapter 3, South–North Exchanges and Cooperation, of the Agreement on Reconciliation, Nonaggression and Exchanges and Cooperation
11	09/17/92		Protocol on the Implementation and Observance of chapter 2, Nonaggression, of the Agreement on Reconciliation, Nonaggression and Exchanges and Cooperation

Table 4.4 Continued

#	Date[b]	Place	Agreement
12	09/17/92		Protocol on the Implementation and Observance of chapter 1, Reconciliation, of the Agreement of Reconciliation, Nonaggression and Exchanges and Cooperation
13	06/28/94		Agreement for the Holding of a Summit meeting between South and North Korea
14	07/02/94		Agreement of the Procedure for Holding a Summit Meeting between South and North Korea
15	04/08/00	Pyongyang	South–North Agreement (on Summit Meeting)
16	05/18/00	Panmunjom	Agreement on Working Procedures for Implementing the April 8 South–North Agreement on Inter-Korean Summit
17	06/15/00	Pyongyang	South–North Joint Declaration
18	06/30/00	Mt. Kumgang	Agreement to Exchange Visits by Separated Families, Establish and Operate a Reunion Center and Repatriate Unconverted Long-Term Prisoners
19	12/16/00	Pyongyang	Agreement on Procedures for Resolution of Commercial Disputes between the South and the North
20	12/16/00	Pyongyang	Agreement on Prevention of Double Taxation of Income between the South and the North
21	12/16/00	Pyongyang	Agreement on Clearing Settlement between the South and the North
22	12/16/00	Pyongyang	Agreement on Investment Protection between the South and the North
23	08/28/02	Mt. Kumgang	Agreement on North Korea's Participation in Pusan Asian Games (Asiad)
24	08/30/02	Seoul	Agreement at the Second Meeting of the Inter-Korean Economic Cooperation Promotion Committee
25	09/08/02	Mt. Kumgang	Agreement at the Fourth Inter-Korean Red Cross Meeting
26	09/17/02	Mt. Kumgang	Agreement on Provision of Materials for Inter-Korean Linkage
27	09/17/02	Mt. Kumgang	Agreement Reached at the First Round of Working-Level Talks on Inter-Korean Railways and Highways
28	11/09/02	Pyongyang	Agreement at the Third Inter-Korean Economic Cooperation Promotion Committee
29	01/22/03	Mt. Kumgang	Agreement Made at the Third South–North Korean Red Cross Working-Level Contact

Table 4.4 Continued

#	*Date*[b]	*Place*	*Agreement*
30	01/25/03	Pyongyang	Agreement Made at the Second Meeting of Working-Level Consultations on the Connection of South–North Railways and Roads
31	01/27/03	Panmunjom	An Interim Military Guarantee Agreement for the Use of Temporary Roads between South–North Control Zones in the Eastern and Western Coastal Districts
32	05/23/03	Pyongyang	Agreement reached at the end of the Fifth Meeting of Inter-Korean Economic Cooperation Promotion Committee
33	06/09/03	Kaesong	Agreement on Connection of Inter-Korean Rails and Roads
34	07/04/03	Munsan	Third Meeting Agreement on Connection of Inter-Korean Rails and Roads
35	07/31/03	Kaesong	Agreement of Second Meeting of Inter-Korean Consultation on Economic Cooperation System
36	08/28/03	Seoul	Agreement reached at the end of the Sixth Meeting of the South–North Economic Cooperation Promotion Committee
37	10/28/03	Kaesong	Agreement of Seventh Working-Level Contact on Connection of Inter-Korean Railways and Roads
38	11/08/03	Pyongyang	Agreement of Seventh Meeting of Inter-Korean Economic Cooperation Promotion Committee
39	11/21/03	Mt. Kumgang	Agreement from the Second Inter-Korean Red Cross Talks

[a] Agreements between the DPRK and KEDO (of which the ROK is a member) as well as numerous "joint press statements" are excluded.
[b] Date signed or entered into force.

Source: The ROK Ministry of Unification at http://www.unikorea.go.kr.

The fact that this third phase continued through the DPRK's nuclear revelations of October 2002 speaks to the strength of the functional relations between the two Koreas. Consistent with a conflict management approach, Seoul opted to continue its dialogues and the issuance of formal agreements with the North despite the revived security challenge of nuclear proliferation.

The agreements on roads and railways are indicative of one of the problems of expanding trade with the DPRK: the lack of infrastructure. Because of the underdevelopment of transportation infrastructure in the North and the lack of connections across the DMZ, President Kim Dae Jung proclaimed in March 2000, in a speech dubbed the Berlin Declaration, "To realize meaningful economic collaboration, the social infrastructure, including highways, harbors, railroads and electric and communications facilities, must be expanded. . . . The Government of the Republic of Korea is ready to respond positively to any North Korean request in this regard."[28] These projects are considered more fully in the next section.

Inter-Korean trade has served an economic purpose for North Korea and a broader functional purpose for South Korea. Ultimately, however, inter-Korean trade is constrained by several structural factors. Both production facilities and infrastructure in the DPRK are dilapidated and in need of serious updating. Pyongyang's lack of hard currency reserves mean that it cannot import as much as it otherwise might from the ROK, and because of the state's control of the economy and the general poverty in the country, there are no free domestic markets for South Korean products. To increase the efficiency of trade and the willingness of South Korean companies to engage in trade with the DPRK, Pyongyang will need to continue revising its laws, institutionalizing its commercial practices, and demonstrating rule of law. For Seoul to continue using trade in a functional way, it will need to see progress of this sort in the North. Marcus Noland calculated that the normalization of trade between the two Korean states—as if they were just two contiguous states in the international system—would imply that 35 percent of the DPRK's total trade volume would be with the ROK; this leaves room for current trade to almost double and implies an increase of significantly more if the DPRK economy improves.[29]

Inter-Korean Investment

The prospects for inter-Korean investment, however, are less clear. While the DPRK certainly needs investment to the same degree that it needs trade—if not to a greater degree—ROK firms, especially the chaebols, are less willing to pursue investment given uncertainties surrounding the rate of return, liquidity, and ultimate safety of any investment in the North. Establishing the economic institutions for trade that provide the necessary perception of certainty has been difficult enough; establishing institutions that will make investors feel secure in North Korea is even more problematic. South Korean investors have been content thus far to observe the North as a potential investment partner and not actually to invest in it.[30] Nonetheless, there is evidence of tentative investment by South Korean companies, and the Kaesong Industrial Complex represents the DPRK's latest and best push to catalyze Southern investment. Given the DPRK's status as self-styled socialist hermit kingdom in the global economic system, ROK investment remains North Korea's best hope for capturing flows of productive investment.

Inter-Korean investment has not only lacked the two-way flows of inter-Korean trade but has also lacked the progressive time frame of that trade. Only after Kim Dae Jung inaugurated the Sunshine Policy was the possibility of investment in North Korea effectively opened. Kim removed the upper limit on the amount of investment possible for South Korean companies, allowed for investment in all fields unless strictly prohibited (as opposed to maintaining a list of the only acceptable sectors for investment), and simplified the approval process. Yet a survey two-and-a-half years later found that ROK companies were alarmed by the lack of institutional framework, the possibility of double taxation, and the impossibility of investment guarantees.[31]

These concerns have been addressed both at the domestic level within the DPRK and at the dyadic level. Congruent with the launch of the Sunshine Policy in the South, the DPRK promulgated its 1998 Constitution and then three subsequent laws focused on external economic cooperation: the Foreign Equity Law, the Contractual Joint Venture Law, and the Foreign Enterprises Law.[32] At the inter-Korean level, four agreements were signed in December 2000 on commercial disputes, double taxation, transactions clearing settlement, and investment protection (see table 4.4). It took another three years, however, for negotiators to agree to implement these agreements, leading many to question the worth of the Inter-Korean Economic Cooperation Promotion Committee, which should have been exactly the institutional mechanism needed to spur investment.[33] (In the interim, though, the DPRK did pass domestically the Foreign Trade Act of February 2001 and the Enforcement Decree of the Foreign Investment Protection Act of December 2001.) The Committee finally issued a declaration in August 2003: "The South and the North will take follow-up steps to the 'four agreements,' which institutionally guarantee inter-Korean economic cooperation."[34] One auspicious component of the June and July 2003 talks leading to the August declaration was that the South Korean negotiating team "commuted" each day through the DMZ on land in June, while the North Korean team made the journey southward through the DMZ in July.

The slow pace of these developments is not at all remarkable. Laws about taxation of foreign investment, control over foreign exchange, the role of foreign banks, leasing of land, and customs are in many ways discordant with the *juche* philosophy that undergirds the DPRK. As Harry Eckstein pointed out as part of his theory of congruence, the dissonance created by incongruent organizations of state and society runs the risk of destabilizing an entire system.[35] The North Korean regime is certainly aware of this threat, and this explains some of the foot-dragging that has occurred. The investment that is indeed allowed is not completely divorced from *juche* principles. For instance, a Hyundai-financed greenhouse in North Korea belongs not to Hyundai but to the DPRK, which also claims 40 percent of the produce grown there for state use.[36] According to a Korean Development Institute survey, of 672 companies that started doing business in the DPRK in 2000 or 2001, only 171 were still involved in North Korea in November 2001, and only one-third of the 115 firms who responded said that they were making a profit in their Northern ventures.[37] While some companies are willing to overlook these low returns either in deference to the grander goals of peaceful coexistence and reunification or because of a belief that they can capture market share at an early stage, others are not so willing.

South Korean companies have also cited the lack of transportation infrastructure as a factor militating against investment. Negotiators undertook this issue in 2003, signing in January an agreement for "military assurances" that would allow for work to begin on roads and railways crossing the DMZ.[38] The unpaved tracks that are to be turned into roads have seen some use, as noted earlier, as conduits for negotiating teams, and this carries serious symbolic import: Kim Dae Jung referred to the reconnection of the lines, severed just before the Korean War in 1950, as *de facto* reunification. Road and rail reconnection is both a component of the developing trade and investment linkages and also a functional connection between the ROK and the DPRK in its own right. The fact that the two Korean states can cooperate to build transportation infrastructure across the most heavily militarized border in the world is a powerful statement at several levels and one rightly judged as a contribution to a broad program of functionalist engagement.

As an indicator of the seriousness of the rail and road projects, 12 out of 17 inter-Korean agreements signed between August 2002 and November 2003 dealt with the procedural and operational details of the work on the Sinuiju–Seoul (Kyonggui) and Donghae rail lines and highways. The completion of de-mining work in December 2002 was described by the North as "a shining fruition of the June 15 North-South Joint Declaration, a landmark of national reunification, and product of the desire of all the Koreans."[39]

The investment in rail—the creation of the "Iron Silk Road"—is one that could stand to reap great gains for both North and South Korea and also Russia. Reconnecting railroads through the Korean peninsula would reduce the time it takes a South Korean shipment to get to Europe by half—from 30 days by sea to 15 days by rail—and the cost by a quarter.[40] Russia sees reconnected railways as its route to the South Korean consumer market and also holds out hope for the DPRK's repayment of $3.6 billion in Soviet era debt. Shipping costs on the peninsula would drop significantly, increasing the profitability of and capacity for POC trade. However, despite all these motivating factors there is little progress on the rail project in the northern half of the peninsula because of a simple lack of investment.[41] There is a developing chicken-and-egg conundrum, whereby the DPRK needs better infrastructure in order to get investment but needs investment in order to improve its infrastructure. The recent decision by a multinational consortium to route a 3,035-mile natural gas pipeline around the DPRK, despite South Korea's eagerness for the pipeline to go through North Korea, feeding thermal plants along the way, suggests that international investors are generally casting a wary eye toward the DPRK.[42] Inter-Korean investment is likely to be the most significant investment in the DPRK in the near future.

In this light, the Kaesong Industrial Complex (KIC)—the largest inter-Korean economic project in development—becomes all the more important. Forty miles north of Seoul, the KIC is designed to lure South Korean businesses to use cheap North Korean labor, with the expectation of the kind of effects that China's SEZ reaped from its proximity to Hong Kong—the stimulation of a hinterland.[43] With 22,000 Korean companies having set up factories in China, it would appear that there is an ample investment base waiting to move into the KIC. Hyundai announced the project in February 2001 as part of the Mt. Kumgang tourism agreement, and so far over 1,300 small- and medium-sized companies have applied to set up factories.[44] According to Hyundai Asan, Hyundai's North Korean arm, production at the KIC should be around $2 billion in its first year and reach $14.5 billion in its ninth year.[45] Exportation from Kaesong to the EU and even Japan is likely, although the "Made in North Korea" label probably will prohibit entry to U.S. markets.[46] The KIC certainly appears better positioned to reap gains than the remote and infrastructure-less Rajin-Sonbong Free Economic Zone, which, despite having been in existence for over a decade, boasts of only a hotel and casino as its main investments.[47] And the future of the Sinuiju Special Administrative Region is highly uncertain since the arrest in China of Yang Bin, the Chinese tycoon selected by Kim Jong Il to run the zone. This leaves the KIC as the most attractive region for investment in North Korea.

However, enthusiasm for the possibilities of the KIC must be tempered. Companies that wish to locate in Kaesong will need to supply their own infrastructure, which could be quite expensive in the face of North Korea's dysfunctional road system and decrepit electricity grid. The fact that exports from Kaesong are likely to prove unsuitable for the United States—and perhaps Japanese—markets will also dissuade many investors. If the KIC were to become a major producer, the international community might then begin to protest the tax-free trade between the two Korean states, creating problems within the WTO. The challenges to Kaesong's success are evidenced in the lack of a marquis investor beyond Hyundai. The industrial park has not attracted interest from the chaebols—although Hyundai at one point claimed Samsung would invest in Kaesong, meeting with Samsung's denial[48]—but rather from small- and medium-sized enterprises. Whether because of the questionable interest in the project or because of fear of negative attention from Washington, the primary actors in Kaesong have tried to keep a low profile, for instance by not publicizing the June 2003 groundbreaking ceremony.[49] The most important factor in determining the ultimate success or failure of the KIC will be the DPRK's ability to convince South Korean companies of the safety of their investment and the sanctity of rule of law in North Korea: Pyongyang must actually implement the business laws that it has been passing.[50]

Of particular interest for Kaesong and elsewhere will be the possibility of developing inter-Korean collaboration on information technology (IT) projects. The DPRK has shown significant interest in increasing the amount of IT production within its borders, presumably in part because of the technology sharing that would accompany such production. While South Korean companies have shown interest in bringing IT production to the North, it is unclear whether the North has the human capital to make these projects worthwhile. In addition, there are some significant path-dependent differences between the computer systems used in the DPRK and those used in the ROK, including even keyboard layouts.

The importance of investment growth or lack thereof in terms of the broader issue of creating a secure environment on the Korean peninsula has recently been substantiated in work by Erik Gartzke, Quan Li, and Charles Boehmer. Beginning from basic liberal contentions about interdependence and the economic opportunity costs of military conflict, the authors discover that capital interdependence sometimes matters more than trade in reducing the resort of states to violence.[51] Using a set of statistical models, the authors demonstrate that in different models either trade or, surprisingly, regime type loses significance in the face of monetary and capital variables.[52] Using coefficient estimates from one model, the work shows that starting from a baseline of two contiguous countries—one democratic and one undemocratic—with low trade dependency, low economic growth, and average capital flows, the probability of militarized dispute can be reduced to only 27 percent if exposure to capital flows and capital openness increase by one standard deviation on their statistical scale, or to only 12 percent if trade dependence also increases by one standard deviation and a joint currency area is formed.[53] These results indicate the potential benefits of increased inter-Korean investment and suggest the possibility of a joint currency zone as a mechanism for both further integrating the two Korean economies and furthering the causes of security, peace, and reunification. At the very least, they demand that the low degree of inter-Korean investment be regarded as a limitation on the functional effects of inter-Korean economic relations.

Inter-Korean Social and Cultural Exchanges

The economically least successful investment in North Korea has been the most successful in terms of publicity: the Mt. Kumgang resort area. Under the sponsorship of Hyundai, Mt. Kumgang tours began in November 1998. Hyundai paid a $400 million business fee for the privilege and has lost additional millions of dollars ever since.[54] This led to the need for financial restructuring with significant contributions from the ROK government to keep the tourism project going, something that proved mildly difficult in the face of embarrassing revelations about a $450 million payment—some say "bribe"—from Seoul to Pyongyang channeled through Hyundai prior to the June 2000 Summit. Nonetheless, calls to keep the Mt. Kumgang tourist visits alive have been strong. For instance, on the five-year anniversary of the project, the *Korea Herald* editorialized that the visits to Mt. Kumgang had "served as a catalyst for other forms of inter-Korean exchanges and certainly narrowed the distance between the peoples of the divided nation, geographically and emotionally."[55] Figure 4.5 indicates the tremendous growth in the number of ROK citizens visiting the DPRK since the opening of Mt. Kumgang. Out of the Mt. Kumgang project have grown an overland route to the mountain, tours of Pyongyang, tours of the town of Kosong near Mt. Kumgang, and conversations about opening Mt. Paekdu.[56] On the other hand, the hotel at Mt. Kumgang is staffed mostly by ethnic Koreans who live in China, demonstrating Pyongyang's willingness to forsake microeconomic gains in favor of preventing what it views as cultural pollution.[57]

In some ways, the sterile atmosphere that the DPRK maintains—government agents closely monitor tourists, preventing conversations with locals and even certain photographs—defeats the functionalist mission inherent in the tourism project.[58] While the hope is that the tourism and its investment component would spread cultural contacts and help form inter-Korean social relations, the DPRK agitates and protects against this.

Likewise the other spectacular media event, the reunions of separated families, has found its lasting impact limited by the strictures and slowness surrounding it. Through the end of 2003, eight rounds of family reunions had occurred, and in November 2003 North and South Korea agreed to build, using North Korean labor and South Korean capital, a permanent facility for the hosting of the reunions near Mt. Kumgang that could also be used as a hotel.[59] Nonetheless, the meetings are brief, occur only once, and do not include allowances for future contact, and at the current rate, most of the 122,000 aged South Koreans who have applied to participate will die before given the opportunity, as some 20,000 already have.[60] Like the Mt. Kumgang tourist visits, these reunions, while symbolically important and emotionally moving, are strictly containerized so as to limit the functional outgrowths it is hoped they will produce.

Given Pyongyang's penchant for restricting the benefits that might come from these cultural and social exchanges, economic activity and exchange becomes more important, albeit more difficult. While the North can control and restrict tourists and family reunions, it is more limited in its capacity to do so with investors and factory managers, since there are direct economic consequences if they are too restricted. Therefore inter-Korean economic relations provide a type of leverage that cannot be found in more glamorous interactions between North and South. As long as social interaction remains circumscribed, it is economic interaction that can be expected to do the heavy lifting in inter-Korean relations.

Conclusions

The development of inter-Korean economic relations has been a cautious and speculative one, marked by occasional bumps, either endogenous (e.g., DPRK foot-dragging) or exogenous (e.g., the Asian Financial Crisis). However, the fact that there is cross-border trade, South Korean investment and tourism in the North, and the reopening of transportation connections across the DMZ is nothing short of incredible. And the impressiveness of this is increased by the fact that it has been sustained through the development of a new nuclear crisis and several naval provocations by the DPRK.

Drawing from several theoretical traditions in international relations, we propose a set of causes for this seemingly nonchalant continuation of inter-Korean economic relations. The liberal school of thought relies on the notion of economic opportunity costs to explain why trading interdependence will decrease the chances of military dispute, while liberalism's sometimes polar companion realism proclaims that states will fail to trade or that trade will inspire military conflict because of concerns about relative gains, as one state becomes more powerful because of its trading habits. As the aforementioned evidence shows, North Korea certainly has much to lose from an interruption of trade with the country that has become its second largest trading partner, while South Korea has little to fear in terms of relative gains by North Korea because the DPRK would need to make tremendous absolute gains in economic ability before it would begin to seriously intimidate the South again. While these observations provide a logic as to why an environment exists where trade might persist, they do not explain why trade began or continues to increase in the face of an often uncertain security situation.

A functionalist explanation stresses the use of multiple pathways to create a peaceful, highly interconnected environment. South Korea, beginning particularly with Kim Dae Jung's Sunshine Policy, has attempted to expand the depth and number of types of links between itself and the DPRK precisely in the name of developing a safer, less perilous environment on the Korean peninsula. For the reasons noted earlier, inter-Korean economic relations—and inter-Korean trade in particular—have been the most successful route for pursuing functional linkages. The post–Cold War environment has aided this endeavor, and inter-Korean trade numbers have maintained a steady upward trend over the past decade. Inter-Korean economic relations, therefore, can be said to have provided a set of successful functional linkages on the Korean peninsula.

However, this conclusion must be tempered with a caution endemic to any discussion involving North Korea. As the limited degree of investment demonstrates, much is still holding back inter-Korean economic relations, and there is still significant uncertainty on the peninsula, which is detrimental to profitable investment. For inter-Korean economic relations to continue to progress, there must be a willing acceptance on the part of the North to be a full participant and to work toward making economic ties mutually beneficial. Most importantly, Pyongyang will have to demonstrate the prevalence of rule of law and its willingness to undertake continued economic reforms. In addition, economic relations must eventually expand and intensify social and cultural relations, since these are the more effective functional linkages in the pursuit of which the ROK is willing to undertake economic relations. The functionalist analysis implies a full system of connections, and inter-Korean economic relations can only carry the majority of the weight for so long.

Notes

1. Charles Montesquieu, *The Spirit of the Laws* (Cambridge: Cambridge University Press, 1989 [1748]), p. 338.
2. Immanuel Kant, *Perpetual Peace: A Philosophical Sketch*. Reprinted in *Kant's Political Writings*, ed. Hans Reiss (Cambridge: Cambridge University Press, 1970 [originally published in 1795]), p. 114; italics in original.
3. Norman Angell, *The Great Illusion: A Study of the Relation of Military Power in Nations to Their Economic and Social Advantages* (London: Heinemann, 1912).
4. See Bruce Russett and John R. Oneal, *Triangulating Peace: Democracy, Interdependence and International Organizations* (New York: Norton, 2001) and John R. Oneal, Frances Oneal, Zeev Maoz, and Bruce Russett, "The Liberal Peace: Interdependence, Democracy and International Conflict, 1950–1986," *Journal of Peace Research* 33: 1 (1996): 11–28.
5. See Solomon W. Polachek, "Conflict and Trade," *Journal of Conflict Resolution* 24: 1 (1980): 57–78 and Solomon W. Polachek, John Robst, and Yuan-Ching Chang, "Liberalism and Interdependence: Extending the Trade-Conflict Model," *Journal of Peace Research* 36: 4 (1999): 405–422.
6. Albert O. Hirschman, *National Power and the Structure of Foreign Trade*, expanded edition (Berkeley: University of California Press, 1980), chapter 1.
7. See Kenneth Waltz, *Theory of International Politics* (New York: Random House, 1979); Joseph M. Grieco, "Anarchy and the Limits of Cooperation: A Realist Critique of the Newest Liberal Institutionalism," *International Organization* 42 (Summer 1988): 485–529; and James D. Morrow, "When Do 'Relative Gains' Impede Trade?" *Journal of Conflict Resolution* 41: 1 (1997): 12–37. Morrow's is the most advanced statement, demonstrating that conflict propensity relies on a host of intervening factors ranging from risk attitudes to the size of a first-strike advantage.
8. David Mitrany, *A Working Peace System* (Chicago: Quadrangle Books, 1966), p. 96. This is an expanded edition of the pamphlet originally published in 1943.
9. See Bradley O. Babson, "Inter-Korean Economic Relations in a Regional Context," *Asian Perspective* 26: 3 (2002): 71–89.
10. Davnet Cassidy, "A Critique of European Integration Using Mitrany's Functionalist Approach," *University of Limerick Political & Economic Review* 3 (1996), available on-line at http://www.ul.ie/~govsoc/ulper/1996/ARTICLES/Dav.htm.
11. For a summary of conflict management, see the introductory chapter to this volume. For a more detailed analysis, see Samuel S. Kim and Abraham Kim, "Conflict Management," in *Encyclopedia of Government and Politics*, 2nd ed., ed. Mary Hawkesworth and Maurice Kogan (London and New York: Routledge 2004), pp. 980–993.
12. Nicholas Eberstadt, "Inter-Korean Economic Cooperation: Rapprochement through Trade?" *Korea and World Affairs* 18: 4 (Winter 1994): 642–661.

13. Laura L. Sowinski, "Maquiladoras," *World Trade* (September 2000): 88–92, cited in Sang T. Choe and Kelly D. Huff, "Five Reasons to Do Business with North Korea," *International Journal of Commerce & Management* 12: 2 (2002): 35.

14. Aidan Foster-Carter, "Seoul's Secret Success," *Asia Times Online*, November 19, 2003, on-line at http://www.atimes.com/atimes/Korea/EK19DG01.html. See also Aidan Foster-Carter, "Never Mind the Nukes?" Comparative connections 4: 3(October 2003): 97–112, online at http://www.csis.org/pacfor/cc/0303Q.pdf.

15. See James Brooke, "Quietly, North Korea Opens Markets," *New York Times*, November 19, 2003, W1, W7.

16. See Dong Yong-seung, "After the Summit: The Future of Inter-Korean Economic Cooperation," *East Asian Review* 13: 2 (Summer 2001): 83 and Brooke, "Quietly."

17. See Charles Armstrong's comments in chapter 3 of this volume.

18. Dong, "After the Summit," 90–91.

19. Brooke, "Quietly."

20. "Agreement of 7th Meeting of Inter-Korean Economic Cooperation Promotion Committee," November 8, 2003, on-line at http://www.unikorea.go.kr/en/.

21. Marcus Noland, *Avoiding the Apocalypse: The Future of the Two Koreas* (Washington: Institute for International Economics, 2000), p. 113.

22. See Marcus Noland, "Economic Strategies for Reunification," in *Korea's Future and the Great Powers*, ed. Nicholas Eberstadt and Richard J. Ellings (Seattle: The National Bureau of Asian Research and University of Washington Press, 2001).

23. Richard Tait, "Playing by the Rules in Korea: Lessons Learned in the North–South Economic Engagement," *Asian Survey* 43: 2 (March/April 2003): 316.

24. Marcus Noland, "Famine and Reform in North Korea," Institute for International Economics Working Paper WP 03-5, July 2003, 14ff.; Brooke, "Quietly."

25. President Kim Dae Jung's remarks at the American Enterprise Institute and the Council on Foreign Relations luncheon, March 8, 2001, on-line at http://www.aei.org/sp/spkim010308.htm.

26. See chapter 3 in this volume.

27. Chung-in Moon, "Sustaining Inter-Korean Reconciliation: North-South Korea Cooperation," *Joint U.S.-Korea Academic Studies* 12 (2002): 225–250 at 231–232.

28. For an English text, see www.korea.net/issue/sn/summit/summit 012109.asp.

29. Marcus Noland, Sherman Robinson, and Monica Scatasta, *Modeling Economic Reform in North Korea* (Washington, DC: Institute for International Economics, 1996). On improvement of the DPRK economy, note that foreign trade as a percentage of GDP was 11% for the DPRK in 2001, compared to 18% for Japan, 44% for China, 51% for Russia, 69% for the ROK, and 95% for Vietnam. World Bank, *World Development Report 2003*, pp. 238–241.

30. L. Gordon Flake, "Patterns of Inter-Korean Economic Relations," in *Patterns of Inter-Korean Relations*, ed. Bae Ho Hahn and Chae-Jin Lee (Seoul: The Sejong Institute, 1999), p. 145.

31. The survey was conducted by the Federation of Korean Industries (FKI) in August 2001.

32. See Eric Yong-Joong Lee, "Development of North Korea's Legal Regime Governing Foreign Business Cooperation: A Revisit Under the New Socialist Constitution of 1998," *Northwestern Journal of International Law and Business* 21: 1 (Fall 2000): 199–242.

33. See Dong, "After the Summit," 89.

34. See "Inter-Korean Economic Cooperation Committee Meets for 6th Round," on-line at http://www.unikorea.go.kr/en/.

35. Harry Eckstein, *The Natural History of Congruence Theory* (Denver: Graduate School of International Studies Monograph, University of Denver, 1980) and Harry Eckstein, *Division and Cohesion in Democracy: A Study of Norway* (Princeton: Princeton University Press, 1966), pp. 234–253. For an application to North Korea, see Samuel S. Kim, "Informal Politics in

North Korea," in *Informal Politics in East Asia*, ed. Lowell Ditmer, Haruhiro Fukui, and Peter N.S. Lee (New York: Cambridge University Press, 2000), pp. 237–268.

36. Anthony Faiola, "A Crack in the Door in N. Korea," *Washington Post*, November 24, 2003, A10.

37. Tait, "Playing," 311.

38. The full name of the document is the Interim Agreement to Provide Military Assurances for Transit of the Temporary Roads Inside the South–North Administrative Areas in the East and West Zones, available on-line at http://www.unikorea.go.kr/en/.

39. *Korean Central News Agency* (KCNA), December 17, 2002.

40. Choe and Huff, "Five Reasons," 39, citing Beth McMullan, "Waiting for the North: The Inter-Korean Railway Project Gets a Boost from Russia," *The Korea Herald*, November 6, 2000.

41. Brooke, "Quietly."

42. Brooke, "Quietly."

43. Aidan Foster-Carter, "Symbolic Links, Real Gaps," *Comparative Connections* 5: 2 (July 2003): 93, on-line at http://www.csis.org/pacfor/cc/0302Q.pdf.

44. Brooke, "Quietly."

45. *Korea Times*, November 5, 2003.

46. Brooke, "Quietly."

47. Marcus Noland describes Rajin-Sonbong as "less Hong Kong than Macau North." Noland, "Famine," 22.

48. Foster-Carter, "Never Mind," 108.

49. Brooke, "Quietly."

50. Tait, "Playing," 326.

51. Erik Gartzke, Quan Li, and Charles Boehmer, "Investing in the Peace: Economic Interdependence and International Conflict," *International Organization* 55: 2 (Spring 2001): 391–438.

52. Gartzke et al., "Investing," 411–416.

53. Gartzke et al., "Investing," 412, 415–416.

54. Tait, "Playing," 306.

55. *Korea Herald*, November 19, 2003.

56. See Foster-Carter, "Never Mind" and Faiola, "A Crack."

57. Faiola, "A Crack."

58. See Faiola, "A Crack."

59. Young-sik Kim, "Constructing a 6,000-Pyong Family Reunion Center," *Dong-A Ilbo*, November 6, 2003, on-line at http://english.donga.com/srv/service.php3?bicode=050000&biid=2003110707348.

60. Foster-Carter, "Never Mind," 105.

CHAPTER FIVE

CHINA AND INTER-KOREAN RELATIONS:
BEIJING AS BALANCER*

Andrew Scobell

Since 1949 the People's Republic of China (PRC) has played an important function as balancer on the Korean peninsula. Particularly since the late 1980s, Beijing has served a key constructive role in reducing tensions and facilitating reconciliation between Seoul and Pyongyang. There are, however, limitations to China's role in Korean conflict management linked to its policy preferences vis-à-vis the Korean peninsula and desired political outcomes on the peninsula. While Beijing's enlightened self-interest has fueled its constructive involvement on the peninsula, self-interest and extreme aversion to rapid major change also constrain the extent of its contribution. Indeed, Chinese diplomacy tends to eschew bold transformational initiatives in preference for efforts that are far more conservative and aimed at maintaining the status quo. This tendency by Beijing toward excessive caution is even more in evidence as a leadership transition from the so-called third generation headed by Jiang Zemin to the fourth generation headed by Hu Jintao is underway. And China's national interests vis-à-vis inter-Korean relations dictate a preference for what might be dubbed peninsular conflict management without swift resolution.

China plays a key role as balancer and stabilizer on the peninsula but always operates on the sidelines and never at center stage. Beijing has a unique status in inter-Korean relations as the only capital since the 1980s to have consistently enjoyed cordial relations with both Seoul and Pyongyang. Moreover, China is geographically proximate, with strong cultural affinities and an unresolved divided nation issue of its own. China also conducts significant trade with both North and South Korea. Bonds of socialist ideology and a history of military alliance link China with the North. But China has developed burgeoning ties with the South, driven increasingly by its own economic and strategic interests.

While China is arguably the key balancer on the Korean peninsula, its constructive role in inter-Korean conflict management has significant limitations. This chapter reviews the history of Beijing's relations with Pyongyang and Seoul and then surveys China's contribution to conflict management on the peninsula in the areas of diplomacy, economics, security, and unification. In each area China's contribution is limited because its policy preferences on the peninsula are restrained by its conservative risk-averse logic and guided by China's own national interests. Furthermore, Beijing's immediate term policy is constrained by its long-term designs for the peninsula.

China is intent on maintaining its influence over Korea in future decades, and current policy is crafted with a view to hedging its bets so that Beijing does not alienate or unnecessarily antagonize either Pyongyang or Seoul. The result is that China pursues a policy that is cautious, low-keyed, and that avoids overreaction or excessive drama, anything that might adversely affect future ties. Beijing views Korea as a "natural [Chinese] sphere of influence" and sees the peninsula's future as being inexorably linked with that of China.[1]

Continuity and Change in China's Korea Policy

There has been both continuity and change in China's policy toward the Korean peninsula. The continuity has been in Beijing's support for Pyongyang, although the direction and context of this support has undergone considerable change. There has also been continuity in the challenge that the Korean peninsula has presented to China over the past half century. The PRC faced a dilemma over Korea right from the start and this was evident in late 1950 as Beijing's top leaders agonized over whether or not to intervene in the Korean War. While China's paramount leader Mao Zedong was clearly predisposed to intervene, many leaders had serious reservations and still others strongly opposed intervention. Nothing short of a high-level policy debate ensued.[2] The major changes in China's outlook toward the peninsula have been its shift from a "One-Korea" to a "Two-Korea" policy, and from a strictly military/security focus to a broader strategic context with an emphasis on economics.

Two main phases can be discerned in China's Korea policy since 1949: a one-Korea policy (1949–mid-1980s) and a two-Korea policy (1980s–present). These main phases can each be further divided into two subphases. China was a de facto military ally of North Korea from the late 1940s—a role cemented during the Korean War (1950–53) and formalized by the Treaty of Friendship, Cooperation, and Mutual Assistance signed in 1961. By the 1970s, Beijing's support of Pyongyang had become more restrained and qualified. Then in the mid-1980s—in tandem with China's broader strategic reorientation from preparing for imminent global conflict in the era of Mao Zedong to anticipating an epoch of overall peace and economic development in the Deng Xiaoping era—Beijing adopted a more pragmatic, less doctrinaire approach to the Korean peninsula. At first, the "two Koreas" approach was de facto, but in 1992 the approach became de jure when China established full diplomatic relations with South Korea.

China's contribution to inter-Korea conflict management has been significant. Since 1999, in particular, Chinese influence on North Korea has resulted in decreased tensions as a more confident and seemingly moderate Pyongyang has begun to engage Seoul. Admittedly, North Korea's shift has not been smooth or without setbacks: indeed it has come in fits and starts with periodic reversals and frequent holding patterns. It is unclear whether this is a strategic shift or merely a tactical tap dance by Pyongyang. In any event, this apparent change did not translate into a less threatening or forward deployed Korean People's Army (KPA) along the DMZ.[3] Nor has this change resulted in North Korea curtailing its nuclear or ballistic and cruise missile programs as the revelation of October 2002 and subsequent actions, such as the cruise missile tests in the Sea of Japan in February and March 2003, have shown.

Nevertheless, Beijing without a doubt has been invaluable in encouraging and reinforcing Pyongyang's inclinations toward moderation, Pyongyang's engagement with Seoul, and North Korea's baby steps toward reforming and opening its economy. China has also contributed to its balancing role in inter-Korean relations by expanding its ties with South Korea: Seoul began viewing Beijing as a more or less honest broker playing a critical role in facilitating moderate and incremental change in North Korea.

To the Summit (and Beyond?)

Since the 1980s Beijing has proved remarkably successful at maintaining cordial relations with both Pyongyang and Seoul. China has managed to balance its rapprochement with South Korea in the late 1980s and early 1990s all the while maintaining good relations with North Korea. By most accounts, China has played a critical role in coaxing and pressuring North Korea to come out of its shell. Beijing appears to have been instrumental, for example, in getting Pyongyang to agree to enter the United Nations simultaneously with Seoul in 1991.[4] Then, the following year China was able to establish full diplomatic relations with South Korea without sabotaging its relations with North Korea.[5] While Beijing's relations with Pyongyang did cool markedly following the death of Kim Il Sung in 1994, ties were never severed and Beijing continued to be viewed as a critically important, if independent-minded, patron to balance against the Washington–Seoul axis. Very likely, for example, China's inclusion in the so-called "Four Party Talks" initiated in 1996 was the necessary precondition for North Korea's participation in the same venue with both South Korea and the United States.[6] Still, Beijing has played a neutral but decidedly negative role vetoing one proposal by North Korea that a Washington–Pyongyang peace treaty be included on the agenda and another proposal by South Korea and the United States to include discussion of tension reduction and confidence-building measures.[7]

Relations between Beijing and Pyongyang quickly thawed out in 1999 with the onset of the Kosovo crisis, in which the U.S. military demonstrated the ability to strike at will against targets in a country anywhere in the world.[8] During this crisis both communist party–states sought to respond to their growing insecurities. In April Chinese Foreign Minister Tang Jiaxuan paid a five-day visit to the North Korean capital, and this was followed in June by the visit of a large delegation to China headed by President Kim Yong Nam of Pyongyang's Supreme People's Assembly. These visits paved the way for Jiang Zemin's visit to North Korea in September 2001—the first by a Chinese head of state in a decade. Both Jiang and Kim used the adjective "friendly" to describe Beijing–Pyongyang relations.[9]

Beijing has also been able to reassure Seoul and encourage South Korean President Kim Dae Jung to pursue his so-called "Sunshine Policy" in the face of an uneven and unresponsive North Korea and the growing unpopularity of this policy in the South. Beijing wholeheartedly supports this policy.[10] But China declined to join KEDO insisting that it could do more good by remaining outside of the organization.[11]

Without a doubt China's greatest triumph to date has been the three-day inter-Korean Summit between Kim Dae Jung and Kim Jong Il held in Pyongyang in June 2000. It seems fair to say that the North Korean leader would never have had the confidence and courage to go through with this without considerable encouragement and input from his socialist comrades in Beijing. His extended trip to China a month prior to the summit paved the way for what I label "Kim Jong Il's Coming Out Party."[12]

China has become far more active and engaged in inter-Korean conflict management initiatives quite recently. Since January 2003 Beijing and Seoul have been actively engaged in dialogue attempting to coordinate efforts to improve the overall climate of relations between the two Koreas and more specifically to try to resolve the ongoing nuclear crisis. This is in addition to the mid–April 2003 meeting between representatives of the United States and North Korea that was facilitated and hosted by, and participated in by China.[13] However, the results of these initiatives remain unclear at this point.

China and North Korea: A Virtual Alliance?

Since the mid-1980s Beijing has appeared to view its erstwhile ally Pyongyang as a major liability and in one sense a time bomb. China seems to see North Korea as the "powder keg" of Northeast Asia—the country with the greatest potential to destabilize the region through implosion or explosion.[14] Nevertheless, Beijing faces a dilemma because it fears that the end of North Korea will only produce even greater problems for China. Hence, for the foreseeable future the Pyongyang regime should be shored up no matter what the cost.

China technically remains an ally of North Korea although since the mid-1990s Beijing has made clear to Pyongyang both publicly and privately that it can no longer count on China to rush to its defense in the event of a conflict on the Korean peninsula.[15] The Chinese People's Volunteers (CPV) fought side by side with their North Korean comrades in arms from October 1950 until the armistice of July 1953. According to Chinese military estimates, some 360,000 soldiers gave their lives in combat and some additional 380,000 died from disease and the elements. In all, more than 2.9 million Chinese soldiers served in the conflict.[16] CPV units remained on the peninsula for an additional five years following the armistice.

The Armistice concluded on July 27, 1953, signed by three battlefield commanders: Mark W. Clark, Kim Il Sung, and Peng Dehuai, is a military accord not a peace treaty between governments. Each man signed in his official capacity as the commanding general of one of the major belligerents. Thus Peng Dehuai signed in his formal capacity as the commander of the CPV just as Clark signed as commander of the UN Command and Kim signed as commander of the KPA. The Armistice Agreement relates purely to military matters concerned with the cessation of hostilities but does include a recommendation that the "governments of the countries concerned" resolve the political issues by negotiation. Chinese officers did serve on the Korean Military Armistice Commission until September 1994 when it withdrew under pressure from North Korea.[17] It was not until eight years after the armistice, in July 1961, that Beijing and Pyongyang formally became allies when Zhou Enlai and Kim Il Sung signed the alliance treaty, formally committing one country to aid the other if attacked.

In the first decade of the twenty-first century, China might be said to have what amounts to a "virtual" alliance with North Korea.[18] On the one hand the ongoing military-to-military links between the PLA and the KPA seem more superficial than substantial but these do provide at least token reassurances to Pyongyang and suggest some form of continuing minimal Chinese commitment to safeguard North Korea's security. On the other hand by getting the message across to Pyongyang that the alliance has essentially lapsed, Beijing also serves as a useful check on any North Korean military adventurism.[19] In short, China plays a valuable conflict management role. Some Chinese analysts privately also express the view that the U.S. military presence south of the DMZ serves as a useful deterrent to any thoughts North Korea might have on launching an attack on South Korea.[20] There is also likely a reticence on the part of North Korea to get too close to China militarily because of concerns that this might risk revealing intelligence about the KPA's capabilities, readiness, and intentions. Certainly Pyongyang's rulers are extremely paranoid and strongly averse to sharing too much information with foreigners. North Korea is suspicious of all outsiders including Russia and China and unwilling fully to trust any country.

What are the dimensions of this virtual alliance? It appears to consist of three elements: largely ceremonial, reciprocal military visits, curtailed educational exchanges, and limited cooperation on research and development of defense technology and weapons systems. Since the 1990s there have been approximately a dozen annual visits by military delegations that are long on ceremony and symbolism but short on substance.[21] For example, in September 2000 Chinese Defense Minister Chi Haotian visited North Korea to commemorate the fiftieth anniversary of the intervention of the CPV into the Korean War. As of 2002, there are reportedly at most a handful of ("not many [*bu duo*]") KPA members attending Chinese military education institutions and none at the National Defense University (NDU) on the outskirts of Beijing, including no North Korean representatives in the special course for foreign military officers hosted annually by NDU.[22] The most promising KPA officers used to be sent to military schools in China (and the Soviet Union) but this practice reportedly ended in the 1990s.[23]

China and North Korean WMD and Ballistic Missile Programs

While China does appear to continue to supply limited military items and know-how to North Korea, possibly including ballistic missile technology, in the first decade of the twenty-first century, the scope and volume of such assistance has decreased significantly over what it was in previous decades.[24] Beijing, for example, was particularly active in the mid-1970s in providing extensive help to Pyongyang to develop its short-range ballistic missile capability. This particular effort was reportedly shelved in the late 1970s when Deng Xiaoping rose to power.[25] Chinese analysts claim that Beijing ended its support for Pyongyang's missile programs with the close of the Cold War.[26] While in the past China appears to have provided assistance to North Korea in its chemical weapons program, by the 1990s this—along with other weapon deliveries—seems to have ceased.[27] Moreover, China is not believed to have helped North Korea develop biological agents.[28]

Beijing appears to oppose Pyongyang's efforts to acquire nuclear weapons and is unlikely to have assisted in this regard, at least since the reform era. According to Jiang Zemin, speaking on October 25, 2002, at a joint press conference with George W. Bush in Crawford, Texas, China was "completely in the dark" about North Korea's nuclear program.[29] Beijing is strongly opposed to either Korea acquiring nuclear weapons. China fears this would only increase the potential for regional instability and almost certainly trigger a domino effect as other states, notably Japan, follow suit. Indeed, China's official position is that it wishes the Korean peninsula to be a nuclear free zone.[30] China was relieved when the 1993–94 nuclear crisis with the United States was resolved and the Agreed Framework was signed, viewing this as an agreeable solution to a sticky crisis that could have very possibly resulted in outright hostilities between Pyongyang and Washington, a conflict that could have escalated to an all-out war on the peninsula in the early 1990s.[31]

China is clearly alarmed by the rhetoric and actions of North Korea since October 2002—especially Pyongyang's announcement on January 10, 2003, of its intention to withdraw from the NPT. Meanwhile, Chinese analysts also contend that Washington's "Axis of Evil" rhetoric has been most unhelpful, only succeeding in raising tensions on the Korean peninsula and heightening Pyongyang's paranoia. Beijing appears to believe that only direct talks between Pyongyang and Washington hold any hope of resolving the issue. Significantly, a Foreign Ministry spokeswoman told reporters in Beijing on January 14, 2003, that China was willing to host talks, and a Pyongyang official later indicated an interest in such an option.[32] Then on April 13, after months of insisting on one-on-one face-to-face dialogue with the United States, North Korea announced that it was open to the format of talks with the United States. This announcement paved the way for three-party talks in Beijing on April 23–25 involving North Korea, the United States, and China. China deserves considerable credit for bringing the two sides together. While beyond question Beijing's persistence with Pyongyang made a critical difference, the extent of the pressure China applied to North Korea remains unclear.[33]

At the same time China has developed modest but budding military-to-military ties with South Korea.[34] Clear indications of this are the reciprocal visits of defense ministers at the turn of the century: Seoul's minister visited Beijing in August 1999 and his Chinese counterpart visited South Korea in January 2000. Analysts from an influential Beijing military think tank, the Chinese Institute for International Strategic Studies, now hold annual seminars with counterparts from Seoul's most prominent research institute on national security affairs, the Korean Institute for Defense Analyses. China's PLA Navy paid its first-ever port visit to South Korea in May 2002 when two missile frigates docked at the Republic of Korea's naval base at Inchon reciprocating a visit by South Korean naval vessels to Shanghai in October 2001.

The "Iron Silk Road" and the "Underground Railroad"

Since the economic crisis in North Korea that began in the early 1990s, China has become deeply mired in dealing with the fallout from this, providing desperately needed food and fuel to Pyongyang and playing unwilling host to hundreds of thousands of refugees. Beijing is particularly adamant about maintaining oversight of the scope and direction of Pyongyang's externally oriented economic initiatives, and limiting the flow of humanity across their common border. At the same time Beijing has sought to promote its burgeoning economic relationship with Seoul and sustain the steady stream of students, entrepreneurs, and tourists between China and South Korea. Despite asymmetry involving its economic and people-to-people relations with Pyongyang and Seoul, Beijing has managed to maintain an uneven but steady equilibrium in its balancing role on the Korean peninsula.

Economics

There is a major imbalance in China's economic interaction with North and South Korea. For Pyongyang, Beijing is a vital source of foreign aid, and China is North Korea's most important trading partner. Aid from Beijing fluctuates from year to year, but remains crucial. In October 2000 China reportedly agreed to provide North Korea with 200,000 tons of food aid and as much as 500,000 tons of fuel.[35] But Pyongyang can no longer expect imports at concessionary prices or no cost from its socialist neighbor: since the 1990s, Beijing has required payments in hard currency from Pyongyang. China–North Korean trade is extremely lopsided: while bilateral trade may constitute as much as one-third of Pyongyang's total trade volume, it represents less than 1 percent of China's total foreign trade. Meanwhile, China may do more than 60 times as much trade volume with South Korea than it does with the North.[36] In recent years Beijing has maintained a significant bilateral trade deficit with Seoul while running a sizable surplus with Pyongyang.[37] Nevertheless, China derives many more benefits from its economic relations with South Korea than it does with North Korea. Beijing is Seoul's second largest export market and Seoul is Beijing's second largest source for foreign direct investment.[38] China also views South Korea as a vital source of capital and expertise to develop North Korea's virtually nonexistent infrastructure and integrate Pyongyang into the regional and global economy.

China appears to want to approve North Korea's major foreign trade and investment activities. The curious case of Yang Bin, a naturalized Dutch citizen and resident of China, seems to bear this out. In September 2002—apparently without prior consultation with Beijing—Pyongyang announced the establishment of a new foreign trade and investment zone at Sinuiju, directly across the border from China, with Yang as its director. Then, several weeks later, in October 2002, Yang was detained by Chinese police in Shenyang and later charged with bribery, fraud, and illegally appropriating land.[39] China's actions amounted to a veto of this project. Although the reasons behind this action are unclear China does appear to want to approve all major North Korean projects (but domestic issues such as corruption probably played a significant role).

Beijing has pushed one project in particular: the TRADP and voiced support for another: the so-called "Iron Silk Road". In fact the two seem to be viewed as complementary and interconnected. Since the early 1990s China has advocated what is called a "Tumen River Golden Triangle" and Tumen River Area Development Program (TRADP) was officially launched in 1992 in Beijing.[40] TRADP's strongest promoter has been the provincial government of Jilin, which would be one of the prime beneficiaries of a successful economic zone. The project envisions extensive investment in infrastructure, including road, railway, and port facilities. The ambitious plans call for investment from Japan, South Korea, Russia, and China.[41] The biggest booster of the Iron Silk Road has been former South Korean president Kim Dae Jung who envisioned a railroad running from Pusan to Paris—a latter day version of the silk route. It would be an overland trade route linking Northeast Asia with Europe. This would be a shorter, more convenient, and less extensive route for cargo than the current ocean one. China is strongly supportive of the reconnection of a rail link between North and South Korea. The issue for China for the larger project is the precise route of the railway from the peninsula to Europe. Beijing would clearly prefer the route to go through rather than around China.

North Korean Asylum Seekers/Refugees

The problem of North Korean refugees and asylum seekers emerged in the mid-1990s and by mid-2002 had become acute. The problem confronts Beijing with a dilemma: a no-win situation that threatens to aggravate both Pyongyang and Seoul. On the one hand China is required by a bilateral agreement with North Korea to return all North Koreans who enter China illegally. On the other hand China has to deal with South Korea that while appearing to be constitutionally obligated to take North Korean asylum seekers,[42] is not eager to see a constant wave of North Korean migrants flood into the country via China. In addition Beijing has to contend with and tolerate South Korean humanitarian organizations that operate inside China to assist refugees. Particularly since 2001 some of these groups have organized "underground railroads" to move groups of their North Korean bretheren out of China to eventual resettlement in South Korea (see later). In short, neither Seoul nor Pyongyang wants this problem to become more acute or high profile. Moreover, Beijing has sought to play balancer and do its best to make sure this refugee/asylum problem does not become a major bone of contention between the two Koreas.

In the late 1990s, there was a trickle of asylum seekers seeking temporary refuge in China and resettlement in South Korea. The most famous of these defectors was Hwang Jang Yop, Pyongyang's primary theoretician of Juche ideology, who fled to South Korea via China in 1997. At the same time refugees continued to cross the porous border into China in search of food and a better life. By 2000, hundreds of thousands of illegal migrants were estimated to be in China, mostly living in the provinces directly adjacent to the peninsula: Liaoning and Jilin. The Chinese authorities tended to tolerate them as long as they maintained a low profile. China also permitted South Korean humanitarian organizations to operate in these areas assisting their ethnic brethren as long as they quietly went about their business.

However, Beijing has launched at least two major crackdowns on North Korean refugees in China and the South Korean citizens who have come to help them. The first of these crackdowns came in 2001 following a group of North Korean refugees who sought asylum in the Beijing offices of the United Nations High Commission for Refugees. The high-profile case, which involved members of one family, resulted in unwanted publicity for the Chinese government and tensions with North Korea. The final outcome was that the entire group was allowed to leave China and eventually resettle in South Korea.

This fragile status quo regarding North Korean refugees in China was again upset in spring 2002 when groups of desperate asylum seekers rushed the gates and jumped the fences of foreign diplomatic compounds of five different countries in the northeastern cities of Beijing and Shenyang. China was caught unawares by this wave of defections. The actions were apparently coordinated by South Korean relief workers who established a latter day "underground railroad" for their North Korean compatriots.[43] Clumsy and heavy-handed attempts by Chinese police to seize these people, including some who had succeeded in entering some of these compounds prompted outraged protests from several of the countries concerned: notably Japan and South Korea.[44] North Korea also apparently made its displeasure known. Under the terms of a bilateral extradition treaty, all DPRK citizens found illegally in China must be repatriated. For China this was a no-win situation where the authorities looked heartless under the glare of the international media. Moreover, relations with both Koreas were severely strained causing "a lot of trouble (*hen duo mafan*)" between Beijing and Seoul and Beijing and Pyongyang.[45] In seeking to make the best of a bad situation China, on the one hand launched a crackdown on North Korean illegals and repatriated many back across the Yalu, while on the other hand permitted more than 60 asylum seekers who had entered Japanese, South Korean, German, the United States, and Canadian diplomatic compounds in 2002 to leave China for resettlement in South Korea.

In early May 2002 the author observed firsthand security being rapidly tightened in diplomatic districts in Beijing. Large contingents of nervous, uniformed police armed with clubs stood guard at intervals of several yards as other personnel constructed barbed wire fences on the sidewalks outside embassy compounds in Sanlitun. The wave of North Koreans seeking asylum in foreign diplomatic missions in China appeared to have crested by mid-2002, but it did not completely subside: another flurry of defections occurred in August and September 2002 and a trickle in early 2003.[46]

South Korean Students and Entrepreneurs
In contrast to the illegal flood of refugees from North Korea into China, most South Koreans in China are there legally—studying, for tourism, or conducting business. In fact, South Koreans constitute the largest group of foreign students studying at Chinese universities. There are an estimated 20,000 of them, including some 400 each at Beijing University and Qinghua University. By contrast there are only a small number of North Korean students—reportedly some several dozen—mainly studying foreign languages and business.[47] In addition, tens of thousands of ROK citizens reside in China working for more than 1,500 South Korean companies.[48]

Chinese Visitors to Korea
A similar imbalance exists in the flow of Chinese citizens to the Korean peninsula for business and pleasure. In recent years hundreds of thousands of Chinese have visited South Korea annually—most as tourists. By contrast the traffic to North Korea is a mere fraction of this. The 2002 World Cup soccer tournament, jointly hosted by Japan and South Korea, should have witnessed an even larger number of Chinese visitors to South Korea. At least 50,000 Chinese fans were expected to follow their national team to South Korea and cheer them on. However, Beijing was concerned about the specter of thousands of Chinese overstaying their visas and sought to avoid

potential embarrassment by severely restricting travel by soccer fans. The result was that less than 15,000 Chinese made the trip to support their team.[49]

Reconciliation Without Unification

China's preferred policy outcome is inter-Korean reconciliation without unification. Beijing assumes that unification, if it occurs, will be under Seoul's auspices. Because of this, China prefers what might be called the "status quo plus" outcome: the continued existence of two Korean states but with greatly decreased tensions on the peninsula. This would mean that North Korea moderates its hard-line stance, becomes reconciled with South Korea, and ameliorates its economic situation through reforms and greater trade, investment, and aid from South Korea. This would necessitate less Chinese aid, produce a more stable Pyongyang regime, and likely result in the peninsula being drawn into a Chinese sphere of influence.[50]

But China does not want inter-Korean rapprochement to be too successful or proceed too quickly—conflict management without swift resolution. Beijing's Defense White Paper issued in December 2002 observes: "Reconciliation on the Korean peninsula is moving haltingly."[51] While China is clearly not satisfied with the progress of North Korea, Beijing would prefer a slow pace of reconciliation rather than a fast one. On the one hand, for China, North Korea is "too close for comfort."[52] Pyongyang is largely a liability in Beijing's eyes: a socialist buffer that requires considerable handholding and substantial resources. On the other hand, China does not want the North Korean regime to collapse—this would mean the disappearance of a socialist buffer state and very likely mean the emergence of a single larger and stronger Korean state that is democratic, capitalist, and a U.S. ally. Beijing's leaders have tended to view Korea's relationship with China as being one of "lips and teeth": when the lips (i.e., Korea) are gone then the teeth (i.e., China) get cold. Since 1949, PRC leaders have viewed North Korea as a crucial buffer state.[53] Jiang Zemin reportedly told his North Korean hosts in September 2001 during his three-day visit to Pyongyang, that because China is "close to the Korean peninsula, [it] is always concerned about the development of the situation on the peninsula and has consistently worked to maintain peace and stability on the peninsula."[54]

The collapse of the North Korean regime would not be conducive to peace and stability in China's view. It would also mean that China is one of the ever-shrinking handful of Leninist party–states—not a comforting thought for Beijing. Moreover, the end of the Pyongyang regime would further weaken the ideological underpinnings of communist party rule in China. A de facto core element of CCP legitimacy is a devoted commitment to national unification with Taiwan. A Korea unified under democratic capitalism would invite obvious comparisons to the Taiwan Strait standoff and fuel speculation about the future of Chinese unification. Although it is difficult to forecast with any degree of accuracy what the actual impact of Korean unification would have on a divided China, it is definitely a complicated situation that the Beijing regime would prefer not to confront in the near future.[55]

Similarly, on the one hand, China views South Korea mostly in a positive light—an economic powerhouse that conducts substantial trade with, and has valuable investments in, China. So where Seoul is concerned, Beijing can be said to be "taking care of business." On the other hand, however, China also views South Korea as a potential security concern. If the Koreas were unified, the result would be a larger, stronger, and more populous state that borders China. This unified Korea would be a putative challenge to China in Northeast Asia as a lively democracy (that sent two former heads of state of prison for corruption), and a key U.S. ally (with tens of thousands of U.S. troops stationed on its soil). Moreover, there are latent territorial disputes and China is home to a significant ethnic Korean minority who may aspire to be citizens of a greater Korea.[56] However, it is not preordained that a unified Korea would maintain an alliance with the United States. A unified Korea might seek a different security arrangement, possibly Finlandization, or even move into Beijing's orbit.

Conclusion

Beijing seems destined to try and continue to maintain an uneasy balance between the socialist outpost of Pyongyang and capitalist dynamo of Seoul. At the very least China desires continuity and stability on the Korean peninsula. Ideally China would like to see a resolution of the creeping nuclear crisis that has been simmering since October 2002, a lessening of regional tensions, increased economic interaction between North and South Korea, and a more moderate reform-minded Pyongyang getting its economy in order with South Korea's assistance. If the North Korean economy ameliorates this will mean a lessening of China's burden to provide economic aid. For Beijing, it is very desirable that Pyongyang institute reforms to better meet its own people's basic needs and provides them greater economic opportunities. This would ease the pressure on China from refugees and asylum seekers.

China will seek to build on the April 2003 meeting in Beijing with North Korea and the United States. However, there are a number of challenges China faces. First, China wants to do its best to make sure this is not a flash in the pan much like the inter-Korean Summit of 2000. It will be enough of a challenge just to have a follow-up meeting. But beyond this, it remains to be seen if China is successful in bringing more parties to the table. The most important addition would be South Korea. Because of its balancing role and record of cordial relations with both Koreas, China is uniquely placed to make this happen. But larger questions remain unanswered: will Beijing continue its more activist role in peninsular conflict management? Can China persuade North Korea that the road to real economic reform runs through the KPA? On this latter question, Beijing is again uniquely qualified to guide Pyongyang through the process of economic reform of a party–army–state regime. Downsizing the KPA and co-opting it into the reform process is vital if the Koreas are to have a viable chance at getting beyond managing the conflict to mitigating and then resolving the conflict.

China's Potential Role in Downsizing the
North Korean Garrison State

China seeks to nurture the emergence of a reform-minded North Korea that would resuscitate its economy, draw down its massive military, and reconcile with South Korea.[57] How realistic this goal is and how far Beijing is willing to pursue it remains unclear.[58] Beijing can certainly preach to Pyongyang the virtues of conceptualizing national security in broad and comprehensive terms. Chinese strategists have tended to emphasize since the 1980s the importance of the "comprehensive national power (*zonghe guoli*)" concept and paying greater attention to economic factors beyond simply the traditional quantitative measure of military power. Many Chinese analysts attribute the dramatic collapse of the Soviet Union to that country's leaders spending excessively on defense and not paying sufficient attention to their country's overall economic well being. Certainly North Korea can be seen as being in great danger of falling into the "Soviet trap."

China is a living, breathing case study of a country that has thus far managed skillfully to avoid this pitfall. Indeed, it is a fascinating—albeit not blemish-free—model of how to demilitarize or at least shrink a garrison state. For systemic economic reform to have a hope of actually succeeding in North Korea, it must start with the KPA and the PLA can help here. Without a doubt, North Korea is an extreme case of a garrison state—what I have called the "party-military-state," and the "most militarized society in the world."[59] Pyongyang has more than one million men and women in its standing armed forces (with millions more in the reserves), a defense budget that probably comprises at least one-third of the central government's expenditure, and a "second" or defense economic sector that constitutes as much as 40 percent of the total economy.[60] The road to meaningful reform in North Korea runs through that country's massive defense establishment.[61] And the PLA represents a relatively successful example of the opportunities available to the military in a reforming socialist state.[62]

However, all this advice may well fall on deaf ears. As many Chinese stress: you cannot tell North Koreans anything. Chinese analysts insist that their North Korean counterparts are very proud people and one can only suggest things to them and hope they listen.[63] North Korea's paranoid leaders may also be extremely suspicious of China's motives in urging demilitarization. In any event, change in Pyongyang often moves at a glacial pace while follow-through on conciliatory rhetoric and brokered agreements is difficult if not impossible to discern.

To conclude, China is a key balancer on the Korean peninsula. However, a combination of a risk-averse mind-set and long-term ambitions for Korea to be a Chinese sphere of influence result in a policy that tries to be extremely restrained because Beijing is fearful of overplaying its hand. While China remains relatively confident of growing Chinese dominance on the peninsula, Beijing is concerned that swift unification might not be in its interests, China would prefer not to see a political union of the two Koreas in the near future: this would result in the emergence of a unified, economically and militarily more powerful Korean state next door that might be less prone to China's influence. What Beijing desires for the immediate future is reconciliation without unification. China's own national interests suggest that there are important limitations as to what China can be expected to contribute to inter-Korean conflict management.[64] Still, Beijing will continue to play a key balancing role between Seoul and Pyongyang, and for the foreseeable future China will be the last best hope as the one external actor capable of prodding the North Korean garrison state to moderate its policies and downsize its defense sector.

Notes

* The views expressed here are solely those of the author and do not represent those of the U.S. government, Department of Defense, or U.S. Army.

1. See, e.g., David Shambaugh, "China and the Korean Peninsula: Playing for the Long Term," *Washington Quarterly* 26: 2 (Spring 2003): 43–56. The quotation is from p. 50.

2. Andrew Scobell, "Soldiers, Statesmen, Strategic Culture and China's 1950 Intervention in Korea," *Journal of Contemporary China* 8 (1999): 477–497.

3. Andrew Scobell, "Making Headway on the Korean Peninsula," in *U.S. Strategies for Regional Security: Report of the 42nd Annual Strategic for Peace Conference* (Muscatine, IA: The Stanley Foundation, 2002), p. 45.

4. Chae-Jin Lee, *China and Korea: Dynamic Relations* (Stanford, CA: Hoover Institution Press, 1996), pp. 121–122; Samuel S. Kim, "The Making of China's Korea Policy in the Era of Reform," in *Chinese Foreign and Security Policy in the Reform Era*, ed. David M. Lampton (Stanford, CA: Stanford University Press, 2001), p. 379.

5. Samuel S. Kim, "The Making of China's Korea Policy," p. 383.

6. Nevertheless, by some accounts, Pyongyang was at least initially almost as suspicious of Beijing's involvement as it was of Seoul's and Washington's. North Korea reportedly looked at the Four Party Talks as an arena in which the other three parties might gang up on it. Almost certainly, however, in the end it was China that was instrumental in coaxing North Korea to join the forum. Eric A. McVadon "Chinese Military Strategy for the Korean Peninsula," in *China's Military Faces the Future*, ed. James R. Lilley and David Shambaugh (Armonk, NY: M.E. Sharpe, Inc., 1999), pp. 273–274, 289.

7. Samuel S. Kim, "The Making of China's Korea Policy," p. 395.

8. Experts agree that the key year in the rapprochement between Beijing and Pyongyang is 1999. See Tom Hart, "The PRC-DPRK Rapprochement and China's Dilemma in Korea," *Asian Perspective* 25 (2001): 247–259 and Jonathan D. Pollack, "China and a Changing North Korea: Issues, Uncertainties, and Implications," paper presented to Conference on North Korea's Engagement-Perspectives, Outlook, and Implications," held in Washington, DC, February 23, 2001 accessed at http://www.nwc.navy.mil/apsg/papers/Pollack%20NORTH%20KOREA%20PAPER.htm. On the impact of Kosovo, see Samuel S. Kim and Tai Hwan Lee, "China-North Korean Relations: Managing Asymmetrical Interdependence" (unpublished manuscript) and Eric A. McVadon, "China's Goals and Strategies for the Korean Peninsula," in *Planning for a Peaceful Korea*, ed. Henry D. Sokolski (Carlisle Barracks, PA: U.S. Army War College, 2001), pp. 170–171.

9. Lin Dequan and Huang Hanmin, "Jiang Zemin Meets with President Kim Yong Nam and Hang Song Nam of the Democratic People's Republic of Korea," *Xinhua Domestic Service* (in Chinese) September 4, 2001 translated in *FBIS-CHI* September 4, 2001.

10. Samuel S. Kim, "China, Japan, and Russia in Inter-Korean Relations," *Korea Briefing 2000–2001* (Armonk, NY: M.E. Sharpe, 2002).

11. Kim and Lee, "China-North Korea Relations."

12. Andrew Scobell, "North Korea on the Brink: Breakdown or Breakthrough?" in *The Rise of China in Asia: Security Implications*, ed. Carolyn Pumphrey (Carlisle Barracks, PA: U.S. Army War College, 2002), p. 213.

13. For more details on these efforts by China, see Scott Snyder, "China-Korea Relations: Regime Change and Another Nuclear Crisis," *Comparative Connections* 5 (Spring 2003): 93–100.

14. This is certainly the U.S. perspective and the author is convinced that this is also the Chinese perspective based on interviews with Chinese civilian and military analysts in spring and summer 2002 [hereafter "Author Interviews."]. For the U.S. perspective, see Andrew Scobell, *U.S. Army and the Asia Pacific* (Carlisle Barracks, PA: U.S. Army War College, May 2001), pp. 19–20.

15. Kim, "The Making of China's Korea Policy," p. 397; McVadon, "China's Military Strategy for the Korean Peninsula," pp. 279–281; Author's interviews.

16. The combat and noncombat casualties are taken from Zhang Aiping, Chief Compiler, *Zhongguo Renmin Jiefang Jun* (China's People's Liberation Army) vol. 1, Contemporary China Series (Beijing: Dangdai Zhongguo Chubanshe, 1994), p. 137. This source claims that the figures include combat-wounded and noncombat incapacitated, respectively. I count all figures as fatalities since I believe these numbers underestimate the deaths. An article written by two distinguished veterans of the conflict, Zhang Wannian and Chi Haotian, commemorating the anniversary of the Korean War published in 2001, gives a slightly higher figure of combat deaths: 366,000. The figure on the total number of Chinese who served in Korea is also taken from this article. See Zhang Wannian and Chi Haotian, "Great Victory, Valuable Asset—Commemorating the 50th Anniversary of the Chinese People's Volunteers' Participation in the War to Resist U.S. Aggression and Aid Korea," *Qiushi* (Internet version), November 1, 2001 translated in *FBIS* November 13, 2001.

17. Samuel S. Kim, "North Korea and the United Nations," *International Journal of Korean Studies* 1 (Spring 1997): 78–105.

18. Taeho Kim argues the military alliance still remains in effect but only "in name." See Taeho Kim, "Strategic Relations Between Beijing and Pyongyang: Growing Strains and Lingering Ties," in *China's Military Modernization*, ed. Lilley and Shambaugh, p. 296.

19. McVadon, "China's Military Strategy for the Korean Peninsula," pp. 280–281.

20. Author's Interviews.

21. See, e.g., McVadon, "China's Military Strategy for the Korean Peninsula," p. 288 and Taeho Kim, "Beijing Strategic Relations with Pyongyang," pp. 305–309; and author's interviews.

22. Author's Interviews.

23. Joseph S. Bermudez, Jr., *The Armed Forces of North Korea* (London and New York: I.B. Taurus, 2001), p. 103.

24. Hart, "The PRC-DPRK Rapprochement and China's Dilemma in Korea," p. 249; McVadon, "China's Goals and Strategies," p. 147.

25. Bermudez, *The Armed Forces of North Korea*, pp. 245–246. For extensive coverage of North Korea's ballistic missile program, see ibid., chapter nine.

26. McVadon, "China's Goals and Strategies for the Korean Peninsula," p. 154.

27. On the curtailment of the Chinese weapons pipeline to North Korea, see Taeho Kim, "Strategic Relations Between Beijing and Pyongyang," pp. 304–305.

28. Bermudez, *The Armed Forces of North Korea*, p. 231.

29. "Remarks by the President and Chinese President Jiang Zemin in Press Conference, Bush, Ranch, Crawford, Texas available at http://www.whitehouse.gov/news/reseases/2002/10/print/20021025.html.

30. Indeed Jiang Zemin stated this at his October 25, 2002 joint press conference with President Bush in Crawford, Texas. See also McVadon, "Chinese Military Strategy for the Korean Peninsula," p. 273.

31. Kim, "China's Korea Policy Making," pp. 393–394.

32. Erik Eckholm, "China Offers to be Host of Direct U.S.-North Korea Talks," *New York Times*, January 15, 2003. A DPRK foreign ministry official was quoted as saying: "We can review mediation offers from neighboring countries . . ." He remarked it would be "a good thing if . . . our neighboring countries . . . play positive roles." The official was quoted in "Pyongyang May Accept Neighbors' Mediation," *Japan Times* January 25, 2003 cited in Northeast Asian Peace and Security Network accessed at http://nautilus.org/napsnet/dr/0301/JAN29.html#item15.

33. There is speculation that China shut off a key oil pipeline for three days in February 2003 to apply direct political pressure on North Korea but this cannot be verified. Significantly Beijing refuses to confirm or deny the report. My interpretation is that the pipeline was

indeed shutdown for "technical reasons" and China decided it best interests would be served by allowing both North Korea and the United States to believe this was an act of intention pressure. See the analysis in Andrew Scobell "China and North Korea: The Limits of Influence," *Current History* 102 (September 2003): 278.

34. Kenneth W. Allen and Eric A. McVadon, *China's Foreign Military Relations* Report No. 32 (Washington, DC: Henry L. Stimson Center, 1999), pp. 66–67.
35. Nicholas Eberstadt, "Korea," in *Strategic Asia: Power and Purpose, 2001–02*, ed. Richard J. Ellings and Aaron L. Friedberg (Seattle: National Bureau of Asian Research, 2001), p. 138.
36. Kim, "The Making of China's Korea Policy," pp. 385, 387.
37. Kim and Lee, "China-North Korean Relations."
38. "Article Marks Tenth Anniversary of Sino-ROK Relations." *Renmin Ribao* (Internet version) August 24, 2002 translated in *FBIS* August 24, 2002.
39. Joseph Kahn, "China Seizes Entrepreneur Named to Run North Korea Enclave," *New York Times*, October 4, 2002; Peter S. Goodman, "China Arrests Head of N. Korean Project," *Washington Post*, November 28, 2002.
40. Jean-Marc F. Blanchard, "The Heyday of Beijing's Participation in the Tumen River Area Development Programme, 1990–1995: A Political Explanation," *Journal of Contemporary China* 9 (July 2000): 271–290.
41. Kim, "The Making of China's Korea Policy," pp. 388–389; ed., Catharin Dalpino and Bates Gill, *Brookings Northeast Asia Survey 2001–02* (Washington, DC: Brookings Institution, n.d.), pp. 93–95.
42. On this point, see Benjamin Neaderland, "Quandary on the Yalu: International Law, Politics, and China's North Korean Refugee Crisis," *Stanford Journal of International Law* 40:1 (2004): 143–177.
43. See, e.g., Robert Marquand, "A Refugee's Perilous Odyssey from North Korea," *Christian Science Monitor*, August 16, 2002.
44. For more on this see, Andrew Scobell, "China and North Korea: The Close but Uncomfortable Relationship," *Current History* 101 (September 2002): s280–281.
45. Author's Interviews.
46. "N. Korean Bids for Asylum Continue," *Los Angeles Times*, September 4, 2002.
47. There are apparently a few North Koreans studying at the Beijing Foreign Languages Institute. Several dozen others are reportedly studying business at institutions in Shanghai, including Fudan University and Tongji University. See Author's Interviews"; "Article Marks Tenth Anniversary of Sino-ROK Relations," *Renmin Ribao* (Internet edition) August 24, 2002 translated in *FBIS* August 24, 2002; and "North Korean Students Re-appear in Shanghai," *Joong Ang Ilbo*, October 5, 2001 accessed on North Korean Net at http://english.joins.com/nk/article.asp?aid=20011005141730&sid=E00.
48. Taeho Kim, "A Testing Ground for China's Power, Prosperity and Preferences: China's Post-Cold War Relations with the Korean Peninsula," *Pacifica Review* 13 (February 2001): 35.
49. "More Chinese Tourists Visit South Korea," http://english.peopledaily.com.cn/200112/25eng20011225_87433.shtml (posted December 25, 2001); James Brooke, "Hosts' Big Hopes Are Let Down By World Cup," *New York Times*, June 29, 2002.
50. Kim, "The Making of China's Korea Policy," p. 404.
51. *China's National Defense in 2002* (Beijing: Information Office of the State Council of the People's Republic of China, December 2002), p. 7.
52. Scobell, "China and North Korea: The Close But Uncomfortable Relationship."
53. Lee, *China and Korea*.
54. Lin Dequan and Huang Hanmin, "Jiang Zemin Meets with President Kim Yong Nam and Hang Song Nam of the Democratic People's Republic of Korea," *Xinhua Domestic Service* (in Chinese) September 4, 2001 in *FBIS-CHI* September 4, 2001.
55. Scobell, "China and North Korea: The Close But Uncomfortable Relationship," 279, pp. 281–283.
56. Kim, "The Making of China's Korea Policy," pp. 403–404.

57. Ibid., pp. 402–403.

58. Pollack, "China and a Changing North Korea."

59. For the first quote, see Scobell, "North Korea on the Brink," 199; for the second quote, see Andrew Scobell, *Going Out of Business: Divesting the Commercial Interests of Asia's Socialist Soldiers* Politics and Security Occasional Papers no. 3 (Honolulu, HI: East-West Center, 2000), p. 16.

60. Scobell, *Going Out of Business*, p. 14, table 2, and pp. 16–17 and Marcus Noland, "Prospects for the North Korean Economy," in *North Korea After Kim Il Sung*, ed. Dae-Sook Suh and Chae-Jun Lee (Boulder, CO: Lynne Rienner, 1998), p. 53, note 5.

61. Andrew Scobell, "Making Headway on the Korean Peninsula," p. 48.

62. Scobell, "North Korea on the Brink," pp. 211–212.

63. Author's Interviews.

64. This is also true of the China's potential to influence North Korea. See Scobell, "China and North Korea: The Limits of Influence."

Chapter Six
Japan in Inter-Korean Relations

C.S. Eliot Kang

Great powers surrounding divided Korea pay lip service to the cherished Korean notion that inter-Korean relations are the affairs of the Korean people alone. The truth of the matter is that these great powers bear much responsibility for the vicissitudes of "inter-Korean relations," as their ambitions and fears have contributed to the creation and perpetuation of a divided Korea. For more than a half century, China, Russia, the United States, and Japan have all stirred the volatile caldron that is inter-Korean relations, sometimes playing the role of instigator, guarantor, or mediator. However, compared to other great powers that have interests at stake in Korea, Japan has played the most passive role in inter-Korean relations. While the United States, China, and Russia (particularly as the Soviet Union) have openly asserted their interests in inter-Korean relations, Japan has been relatively quiescent.

Undoubtedly, the legacy of Japan's imperialist past has contributed to Japan's long-standing reluctance to take an active role in inter-Korean relations. For one, Japan's failed drive for an empire, resulting in devastation for Japan and division for Korea, has imparted a high degree of self-consciousness and circumspection in its diplomacy toward the divided Korea. For another, Japan's colonization of Korea left a searing memory among Koreans who are only eager to remind the Japanese and the world about Japan's misdeeds and cruelty during its imperium. And this has acted to contain any residual Japanese impulse, unchecked by Japan's own self-restraint, to play a leading role in inter-Korean relations.

Nonetheless, Japan's detachment may be more a function of self-interested calculation than a complication arising out of history. The fact is, its unique lopsided alliance with the United States and the intense zero–sum nature of the inter-Korean rivalry have long shielded Japan from hazards arising out of often volatile inter-Korean relations, allowing Japan to maintain a comfortable degree of aloofness from Korean affairs. However, the end of the Cold War and emergence of new threats emanating from inter-Korean relations have made such a passive role no longer tenable for Japan. Consequently, Japan is taking a more proactive role in inter-Korean relations, participating more visibly in conflict management to preserve peace and foster reconciliation between the two Koreas.

This chapter seeks to capture the logic of the changing Japanese role in inter-Korean relations in several separate but interrelated dimensions—the political/diplomatic, military/security, economic, and functional. The analysis begins with a focus on Japan's long-standing passive role in inter-Korean relations, but it details the post–Cold War transformation of Japan's role in key dimensions of inter-Korean relations. The chapter offers a "defensive realist" explanation of this change that stresses the importance of threat management over balance of power in international relations.[1] It concludes by considering the implications of a defensive realist Japan on the prospect of Korean reunification. While it is impossible to predict exactly what role Japan will play in Korean reunification, there can be little doubt, as Japan pursues its own interests in an increasingly challenging threat environment, it will have a significant impact on the prospect and, if it happens, the nature of Korean reunification.

The Political/Diplomatic Dimension

The geographical proximity of the Korean peninsula to the Japanese archipelago makes inter-Korean relations a vital matter for Japan. Yet compared to China, Russia, and the United States, Japan has played a markedly passive role in inter-Korean political affairs. Only in recent years has Japan played a key, if often reactive and sometimes erratic, role in the conflict management process between South Korea and North Korea.

Cold War Passivity

Koreans remember well a time when the Japanese acted with vigor and ruthlessness toward them. More than a century ago, when Korea was technologically and economically backward and militarily weak, Japan was deeply involved in Korean affairs, coveting the strategic benefits of controlling the peninsular neighbor in great power competition against China and Russia. Through a series of successful wars against China and Russia, Japan compelled Korea into its orbit by the early part of the last century. With no national liberation movement of consequence challenging complete Japanese absorption, only the unconditional surrender of Japan in World War II brought about the recovery of Korean sovereignty.

Unfortunately for the Koreans, the "temporary" division of their country into two zones of occupation by Japan's foes (the United States and the Soviet Union, a late and opportunistic entrant to the Pacific war) resulted in the development of two rival Korean states hostile to each other, producing war in 1950. For Japan, economically fragile and still under foreign occupation, the Korean War could have presented a serious existential threat. After all, if victory by the communists had produced a revanchist Korea allied with the Soviet Union and newly communized China, Japan would have suffered a grave strategic blow.

Fortunately for the Japanese, the United States took on the burden of South Korea's defense for its own strategic reasons, and there was little that the Japanese had to do directly about the savage and costly war raging next door. Although the conflict became stalemated, the United States committed itself to an indefinite military presence on the Korean peninsula. Furthermore, the United States entered into a mutual security treaty with Japan that was skillfully negotiated by the Japanese, providing for U.S. protection of Japan but allowing Japan to escape the burden of collective defense. Given these circumstances, although it stood nominally with the United

States against communist expansionism in Asia and adopted the obligatory "one-Korea" policy favoring South Korea, Japan could and did take a detached role in inter-Korean political competition throughout the Cold War.

In addition, the fierce inter-Korean rivalry of the 1950s and the 1960s left no room for an independent Japanese role in inter-Korean conflict and rivalry during that time. In fact, inter-Korean relations were essentially war by other means and were severely limited by the security challenge the two Koreas posed to each other and to the complex but stable balance of power among their great power patrons, the United States, China, and the Soviet Union. Hence, Japan's insertion into the deadlocked inter-Korean relations would have upset the unforgiving zero–sum calculations of the rival Koreas and their great power allies, making any Japanese initiative potentially costly and dangerous.

Of course, the retreat of American power in the early 1970s led to a brief reassessment of Japan's role in what was still a volatile and intense inter-Korean rivalry, despite the beginnings of formal inter-Korean talks as Seoul and Pyongyang took in the new strategic reality in Asia. As the United States began to pull out of Southeast Asia, having achieved a rapprochement with China and détente with the Soviet Union, Washington also reduced and restructured the U.S. military presence in South Korea and Japan. If many ordinary Japanese were not alarmed about reductions in U.S. troops and bases in East Asia—particularly on Okinawa, which was being reverted to Japan—the Japanese leadership became concerned enough to contemplate playing a more active role in supporting South Korea in its competition with North Korea. Following an extended period of extreme volatility in inter-Korean relations and faced with the reduction of U.S. troops, the Japanese leadership went as far as to verbally acknowledge how strategically important to Japan was the security of South Korea.

However, as it became clear that a significant contingent of U.S. forces would remain in South Korea to act as a "tripwire," and as Washington took pains to reaffirm its security commitment to Japan, Tokyo quickly lost interest in doing anything further to give substance to this acknowledgment. By choice as well as by circumstance, Japan remained contentedly ensconced in a passive role in inter-Korean diplomacy until the end of the Cold War.[2]

Post–Cold War Rethinking
The end of the Cold War made detachment no longer tenable for Japan. It raised once again the question of America's security commitment to East Asia and doubts about the U.S.–Japan mutual security treaty, which underpinned Japan's stance toward not just Korea but the entire Asia Pacific region. More importantly, collapsing communism in Europe fundamentally transformed the focus of inter-Korean relations from a zero–sum contest between more or less evenly matched rivals to a conflict management effort between a rich and confident South Korea and an isolated and impoverished North Korea. The ups and downs of inter-Korean relations now held the possibility of a sudden reunification of Korea under terms favorable to increasingly powerful South Korea, and of a desperate North Korea lashing out with weapons of mass destruction (WMD).

Under these changed conditions, Japan has found it more and more difficult to be a bystander in the inter-Korean relations that now have the potential to directly impact Japan and to be the driving force of new and uncertain international relations throughout the Asia Pacific region. That is, without the stability and strategic clarity of the Cold War, Japan has had to contemplate the possibility of another destructive inter-Korean war, which would this time more directly involve Japan, and/or a sudden reunification of Korea with uncertain consequences for Japan. Hence, motivated by a sense of anxiety not felt during the Cold War, Japan has been pushing and has been pulled to play the direct role that it avoided during the Cold War.

As argued earlier, one of the conditions that allowed Japan to take a passive stance in inter-Korean relations during the Cold War was the security commitment of the United States to Japan and its surrounding areas. However, the end of the Cold War led to another round of U.S. troop reduction in East Asia.[3] In fact, with the disappearance of a direct Soviet military threat to Japan, questions arose about the U.S.–Japan alliance itself, the bedrock of Japanese diplomacy.

In the United States, skepticism about the trans-Pacific alliance had been building for some time, as many believed that the Japanese were "free riding" on the United States, enjoying the security of U.S. military protection while annihilating key U.S. industries, one after another. Especially in the aftermath of the Persian Gulf War, some critics of Japan began to voice doubts about Japan's ability and willingness to share the burdens of the alliance in the post–Cold War security environment, when Japan is no longer directly threatened by a hostile adversary.[4] Indeed, doubts began mounting in Japan about the need for continuing security cooperation in the absence of the kind of mortal threat once posed by the Soviet Union.[5]

This centrifugal trend forced Japanese and U.S. policy-makers to recast the bilateral security relationship from a new perspective, resulting in the 1997 issuance of new defense guidelines that emphasized the alliance's utility in preserving stability and in lowering uncertainty in East Asia.[6] The alliance was essentially recast to deal with unknowns associated with the rise of China and contingencies related to Korea.

However, because of the desire to avoid unduly antagonizing China and the need to win over the Japanese public, the new guidelines have been justified as an insurance against the palpable and mounting threat posed by North Korea. While many members of the policy elite in Japan understand the logic of the U.S.–Japan alliance balancing the growth of Chinese power, the ordinary Japanese generally do not. However, as detailed later, the Japanese people have come to understand the clear and present danger represented by North Korea's nuclear and ballistic missile programs.[7]

The concrete operational language of the new guidelines has therefore been explained and justified in terms of dealing with some emergency on the Korean peninsula. Consequently, the reformulation of the U.S.–Japan alliance has significantly altered Japan's role in inter-Korean relations from that of a bystander to one of a more committed backer of South Korea.

However, and with implications for Japan's role in Korean reunification, the Korea that Japan appeared to be more concerned about in the waning days of the Cold War was not North Korea but the militarily powerful and economically dynamic South Korea. As the simpler logic of bipolar competition between the United States and the Soviet Union was replaced with a new, more complex multipolar regional dynamic, some Japanese strategic thinkers began to privately express worries about the intentions of the apparent victor of the inter-Korean rivalry, South Korea.[8]

Indeed, sensing new opportunities in the decades-old inter-Korean rivalry, South Korea moderated and intensified its Northern policy, supported by Washington's conciliatory diplomatic probes toward Pyongyang.[9] While some in Japan applauded this warming trend in inter-Korean relations, others became uneasy as they contemplated the reunification of Korea, having just witnessed the sudden and swift reunification of Germany.

In fact, South Korea's unexpected and rapid normalization of relations with the Soviet Union in 1990 had already taken many Japanese by surprise. It caused them to worry that the rapidly improving relations between Seoul and Moscow might put additional pressure on the more frigid Japanese–Soviet ties, by giving Moscow a "South Korean card" to play against Tokyo.[10] It also raised the specter of inevitable normalization of relations between South Korea and China (which took place in 1992), further isolating North Korea diplomatically and putting South Korea in the driver's seat of Korean reunification.

In late January 1991, as it was seemingly being overtaken by events with uncertain but serious implications, Japan launched normalization talks with North Korea. This rather clumsy and hasty initiative was undertaken in order to gain some control over rapidly evolving inter-Korean relations. However, Prime Minister Kaifu Toshiki—guided by Kanemaru Shin, a powerbroker in Japanese domestic politics— plunged into normalization talks with North Korea without sufficient consultation with South Korea. Consequently, Japan's abrupt overture to North Korea raised suspicions in South Korea and fed a North Korean hope of now playing South Korea, Japan, and the United States off against one another. Since Japan was in the position to provide massive economic assistance to North Korea if normalization of relations occurred, Japan's initiative fed the popular paranoia in South Korea that the Japanese were trying to prop up Pyongyang because of their desire to keep Korea divided. At the same time, the overture no doubt whetted the appetite of the North Korean leadership for a huge Japanese reparation payment, particularly in case South Korean or American economic aid were to be rejected or denied.

However, the negative fallout from this ham-fisted Japanese initiative became inconsequential as North Korea, apparently for strategic and tactical reasons, decided to take a more confrontational approach in its relations with South Korea, the United States, and Japan. Despite overtures by South Korea (with U.S. blessings) and Japan's own initiative, North Korea gave up its engagement approach as it apparently weighed the costs and benefits of opening up its economy and society to the West.

Emergence of the North Korean Threat
Unwilling to carry out reforms, North Korea ignored the framework for inter-Korean relations embodied in two agreements (the December 1991 Agreement on Reconciliation, Non-aggression, and Exchanges and Cooperation Between South and North Korea and the January 1992 Joint Declaration of the Denuclearization of the Korean Peninsula). Instead, Pyongyang placed its faith in building up asymmetrical power capabilities. North Korea forged ahead with its nuclear

weapon and long-range ballistic missiles programs in order to deter and to gain a better leverage over its richer and more developed neighbors.

The negative externalities arising out of North Korea's recalcitrance and "internal balancing strategy"[11] dampened the concern that many Japanese were beginning to have about South Korea's intentions in the post–Cold War era. With North Korea's hardball negotiating tactics and brinkmanship, a sharply felt, common "North Korea problem" emerged for Japan and South Korea, pushing them closer together, even as Tokyo's normalization talks proceeded fruitlessly with Pyongyang.

To be sure, as Tokyo has moved nearer to Seoul, Japan has not sought a role comparable to that of the United States in inter-Korean affairs. With the missteps of the early 1990s, Tokyo has been considerate of the South Korean people's sensitivity to what may be perceived as Japan's interference in inter-Korean relations.[12]

In fact, Japan has been shut out of the formal workings of the Four Party Peace Talks, an attempt to negotiate a formal peace treaty ending the Korean War to replace the 1953 Armistice Agreement, building confidence between the two Koreas in the process.[13] The principals in the talks are the two Koreas, the United States, and China. Although its exclusion has been a source of unhappiness, Japan has consistently supported the talks.[14]

Of course, the Four Party Peace Talks have not worked as originally envisioned, particularly from the South Korean perspective. To the annoyance of South Korea, North Korea has maneuvered with much success to make the talks more bilateral between itself and the United States. Sensing a diplomatic opening, Japan has proposed a six-party security forum consisting of the two Koreas, Japan, China, Russia, and the United States.[15] Although the six-party scheme has received the diplomatic support of South Korea (and, not surprisingly, Russia), the proposal has languished.[16]

Nonetheless, despite certain limitations, Japan's diplomacy has become increasingly more proactive in the management of inter-Korean conflict. As matter of fact, Tokyo has played a crucial supporting role in Washington and Seoul's "engagement" strategy toward Pyongyang, as exemplified by the 1994 "Agreed Framework," which provides economic and political incentives for North Korea to disarm its plutonium-based nuclear weapon programs and to moderate its behavior. In 1999, its diplomacy became embedded in the trilateral policy coordination mechanism associated with the "Perry Process" of engagement initiated by President Clinton and supported by South Korean President Kim Dae Jung.[17]

Of course, the October 2002 North Korean admission that it has a clandestine highly enriched uranium (HEU) nuclear weapon program and its subsequent brinkmanship have called into question the viability of engagement with North Korea. However, the TCOG, inspired by the Perry Process, has continued to function and prove useful in managing inter-Korean relations.

While the United States and South Korea have long enjoyed well-established channels of communication (ranging from the Combined Forces Command to the Four Party Peace Talks process) to coordinate their North Korea policies, Japan has not been well integrated into this allied network. Japan does not have a formal alliance relationship with South Korea, and it is a newcomer to managing North Korean belligerence. Before the creation of the TCOG, Tokyo dealt with Pyongyang on its own, and this sometimes complicated Seoul and Washington's handling of the North Korean threat.

For example, when Pyongyang test-fired a Taepodong-1 long-range ballistic missile over Japan in late August 1998, Tokyo reacted viscerally. In early September 1998, the Japanese government announced its decision to halt its involvement with KEDO (discussed in the following section), to suspend its effort to restart the normalization talks with North Korea, and to freeze its food and other support to North Korea.[18]

These unilateral actions, particularly the threat to stop financial contributions to KEDO, alarmed South Korea's President Kim Dae Jung who was trying to sustain its "Sunshine Policy," a strategy of offering North Korea steady positive inducements to reform itself. They also annoyed the Clinton administration that was trying to protect its own engagement policy for the sake of regional stability and its anti-proliferation strategy. Seoul and Washington were ultimately able to persuade Tokyo to withdraw the suspension of its financial commitment to KEDO. However, from this episode, Tokyo, Seoul, and Washington saw that a high-level trilateral policy coordinating mechanism was needed to deal more effectively with North Korea, and in April 1999 they established the TCOG to bring about a more united front to deal with the North Korean threat.

The resulting solidarity was clearly evident in their coordinated response to North Korea's plan to launch another ballistic missile, which was expected on or around September 9, 1999, the fifty-first anniversary of the North Korean regime. When it became apparent that North Korea was readying another missile test, the three countries intensified consultations and formed a united front against another missile launch. The trilateral coordination reached a high point in the summit meeting of Prime Minister Obuchi Keizo, President Kim Dae Jung, and President Bill Clinton in Auckland, New Zealand. On the occasion of the Asia Pacific Economic Cooperation (APEC) meeting on September 12, 1999, the three leaders reiterated their determination to penalize North Korea if it proceeded with the planned missile launch.

Trilateral unity greatly facilitated the Berlin agreement on September 13, 1999, in which North Korea agreed to halt testing of its long-range ballistic missiles in exchange for a commitment from the United States and Japan to move forward with economic assistance for Pyongyang. After the agreement, Japan began lifting the sanctions it had imposed on North Korea after the August 1998 missile launch. Forming a cohesive front, Japan joined South Korea and the United States in sending North Korea the message that it had more to gain through cooperation than confrontation and that the three countries were united in their resolve to counter any North Korean provocation.

In fact, there was a great deal of optimism when Japan, in consultation with South Korea and the United States, reenergized its normalization diplomacy toward North Korea in 2000. For some time, many have believed that Japan's normalization diplomacy, with its promise of billions of dollars of economic assistance to North Korea, would be an important catalyst in bringing about far-reaching changes in North Korea.

And unlike its decade-earlier effort, this time around, Tokyo's diplomacy had the full blessing of Seoul. South Korean President Kim Dae Jung, the recipient of a Nobel Peace Prize for his unflagging, if overly hopeful, effort to bringing about the reconciliation of the two Koreas, encouraged bold Japanese initiatives toward Pyongyang. Though the more hard-nosed Bush administration came to replace the more conciliation-inclined Clinton one by early 2001, despite its initial tough attitude toward North Korea, it placed no obstacles in the way of Japan's reenergized normalization diplomacy. Indeed, after the shocking events of September 11, 2001, no doubt, the Bush administration was hoping for some kind of forward movement in relations with North Korea, as the United States faced a plethora of security challenges throughout the world.

For a time, Japan's diplomacy appeared to be making progress toward a breakthrough. It resulted in the historic summit meeting between Japanese Prime Minister Koizumi Junichiro and the North Korean leader, Kim Jong Il, in Pyongyang on September 17, 2002. And during the summit, Prime Minister Koizumi raised issues and concerns that were common to Tokyo, Seoul, and the United States. These common agenda items, aired and weighed in various TCOG meetings, included nuclear and missile proliferation issues and continued progress in the dialogue between the two Koreas.

However, Japan had its own agenda items going into the summit, one of them being the resolution of issues stemming from the kidnapping of Japanese nationals by North Korean agents. Pyongyang had always denied it abducted Japanese citizens. Kim Jong Il, however, admitted to the Japanese prime minister that, supposedly, a rogue element in North Korean intelligence had kidnapped a small number of Japanese citizens to further espionage operations. Undoubtedly, the North Korean leadership as well as some Japanese officials felt Kim's acknowledgment would clear the way for better relations. This has not proved to be the case.

The admission of guilt and particularly the revelation that eight of the thirteen abductees had died outraged the Japanese public. Ordinary people as well as the mass media reacted with a surprising degree of indignation.[19] The animosity toward North Korea converged with sharp fear when Pyongyang acknowledged in October 2002 that it has a secret nuclear weapon program. Not surprisingly, the negative fallout of the kidnapping admission and the nuclear confession have taken the wind out of Japan's normalization diplomacy to the disappointment of South Korea, now under the leadership of President Roh Moo Hyun, if not the Bush administration, especially its hard-liners.

Indeed, North Korea's nuclear admission has complicated trilateral cooperation among Japan, South Korea, and the United States. North Korea's startling admission and its renewed brinkmanship have reignited the political debate in Japan, South Korea, and the United States about how to deal with North Korea. With the signing of the 1994 Agreed Framework, the debate among allies had been settled largely in favor of engagement, drawing out North Korea and disarming its WMD and ballistic missile capabilities with economic enticements and various conflict management measures. The October 2002 surprise, however, has reopened the debate and strengthened those, especially in Washington, that argue North Korea is aggressive by nature and not serious about engagement and, therefore, must be confronted or undermined.

However, in December 2002, South Korean voters elected Roh Moo Hyun, a staunch advocate of rapprochement toward North Korea, as their new president. Riding a wave of surging anti-American nationalism to office, Roh has promised the continuation of the Sunshine Policy. Arguing that coercion does not work with North Korea and war is simply not an option, Roh and other South Koreans have urged U.S. restraint in dealing with North Korea to the annoyance and displeasure of many hawks in Washington.

What is interesting in the evolution of Japan's role in inter-Korean relations is that Japan has now come to play an important mediating role between South Korea and the United States in dealing with the North Korean threat. Because of North Korea's continuing pursuit of WMD and ballistic missile programs, "spy ship" provocations (discussed later), and kidnappings of Japanese citizens, the Japanese leadership and the people have never been more receptive to a tougher, more punitive approach toward North Korea. However, they are also sympathetic toward Seoul to the extent that they share, of course not to the same extent, an immediate sense of vulnerability to a unwanted war initiated by a third party, North Korea or the United States. Hence, during bilateral summit meetings with President Bush and President Roh in May and June 2003, Prime Minister Koizumi tried to bridge the gap between South Korea and the United States. In addition, Japan has used its central role in the TCOG to further help the harmonization of the disparate views and attitudes of South Korea and the United States.[20]

Of course, even with out Japanese mediation, the Bush administration's actual behavior has been measured and considerate of the interests of South Korea. Despite its willingness to use force against Iraq and its earlier declared policy of employing U.S. armed forces, if necessary, unilaterally and preemptively in protecting vital U.S. national interests, the Bush administration has been calling for coordinated diplomacy to deal with North Korea.

Although North Korea has declared that it is uncapping its plutonium-based nuclear program, the reality is that, as key allies of the United States, South Korea and Japan limit the range of realistic policy options for the United States. If the Bush administration decides to take a robust coercive approach to North Korea, it would have to take into account serious consequences for the U.S.–South Korea and U.S.–Japan alliances. Consequences could be severe if Washington's confrontational approach leads to North Korean artillery bombardment of Seoul and/or missile attacks against Japanese cities.

Unless Washington is prepared to risk its key trans-Pacific bilateral alliances, it appears likely that the reopened debate will settle on some form of renewed engagement with North Korea. Undoubtedly, if it comes to pass, this second try at engagement will be a fragile and contentious one: A highly skeptical United States will demand stricter compliance and verification from North Korea regarding the terms of engagement while anxious and ambivalent Japan will, most likely, side with South Korea in urging North Korea as well as the United States for greater flexibility.

The Military/Security Dimension

It is clear from the earlier discussion that the emergence of a direct threat emanating from the Korean peninsula has been a key force in shaping Japan's post–Cold War role in inter-Korean relations. In addition to diplomatic adaptations discussed earlier, this keenly felt threat has brought about changes in Japan's military posture as well.

Indeed, it could be argued that Japan has felt the threat emanating from North Korea more acutely than South Korea. When the nuclear and ballistic missile threats began manifesting themselves in the 1990s, Japan may have been the country more distressed than South Korea.

While South Korean leaders were concerned by the rapidly advancing North Korean nuclear and ballistic missile capabilities, ordinary South Korean citizens—many having lived a long time within the range of massed North Korean conventional artillery—did not appear particularly troubled. More than a few, in fact, took pride in North Korea's nuclear and ballistic missile advancements as national accomplishments. The Japanese, however, having suffered atomic attacks in World War II, were alarmed and felt a degree of anxiety they had perhaps never felt during the Cold War.

Japanese fear became palpable during the nuclear crisis of April 1994 when North Korea removed spent fuel rods from its nuclear reactor in Yongbyon and refused to segregate rods that could provide evidence of a plutonium-based nuclear weapon program.[21] Japanese leaders let out a sigh of relief when the crisis was defused by Jimmy Carter's June 1994 visit to Pyongyang, and Carter's meeting with Kim Il Sung paved the way for the signing of the Agreed Framework between the United States and North Korea in October 1994.[22] However, with North Korea's October 2002 acknowledgment that it has a clandestine alternative HEU nuclear weapon program and its repudiation of the Agreed Framework, Japan now faces the possibility of massive proliferation of nuclear weapons on the Korean peninsula.

Amplifying Japan's fear has been the advancement of North Korea's long-range ballistic missile capability. In May 1993, Pyongyang test-launched a missile, Nodong-1, into the East Sea/Sea of Japan. Though not widely publicized at the time, this test signaled to Japanese security planners that North Korea now possessed the missile capability to attack cities in the southern half of Japan, including Osaka.

North Korea's testing of a more advanced missile, Taepodong-1, in late August 1998 dramatically heightened Japan's awareness of North Korean missile capabilities. This time, ordinary Japanese citizens could not help but to take notice. Longer-ranged than Nodong, Taepodong missile entered the stratosphere in Japanese airspace and, according to Funabashi Yoichi, had a psychological impact on the Japanese equivalent to the Sputnik shock on the American people in 1957.[23] This event heightened Japan's sense of vulnerability now that all of its cities, including Tokyo, fell within the reach of North Korean missiles possibly armed with WMD.

The dramatic summit diplomacy of the two Koreas in June 2000 gave some comfort to the Japanese regarding the prospect of a more reasonable and responsible North Korea.[24] However, since then, the lack of progress in inter-Korean relations, continuing North Korean provocations, and renewed nuclear brinkmanship have kept the Japanese anxious. In sum, in the post–Cold War era, Japan has come to see North Korea as a clear and present danger, and this threat perception has added a new Japanese variable to the military/security dimension of inter-Korean relations.[25]

Indeed, it is critical to note that Japan has been developing military options that could impact inter-Korean relations, a fact that was most dramatically demonstrated in Japan's sinking of a suspected North Korean spy vessel that was fleeing from Japanese territorial waters in late 2001. Despite the enduring pacifist inclination of many Japanese, the fact is that Japan is now susceptible to North Korea's WMD and its long-range ballistic missiles. Japan is particularly vulnerable because its military lacks offensive capacities to deter or counter North Korean attacks, in contrast to the strong retaliatory capabilities possessed by the United States and, to a lesser extent, South Korea.

With Japanese citizens feeling more and more vulnerable to North Korea, like-minded Japanese leaders in the Diet and the defense bureaucracies have initiated self-help security measures that might have been considered unthinkable only a decade earlier. For example, in November 1998, following the Taepodong shock, Japan decided to acquire spy satellites for the first time. Although they have been billed as "multipurpose" satellites and therefore have not been included in the official defense budget, the decision to acquire them required the Japanese government to override the Diet resolution of 1969 that limits the use of space technology to nonmilitary activities.[26]

In addition, in March 1999, Defense Agency Director General Norota Hosei told a Diet defense panel that Japan had the right to make preemptive military strikes if it felt a missile attack on Japan was imminent.[27] This was a remarkable development in Japan's post–World War II security policy. Although Japan at present does not have the capability to carry out such a threat, the statement was clearly made to warn North Korea against testing another missile over Japan. To demonstrate its resolve, Japan decided to acquire mid-air refueling aircraft to enable its Air Self-Defense Force (ASDF) to conduct long-range strike missions. Originally contemplated when Pyongyang test-fired its Nodong-1 missile into to the East Sea/Sea of Japan in 1993, the decision to acquire the capacity was announced by Prime Minister Obuchi during a meeting of the Japanese National Security Council in December 1999.[28]

Further, as mentioned earlier, Japan moved to solidify its alliance with the United States by revising the guidelines for their security cooperation of 1976. Despite some lingering concerns about "entrapment," Japan has come to feel that the benefits of a closer military alignment with the United States in case of a contingency on the Korean peninsula outweigh potential costs.[29]

The new guidelines indeed represent a milestone in U.S.–Japan security relations since the mutual security treaty was signed during the Korean War. Whereas Article 6 of the mutual security treaty limited Japan's cooperation to little more than allowing U.S. forces to use bases in Japan, the new guidelines allow Japan during crises to supply those forces with nonlethal material assistance as well as open civilian ports and airfields, and they also allow new missions for Japan's Self-Defense Forces (SDFs). For example, Japan's naval forces could resupply U.S. warships during a crisis, evacuate civilians and U.S. military personnel from dangerous situations, remove mines from the high seas, or enforce UN sanctions. The concrete operational language of the new guidelines is clearly designed to deal with a contingency on the Korean peninsula.

In September 1998, on the heels of the Taepodong-1 test, Japan also agreed to cooperate with the United States on a joint project to develop a theater missile defense (TMD) system.[30] Japan's decision to make a significant financial commitment to the TMD project is noteworthy given its previous reluctance to do so because of doubts about technological viability and the large expected cost of the project.[31] Further, in the wake of the October 2002 revelation about North Korea's secret HEU nuclear weapon program, among other physical and legal measures taken to increase its defensive capabilities, Japan readily agreed with the United States to increase funding and research for the missile defense project. It is not surprising that, compared to Europe, Japan has little misgiving about the global security implications of deploying a ballistic missile defense system.

It is also not surprising that Prime Minister Koizumi specifically raised the issue of North Korean missiles capable of reaching Japan during his summit meeting with Kim Jong Il. It is unlikely that normalization of relations between Japan and North Korea would take place unless Pyongyang somehow satisfies Tokyo's concern about these missiles. If North Korea does not yield sufficiently on this issue, Japan will undoubtedly further accelerate its self-help and collective defense measures to deter North Korea.

Indeed, obscured in the ongoing political debate about "collective defense" in Japanese domestic politics is the fact that, since the emergence of direct threat from North Korea, Japan has initiated and increased security cooperation with South Korea. This is a sharp departure from Japan's lack of interest in closer security ties with South Korea during the Cold War.

Despite Japan's long-standing allergy to anything that smacks of collective defense, during the historic state visit of President Kim Dae Jung to Japan in October 1998, Prime Minister Obuchi agreed with President Kim to increase bilateral security cooperation to handle the mutual North Korean threat.[32] Japan's eagerness to improve relations with South Korea was reflected in the decision to include in the summit joint statement its first-ever written apology to the South Koreans for Japan's oppressive colonial rule.

The summit was followed by such cooperative security measures as establishing military hotlines in May 1999 and conducting the first joint naval "search and rescue exercise" in August 1999 when Japan, South Korea, and the United States were urging North Korea to abandon its plan to launch a Taepodong-2.[33] This joint naval exercise is particularly noteworthy because it was no ordinary search and rescue exercise. The five-day mission involved three Maritime Self-Defense Force destroyers, two ROK Navy destroyers, and aerial and intelligence support. The search and rescue component of the exercise was followed by joint formation training and tactical maneuvers. The latter part of the exercise was no doubt conducted with a contingency involving North Korea in mind.

These measures do not amount to Japan formally embracing collective defense, however, and inescapable tensions stemming from Japan's colonial rule of Korea continue to plague Japan–South Korea bilateral relations. Predictably, some of the informal cooperative security measures have been held hostage to the attraction/repulsion dynamics of Japan–South Korea relations. For example, with Prime Minister Koizumi's 2001 visit to the controversial Yasukuni Shrine honoring Japan's war dead, including those convicted of war crimes, tensions flared between South Korea and Japan, placing bilateral security cooperation at risk. However, with sufficient time to cool off and the general positive trajectory of burgeoning bilateral economic and cultural ties (exemplified by the highly successful joint hosting of the 2002 World Cup), canceled exercises and exchanges have been reinstated. The trend is toward more cooperation, not less.

The Economic and Functional Dimensions

Although less dramatically than with the developments in Japan's role in the political/diplomatic and military/security dimensions of inter-Korean relations, Japan has become more active in economic and functional dimensions as well, bringing to bear its wealth and regional diplomatic clout. Particularly since the nuclear crisis of 1994, Japan has been a strong supporter of multilateral efforts to stabilize and improve inter-Korean relations.

Two examples stand out for their impact. First, although Japan has contributed to and participated in a number of aid programs (such as rice shipments to North Korea) and developmental schemes (e.g., the TRADP) to stabilize inter-Korean relations, its generous contribution to KEDO stands out for financial and political significance. The second is Japan's role in facilitating North Korean involvement in the ARF[34], which has added another point of contact between North Korea and South Korea as well as between North Korea and the United States.

In general, Japan has been more a follower or supporter of others' initiatives than a leader—Tokyo has tended to follow cues coming from Seoul and Washington. For example, until the establishment of KEDO in March 1995, the United States had shunned multilateral peace-building efforts on the Korean peninsula. During the Cold War, almost all initiatives of this type came from the Soviet Union, as it attempted to drive a wedge between the United States and its East Asian allies.[35] The U.S. attitude toward multilateralism in security matters did not change much after the collapse of the Soviet Union. The George H.W. Bush administration saw multilateralism as at best a distraction and at worst a threat to the San Francisco system of bilateral security alliances linking the United States to its Pacific allies. The Clinton administration did give more rhetorical support for multilateralism, but it also saw key bilateral alliances and robust deterrence as the key to peace and stability in East Asia.

KEDO, however, is an exception to the rule. The multilateralism embedded in KEDO is necessitated by the U.S. need for a huge sum of money to finance the goal of the organization. Although an American heads KEDO, Japan has taken a prominent role in the organization that includes South Korea as well as European members. When the United States requested that Japan become an executive member of the organization and contribute a portion of the needed funds, Japan readily agreed.[36] Japan took responsibility for a large sum of the money needed for providing North Korea with "safe" nuclear reactors, and in early 2000 Japan signed a formal agreement with KEDO to provide about one billion dollars to fulfill its commitment.[37]

Of course, it remains to be seen what will happen to KEDO as consequences of North Korea's October 2002 nuclear confession play out. However, while both North Korea and the United States have expressed doubts about the Agreed Framework, KEDO remains in operation and there is no serious talk of dissolving the organization. In fact, despite President George W. Bush's stronger skepticism of multilateralism than even his father's, it is conceivable that KEDO's charter may be enlarged to facilitate a new bargain between North Korea and the West if engagement gets back on track.[38]

Japan has also brought to bear its considerable diplomatic clout throughout the Asia Pacific, specifically Southeast Asia, to add a regional dimension to inter-Korean relations. With the support of South Korea, Japan took a leadership role in persuading its ASEAN friends to invite North Korea into the activities of the ARF, the only existing official multilateral security organization in the Asia Pacific, created by ASEAN with Japanese instigation.[39] And again with South Korea, Japan played a critical role in convincing North Korea to seek membership in the ARF.

Although North Korea's participation in the ARF has been spotty, the promise remains that North Korea will take a more active part in the confidence-building activities of the organization, adding a multilateral, regional dimension to Pyongyang's thinking and thus drawing North Korea out of isolation. The late July 2002 contact between North Korea's foreign minister and his South Korean, Japanese, and U.S. counterparts during the Brunei ARF meeting demonstrates the usefulness of this multilateral mechanism. Particularly important during this occasion was the informal exchange between North Korean Foreign Minister Paek Nam Sun and U.S. Secretary of State Colin Powell. This meeting constituted, after a number of failed attempts at high-level bilateral talks, the most significant contact between Pyongyang and Washington from the time that President Bush took office and the October 2002 meeting in Pyongyang between Assistant Secretary of State James Kelly and North Korean officials.

However, as important as Japan's multilateral diplomacy and financial muscle in KEDO and the ARF have been, the most significant function Japan has been playing in inter-Korean relations is, as discussed earlier, its role as a potential underwriter of North Korean economic reform. If North Korea chooses to reciprocate Western engagement, the general assumption is that Japan will provide North Korea with around ten billion dollars worth of grants and credit when Japan normalizes relations with North Korea.[40] This understanding remains despite the perceived failure of the Koizumi–Kim summit of September 2002. Indeed, in engaging North Korea, Japan's possible economic aid has acted as the biggest bunch of carrots dangling before Pyongyang in trying to improve inter-Korean relations and ensure peace and stability in Northeast Asia.

Japan's Changing Role and Korean Reunification

With continuing uncertainties in inter-Korean relations and lingering questions about the U.S. security commitment to East Asia further complicated by increasing anti-Americanism in South Korea,[41] it is all but certain that Japan will be both pushed and pulled to take a more assertive role in inter-Korean affairs. This is particularly true in the area of security, and this prospect raises questions about the immutability of Japanese pacifism or Japan's self-image as a "civilian power," with obvious implications for Japan's role in Korean reunification, if and when it occurs.[42]

The Logic of Increasing Japanese Activism

A group of scholars has argued that for Japan's formulation of foreign policy, domestic and international normative determinants matter more than material interests.[43] These "constructivists" find in Japan's post–World War II diplomacy the strongest case that "national identity" trumps "national interest." Drawing from a growing literature in the social sciences that highlights the role of norms and ideas in human endeavors, these scholars claim that state security policy varies according to the normative context that defines standards of acceptable action.[44]

The constructivists argue that Japan's devastating defeat in World War II transformed its "strategic culture." They highlight the enduring legacy of the Hiroshima and Nagasaki atomic attacks on the psyche of the Japanese people, and they argue that this created a "culture of anti-militarism" in Japan. This culture is said to have become so deeply embedded in domestic politics and institutions that Japan is unlikely to become a great power with a complement of military capabilities in line with its economic superpower status.[45] Although they have varying views about how much causal importance to assign to the international power structure, constructivists generally agree that Japan will not engage in self-help behavior.[46]

But what about Japan's more proactive role in inter-Korean relations in the post–Cold War period, particularly its self-help behavior regarding security? As discussed earlier, for example, the Japanese government has responded to the rise of the North Korean threat with the initiation of self-help measures to strengthen the capabilities of the SDFs. Do such measures indicate the reemergence of Japan as a normally armed great power, as anticipated by the realists? Do they foreshadow the return of Japan's realpolitik Korea policy of a century ago?

Realists of various stripes have argued that in East Asia the end of superpower competition between the United States and the Soviet Union may push Japan to seek a more self-assertive security strategy.[47] "Offensive realists," who argue that states are compelled to balance "capabilities" of others, have been more insistent.[48] For example, Kenneth Waltz has argued that Japan will be forced to deal more aggressively and unilaterally with the emergent security system in Northeast Asia, a multipolar system that contains up to four great powers.[49] And many South Korean realists believe that the rise of a more aggressive and unilateral Japan would surely mean a Japan that actively opposes Korean reunification.[50]

If the account in this chapter of a more assertive role for Japan in inter-Korean relations complicates the constructivist explanation of Japan's "security culture," it does not validate the offensive realist prognosis or the paranoia of many Koreans. There is no compelling evidence to indicate that Japan's self-help measures have been premeditated or that its Korea policy is based on some grand design or strategy. Furthermore, private expressions of anxiety by Japanese leaders and strategic thinkers about the prospect of Korean reunification hardly amount to convincing proof of Japanese opposition to a unified Korea.

Rather, the present account of the changing role of Japan in inter-Korean relations suggests that Japan has been reactive, responding to probable "threats" more than "capabilities," a course of action more in line with defensive realist thinking than with offensive realism.[51] Indeed, if Japan were responding to "capabilities," it would be trying to balance the rising power of South Korea rather than bandwagoning with South Korea against a common North Korean threat.

With North Korea backtracking on its moderating stance and returning to its provocative ways, it is likely that political leaders in Tokyo will respond with an ever more active role in inter-Korean affairs. If the recent past is a reliable guide, Japan will make changes facilitating the production of new military and political capabilities to deal with the perceived threat. And it is probable that Japan's virtual alliance with South Korea will be further strengthened, despite Japan's continuing internal political debate about collective defense.

This dynamic is unlikely to transform Japan into a "normal" nation of offensive realist prognostication, but it could erode what constructivists consider the cultural and institutional basis of Japan's post–World War II pacifism. It may very well push Japan toward Ozawa Ichiro's conception of a normal nation, which envisions for Japan a greater political and military role in the world but with its overseas operations limited to missions sponsored and directed by the United Nations.[52]

If Pyongyang fails to moderate its belligerent behavior, urged on by hard-liners in Washington, Tokyo is likely to increase its military options in case things go very wrong on the Korean peninsula. However, if Pyongyang pursues earnest engagement with South Korea and satisfies Japan's security concerns, Tokyo would no doubt employ its vast economic resources to greatly augment the material rewards of engagement.

Implication for Reunification

In either case, Japan has a vital and undeniable role to play in inter-Korean relations. Whatever the direction of inter-Korean relations, in order to encourage North Korea to be realistic about its options, Japan's active diplomatic engagement and its security cooperation with South Korea and the United States should continue.[53] Indeed, Japan's continuing cooperation with South Korea, not just in military and political spheres but also in economic and cultural spheres should prove invaluable in the event of Korean reunification.[54] Undoubtedly, trust and goodwill developed between Tokyo and Seoul will mitigate any misunderstanding and lingering apprehension that the two may have about each other during a crucial turning point in history.

Without question, Japan will find Korean reunification a cause of great anxiety. The Korean peninsula has been a strategically vital area for Japan's national interest, and some speculate that one thing that will trigger the rearmament of Japan would be the reunification of Korea. Indeed, from an offensive realist perspective that emphasizes balance of power, Japan would feel insecure with a powerful unified Korea as its neighbor. And from the perspective of those who point to the determining nature of the bitter legacy of Japanese colonization of Korea, Japan should be wary of a reunified Korea. However, from the defense realist perspective, the primary worry would be Japan and Korea's threat perception of each other, particularly just prior to and during the reunification process, not unified Korea's power resources and capabilities.

Hence, as Japan plays a more central role in conflict management in inter-Korean relations, it must think and act strategically to build confidence and trust with South Korea, as most likely reunification will be on South Korea's terms. Of course, South Korea must do the same with Japan to assuage latent Japanese fears about revanchist Korea. In other words, as Japan and South Korea engage in conflict management with North Korea, they must also build confidence and security with each other to prepare the ground for Korean reunification. Indeed, as Zbigniew Brzezinski argues, "a true Japanese-Korean reconciliation would contribute significantly to a stable setting for Korea's eventual reunification, mitigating the international complications that could ensue from the end of the country's division."[55]

Notes

1. The analysis in this chapter is framed by a variant of defensive realism, "postclassical realism." This modification of realism posits that states base their national security policy on the probability, not simply the possibility, of aggression. See Stephen G. Brooks, "Dueling Realisms," *International Organization* 51: 3 (Summer 1997): 445–477.

2. In the early 1980s, Prime Minister Nakasone Yasuhiro, an unusually forceful Japanese leader, championed a closer relationship between Japan and South Korea (largely for domestic economic reasons), but he did not alter Japan's basic aloofness toward inter-Korean relations.

3. In its East Asian Strategic Initiatives (EASI) of April 1990, the United States outlined a blueprint for a force reduction in East Asia to be implemented in two phases (1990–92 and 1992–95). The first phase reduction was completed as planned. The reduction consisted of nearly 4,800 from Japan, about 7,000 from South Korea, and a total withdrawal from the Philippines (nearly 15,000), bringing down the U.S. force level in the three countries to 83,640 from 109,200 in 1993.

4. See Chalmers Johnson and E.B. Keehn's "The Pentagon's Ossified Strategy," *Foreign Affairs* 74: 4 (July/August 1995): 103–114.

5. For one Japanese perspective, see the 1998 *Foreign Affairs* essay by a former prime minister of Japan. Morihiro Hosokawa, "Are US Troops in Japan Needed?: Reforming the Alliance," *Foreign Affairs* 77: 4 (July/August 1998): 2–5.

6. Of course, it should be noted that what gave much impetus to the drafting of the new guidelines in the first place was the 1995 rape of a Japanese schoolgirl by U.S. marines stationed in Okinawa, an incident that focused intense Japanese public scrutiny on the continuing U.S. military presence in Japan.

7. See the *Yomiuri Shimbun/Gallup* opinion survey published in *The Daily Yomiuri*, November 30, 1997.

8. Author's interviews with leading Japanese Korea specialists and national security specialists. Tokyo, summer 1997–98.

9. Namely, Ronald Reagan's "modest initiative" to start a dialogue with North Korea, a process that George H.W. Bush continued during his presidency.

10. Author's interview with a Japanese diplomat. Chicago, summer 1996.

11. States balance power, either "internally" by arms race or "externally" by forging military alliances.

12. Author's interviews with Japanese foreign ministry officials, Tokyo, Japan, Spring 1998.

13. C.S. Eliot Kang, "The Four-Party Peace Talks: Lost Without a Map," *Comparative Strategy* 17: 4 (October/December 1998): 327–344.

14. Author's interviews with Japanese foreign ministry officials, Tokyo, Japan, summer 1997.

15. For details, see C.S. Eliot Kang and Yoshinori Kaseda, "Japanese Security and Peace Regime on the Korean Peninsula," *International Journal of Korean Unification Studies* 9: 1 (2000): 117–135.

16. During his tenure, at various times, South Korean President Kim Dae Jung voiced support for the six-party talks proposal.

17. The Perry Process has its origin in President Clinton's attempt to defuse congressional criticism of his North Korea policy. In November 1998, President Clinton named William S. Perry, a former Secretary of Defense respected by Congress, as the North Korea Policy Coordinator. Perry was charged with a full and complete review of U.S. policy toward North Korea and with producing a policy report by May 1999. The Perry Report, issued only in September 1999, concluded that the United States should intensify its engagement with North Korea. The report recommended that the United States establish diplomatic relations with North Korea. As a short-term measure, it advocated that the United States lift some economic sanctions in exchange for North Korea's suspension of its missile testing. It recommended that the mid-term goal of the United States

should be getting the North Koreans to agree to cease engaging in nuclear and missile development. The ultimate goal, it stated, was the dismantling of the Cold War structure on the Korean peninsula.

18. In addition, the Japanese government revoked its permission to North Korea's Air Koryo for nine chartered flights between Pyongyang and Nagoya and decided not to permit any further chartered flights. Tokyo then threatened to impose additional unilateral sanctions on Pyongyang if the North Koreans tested another missile over the Japanese territory. Japan Ministry of Foreign Affairs, *Diplomatic Blue Book 1998*.

19. Complications arising from North Korea's attempt to assuage Japanese anger by having some kidnapped victims visit Japan, while leaving behind in North Korea their spouses and children as hostages, only further inflamed anti–North Korean sentiments in Japan.

20. Author's interviews with Japanese officials. Washington, DC, May 2003.

21. For a comprehensive discussion of the 1994 nuclear crisis, see Leon V. Sigal, *Disarming Strangers: Nuclear Diplomacy with North Korea* (Princeton, NJ: Princeton University Press, 1998). See also Young Whan Kihl and Peter Hayes, eds., *Peace and Security in Northeast Asia: The Nuclear Issue and the Korean Peninsula* (Armonk, NY: M.E. Sharpe, 1997).

22. In the Agreed Framework, North Korea pledged to freeze its nuclear program under the International Atomic Energy Agency (IAEA) supervision. Essentially, Pyongyang agreed to stop the operation of its graphite reactors in exchange for the provision of light-water ones with much lower weaponization potential. The Agreed Framework calls for the West to supply North Korea with two 1,000-megawatt proliferation-resistant light-water reactors (costing about $4.5 billion and largely to be financed by South Korea and Japan) and 500,000 tons of heavy fuel oil per year until the completion of the first reactor. In return, North Korea agreed to close down its existing reactor at Yongbyon.

23. Yoichi Funabashi, "The Question of What Constitutes Deterrence," *Asahi Shimbun*, February 15, 1999.

24. Following the summit, hopeful but also cautious sentiments were expressed in editorials in leading Japanese dailies such as the *Mainichi Shimbun, Yomiuri Shimbun*, and *Asahi Shimbun*.

25. Citing the results of a survey revealed by the Prime Minister's Office concerning the SDF and defense issues, an editorial in the *Yomiuri Shimbun* argued that "North Korea was a predominant destabilizing factor for this nation [Japan] and surrounding areas . . ." *Yomiuri Shimbun*, May 22, 2000. See also the concern expressed in the 1999 defense white paper published by the Japan Self-Defense Agency, *Boei Hakusho, Heisei 11 nen ban* [Defense of Japan 1999] (Tokyo: Okura-sho Insatsu-kyoku, 1999).

26. *Japan Times*, September 10, 1998.

27. *Yomiuri Shimbun*, March 5, 1999.

28. Following North Korea's first test-launch of a missile in May 1993, Japan included in its 1996–2000 Mid-Term Defense Program a plan to study and decide on the acquisition of airborne refueling capacity. See Boei-cho, *Boei Hakusho*, Heisei 10 nen ban [Defense White Paper, 1998] (Tokyo: Okura-sho Insatsu-kyoku, 1998), p. 118.

29. For a discussion on the concept of "entrapment," see Victor D. Cha, *Alignment Despite Antagonism: The United States-Korea-Japan Security Triangle* (Stanford: Stanford University Press, 1999), pp. 38–43.

30. *Asahi Shimbun*, September 21, 1998.

31. For more on Japan's previous reluctance about the TMD project, see Patrick M. Cronin and Michael J. Green, *Redefining the US-Japan Alliance: Tokyo's National Defense Program*, McNair Paper 31 (Washington, DC: Institute for National Strategic Studies, 1994), pp. 12–13.

32. *21 seiki ni muketa aratana nikkan paatonaashippu no tameno koudou keikaku* [The *Action Plan for the New Japan-Korea Partnership for the 21st Century. Gaimusho* [the Ministry of Foreign Affairs].

33. For a comprehensive discussion of confidence- and security-building measures between Japan and South Korea, see C.S. Eliot Kang and Yoshinori Kaseda, "Confidence and

Security Building Between South Korea and Japan," *Journal of Political and Military Sociology* 28: 1 (Summer 2000): 93–108.

34. Association of South East Asian Nations.

35. See David Youtz and Paul Midford, *A Northeast Asian Security Regime: Prospects After the Cold War* (Public Policy Paper 5) (New York: Institute for EastWest Studies, 1992).

36. Hang Nack Kim, "Japan's Policy Toward the Two Koreas in the Post-Cold War Era," *International Journal of Korean Studies* 1: 1 (Spring 1997): 143.

37. This figure represents the second largest contribution to the KEDO after that of South Korea. Of the estimated cost of 4.5 billion dollars, Seoul pledged to provide 70% of the total, while Tokyo has committed 116.5 billion yen, about 1 billion dollars.

38. Over the years, various schemes have been aired to provide agricultural, electrical, and other needs of North Korea through KEDO or KEDO-like organizations.

39. The original Japanese proposal of the ARF to ASEAN countries in July 1991 was made "despite American reservations about creating new security organizations." See Mike M. Mochizuki, "Japan as an Asia-Pacific Power," in *East Asia in Transition: Toward a New Regional Order*, ed. Robert S. Ross (Armonk, NY: M.E. Sharpe, 1995), pp. 152–153.

40. The figure of 10 billion dollars is the consensus of Japanese scholars, journalists, and diplomats interviewed by the author. Washington, DC, March and May 2000.

41. On growing anti-Americanism in South Korea, see Seung-Hwan Kim, "Anti-Americanism in Korea," *The Washington Quarterly* 26: 1 (Winter 2002–03): 109–122.

42. On Japan as a "civilian power," see Yoichi Funabashi, "Japan and the New World Order," *Foreign Affairs* 70: 5 (Winter 1991/92): 58–74.

43. Thomas U. Berger, "From Sword to Chrysanthemum: Japan's Culture of Anti-militarism," *International Security* 17: 4 (Spring 1993): 119–150; Thomas Berger, "Unsheathing the Sword? Germany and Japan's Fractured Political-Military Cultures and the Problem of Burden Sharing," *World Affairs* 158 (Spring 1996): 174–191; and Peter J. Katzenstein and Nobuo Okawara, "Japan's National Security," *International Security* 17 (Spring 1993): 84–118.

44. For a more general discussion of "constructivism," see the pioneering work of Alexander Wendt, "Anarchy is What States Make of It: The Social Construction of Power Politics," *International Organization* 46: 2 (Spring 1992): 391–425. See also Jeffrey T. Checkel, "The Constructivist Turn in International Relations Theory," *World Politics* 50: 2 (January 1998): 324–348, and Ted Hopf, "The Promise of Constructivism in International Relations Theory," *International Security* 23: 1 (Summer 1998): 171–200.

45. To be sure, Japan is already well armed; its absolute defense expenditure is one of the highest in the world. However, Japan clearly does not have a level of military capability commensurate with its economic power and stake in the status quo of the international system.

46. Berger hedges that "Japan's anti-militarism in its present form could not survive both a weakening of its alliance with the United States and the emergence of a new region security threat." Berger, "From Sword to Chrysanthemum," 120. Katzenstein and Okawara are more convinced that "the record of the last forty years makes such change [rearmament] highly improbable, for Japan's security policy is shaped largely by domestic rather than international determinants." Katzenstein and Okawara, "Japan's National Security," 117.

47. Aaron L. Friedberg, "Ripe for Rivalry: Prospects for Peace in a Multipolar Asia," *International Security* 18: 3 (Winter 1993/94): 5–33; Richard K. Betts, "Wealth, Power, and Instability," *International Security* 18: 3 (Winter 1993/94): 34–77; James Goldgeier and Michael McFaul, "A Tale of Two World," *International Organization* 46: 2 (Spring 1992): 467–492; and Douglas T. Stuart and William T. Tow, "A US Strategy for the Asia Pacific," *Adelphi Paper* 299, pp. 17–20.

48. Hard-core neorealists are offensive realists. See Kenneth N. Waltz, "The Emerging Structure of International Politics," *International Security* 18: 2 (Fall 1993): 44–79; John Mearsheimer, "Back to the Future: Instability in Europe After the Cold War,"

International Security 15: 1 (Summer 1990): 5–56; and Christopher Layne, "The Unipolar Illusion: Why New Great Powers Will Rise," *International Security* 17: 4 (Spring 1993): 130–76.

49. Waltz, "The Emerging Structure of International Politics."
50. Author's informal survey of various South Korean officials, journalists, and academics. Seoul, Tokyo, New York, Chicago, and Washington, DC, 1992–2002.
51. Defensive realists try to avoid the neorealist fallacy that states always employ worst-case reasoning and prepare for imminent hostilities. See Brooks, "Dueling Realisms."
52. See Ichiro Ozawa, *Blueprint for a New Japan* (Tokyo: Kodansha, 1994).
53. The downside of trilateral cooperation is its impact on China. Tokyo's security cooperation with Seoul and Washington is an unwelcomed development for Beijing. Many in China see the recent increased trilateral security cooperation as a precursor to a new collective defense arrangement aimed at China. Author's interviews with Chinese security analysts and officials, Tokyo, Japan, Spring 1998. Also, for China's concern over a closer U.S.–Japan alliance, see Thomas J. Christensen, "China, the US–Japan Alliance, and the Security Dilemma in East Asia," *International Security* 23: 4 (Spring 1999): 49–80.
54. It is assumed here that the reunification will take place under terms favorable to South Korea. It is currently difficult to imagine a reunification scenario favorable to North Korea.
55. Zbigniew Brzezinski, "A Geostrategy for Eurasia," *Foreign Affairs* 76: 5 (September/October 1997): 62.

CHAPTER SEVEN

RUSSIA IN INTER-KOREAN RELATIONS

Elizabeth Wishnick

The Korean peninsula is one of many areas where President Vladimir Putin sees Russia playing a key role in conflict resolution.[1] Russia's determination to make its influence felt on Korean issues was much in evidence during the 2002–03 crisis over the resumption of North Korea's nuclear program in violation of international agreements, when Russian diplomats worked hard to reduce tensions between the United States and North Korea and bring them to the negotiating table. Deputy Foreign Minister Aleksandr Losyukov went so far as to say that "Without taking Russia's interest into account, it is almost impossible" to resolve the nuclear crisis in North Korea.[2]

Russia has been staking out a more active mediating role in inter-Korean relations since the mid-1990s, however. Russian officials have pursued a three-pronged diplomatic strategy on Korean issues, involving summits, proposals for multilateral negotiations, and regional economic cooperation. Russia also has been encouraging other powers, particularly Japan and the United Sates, to end North Korea's isolation.

This chapter evaluates the progress achieved in Russian diplomacy on inter-Korean relations, focusing on the period of most intensive diplomatic efforts from 2000 to mid-2003. In particular Moscow's efforts to expand Russian influence over diplomatic efforts, security matters, and economic development on the Korean peninsula are examined. While Moscow has aspired to mediate in conflicts in inter-Korean relations, such as the 2002–03 crisis, Russia's role thus far has been limited and is likely to remain so due its relative lack of leverage.

Russia as a Mediator in Inter-Korean Relations

Russia has taken greater initiative in inter-Korean relations as part of a broader effort to enhance Russian influence in Asian affairs and expand economic cooperation with Asian states. By late 1992, once disillusionment with Russia's new relationship with the West set in, President Boris Yeltsin announced a foreign policy balanced between East and West. This policy focused on expanding cooperation with China and developing a partnership with South Korea. Russia downgraded relations with North Korea, prompting strong criticism, first from Yeltsin's communist opponents, and then from an expanding political Center that sought to promote Russian national interests more actively. By the late 1990s, and especially once Putin became president, Russian policy-makers viewed recovering Russia's lost influence in Pyongyang as a precondition for ending Russia's exclusion from great power talks on inter-Korean relations and justifying a Russian role in any Korean settlement.

During the 2002–03 crisis, officials in the United States, Japan, and South Korea have looked to China and Russia as potential mediators because they are unique in maintaining relations with both North and South Korea. Nevertheless Sino-Russian cooperation in the Korean crisis largely has been confined to joint statements, as the subsequent discussion will show. Although such expectations by the United States, Japan, and South Korea would seem to bolster Russia's effort to increase its influence over developments on the Korean peninsula, Russia's leverage is more limited than China's due to North Korea's dependence on Chinese energy and food aid. China has been a most reluctant mediator, however agreeing to host tripartite talks with the United States and North Korea in April 2003, but not willing to apply pressure on Pyongyang prematurely through United Nations sanctions or blockades.

One of the reasons why China and Russia have not lived up to international expectations of their roles as mediators is because there is little agreement regarding what mediation should accomplish in general. Mediation may involve a range of actions, from the disruption of conflict behavior to the achievement of a compromise among the parties. Typically mediation is distinguished from the negotiation process itself, a "pre-negotiation" phase in which third parties facilitate the initiation of negotiations.[3]

Moreover, not all mediators are created equal. Some, like Russia in the 2002–03 Korean crisis, are "powerless" and lack any enforcement capacity.[4] As we will see later Russia's role in this instance has been to facilitate communication among the parties and to formulate alternatives for conflict resolution. China is closer to the model of the "mediator with muscle,"[5] since its substantial economic assistance to North Korea gives Chinese leaders some means of applying pressure (should they seek to use it) to change Kim Jong Il's cost–benefit calculations of noncompliance with international nuclear standards. To build up its "mediating muscle," Russia has been trying to enhance its economic leverage, mostly by proposing to involve North Korea in its plans to develop a Northeast Asian energy network, relying on Russian oil, gas, and electricity.

Russia in Inter-Korean Political and Diplomatic Relations

Moscow's reassessment of its role in inter-Korean relations dates back to the Gorbachev era. Initially, in his first years as Soviet Communist Party General Secretary, Mikhail Gorbachev paid scant attention to Korean diplomacy. Gorbachev's July 1986 speech in Vladivostok—his first major statement on Soviet Asia policy—reiterated Soviet support for the DPRK and its proposal for a nuclear-free zone on the Korean peninsula.[6] Beginning in 1988, however, Gorbachev took a series of steps that would have a profound impact on great power relations on the Korean peninsula.[7] In March 1998 the Soviet foreign minister created a loophole in the ban on Soviet travel to South Korea by allowing ethnic Koreans from Sakhalin to visit their homeland via third countries. Six months later, in August 1988, 6,000 Soviet athletes and tourists, accompanied by the Bolshoi Chorus and the Moscow Philharmonic, traveled to Seoul for the 1988 summer Olympics, despite Moscow's prior support for Pyongyang's bid to co-host the event.[8] Just as "ping-pong diplomacy" helped stimulate U.S.–China relations, so did the Soviet Union's enthusiastic participation in the 1988 Olympics pave the way for expanded economic cooperation between Moscow and Seoul.

In a speech in Krasnoyarsk in September 1988, for the first time Gorbachev advocated improved economic and trade ties with South Korea, as a part of his broader effort to reform the Soviet economy and expand economic cooperation with a wide range of countries.[9] Meanwhile, in July 1988 newly elected South Korean President Roh Tae Woo announced his *Nordpolitik*, a major policy initiative aimed at improving North–South relations by expanding political, economic, and cultural ties with the Soviet Union, China, and other socialist states, and urging Japan and the United States to develop better relations with North Korea. As Sino-Soviet rapprochement proceeded, leading to normalization at the Beijing summit in May 1989, Sino-Soviet competition for influence in North Korea diminished, thereby enabling both Moscow and Beijing to follow their economic interests and open diplomatic relations with Seoul. First Moscow and Seoul normalized relations in 1990, with Beijing following suit in 1992.

Gorbachev took advantage of a visit to San Francisco in June 1990 to meet with Roh Tae Woo, the first meeting ever between leaders of the USSR and South Korea. Although Gorbachev pledged to open diplomatic relations with South Korea, he delayed making a final decision for several months.[10] In early September, Foreign Minister Eduard Shevardnadze went to Pyongyang to inform Kim Il Sung of Soviet plans to normalize ties with Seoul, but the North Korean leader refused to meet him. Instead Shevardnadze met with North Korean Foreign Minister Kim Yong Nam, talks that the foreign minister would later describe as among the most difficult of his career.[11] According to the Soviet foreign minister, eliminating confrontation and promoting peaceful unification were top priorities for Moscow and could best be accomplished by establishing diplomatic ties with Seoul, while maintaining alliance relations with Pyongyang.[12]

On September 30, 1990, the Soviet Union established formal diplomatic relations with South Korea and, within months, in December 1990, Roh Tae Woo traveled to Moscow to meet with Gorbachev. The two leaders outlined the general principles of Soviet–Korean relations—nonuse of force, good neighborliness, and cooperation—and noted that the development of relations between Seoul and Moscow would help promote peace and security and eliminate the vestiges of the Cold War in Asia.[13] In January 1991, South Korea extended a $3 billion loan to the USSR, half in cash and half in Korean products.

Following the summit, the Soviet Union stopped its assistance to Pyongyang's nuclear program in an effort to persuade North Korean leaders to allow International Atomic Energy Agency (IAEA) inspections.[14] Gorbachev then chose South Korea for his first destination on the Korean peninsula, a further snub to Pyongyang. During his meeting with President Roh at Cheju island in April 1991, Gorbachev made a series of startling announcements attesting to the dramatic improvement in Soviet–South Korean relations over the past three years. First Gorbachev told the South Korean president that he would support Seoul's membership in the United Nations, regardless of Pyongyang's opposition. The Soviet leader also expressed support for North Korean dialogue with the South (as well as with Japan and the United States) in an effort to reduce tensions on the peninsula. He proposed codifying the improved Soviet–South Korean relationship in a new treaty and, in support of U.S. and South Korean positions, called on Pyongyang to submit to IAEA inspections of its nuclear power plants.[15]

At a time when North Korea was no longer assured of Soviet support for its international positions, Li Peng traveled to Pyongyang on May 3–6, 1991 to inform North Korean leaders of China's intention to support separate Korean membership in the United Nations.[16] Fearing diplomatic isolation, on May 27, 1991, Kim Il Sung applied for membership in the United Nations, a major reversal of North Korea's position that Korea should only occupy one seat in the organization. With the simultaneous improvement of relations between China and South Korea and the Soviet Union and South Korea, neither Moscow nor Beijing had further cause to veto Seoul's entry into the United Nations and both Koreas were able to obtain seats in September 1991.[17]

During Yeltsin's November 1992 visit to Seoul, Russian and South Korean leaders signed the Treaty on Principles of Relations between the Russian Federation and the ROK. The 1992 treaty states that relations between the two partners are based on shared commitment to ideals of freedom, democracy, human rights, and a market economy. While claiming that the treaty was not intended to be detrimental to Pyongyang's interests, Yeltsin noted that as a result of the improvement in relations with Seoul, Russia had altered certain aspects of policy toward North Korea. Deliveries of offensive weapons and nuclear equipment were halted and the mutual defense clause in the 1961 treaty with Pyongyang would have to be reconsidered, a change that the Russian president believed would contribute to the improvement of inter-Korean relations.[18]

On June 2, 1994, during South Korean president Kim Young Sam's visit to Moscow, Russia, and South Korea issued a joint declaration, proclaiming their "constructive mutually complementary partnership." Yeltsin and Kim pledged to enhance their economic cooperation, agreed to establish a hot line between the Kremlin and the Blue House, and stated that Korean unification should take place in a peaceful and democratic way, through inter-Korean dialogue. South Korea expressed support for ongoing reforms in Russia and its future membership in Asia-Pacific Economic Cooperation (APEC), while Russia reaffirmed its commitment to ensure the denuclearization of the Korean peninsula.[19] As was the case with Russia's relationship with China, however, it turned out to be far easier to declare a partnership with South Korea than to implement one. Some outstanding bilateral issues—Seoul's demand that Moscow pay reparations for the downing of the KAL airliner in 1983, the repayment of the Soviet era debt to South Korea, a dispute over the ownership of some diplomatic property in Seoul, the reciprocal expulsion of diplomats on espionage charges in 1998, and Russia's decision to return North Korean migrants to China (for eventual repatriation in North Korea)—have clouded the new Russian–South Korean relationship.

Nevertheless, since the mid-1990s, Russian leaders have used bilateral meetings with South Korean and North Korean leaders to enhance Russia's role in conflict resolution on the Korean peninsula. Although Putin's diplomacy on the Korean peninsula has been particularly active in staking out a role for Russia in inter-Korean relations, the process began during the Yeltsin era.[20] In a May 1999 visit to Moscow,

South Korean leader Kim Dae Jung, noting the improvement of Russian–North Korean relations in the late 1990s, stated that Russia could play the role of mediator in inter-Korean relations.[21] Yeltsin took the opportunity to express Russia's support for South Korea's engagement policy toward North Korea.[22] In their concluding visit, the two leaders came out in favor of six-party talks on the Korean peninsula, including Russia and Japan.[23] Despite their apparent agreement, the Russian press soon reported some fundamental differences of views on the future of the Korean peninsula. Russian diplomats took issue with what they viewed as politically motivated coverage of Kim Dae Jung's visit to Moscow by the Korean press, which sought to show Russian support for regime change in North Korea and its abandonment of its missile program.[24]

During Russian Foreign Minister Igor Ivanov's visit to Pyongyang, on February 9, 2000, Russia and North Korea signed a new Treaty of Friendship, Good Neighborliness and Cooperation, replacing their 1961 agreement. Korean officials claimed that the new treaty would have no adverse impact on Russian–South Korean relations.[25] To the contrary, Russian officials saw the treaty with Pyongyang as symbolizing the restoration of balance in Moscow's relations with North and South Korea.[26] According to Russian ambassador to South Korea, Evgenii Afanasiev, the improvement of Russian–North Korean relations would help promote peace and stability on the peninsula as well as a more prominent role for Russia in the region.[27]

President Vladimir Putin was the first Russian president to visit North Korea. Coming directly after Putin's summit in Beijing, the Russian president's active diplomacy aimed to boost Russia's profile in Northeast Asia. The final communiqué noted Russia's support for the results of the North–South summit, the commitment of both sides to the development of a multipolar world order, the process of Korean unification without outside interference, noninterference in internal affairs, and support for sovereignty, independence, and territorial integrity.[28]

During the Russian president's subsequent visit to Seoul on February 26–28, 2000, Putin and Kim Dae Jung noted their support for the results of the inter-Korean summit. The communiqué issued after Putin's visit reiterated many of the points made during the May 1999 Moscow summit, including Russian support for the 1992 declaration by North and South Korea about the denuclearization of the Korean peninsula, Kim Dae Jung's efforts to ease North–South tensions, and Russia's readiness to facilitate inter-Korean cooperation.[29] The two presidents also noted that the improved climate of inter-Korean relations created favorable conditions for trilateral projects (involving Russia) in energy and transportation.[30] Much to Moscow's satisfaction, Kim's "Sunshine Policy" involved both a renewed interest in regional development projects including the Russian Far East and greater consultation with Russian officials over strategies to engage the North. Russian officials saw the inter-Korean summit as a very positive step and noted that Russia would do whatever possible to continue this dialogue and support a peaceful settlement on the Korean peninsula.[31]

Plans for Kim Jong Il's visit to Russia took more than a year to organize, due to the North Korean leader's security concerns and aversion to air travel, and the summit meeting ultimately took place in August 2001. At the end of his visit, Russia and North Korea signed an accord (known as "the Moscow declaration"), highlighting both areas of Russian–North Korean agreement and their differences. Putin and Kim pledged their support for the inter-Korean dialogue begun at the June 2000 Summit and the Russian president said he was prepared to play a constructive role in this process. The Russian president urged his counterpart to pay another visit to Seoul, but the North Korean leader stated that "certain conditions" had not yet been met.[32]

Putin and Kim agreed to disagree on other key issues as well: North Korea stated that the withdrawal of U.S. forces from South Korea was a pressing issue, while the Russian side expressed understanding of the North Korean position (rather than agreement) and underscored the need for nonmilitary means to help ensure stability and peace on the Korean peninsula. The North Korean side also stated that its missile program is peaceful and does not threaten any country recognizing its sovereignty, while the Russian agreement was limited to recognition of the right of every state to equal security.[33]

After talks between South Korean Deputy Foreign Minister Choi Sung Hong in Moscow, Russia and South Korea pledged to make joint efforts to move forward with inter-Korean talks, which they termed essential to preserving the peace and stability of the Korean peninsula.[34] Following up on the initiative in a letter to Kim Jong-Il in honor of his sixtieth birthday, Putin urged the North Korean leader to pursue dialogue with South Korea.[35]

During Kim Jong Il's visit, a new back channel to Pyongyang was established—ever since Putin's representative to the Russian Far East federal district, Konstantin Pulikovskii, accompanied Kim Jong Il on his lengthy train journey across Russia in August 2001, the Russian official has periodically played the role of emissary on inter-Korean relations.[36] In July 2002, almost exactly a year after Kim Jong Il's visit, Pulikovskii revisited the same train route, this time with a 350-member South Korean business delegation. The group took a 17-day rail journey from Vladivostok to St. Petersburg on a train dubbed the "Korea-Russia Friendship Express" to celebrate the twelfth anniversary of the establishment of relations between Moscow and Seoul.[37] In August 2002, Pulikovskii was on hand once again to escort Kim Jong Il on a tour of the Russian Far East in an effort to promote regional economic relations between the two neighboring countries.[38] Pulikovskii also did his part to resolve the 2002–03 nuclear crisis, meeting with visiting Japanese Foreign Minister Yoriko Kawaguchi in June 2003 to discuss the issue.[39]

Russia in Inter-Korean Security and Military Relations

Although Russia has not yet succeeded in playing an integral part in great power talks on Korean issues, Russian actions have had an important influence on North Korea's nuclear policy and inter-Korean security. It was Gorbachev (at U.S. urging) who had succeeded in convincing North Korea to sign the NPT in 1985, a time when Moscow still sold weapons to Pyongyang. After assuming office Gorbachev continued to provide military and technological assistance to Pyongyang, including delivery of MiG-23 fighters promised during Kim Il Sung's May 1984 visit to Moscow, but the new Soviet leader made this support contingent on North Korea's agreement to steps to lower tensions with the United States and South Korea. Thus, the Soviet Union only agreed to help construct a 30-megawatt nuclear reactor in North Korea if Kim would agree to sign the NPT. Once the DPRK signed the NPT in December

1985, the USSR agreed to a five-year aid package, including the construction of the nuclear reactor.[40]

When Gorbachev normalized ties with South Korea in 1990 and cut off military aid to Pyongyang, North Korea hinted that it might need to go nuclear to meet its security needs and delayed signing the IAEA nuclear safeguards agreement.[41] Yeltsin's subsequent statement that the 1961 Soviet–North Korean Mutual defense treaty existed only on paper further exacerbated Pyongyang's security concerns.[42] Nevertheless North Korea finally relented to international pressure and signed the IAEA accord six years later, in January 1992.[43]

Russian officials criticized North Korea's refusal to allow IAEA nuclear inspections and withdrawal from the NPT in March 1993, actions that ran counter to Russian interests in maintaining stability on the Korean peninsula.[44] In response, Russia's Minatom (Ministry of Atomic Energy) halted fuel deliveries promised under the 1985 Soviet–North Korean agreement on economic and technical cooperation for the construction of a nuclear power plant at Yongbyon. Then, on April 19, 1993, Yeltsin issued an order halting all work on Yongbyon project.[45] The Russian position invited North Korean reprisals—Pyongyang threatened to block proposed energy pipelines spanning from Russia through North Korea to South Korea, and publicly denounced Russia for dumping nuclear waste into the Sea of Japan.[46]

Russian Peace Proposals, Four Party Peace Talks, and the KEDO
Russian multilateral initiatives for conflict resolution on the Korean peninsula reflect both Moscow's bid for a greater role on Korean issues as well as Russia's reappraisal of North Korean nuclear intentions. By early 1994, Russian policy-makers and military analysts came to discount concerns in the United States, South Korea, and Japan, that North Korea would soon have an operational nuclear weapon.[47] In August 1994 an expert analysis commissioned by the Russian State Duma concluded that former KGB Chairman Viktor Kryuchkov's 1990 estimate of North Korea's nuclear capability had been exaggerated, possibly due to reliance on disinformation from Pyongyang.[48]

Instead of introducing sanctions against North Korea (a step favored by the United States), on March 24, 1994, Russia proposed holding an eight-party conference, including South Korea, North Korea, the United States, China, Russia, and the two other UN Security Council permanent members (and nuclear powers), France and Britain, plus Japan, to discuss a settlement on the Korean peninsula.[49] The Russian proposal failed to generate a positive response due to concerns that an expanded framework would only complicate the resolution of North–South issues or bind Seoul and Pyongyang to solutions that were not in their own interests.[50]

As Russian officials had feared, the steps ultimately taken to address the 1993–94 nuclear crisis in North Korea dramatized Russia's exclusion from the Korean peninsula. Russia supported the need for North Korean compliance with IAEA inspections of its nuclear facilities and froze its nuclear cooperation with Pyongyang, yet under the Agreed Framework reached in October 1994 only the United States and an international consortium would be responsible for supplying North Korea with light-water reactors (LWRs). Although Moscow extended nearly $2 billion in credits to Pyongyang to construct the Yongbyon reactor, U.S. Ambassador-at-large Robert

Gallucci only invited Russia to participate in the newly created KEDO in a limited way, confining the Russian role to reprocessing the spent fuel from the U.S. and South Korean reactors. Moscow rejected this type of participation in KEDO as "second-rate" and claimed that Russia was being penalized for its compliance with the NPT, while U.S. and South Korean officials countered that those states that were prepared to pay for the LWRs should be the ones to provide them.[51]

Russian officials further contended that commercial interests motivated the parties to the Agreed Framework (which would be a violation of the NPT), and that North Korean compliance with the IAEA was being held hostage to U.S.–North Korean agreements.[52] KEDO and the Agreed Framework still rankle in Moscow— Minatom's 1998 proposal to build a nuclear power plant in the Russian Far East that would supply electricity to North Korea—an idea still discussed today—represents an attempt to gain a meaningful role for Russia in supplying energy to Pyongyang.[53]

In April 1996 U.S. and South Korean leaders proposed four-power peace negotiations that would include North and South Korea, the United States, and, China. The proposal demonstrated to Russian officials that partnership with China and normalization with South Korea delivered few political benefits in terms of Russia's influence over the Korean peninsula. North Korea expressed no interest in involving Russia in the new talks, even in bilateral consultations.[54] As four-party talks— including the United States, South Korea, North Korea, and China—proceeded, Russian officials argued that conflict resolution on the Korean peninsula required Russian and Japanese participation. In the Russian view, mutual recognition among the six would be essential to any settlement, which should not be predicated on regime change in any country.[55] Russia has continued to advocate a multilateral framework for talks. Faced with North Korean opposition to the idea, Foreign Minister Ivanov has noted that Russia's main concern is to promote constructive dialogue on Korean security, not to set the format of the talks.[56]

The Taepodong Missile Issue
Kim Dae Jung welcomed President Putin's more active diplomacy on the Korean peninsula, which provided an additional source of support for his "Sunshine" Policy. For Putin, intervention in inter-Korean relations not only served to expand Russia's influence on the peninsula, but also contributed to broader security interests, such as Moscow's efforts to forestall the U.S. development of national and theater missile defense systems. Nevertheless, Russian officials have had to play a difficult balancing act—urging the development of a nuclear-free zone on the Korean peninsula and welcoming Pyongyang's moratorium on missile testing, while discounting the threat posed by North Korean missiles and claiming that North Korea has the right to develop a missile capability.

Russian diplomacy appeared to have scored a major coup when Putin revealed that the North Korean leader pledged at their July 2000 Summit meeting to eliminate his country's Taepodong missile program—a key rationale for NMD and TMD— if developed countries provided access to rocket boosters for peaceful space research. As it turned out, Putin may have read too much into the offer, which Kim Jong Il later retracted and called "a joke."

During the February 2001 summit meeting between Putin and Kim Dae Jung, the two leaders issued a joint communiqué opposing American plans to develop NMD, a move that complicated the South Korean president's subsequent discussions with George W. Bush. After several awkward attempts to dispel any notions of disagreement between Seoul and Washington and a difficult meeting with President Bush, Kim ordered a shake-up in his cabinet and replaced key officials, including the foreign minister and the unification minister.

Arms Sales

Russia's arms sales to South and North Korea have a significant impact on North–South relations by affecting the military balance between them and their perceptions of security. Soon after normalizing relations with Seoul, Moscow terminated arms sales to Pyongyang at the South's request.[57]

In April 2001 Russia agreed to resume military cooperation with North Korea, although this is limited to upgrading weapons supplied during the Soviet era.[58] North Korean defense officials reportedly requested $500 million in new weapons systems, including fighter aircraft and reconnaissance planes, but Moscow refused given Pyongyang's inability to pay hard currency for the order.[59] North Korea now purchases $10 million in spare parts from Russia annually for Soviet-made weapons.[60]

Despite the limited nature of the resumed Russian–North Korean military relationship, the April 2001 agreements evoked concern in Seoul. According to an editorial in the *JoongAng Ilbo*, Russian arms sales to Pyongyang could fuel a North–South arms race and raise questions in Washington about the merits of Seoul's policy of engaging Pyongyang.[61] In September 2001, the South Korean government asked Russia to exercise caution in its military cooperation with North Korea to avoid exacerbating North–South tensions or creating tensions in South Korean–Russian relations.[62] Reportedly North Korea has been trying to acquire advanced Russian missile and rocket systems through Syria,[63] an effort the Bush administration is seeking to block.

Meanwhile, Russian officials have been seeking to increase arms sales to Seoul. In the mid-1990s Russia offset $460 million of its $2.2 billion debt to South Korea through supplies of weapons (including T-80U tanks, BMP-3 infantry fighting vehicles, antitank and antiaircraft missiles systems, and KA-32 helicopters).[64] President Roh Moo Hyun decided in June 2003 to write off 30 percent of the Soviet debt (approximately $660 million). Another $300 million will be repaid through weapons deliveries in 2003–06.[65]

Russia's arms manufacturers also have been competing for major South Korean contracts. The Russian Sukhoi corporation's prototype Su-35 multipurpose fighter competed with France's Dassault and the U.S. Boeing corporation, but ultimately lost to the American F-15K.[66] Pyongyang has been opposed to Russian arms sales to South Korea, which North Korean officials view as exacerbating the military confrontation on the peninsula.[67]

Nuclear Proliferation

Although Moscow has been a consistent supporter of North Korea's adherence to the NPT and ceased its own nuclear cooperation with Pyongyang after its withdrawal from the treaty and refusal to allow inspections, the possibility of proliferation of nuclear technology and material from military bases in the Russian Far East remains a key concern. Underemployed scientists in the region's ailing military complex make ripe targets for North Korean agents seeking to purchase small pieces of equipment or software, items that would be difficult to detect.[68]

Many of the Russian Pacific fleet's nuclear submarine bases and installations are located within 100 km. of North Korea, providing opportunity for infiltration. Since the mid-1990s several North Korean agents have been caught trying to purchase Russian radioactive materials and the schedules for decommissioning nuclear submarines.[69]

Russian officials and experts are well aware that Russia's ability to play a constructive role in Asian security is inextricably linked to the development of the Russian Far East since regional economic decline creates a whole host of security challenges, while setting limits to regional economic cooperation (discussed later).[70] As one scholar noted, instability in the Russian Far East only serves to compound Russia's peripheral role in Asia.[71] Thus, one of the preconditions for a higher-profile Russian role in inter-Korean relations is the stable economic development of the Russian Far East.

Russia and the 2002–03 Nuclear Crisis
Although Russia initially reacted with caution to the revelation by the United States in October 2002 that North Korea was developing a highly enriched uranium (HEU) nuclear program, by November Russian officials had launched a multifaceted diplomatic effort to ensure that the ensuing crisis would be resolved peacefully and without the intervention of the UN Security Council. American and Russian officials have held several discussions on North Korea. A previously planned summit between Putin and Japan's Prime Minister Koizumi ended up focusing considerable attention on the North Korean crisis. In a joint statement, Russia and Japan urged a peaceful solution to the crisis, involving a nuclear-free Korean peninsula and a renewed North Korean commitment to non-proliferation agreements.[72]

Similarly, during Putin's December summit meeting with Jiang Zemin and Hu Jintao, Russian and Chinese leaders issued a declaration calling for a nonnuclear Korean peninsula and urging the United States to normalize relations with North Korea.[73] In the declaration signed after their May 2003 summit in Moscow, Putin and Hu Jintao stated that the crisis should be resolved through political and diplomatic means. They proposed "to guarantee the nuclear-free status of the Korean peninsula, respect the non-proliferation of weapons of mass destruction, and... guarantee the security of the DPRK as well as to create favorable conditions for its social and economic development."[74] Both Russia and China have viewed any condemnation of North Korea's nuclear program by the UN Security Council as unnecessarily provocative and urged the body to hold off on such actions.[75]

Although South Korea had been less than enthusiastic about Russia's offer in summer 2002 to mediate in inter-Korean relations by hosting a meeting between South and North Korean leaders in Khabarovsk,[76] in January 2003 South Korean officials specifically asked Russian Foreign minister Igor Ivanov to use his influence to persuade North Korea to rescind its decision to withdraw from nuclear non-proliferation frameworks.[77] Nevertheless U.S. and South Korean leaders have viewed China as the key to diffusing the crisis. Chinese leaders proposed holding U.S.–North Korean talks in China, but Russian officials pressed forward with their own three-part initiative. Deputy Foreign Minister Aleksandr Losyukov traveled to Pyongyang in January 2003 to propose a plan involving guarantees of a nuclear-free Korean peninsula, a written security pledge by the United States, and a package of relief and economic assistance.[78] In the end China hosted three-way talks in April 2003, leaving Russia once again on the sidelines of international efforts to diffuse the crisis.

The Sino-Russian partnership notwithstanding, the Chinese leadership has never actively promoted Russia's participation in any future multilateral talks. While the United States has advocated the inclusion of its allies, South Korea and Japan, American support for Russian participation has been lukewarm. North Korea has focused on securing bilateral talks with the United States, although in June 2003 Kim Jong Il wrote to Putin to ask for his help in bringing the Americans back to the negotiating table.[79]

For Russia the crisis has afforded an opportunity to demonstrate Moscow's value as an intermediary on Korean security issues and to stake a Russian claim to a role in postcrisis arrangements. Russia's disappointment with its exclusion from the talks and energy cooperation developed as a result of the 1993 crisis spurred Moscow's efforts to develop a more balanced Korea policy in the latter half of the 1990s. Undoubtedly Russian leaders are hoping that their active diplomacy in 2002–03 will be rewarded. Russian Nuclear Energy Minister Aleksandr Rumiantsev suggested, for example, that Russia could build a nuclear power plant in North Korea as a part of an effort to diffuse the crisis.[80] The Far Eastern Managing Energy Company, a Russian power company based in Primorskii Krai, proposed constructing a power line from Vladivostok to Chongjin in North Korea.[81] Whether or not Russian initiatives will translate into greater long-term influence over Korean security remains an open question, however.

Russian and Inter-Korean Economic Cooperation

Russian regional cooperation with the Koreas has focused on major rail and gas pipeline projects, as well as participation in the TRADP. The presence of a Korean diaspora in the Russian Far East and the use of North Korean labor in regional projects have further highlighted the importance of Russia's Korean diplomacy for the economic development of the Russian Far East.

Energy

Russia's energy strategy, adopted on May 22, 2003, involves a substantial reorientation of Russian energy exports from Europe to Northeast Asia. By 2020, 25–30 percent of Russia's oil exports and 20 percent of its gas exports could be destined for Northeast Asian markets. This shift in Russian energy exports reflects a preference in Europe to avoid undue dependence on gas imports from Russia as well as the Putin leadership's interest in diversifying Russian export markets.[82]

The South Korean natural gas market is one of the most developed in Northeast Asia and is seen as a promising destination for natural gas from East Siberia and Sakhalin. Although largely reliant on coal for energy, North Korea established a natural gas research society in 1998 to encourage natural gas use and promote pipeline projects.[83]

There are three energy pipeline projects that could involve the two Koreas, including one shipping liquid natural gas from Sakhalin to the Russian mainland and then south to the Korean peninsula and possibly to China, and another spanning from the Kovyktinskoe gas fields in East Siberia to China and then to the Korean peninsula. A third project would involve shipping oil from Angarsk in East Siberia principally to China, but possibly also to the Korean peninsula and Japan depending on the routing of the pipeline.[84]

Since North Korea faces an acute energy shortage but lacks the hard currency for energy imports, Pyongyang is likely to support the trans-Korean pipeline projects to benefit from transit revenues. Other potential project participants are concerned that a trans-Korean route would provide Pyongyang with leverage over oil and gas flows and enable it to blackmail other recipients (including China and South Korea) for political purposes.[85] Nevertheless, if implemented, these pipeline projects would contribute significantly to the fulfillment of two of Putin's political goals, ensuring that Russia becomes more of a player in the Northeast Asian economy, and, depending on the routing selected, enhancing Russian leverage on the Korean peninsula.

Transportation

Russia has been active in promoting a link from the inter-Korean railway to the Trans-Siberian railroad, which Russian officials hope would lead to a more than tenfold rise in shipping along the Trans-Siberian, from 45,000 containers per year to 500,000 to 600,000 annually. The rail project also will involve cooperation by Russia, North Korea, and South Korea in unifying and automating customs procedures to eliminate clearance stops at their borders.[86] Russia first proposed the idea to North Korean leaders during Foreign Minister Ivanov's visit to Pyongyang in February 2000 and then at the summit meeting between Putin and Kim Jong Il in June. When North Korean leaders responded positively, Putin raised the issue with Kim Dae Jung during their September 2000 meeting at the UN Millennium summit and Russia and South Korea reached an agreement in principle to connect the trans-Siberian to the inter-Korean railway.[87]

In December 2001, Russia and South Korea discussed the possibility of a connection from Pusan to Pyongyang and then to Khasan in Primorskii Krai. The 950 km. Pyongyang–Khasan line would require a $250 million investment and take about 2 years to complete.[88] The price tag for the project will be considerably higher, since, prior to any new construction, existing North Korean rail lines would require extensive repairs, requiring an additional $2.2 billion, according to the results of a joint Russian–North Korean study completed in April 2002.[89]

During his summit meeting with Kim Dae Jung in February 2001, Putin continued to promote a rail link from the Trans-Siberian railroad to the inter-Korean railway in an effort to encourage tripartite economic cooperation among Russia, South and North Korea.[90] Russia and South Korea established a Committee on Transportation Cooperation to continue their discussions of the proposed link between the two rail lines. Although Putin stated that his government was prepared to invest in the new railway, according to some reports, Russia is hoping to provide the technical expertise for the rail link in exchange for a reduction of the Soviet era debt to South Korea.

Russian Railways Minister Gennadyi Fadeyev, has cautioned that the project represents a huge political risk, requiring major investment.[91] Russia's investment would come in the form of loans to North Korea, to be repaid from revenues from the new rail line. The South Korean government also has called attention to obstacles to the construction of the inter-Korean railway.[92] In an effort to speed up work on the project, delayed in part due to a lack of equipment on the North Korean side, Seoul offered to provide rails and ties to Pyongyang.[93]

De-mining activities begun in September 2002 in the buffer zone between the two Koreas came to a halt in mid-November, when Pyongyang accused Washington of interference due to its insistence that the North first inform the U.S.-led UN Command prior to entering the DMZ. North Korea ultimately decided to resume removing the land mines and the work was completed on schedule in mid-December 2002.

Despite more sober appraisal of the problems involved in completing the inter-Korean railway, Putin has indicated his support for the Donghae line. The Russian president told journalists in the Russian Far East that if Russia failed to support the project, then the Trans-Siberian railway would lose revenue to the Chinese, who would benefit from the increased freight.[94] In preparation for the inter-Korean rail line to the Trans-Siberian via Khasan in Primorskii Krai, in December 2002 Russia completed the electrification of the Far Eastern spur of the trans-Siberian and concluded an agreement with North Korea regarding the reconstruction and modernization of eastern coastal railways.[95]

On June 14, 2003, just before the third anniversary of their historic summit meeting, South Korea and North Korea briefly opened their borders to celebrate the reconnection of their rail link. Despite the symbolism, regular traffic will not begin until later in 2003 at the earliest.[96] Although South Korea has completed work on its side of the border, construction still continues on the North Korean side and its fate will depend on the resolution of the nuclear crisis. The high political risk, as well as the slow speed (an average of 40 km. per hour, compared to 80 km. per hour in the south) and susceptibility of North Korean trains to energy outages, will dissuade shippers from using the new link.[97]

Special Economic Zones

For the past decade, the prospects for Russian–North Korean regional cooperation have been linked to the United Nations Development Program's (UNDP) TRADP, involving Russia, North and South Korea, China, and Mongolia. In its original conception, the $30 billion 20-year project launched in 1991 was designed to transform the Tumen River area into a global trade, transportation, and communications gateway. The project had to be scaled back due to unrealistic expectations about foreign investment (especially from Japan, which is unwilling to invest in TRADP until relations with North Korea are normalized), conflicts of interests among the participants, and instability on the Korean peninsula.[98] The UNDP now is trying to foster the development of regional trade through infrastructure development as well as to promote tourism and environmental protection in the Tumen River area.

Officials in Primorskii Krai, the Russian region bordering on the Tumen River, have not been enthusiastic supporters of the TRADP due to their concern that infrastructure improvements in China, in particular, would increase competition for already scarce cargo now moving through the ports of Pos'et and Zarubino. Although the UNDP decided against building any new Chinese ports, other infrastructure improvements have been made, including the reopening of the Tumen River bridge connecting China and North Korea at Wonjong/Quanhe, and the construction of a railway linking the Chinese city of Hunchun with Kraskino in Primorskii Krai.[99]

Despite its usual reluctance to become involved in multilateral projects, China has been the strongest supporter of the TRADP in an effort to achieve an outlet to the Sea of Japan, by improving rail and road connections to the aforementioned ports in Primorskii Krai as well as to Rajin and Songbong in North Korea. Chinese officials have long complained about excessive fees and duties in Russia and hope that once Rajin and Songbong can compete for cargo, shipping costs will be lowered throughout the Tumen region.[100]

Although earlier in the 1990s Primorskii Krai shippers used the ports of Rajin and Songbong, by the end of the decade they moved their cargo through Pos'et and Zarubino. Primorskii Krai has been trying to promote investment in its southern ports,[101] now being portrayed as ideal hubs for transit trade from Northeast China and South Korea bound for Japan. When Russia and North Korea signed an investment agreement in 1996, the two countries envisaged Russian investment in the Rajin-Songbong zone. Although the South Korean-financed Nakhodka (SEZ) in Russia's Primorskii Krai and the Rajin-Songbong FEZ in North Korea planned to explore joint activities in areas such as the forestry sector, little cooperation ensued due to obstacles on the Russian side to the development of the Nakhodka zone.[102]

The improvement in the political climate on the Korean peninsula has served to revive Russian interest in the TRADP plan. In February 2002, for example, Russia agreed to help modernize Rajin's port and telecommunications infrastructure to facilitate Russian cargo shipment to South Korea, as well as to Japan, China, Canada, and Australia.[103] Nevertheless, without a major improvement in the overall economic health of Northeast China, North Korea, and the Russian Far East, sufficient cargo is unlikely to be generated within the region to make regional economic cooperation viable.

Koreans in the Russian Far East: Socioeconomic Implications
If projects like the TRADP continue to have appeal despite numerous obstacles, this is a reflection of the facts on the ground, especially the shared Tumen River boundary and migration flows. As of 1991, some 15,000 Koreans lived in the Russian Far East and approximately 400,000 remained in Kazakhstan, Uzbekistan, Tajikistan, and other regions of Russia. In early 1993, the Russian Parliament recognized the illegal nature of the repression of Soviet Koreans in the Stalin era and affirmed their right to national development and equal opportunity in the exercise of their political freedoms.[104] Their rehabilitation gave them the right, on an individual basis, to return to their former places of residence, a decision that evoked an immediately negative reaction in Primorskii Krai. South Korea has been monitoring the fate of Korean nationals living in the Russian Far East. A program has been established to

repatriate some older Koreans living on Sakhalin, who had been forced into labor there by the Japanese during World War II. Seoul also has made financial contributions to programs that provide farming land to the small number of Korean exiles returning from Central Asia to the Russian Far East.

Residents of Primorskii Krai and Khabarovskii Krai also have become increasingly concerned about the presence of North Koreans on their territory. At first, Khabarovskii Krai supported the continuation of a forestry agreement with North Korea that provided cheap labor for the regional timber industry—against the opposition of policy-makers in Moscow who were concerned about allegations of human rights abuses in forestry camps, which employed workers in prison-like conditions. When North Korean timber workers were implicated in drug trafficking and their work methods were linked to environmental degradation, regional sentiment turned against the venture and its scope has been narrowed. The Russian–North Korean agreement governing the timber projects was renegotiated so as to provide local officials with greater oversight and a larger share of the harvest (61.5 percent instead of 43 percent).[105] Approximately 12,000 North Koreans are currently employed in the Russian Far East, primarily in the timber industry in Khabarovsk Krai, the construction industry in Primorskii Krai and Khabarovskii Krai, and in agriculture in Amurskaia Oblast.[106]

Russia and Korean Unification

In the early 1990s, Russian officials sought unsuccessfully to contribute to inter-Korean dialogue by proposing various multilateral venues for great power talks. Because Moscow had downgraded relations with Pyongyang, however, Russia lacked sufficient influence in North Korea to play any sort of mediating role in inter-Korean relations. Thus, by the mid-1990s, Russian officials sought to restore balance with North and South Korea to enhance Russia's influence over inter-Korean relations. By boosting Russia's diplomatic role on Korean issues, Russian policy-makers have sought to promote their vision of an inter-Korean settlement.

Russian officials and analysts note that while China, Japan, and the United States all have varying interests in maintaining the status quo on the peninsula, Moscow is the only power to unequivocally support a process of gradual unification.[107] While some Russian experts see Chinese support for Korean unification as an effort to check Japanese influence in the region, others note that a strong unified Korea could also limit Chinese regional ambitions. For Russia, a unified Korea friendly to Moscow would provide a counterbalance to both Chinese and Japanese power and serve as an engine of development for the Russian Far East.[108] For Russia, however, support for unification entails support for the North Korean regime, as unification achieved by North Korean collapse would be detrimental to Russian interests in border security and regional economic development.[109] As a Foreign Ministry official explained, Russia views unification as the endgame of a long-term process involving "the peaceful coexistence of the two Korean states over a prolonged period of time."[110]

With the full restoration of Russian–North Korean relations in the aftermath of the signing of a new friendship treaty in February 2000 and Putin's visit to Pyongyang in July 2000, Russian leaders have become more vocal in outlining a vision of an inter-Korean settlement. Upon his return from North Korea, President

Putin expressed his support for the unprecedented North–South dialogue achieved at the June 2000 inter-Korean Summit and noted that Russia would continue to follow developments on the peninsula closely.[111]

In a speech to the South Korean National Assembly on February 28, 2001, President Putin outlined his vision of unification. According to Putin, an inter-Korean settlement should take place in an atmosphere of peace and stability, on the basis of the June 15, 2000 joint declaration, and be coordinated by Korean leaders without any outside interference. He stated that Moscow would "welcome the creation of a single Korean state friendly toward Russia and other countries" and supported a nonnuclear future for the Korean peninsula. To enhance inter-Korean cooperation and economic development in Northeast Asia in general, Putin expressed Russia's interest in participating in transportation and power engineering projects involving the two Koreas.[112]

Conclusion

Although the improvement of Russian–North Korean relations has provided new opportunities for Moscow to play a more active role in inter-Korean relations, several factors limit Russia's ability to serve as a mediator.[113] While South Korea has welcomed Russian efforts to become more actively involved in promoting conflict resolution in the Korean peninsula, it remains unclear how Russia's new role will evolve. Some South Korean commentary recognizes that Russian policy toward the Korean peninsula may actually be serving broader goals vis-à-vis the United States, for example, reducing the U.S. need to develop a theater missile defense system. There is also some concern in South Korea that North Korea may be trying to use Russian support as a bargaining chip.[114] The brouhaha over Kim Jong Il's reported pledge to Putin in July 2000 that he would cease missile development activities if North Korean access to satellite technology showed that Russia's attempt to mediate could be disruptive, in this case contributing to a rift in U.S.–South Korean relations and a cabinet shake-up in Seoul. Thus, South Korean experts have noted the importance of cooperation with Russia to ensure that great power efforts on inter-Korean issues are coordinated.

One basic problem for Russian officials is how to put more muscle into their mediation efforts. At times Russia has opted for a conciliatory position toward the North, for example, sending Kim Jong Il 3 racehorses for his birthday in the midst of the 2002–03 nuclear crisis, resisting the imposition of UN sanctions, and supporting North Korean demands for U.S. security guarantees. In June 2003 Russia announced its first contribution of $11 million to the World Food Program, a portion of which will go to North Korea.[115] While such efforts earn North Korean goodwill, they reduce Russia's value as a mediator in U.S. eyes, since American officials are seeking to strengthen international pressure on Pyongyang.

Some critics of Putin's policy toward North Korea, such as Georgy Kunadze, a former ambassador to Seoul, contend that the Russian government is going too far in its effort to play a role in Korean security and trying to act as an advocate for the North Korean regime. Kunadze lamented the Soviet-style effusive praise Russian officials have been heaping on Kim Jong Il—Foreign Minister Ivanov referring to his "deep understanding of all the issues," for example—and the inattention to North Korean human rights abuses. In Kunadze's view, Russia should pursue normal relations with North Korea but use these ties to encourage Pyongyang to act more responsibly.[116]

One factor has limited Russia's role above all: both Russia and North Korea are more focused on relations with the United States than they are with each other. North Korea sought Russian support to forestall the development and deployment of U.S. missile defense systems neutralizing the North Korean deterrent. Although Russia has opposed U.S. missile defense plans, Putin had no choice but to acquiesce to the U.S. decision to withdraw from the ABM treaty and signed a new bilateral strategic arms agreement, as part of an overall improvement in Russian–American relations. While North Korea has welcomed greater Russian participation in inter-Korean relations, for Pyongyang, the resumption of dialogue with the United States is of central importance for North Korean security.

Russia has tried to achieve greater balance in its relations with North and South Korea, but this has not meant equidistance—Russian–South Korean bilateral and regional economic relations have been developing much more quickly than ties between Russia and North Korea.[117] Moscow stands to gain much more economically from improved ties with Seoul and lacks the economic resources to subsidize Pyongyang's participation in trilateral cooperation projects, such as the inter-Korean railway. To the contrary, one important motivation for Moscow's interest in such endeavors is to recover as much as possible of Pyongyang's $4 billion Soviet era debt and earn forgiveness for the USSR's debt to Seoul.[118]

Although North Korea is interested in expanding economic cooperation with Russia in energy, transportation, labor contracts, and the renovation of Soviet-built plants, much will depend on the North Korean regime's willingness to undertake the economic reforms necessary to enable it to participate more fully in economic integration projects in Northeast Asia and expanding ties with Seoul.[119]

Moreover, the continued economic decline in the Russian Far East has increased the risk of nuclear proliferation from regional bases to North Korea. Russia's inclusion in regional security dialogue, therefore, may not be a sign of its growing clout in Asia, but of the concern South Korea, Japan, and the United States have about the negative impact of instability in Russia for Asian security.[120]

Finally, the expansion of Russia's role in inter-Korean relations has been contingent on support for this process in both Seoul and Pyongyang, as well as in Washington, Beijing, and Tokyo. Nevertheless, the 2002–03 nuclear crisis, new tensions in U.S.–South Korean relations over the status of forces agreement, and the negative impact of the abduction issue on Japan–North Korean normalization, have made the already precarious security environment on the Korean peninsula even more volatile and perhaps more receptive to new initiatives, such as Russia's, to break existing deadlocks.

Notes

1. Putin Press Conference with Russian and Foreign Media, June 20, 2003, www.kremlin.ru; Dmitry Zaks, "Putin Sees Russia Assuming Global Peacemaker Role," *Agence France-Presse,* June 20, 2003.

2. ITAR-TASS, June 11, 2003.

3. Chester Crocker, Fen Osler Hampson, and Pamela Aal, "Is More Better? The Pros and Cons of Multiparty Mediation," in *Turbulent Peace: The Challenges of Managing International Conflict*, ed. Chester A. Crocker and Fes Osler Hampson et al. (Washington, DC: United States Institute of Peace, 2001), pp. 499–500.

4. On the "powerless" mediator, see Hugh Miall, Oliver Ramsbotham, and Tom Woodhouse, *Contemporary Conflict Resolution* (Cambridge, England: Polity Press, 1999), p. 10.

5. This term comes from Saadia Touval, cited in Chester Crocker, Fen Osler Hampson, and Pamela Aall, "Multiparty Mediation and the Conflict Cycle," in *Herding Cats: Multiparty Mediation in a Complex World*, ed. Crocker et al. (Washington, DC: United States Institute of Peace, 1999), p. 21. On the different roles played by mediators, also see I. William Zartman, "Bargaining and Conflict Resolution," in *Coping with Conflict after the Cold War*, ed. Edward A. Kolodziej and Roger E. Kanet (Baltimore: The Johns Hopkins University Press, 1996), pp. 279–284.

6. M.S. Gorbachev, *Izbrannye rechi i stat'i* [Collected Speeches and Articles], Tom 4 [Vol. 4], "Rech' na torzhestvennom sobranii posvyashchennom vrucheniyu Vladivostok ordena Lenina" [Speech at the Celebratory Meeting in Honor of the Award of the Order of Lenin to Vladivostok], pp. 26, 31.

7. Charles E., Ziegler, *Foreign Policy and East Asia: Learning and Adaptation in the Gorbachev Era* (Cambridge: Cambridge University Press, 1993), pp. 115–116.

8. Peggy Falkenheim Meyer, "Gorbachev and Post-Gorbachev Policy toward the Korean Peninsula: The Impact of Changing Perceptions," *Asian Survey* XXXII: 8 (August 1992), p. 760.

9. M.S. Gorbachev, "Vremya Deistvii, vremya prakticheskoy raboty (Time for Action, Time for Practical Work)," *Izbrannye rechi i stat'i* (Collected Speeches and Articles), Vol. 6, p. 564.

10. Alvin Z. Rubinstein, "Russia's Relations with North Korea," in *Imperial Decline*, ed, Stephen J. Blank and Alvin Z. Rubinstein (Durham: Duke University Press, 1997), p. 159.

11. After his return to Moscow the Soviet Foreign Ministry issued a statement noting that Moscow did not need to ask Pyongyang's permission to make foreign policy changes. Ziegler, *Foreign Policy and East Asia*, p. 123.

12. USSR Minister of Foreign Afffairs E. Shevardnadze, "Dynamics of Positive Change Called Upon to End Confrontation in the Asia-Pacific Region," *Izvestiya* (October 2), 1990: 7, in *CDSP* XLII: 40 (1990): 17.

13. "Declaration of General Principles of Relations between the Union of Soviet Socialist Republics and the Republic of Korea," *Izvestyia* (December 15), 1990: 7, in *Current Digest of the Soviet Press* (CDSP) XLII: 50 (1990): 21.

14. Ziegler, *Foreign Policy and East Asia*, p. 122.

15. Falkenheim Meyer, "Gorbachev and Post-Gorbachev Policy," p. 762.

16. Samuel S. Kim, "The Making of China's Korea Policy," in *The Making of Chinese Foreign and Security Policy in the Era of Reform, 1978–2000,* ed. David M. Lampton (Stanford: Stanford University Press, 2001), p. 379.

17. Rubinstein, "Russia's Relations with North Korea," p. 160; Ziegler, *Foreign Policy and East Asia*, p. 124. The United Nations decided on membership for the two Koreas in a package deal, after only five minutes of debate on August 8, 1991. See Samuel S. Kim, "The Emerging Northeast Asian Order and Chinese and Russian Policies toward the Korean Peninsula," *New Asia* 2: 4 (Winter 1995): 30.

18. Vasily Kononenko, "In Seoul, B. Yeltsin Proposes 23 Projects for Economic Cooperation with South Korea," *Izvestiya*, November 19, 1992, pp. 1, 4, in *CDSP* XLIV: 46 (1992): 16.

19. ITAR-TASS, June 2, 1994.

20. Elizabeth Wishnick, "A New Era in Russian-North Korean Relations?" in *North Korea and Northeast Asia*, ed. Samuel S. Kim (Boulder: Rowman & Littlefield, 2003).

21. *Interfax*, May 28, 1999.

22. *Yonhap*, May 28, 1999.

23. *Interfax*, May 28, 1999.

24. ITAR-TASS, May 30, 1999.
25. *Yonhap*, February 10, 2000.
26. Kim Sok-hwan, "The Meaning of the Russian Foreign Minister's Visit to North Korea," *Chungang Ilbo* (Seoul), FBIS-EAS-20000, February 1, 2000.
27. *Yonhap*, February 15, 2000.
28. DPRK-Russia Joint Declaration, KCNA (Pyongyang), July 20, 2000, in FBIS-SOV-2000, July 21, 2000.
29. *Yonhap* (Seoul), February 27, 2001.
30. Ko Jae-nam, "Pyongyang's Opening and North-South-Russia Cooperation," *Korea Focus* 9: 3 (May–June, 2001): 69.
31. *Interfax*, June 15, 2000.
32. Hyun-ik Hong, "Kim Jong-il's Russia Visit and South Korea's Diplomatic Strategy," *Korea and World Affairs* XXV: 3 (Fall 2001): 343.
33. ITAR-TASS, August 4, 2001.
34. *Yonhap*, January 25, 2002
35. *Agence France-Presse*, February 16, 2002.
36. Portions of Pulikovskii's memoir of the train voyage, *Orient Express,* were published in March 2002 in *Vladivostok*, a regional newspaper. See Ol'ga Mal'tseva and Leonid Vinogradov, "Konstantin Pulikovskii. Po Rossii s Kim Chen Irom (Konstantin Pulikovskii. Across Russia with Kim Jong Il)," *Vladivostok*, March 26, 2002 (Part I); March 29, 2002 (Part II), http:www.vladnew.ru.
37. Sergei Blagov, "Moscow Eyes Role as Korean Mediator," *Asia Times Online*, July 25, 2002, www.atime.com.
38. *BBC Monitoring*, August 18, 2002.
39. *ITAR-TASS*, June 28, 2003.
40. Ziegler, *Foreign Policy and East Asia*, pp. 113–114.
41. Kim, "The Emerging Northeast Asian Order and Chinese and Russian Policies toward the Korean Peninsula," 36.
42. Evgenii Bazhanov, "A Russian Perspective on Korean Peace and Security," *NAPSNet Policy Forum Online*, July 30, 1997, www.nautilus.org.
43. Seung-Ho Joo, "Russian Policy on Korean Unification in the Post-Cold War Era," *Pacific Affairs* (Spring 1996): 43–44.
44. Soo-Heon Park, "Russian Policy toward the Korean Peninsula: From Balancing to Bridge-Building between the Two Koreas," unpublished paper presented at the annual meeting of the International Studies Association, July 26–28, Hong Kong, p. 7.
45. Georgii Kaurov, "A Technical History of Soviet-North Korean Nuclear Relations," in *The North Korean Nuclear Program*, ed. James Clay Moltz and Alexandre Y. Mansourov (New York: Routledge, 2000), pp. 18–19.
46. Eugene [Evgenii] Bazhanov and Natasha Bazhanov, *Asian Survey* XXXIV: 9 (September 1994): 793.
47. Stephen Blank, "Russian Policy and the Changing Korean Question," *Asian Survey* XXXV: 8 (August 1995): 719–723. For an opposing view see Alexander Zhebin, "A Political History of Soviet-North Korean Nuclear Cooperation," in *The North Korean Nuclear Program*, ed. Moltz and Mansourov, pp. 35–36.
48. Vladimir Li, "North Korea and the Nuclear Non-Proliferation Regime," in *The North Korean Nuclear Program*, ed. Moltz and Mansourov, p. 144.
49. Evgenii Bazhanov, "Russian Views of the Agreed Framework and the Four-Party Talks," in *The North Korean Nuclear Program*, ed. Moltz and Mansourov, pp. 229–235.
50. Blank, "Russian Policy and the Changing Korean Question", 723; Vadim Tkachenko, "Russian-Korea Cooperation to Maintain the Peace on the Korean Peninsula," *Far Eastern Affairs* 3 (1999): 48.
51. Kaurov, "A Technical History", p. 20; Zhebin, "A Political History," p. 34; Bazhanov, "Russian Views of the Agreed Framework," p. 226.

52. Bazhanov, "Russian Views of the Agreed Framework," p. 225.

53. Kaurov, "A Technical History," p. 20.

54. Tkachenko, "Russian-Korean Cooperation to Maintain the Peace on the Korean Peninsula," pp. 50–51.

55. Bazhanov, "Russian View of the Agreed Framework," pp. 225–226, 228–229.

56. *Federal News Service*, June 29, 2000.

57. *Yonhap*, August 17, 2001.

58. *Reuters*, April 28, 2001.

59. *Choson Ilbo* (Seoul) April 29, 2001, *BBC Monitoring*.

60. Blagov, "Moscow Eyes Role as Korean Mediator."

61. Editorial, "Take Heed of North Korea-Russia Military Ties," *JoongAng Ilbo*, April 30, 2001, in *Korea Focus*, May–June 2001, pp. 13–14.

62. *Yonhap*, September 6, 2001.

63. *Agence France-Presse*, "North Korea Plans to Upgrade Missiles with Russian Technology: Report," April 3, 2003.

64. Mikhail Kozyrev, "Between Two Koreas," *Vedomosti*, April 27, 2001, p. A3. South Korea subsequently turned down Russian diesel subs and S-300V anti-aircraft systems.

65. *Vedmosti*, June 21, 2003, p. A3.

66. Igor Korotchenko, "Struggling for the South Korean Contract," *Nezavisimoe Voennoe Obozrenie* 40 (October 26–November 1, 2001): 1, 6.

67. Yekaterina Labetskaya and Alexander Timofeyev, "Russia Sells Arms to Seoul," *Moscow News*, September 8, 1999.

68. Michael D. Swaine with Loren H. Rumyon, "Ballistic Missiles and Missile Defense in Asia," *NBR Analysis* 13: 3 (June 2002): 44.

69. James Clay Moltz, "Russian Nuclear Regionalism: Emerging Local Influences over Far Eastern Facilities," *NBR Analysis* II: 4 (December 2000): 13.

70. Oleg Zhunusov, "Konstantin Pulikovskii, polpred president: Na Dal'nem Vostoke (Konstantin Pulikovskii, Presidential Representative to the Russian Far East)," *Izvestiya*, July 24, 2002.

71. Alexei Bogaturov, *Velikie derzhavy na tikhom okeane* (Great Powers in the Pacific), (Moscow: Institute of the USA and Canada, 1997), p. 270.

72. "Text of Japan–Russia Action Plan," *BBC Monitoring*, January 11, 2003 (from Japanese Ministry of Foreign Affairs website).

73. "2 December Sino-Russian Joint Declaration," *Xinhua*, December 2, 2003.

74. "Chinese, Russian Leaders Sign Joint Declaration—Text," *Xinhua*, May 27, 2003.

75. Felicity Barringer and David E. Sanger, "Delay by U.N. on Rebuking North Korea Is Urged," *The New York Times*, July 3, 2003, p. A8.

76. *BBC Monitoring*, July 30, 2002.

77. *Yonhap*, January 11, 2003.

78. Howard W. French, "The Two Koreas Open Cabinet-Level Talks," *The New York Times*, January 22, 2003.

79. *Agence France-Presse*, June 8, 2003.

80. *Prime-Tass News Wire*, January 13, 2003.

81. *ITAR-TASS*, April 10, 2003.

82. Vladimir Ivanov, "Russia Emerging as Energy Powerhouse," *The Daily Yomiuri*, June 14, 2003, p. 8.

83. Kengo Asakura, "Trans-Korean Pipeline Could Help Asia Energy Security, Environmental Problems," *Oil and Gas Journal*, May 15, 2000, pp. 74–77.

84. *Prime-TASS*, May 26, 2003.

85. Institute of World Economy and International Relations (IMEiMO), Moscow, and The National Institute for Research Advancement (NIRA), Tokyo, "The Northeast Asia Energy and Environmental Cooperation: Russian Approach," *Russia and Northeast Asia: Economic and Security Interdependence*, Part II (Moscow: IMEiMO, 1999), p. 15.

86. The inter-Korean rail connection to the trans-Siberian could reduce dramatically the time and cost of shipping goods to Europe, from the current 30–40 days by sea to approximately 12 days by the new train route. *Prime-TASS*, September 21, 2001.

87. *Yonhap*, September 8, 2000 in *FBIS* (East Asia), September 8, 2000. See also, Seung-Hoo Joo, "Russia and Korea: The Summit and After," p. 21. Unpublished paper presented to the 42nd annual convention of the International Studies Association, Chicago, February 20–24, 2001.

88. "Russia Offers South Korea a Shortcut to Europe," *strana.ru*, February 26, 2001.

89. Oh Day-young, "North Rail System Called Dangerous," *Joongang Ilbo*, April 9, 2002, in NAPSNet Daily Report, April 9, 2002, http://www.nautilus.org.

90. O Young-Chin, "Russia Reiterates Support for ROK's DPRK Policy," *The Korea Times* (Internet version), February 27, 2001, in *FBIS* (East Asia), February 27, 2001.

91. *Prime-TASS*, March 19, 2002.

92. Editorial, "Pitiful Expectations for Kyongui Railways," *Tong-a Ilbo*, January 18, 2002, in FBIS-EAS-2002-0118, January 18, 2002.

93. Yoo-Jae-suk, "South Korea Wants Inter-Korea Rail," AP, May 15, 2002, cited in *NAPSNet*, May 15, 2002, www.nautilus.org.

94. Russian Public TV (ORT), August 23, 2002.

95. *KCNA News Agency* (Pyongyang), December 21, 2002.

96. Reuters, "Full Steam Ahead for Rail Line," *The St. Petersburg Times*, June 17, 2003.

97. Bertil Lintner, "A Railway Line in Limbo," *The Far Eastern Economic Review*, June 12, 2003, p. 24.

98. David Aldrich, "If You Build It, They Will Come: A Cautionary Tale about the Tumen River Development Project," *Journal of East Asian Affairs* XI: 1 (Winter/Spring 1997): 303.

99. Ian Davies, "Regional Co-operation in Northeast Asia—The Tumen River Area Development Program, 1990–2000: In Search of a Model for Regional Economic Co-Operation in Northeast Asia," *North Pacific Policy Paper* 4 (Vancouver: University of British Columbia, 2000): 24–25.

100. Interviews with officials, Beijing, November 1999.

101. Larisa Zabrovskaya, *Rossiya i KNDR* (Russia and the DPRK) (Vladivostok: Far Eastern State University, 1998), p. 69.

102. James Clay Moltz, "The Renewal of Russian-North Korean Relations," in *The North Korean Nuclear Program* ed. Mansourov and Moltz, p. 203

103. *Yonhap*, March 21, 2002.

104. *Yonhap*, July 6, 1993, in FBIS-SOV-93-128, July 7, 1993.

105. Moltz, "The Renewal of Russian-North Korean Relations," p. 203.

106. Georgy Kunadze, "The Fluffy Dictator," *Novoye Vremya*, September 1, 2002, pp. 16–18.

107. Zarubin, in *The North Korean Nuclear Program*, ed. Mansourov and Moltz, p. 213; Vladimir Li, Rossiya i Koreia, p. 243; Bazhanov, in "Russian Views of the Agreed Framework", ed. Mansourov and Moltz, p. 227.

108. Joo, "Russian Policy on Korean Unification," pp. 40–41; Seung-Ho Joo, "The New Friendship Treaty between Moscow and Pyongyang," *Comparative Strategy* 20 (2001): 480.

109. Georgii Bulichev, "Koreiskaya politika Rossii: popytka skhematizatsii" (Russia's Korea Policy: An Attempt at Schematization), *Problemy Dal'nego Vostoka* (Far Eastern Affairs) 2 (2000): 9.

110. Interview with Georgiy Toloraya, Deputy Director, Foreign Ministry First Asian Department, *Vremya Novostey*, June 9, 2000, pp. 1, 6.

111. Roald Saveliev, "The New Russian Leadership's Foreign Policy and Russian-Korean Relations," *Far Eastern Affairs* 2 (2001): 11.

112. Cited in Georgiy Toloraya, "Russia and the Republic of Korea after the Seoul Summit," *Far Eastern Affairs* 2 (2001): 5.

113. Hyun-Ik Hong, "Kim Jong-Il's Russia Visit and South Korea's Diplomatic Strategy," *Korea and World Affairs* XXV: 3 (Fall 2001): 348.

114. Kang Won-sik, "South Korea-Russia Ties Neglected," *Tong-a Ilbo*, September 29, 2000, in FBIS-EAS-2000-0929, September 29, 2000; Ko Chae-nam, "Make Russia a Cooperator for National Unification," *Tong-a Ilbo*, July 20, 2000, in FBIS-EAS-2000-0721, July 20, 2000.
115. *Prime-TASS*, June 26, 2003.
116. *Kunadze,* "The Fluffy Dictator."
117. Hong, "Kim Jong-il's Russia Visit," p. 348.
118. Vasily Mikheev, "South-North Reconciliation and Prospects for North Korea-Russian Relations," *Asian Perspective* 25: 2 (2001): 40.
119. Mikheev, "South-North Reconciliation," p. 40.
120. Peggy Falkenheim Meyer, "Russia's Post-Cold War Security Policy in Northeast Asia," *Pacific Affairs* 67: 4 (Winter 1994–95): 511.

Chapter Eight

The U.S. Role in Inter-Korean Relations: Container, Facilitator, or Impeder?

Victor D. Cha

For nearly fifty years, the U.S. role in inter-Korean relations was relatively uncontroversial. The animosity in Seoul–Pyongyang relations and the Cold War structure of regional security dictated one basic algorithm: The United States guaranteed successful deterrence against a North Korean attack of the South; moreover, U.S.–South Korean unity on a policy of diplomatic isolation and non-dialogue toward the North was indisputable. But since the loosening of the diplomatic deadlock on the peninsula,[1] this basic algorithm has been called into question. Despite arguments to the contrary by policy elites, the U.S. role in inter-Korean relations has become a contested one, with the spectrum of views ranging from supporters of the Cold War template to dissenters that see the United States fundamentally as an obstacle to improvement in inter-Korean relations. The contested nature of the U.S. role became increasingly evident in the aftermath of the June 2000 North–South Korea summit's relaxation of peninsular tensions in South Korean eyes, followed by the Bush administration's designation of North Korea as part of an "axis of evil." Moreover as the South Korean presidential elections of 2002 showed, for the general public, the distinction between the United States as security guarantor and ally against the North, and as a spoiler of inter-Korean reconciliation has become muddled at best, destroyed at worst.

This chapter looks at the different roles played by the United States in inter-Korean relations. These roles could be described roughly as uncontested and contested. In the former vein, the United States played a dual role as "co-container." Inter-Korean dialogue was for all intents and purposes nonexistent because the only mode of interaction on the peninsula was one between adversarial sides. In this context, the U.S. role remained primarily one of deterrence and defense of the peninsula's security, and in inter-Korean relations, its role was limited to Washington's support of South Korean containment and isolation of the North. The second role played by the United States is as a "facilitator." Here, the basic dynamic referred to American efforts, through dialogue with the North and through entreaties to the South, to create greater interaction between the two Koreas. This was ostensibly for the purpose of reducing tensions on the peninsula. But it often emerged from alliance management needs, when an anxious South Korea did not want

U.S.–DPRK dialogue to move too far afield from North–South talks for fear that such progress would undercut South Korean leverage. The third role played by the United States is arguably as an "impeder" of North–South relations (these are contested notions). In this view, the United States is seen as the primary obstacle to improvements in inter-Korean relations. Although this view has been held by the radical fringe in Korea for some time (as well as in North Korea), I focus on this role only as it applies to mainstream public opinion in South Korea recently.

Rather than go through a historical description of these three roles for the United States, this chapter attempts to identify the variables at play that might explain the changes in the perceived U.S. role between the two Koreas over time. This forthcoming analysis is not meant to make a monocausal argument that insists dogmatically that there is one and only one variable that explains every degree of change in the U.S. role. Instead, I seek an interpretive explanation that is empirical, inductive, and, some might argue, analytically "eclectic."[2] The explanations roughly include four different factors: structural and relative capabilities-based explanations; alliance management explanations; domestic-politics explanations; and perceptual explanations. Some of these could be seen as competing explanations, others as complementary. But the idea is to provide in this fashion a comprehensive rendering of the important factors in understanding how and under what conditions changes occur in the U.S. role in inter-Korean relations. Future research can draw out from this interpretation any worthwhile testable hypotheses. In the next section, I look historically at each of the variations in the U.S. role, with a discussion of alternative explanations. I conclude with a discussion questioning the purported permanency of the current view of the American "impeder" role that became fashionable after the 2002 presidential election in South Korea.

America as Co-Container During the Cold War

The time periods for the U.S. role as co-container, facilitator, and impeder roughly correspond to major breakpoints in twentieth-century international relations.

As one might expect, the containment phase coincided with the Cold War when North–South tensions were at their height and there was little dispute over what the desired and actual role of the United States was between the two Koreas. There were brief periods during which inter-Korean relations saw some warming (i.e., July 1972 North–South joint communiqué; 1984–85 exchanges), but these were short-lived and did not amount to much change. The predominant relationship was adversarial. The South Koreans had virtually no interest in improving relations with the North. And because of this, the U.S. role in inter-Korean relations was by definition limited to support of the ally's position. On the rare occasion when Washington did pursue small gestures probing the possibility of a thaw on the

Table 8.1 U.S. role in Inter-Korean Relations (IKR)

	Strategic Environment		
	Cold War	Post–Cold War	Post-Summit
U.S. role in IKR	Co-container	Facilitator	Impeder

peninsula (i.e., in the role of facilitator), the South Koreans reacted in a strongly negative way, raising acute fears of allied abandonment in Seoul. During the detente period for example, even while the South had managed the 1972 North–South joint communiqué, they were extremely critical and suspicious of any inkling of detente spreading to the U.S.–DPRK relationship. In March 1972 Seoul immediately contested U.S. intimations that it might lift travel restrictions on North Korea. In July 1972 Foreign Minister Kim Yong-sik filed strong protests over Secretary of State Rogers's use of the formal designation "DPRK" when referring to the North. Both acts by the United States were seen as departures from past practice and were harshly criticized as the first steps toward U.S. recognition of the regime.[3]

The question arises as to why the South Koreans were so strongly opposed to the slightest deviation from the co-container role played by the United States. Part of the answer lies in a capabilities-based argument in which successive South Korean governments from Syngman Rhee to Park Chung Hee to Chun Doo Hwan experienced insecurity as a result of relative parity of power with their northern adversaries. CIA estimates put the North Korean economy, measured in per capita terms, on par with, or higher than, that of South Korea through the 1970s. The North was endowed with more mineral resources and the industrial legacy left by the Japanese. And while the South experienced political instability, coups, and the death of their chief executives, the North experienced a fairly stable leadership under Kim Il Sung. Moreover, while the North experienced the staunch support of Beijing and Moscow, the South faced the prospect of U.S. troop withdrawals contemplated during the Johnson, Nixon, and Carter administrations. This may have given rise to a zero–sum co-containment expectation by the insecure South of its ally in the United States as the only acceptable role in inter-Korean relations.

Such a capabilities-based explanation, however, does not account for the fact that by the 1980s and the 1990s the South was beginning to far outpace the North in material terms. Yet, there continued to be strict adherence to the view of the U.S. as co-container, and strong resistance in the 1990s in particular to the new American role as facilitator in inter-Korean relations.

The "Restraint" Rationale

Before looking at the U.S. role in inter-Korean relations in the 1980s and 1990s, however, it is useful at this point to note an additional role played by the United States in inter-Korean relations in the early Cold War years. In addition to undertaking the explicit function of containing North Korea, Washington also played an implicit role of containment or restraint on its ally's ambitions on the peninsula. Both the Syngman Rhee (1948–60) and Park Chung Hee governments were never shy about their desires for unification, which raised serious concerns in the U.S. government about avoiding entrapment in a second Korean conflict. In this sense, the U.S. role in inter-Korean relations was arguably as "co-container" seeking to restrain both sides while allying strongly with one. In other words, in accordance with the American security commitment to its South Korean ally, the U.S. role in inter-Korean relations was explicit and uncontested. However, there was also an implicit role that the United States played with regard to containing not just North Korea, but also *restraining its South Korean ally.*

Particularly in the early Cold War years, South Korean governments made no secret of their desire for unification by force (*pukch'in t'ongil* or *songong t'ongil*). This ambition was not just manifest in the well-known stories of Syngman Rhee refusing to sign the Armistice Treaty and deliberately trying to sabotage the negotiations during the Korean War because he wanted to prosecute the war with U.S. support to the end. It was also evident during Park Chung Hee's rule. Despite Park's renunciation of Rhee's unification by force principle and acceptance of a unification by peace principle (laid out in the July 4 North–South joint communiqué), the South Korean leader clearly considered North Korean provocations like the failed North Korean commando raid on the ROK presidential Blue House in 1968 as opportunities to retaliate against the North militarily.

The United States saw absolutely no use for inflaming a second conflagration in Asia (given the war in Vietnam), and therefore was hypersensitive to becoming potentially entrapped into a conflict by its ally's overzealous actions. Successive American administrations therefore viewed the alliance relationship with South Korea in dual terms: not merely as containment of the North but also as binding or restraining the South. This restraining rationale was evident in very specific messages sent by the Lyndon Johnson administration during the 1968 crises (e.g., the Vance mission in which Cyrus Vance was dispatched as a special envoy to tell Park that the United States would not tolerate any unilateral military retaliation by the South Koreans for the Blue House Raid).

American archival records, moreover, reveal the extent to which this preoccupation with restraining the ally was interwoven with arguments for the United States holding operational command authority within the alliance.[4] The traditional rationale for the United States holding operational command authority was not just for enhanced defensive warfighting efficiency, but also to keep a leash on unilateral offensive acts by the South Koreans.[5] It was U.S. standing policy established during the Eisenhower administration that any unilateral ROK military actions would prompt Washington to the severest of actions including the immediate cessation of economic and military aid, disassociation of the UN Command from support of ROK actions, and even the use of U.S. forces to impose martial law. NSC 5817 "Statement of U.S. Policy Toward Korea," (August 11, 1958) stated that if the ROK unilaterally initiated military operations against Chinese or North Korean forces in or north of the DMZ, then: (1) UN Command ground, sea, and air forces will not support such operations directly or indirectly; (2) the United States will not furnish any military or logistic support for such operations; (3) all U.S. economic aid to Korea will cease immediately; (4) the UN Commander will take any action necessary to prevent his forces becoming involved in the renewal of hostilities and to provide for their security.[6] In White House deliberations on the issue in the late 1950s, President Eisenhower went so far as to say that the United States would covertly support new leadership, forcibly remove Rhee, or even threaten abrogating the alliance.[7] Retaining operational control of ROK forces therefore was arguably as much a tool of alliance restraint in inter-Korean relations as it was a tool of deterrence and warfighting against the North exclusively. Admittedly, the U.S. concern about South Korean preemptive attack has abated considerably over the years (particularly after democratization in 1987) and the United States transferred peacetime authority to the South in 1994. But the point remains that the U.S. role in inter-Korean relations during the Cold War was a dual one that featured not only containment of the North, but also restraint of the South.

America as Facilitator During the Post–Cold War Era

The second role played by the United States in inter-Korean relations was as a "facilitator." Here, the basic dynamic referred to American efforts, through dialogue with the North and through entreaties to the South, to create greater interaction between the two Koreas. This was ostensibly for the purpose of reducing tensions on the peninsula. But it often emerged from alliance management needs, when an anxious South Korea did not want U.S.–DPRK dialogue to move too far afield from North–South talks for fear that such progress would undercut South Korean leverage. The strongest form of this was when the United States would make inter-Korean dialogue a precondition for improvements in U.S.–DPRK relations.

The United States as a facilitator of inter-Korean relations became most relevant in the immediate post–Cold War years. The height of this phase was probably 1993–96 during the (first) North Korea nuclear crisis and the negotiations and implementation of the Agreed Framework. The official U.S. position has been that it has always supported tension-reduction between the two Koreas. This may be true. This "theology" of American efforts at improving inter-Korean relations, however, has in practice, been greatly informed by the alliance management exigencies that come with American pursuit of non-proliferation objectives on the peninsula. In other words, U.S. desires to facilitate North–South dialogue stemmed not just from benign and ideal desires to see Korean reconciliation, but also from complaints by the allies in Seoul that the United States was pressing too fast in its own bilateral contacts with Pyongyang in a manner that excluded Seoul. The primary reason for U.S. interest in bilaterals with North Korea, in turn, largely derived from U.S. non-proliferation concerns. Hence, the United States was "facilitating" inter-Korean relations for non-proliferation reasons: In order to enable U.S.–DPRK non-proliferation negotiations, Washington needed Seoul's backing, and therefore pressed for its allies desires not to be excluded from negotiations on the peninsula.

This dynamic was especially evident during the Kim Young Sam administration. Seoul opposed any moves forward in U.S.–DPRK relations without corresponding improvements in North–South dialogue. From the ROK's perspective this asymmetry raised fears of abandonment in the context of the alliance. The concern was that the United States by moving too fast with the North was (1) undercutting Seoul's own efforts at inter-Korean dialogue; (2) giving the North the impression, by not consulting with Seoul, that the alliance was not strong; and (3) potentially being lulled into a situation where it might sacrifice South Korean security interests for some quick and easy deal with the North. For this reason, the South Koreans have always been hypersensitive to any asymmetry—real or perceived—in the two tracks. During the Agreed Framework negotiations, for example, American negotiators were acutely sensitive to avoiding any actions or discussions with the North that might be seen as alienating the South. The United States on a daily basis, debriefed its ally about negotiations with the North, and held fast to a clause in the 1994 agreement that required the North to improve North–South relations as a condition of the agreement despite eleventh hour threats by the North Koreans to trash the entire agreement if the United States did not expunge this condition. U.S. officials made deliberate efforts to consult Seoul and urge Pyongyang to dialogue with the South, but very clearly the perception in Seoul was that the inordinate pace of U.S.–DPRK relations undermined North–South dialogue. (Gong Ro-myong's first enunciation of "balance and parallel" (*choul kwa pyonghaeng*) came on the heels of replacing Foreign Minister Han Sung-joo who was unjustly held responsible for allowing the ROK to be "excluded" from talks with North Korea.) With the exception of President Kim Young-sam's first few months in office when he tried to encourage his own "Sunshine Policy," this was the case for much of his administration.

Three effects of this asymmetry in dialogues (U.S.–DPRK leading inter-Korean dialogues) therefore obtained: (1) the South sought de facto veto rights over the pace of U.S.–DPRK dialogue; (2) the leverage Seoul employed was the alliance, and in particular the U.S. obligation to alleviate allied abandonment fears in order to shore up the alliance; and (3) the result was a feeding of latent anti-Americanism at perceived high-handedness and disregard on the part of Washington, which arguably rooted the groundswell of anti-Americanism evident at the end of 2002. The irony of this dynamic was that U.S.–DPRK bilaterals leading to the Agreed Framework arguably was a necessary condition for greatly improved North–South dialogue that culminated in the June 2000 summit, but even before this, in the scheduled 1994 summit between Kim Young Sam and Kim Il Sung (prior to his death in July).

As noted earlier, the source of the South Korean opposition to the United States as "facilitator" cannot be explained purely by power variables. By virtually every measure, the South by the 1980s and 1990s dwarfed the North, yet Seoul continued to pine for the American co-container role in inter-Korean relations. If anything, power asymmetries should tell us that the wider the gap grows as it did in the Post–Cold War era, the less concerned the South should have been about the American facilitating role. In the end, these anxieties had little to do with power, nor the United States somehow "selling out" its ally's interests (how this would happen was never explained) and much more to do with what Sam Kim has termed the zero–sum mentality and the politics of competitive legitimation on the peninsula.[8] Under such conditions, any North Korean diplomatic gain was by definition an ROK loss; thus, any forward movement in U.S.–DPRK dialogue however minimal was necessarily a victory for the North over the South that was intolerable. The ROK (particularly during Kim Young Sam's administration) basically wanted all dialogue channels to Pyongyang to come through Seoul. During the Kim Young Sam years, South Korea wanted American and Japanese humanitarian food aid not to go directly to Pyongyang, but be provided through Seoul after the North first comes to Seoul to request help. During Roh Tae Woo's term there was also apprehension after Kanemaru Shin's mission to Pyongyang that the Japan track was progressing without forcing the North to talk with the South.

Seoul's Attribution Errors
While Washington's controversial role as a facilitator in inter-Korean relations took place with reference to specific issues vis-à-vis the North (e.g., food aid, ballistic

missiles, electricity, etc.), I argue that at the core, the problem was a cognitive or perceptual one. Controversy over the United States forging ahead unilaterally in its facilitating role in inter-Korean relations (i.e., forging ahead with Pyongyang at the expense of the alliance) is met by Seoul's complaints and Washington's subsequent efforts to respond to the ally's complaints and fears of abandonment. But these American efforts are subject to acute attribution errors by Seoul. For example, if the United States responds positively to the complaints—that is, the desirable behavior—this action is *not* seen by Seoul as motivated by a genuine value assigned by Washington to the alliance (dispositional), but by immediate and more pragmatic situational factors (i.e., "they were forced to respond the way we wanted, not that they wanted to"). In other words, the positive behavior is assigned little value, because the belief is that if the situational factors were not compelling, then the ally would have responded negatively rather than positively.[9]

Conversely, if Washington does not respond to the ally's complaints about its uniltateral facilitating role in inter-Korean relations—that is, undesirable behavior—this behavior is seen as representing the true disposition of the ally (assigning no value to the alliance), rather than as motivated by the situation. The result is mutual frustration as neither side feels that the ally is responding in a genuine fashion.

Arguably, this attribution error occurs more consistently on the South Korean side vis-à-vis the American facilitator role in inter-Korean relations. This is a function of power disparities (note: the power disparities here are within the alliance, not between the two Koreas). In general, it is more difficult to placate the abandonment fears of a smaller ally than a larger one. Smaller allies are much more likely to become subject to a spiral of insecurity stemming from the fundamental attribution error. If the great power ally does not address the smaller ally's concerns, this validates fears of abandonment. On the other hand, if the great power does offer reassurance, the smaller ally is still unsatisfied—it sees these reassurances not as dispositionally motivated (i.e., an earnest attempt by the ally to reassure), but as situationally determined (i.e., the ally reassured not because it wanted to but because the situation dictated it).

Attribution errors abound in the history of the U.S. role in inter-Korean relations. As early as 1972, for example, South Korean president Park Chung Hee protested strongly at American intimations at promoting a slight thaw in inter-Korean relations (pursuant to the atmosphere of detente created by Nixon's visit to China, Secretary of State Rogers made reference to North Korea by its official title—DPRK—for the first time).[10] In response to Seoul's complaints, the United States stopped any further initiatives in inter-Korean relations. Rather than taking comfort in the U.S. response, however, Seoul interpreted the American response as situational—that is, Washington discontinued the probes with Pyongyang largely because they realized the dialogue was fruitless, not because of Seoul's complaints. The Park government did not interpret the American response as dispositional—that is, a genuine understanding of allied abandonment concerns.

Attribution errors were evident in the Clinton administration as well. During the U.S.–DPRK negotiations on the Agreed Framework, for example, the Kim Young Sam government complained vigorously about how the United States was pressing forward with dialogue with the DPRK and leaving Seoul behind. National Assembly members screamed about how the Americans were pursuing their own narrow non-proliferation interests on the peninsula at the expense of relations with their South Korean ally.[11]

America as Impeder During the Post-Summit Period

The third role played by the United States on the peninsula is as an "impeder" of North–South relations (these are contested notions). In this view, the United States is seen as the primary obstacle to improvements in inter-Korean relations. Although this view has been held by the radical leftists in South Korea for some time (as well as in North Korea), I focus on this role only as it applies to mainstream public opinion in South Korea recently. The strong form of this is when the United States makes statements or takes actions on the peninsula that not only are seen as impeding relations but also are seen as unnecessarily inflaming tensions on the peninsula.

Most view the role of the United States as impeder becoming salient from mid-2000 after the June inter-Korean summit. It became more salient after January 2001 with the confluence of two critical factors. First, Kim Dae Jung's Sunshine Policy, based firmly in an *ideology of unconditional* engagement with the North facilitated the June 2000 meeting, which at the time far exceeded anyone's expectations. The summit's joint declaration, family reunions, joint infrastructure projects, and ministerial meetings propelled North–South relations forward by leaps and bounds. What distinguished the policy was its explicit nonzero–sum view of interaction with the North. Not only did the South eschew any pretense of making engagement conditional, but also denied any need for dialogue channels to come through Seoul only. The Sunshine Policy had no objection to all forms of world engagement with the reclusive regime. This was a far cry from the fixation of previous South Korean administrations on the relative pace of North–South dialogue compared with others.

The Sunshine Policy had the unintended consequence of creating nation-wide perceptions of the United States as an impediment to inter-Korean relations. As noted earlier, this view started to be cemented with the first summit between Bush and Kim in March 2001. Kim tried to lecture the newly inaugurated Bush administration of the Sunshine Policy's wisdom that was spectacularly unsuccessful. Bush then called a "time-out" on Clinton's engagement with the North and completed a policy review in June 2001 that stated a nominal offer to meet with the North Koreans anytime, anyplace and without precondition. But President Bush's January 2002 "axis of evil" speech reduced the chances for dialogue (even though the North had announced earlier that it was not interested in meeting with the United States because of its high-handed attitude).

What emerged from the Sunshine Policy was therefore a dual dynamic reinforcing the U.S. role as impeder in inter-Korean relations. On the one hand, the success of the policy created the impression that the United States' overbearing military footprint on the Korean peninsula was no longer necessary. Indeed, during summer 2000 in the aftermath of the summit, numerous demonstrations sprouted up at U.S. military facilities protesting the American presence. In addition, the memories of the U.S. role as savior during the Korean War were explicitly extinguished on what was then to be the fiftieth anniversary of the Korean War (the ROK government ordered a toning down of the celebrations because of the newfound detente with the North).

On the other hand, however, when the Sunshine Policy proved to be less successful than initially believed in terms of eliciting North Korean reciprocation, the popular response was to look for scapegoats—of which the U.S. presence and Bush's axis of evil statements were seen as a prime target.

A second critical factor contributing to the view of the United States as impeder was a "decoupling" dynamic in the alliance. In short, U.S. and ROK security interests on the peninsula had always been dissimilar. The ROK's first priority was peninsular defense whereas for the United States, the key concern, particularly in the post–Cold War era, was the proliferation threat posed by the North. The concern about North Korea as a proliferation threat transformed into concern about the North as a homeland security threat after September 11. This is not to argue that the two sides do not share similar security interests in deterring a second North Korean invasion of the peninsula. But while this contingency has been effectively deterred, the gaps in the two allies' views on proliferation have become more clear. The South Koreans' view of the U.S. hard-line policy toward the North is not seen as justified in large part because the Sunshine Policy, in their eyes, reduced the primary threat posed to the South (i.e., another conventional invasion) even though it may not have appeased all American concerns about the longer-range threats still posed by the North. This decoupling of U.S. non-proliferation concerns from that of South Korea contributes to Seoul's view of the United States as unduly "spoiling" the inter-Korean party after the June 2000 summit.

The changes in the roles played by the United States on the peninsula is therefore in good part a function of the current state of combined interests at the time. Whether the United States is a facilitator or impeder at the core is determined by disparate perceptions of what interests are at stake at the given moment. With the containment role, there is little difference in interests. But in the facilitation phase, the United States is often seen in the South as delinking their proliferation interests from South Korea's. And in the impediment phase, is seen as delinking its peninsular interests from U.S. homeland security interests on the peninsula.

America as the Permanent Obstacle?

Is this perception of the United States as an impediment to North–South reconciliation a permanent one in Korea? A snapshot of the political scene at the end of 2002 and beginning of 2003 might lead one to believe so. Political maverick and former labor activist lawyer Roh Moo-hyun was elected upon a clear wave of anti-Americanism

Table 8.2 Images of the United States and North Korea

	United States	*North Korea*
Positive	37.2	47.4
Negative	53.7	37
Don't Know	9.1	15.6

Source: *Gallup Korea Survey* (1054 sample size), December 2002.

Table 8.3 Negative attitudes toward the United States and North Korea by age distribution

Age	United States	North Korea
20s	76	32
30s	67	29
40s	53	39
50s+	26	47

Source: *Gallup Korea* (December 2002).

and his campaign rhetoric, very critical of Bush's "axis of evil" designation of North Korea, appeared to resonate with a broad-based constituency in South Korea. Perhaps for the first time in South Korean political history, it appeared to many, particularly young Koreans, that the Americans were more threatening to the country than the communist threat from across the DMZ. December 2002 polls showed that more South Koreans harbored negative images of the United States than they did of North Korea.

On 2003 New Year's Eve, 23,000 Koreans gathered in the vicinity of the American Embassy in Seoul in a candlelight demonstration demanding the Bush administration's apology for the deaths and revision of the SOFA. Nowhere was this view more epitomized than in the CBS's 60-Minutes story that caught a group of young Koreans self-righteously responding to a loaded question that President Bush was more scary to them than Kim Jong-Il.[12] Public opinion polls a fortnight after the election of Roh painted the picture of a changing demographic in which a younger "post–Korean War" generation informed with a less grateful, more critical view of the United States had risen to political significance.[13] While 26 percent of middle-aged South Koreans held negative images of the United States, an astounding 76 percent of youth in their twenties and 67 percent of those in their thirties responded in a similar fashion (see table 8.3).

Moreover, 51 percent of South Koreans who polled believed that North Korea's nuclear intransigence at the end of 2002 and beginning of 2003 was the result of the Bush administration's hard-line policy (only 24.6 percent attributed the problem to North Korean actions and intentions).[14] Implicit in these numbers, some might argue, is the counter-factual argument that North–South reconciliation post–June 2000 summit would be entirely conceivable if not for the overbearing American preoccupation with proliferation issues role on the peninsula. Or as one conservative commentator characterized the radical position: "There is no task more urgent than the reunification of the Korean nation, and the greatest obstacles to unification are the United States and its politics of strength."[15]

Not Yet

A deeper and nuanced analysis of the situation, however, would look beyond the heat of the presidential election campaign at the end of 2002 and look in particular for longer-term trends that either confirm or disconfirm what had transpired. Here I would argue that the situation may not be as bleak as commonly believed.

For the U.S. role as "impeder" in North–South relations to be permanent, one would expect to observe two continuing trends. At the "street" or general public level, a growing and unconditional dissatisfaction with the U.S. military presence in Korea should be ever present because this would represent the embodiment of the American "impeder" role as viewed by the post–Korean War generation. And at the elite level, a widening gap in policy toward North Korea between Washington and Seoul should be evident as Roh pursues engagement in defiance of a harder-line position taken by the Bush administration.

Neither of these trends are indisputably evident, contrary to the popular perception. First, at the street level, there is no denying the groundswell of dissatisfaction at the U.S. military presence expressed through burnings of flags and effigies of George Bush, and the demonstrations in downtown Seoul. The proximate event fueling this movement was the acquittal by U.S. military trial of two servicemen for the accidental vehicular death of two South Korean schoolgirls in November 2002. The popular outrage over this outcome, fueled by the heat of presidential campaign rhetoric, turned one dimension of election into a choice between the so-called "pro-American" Lee Hoi-chang and so-called "anti-American" Roh Moo-hyun.[16]

What is most interesting, however, about the public anger and demonstrations at Yongsan at the end of 2002 is that they were soon followed by "counterdemonstrations" by other South Korean nongovernmental groups expressing support for the American presence in Korea and calling for continuation of the long-standing alliance. These demonstrations, organized by Korean War veterans groups and religious groups numbering in the tens of thousands, wanted to make clear that the protest activities seen by the world at the end of 2002 did not represent all of Korean public opinion, and that a "silent majority" of Koreans still strongly supported the United States. On January 8, 2003, 1000 Koreans rallied outside the US military base at Osan, burning a North Korean flag and waving pro-U.S. banners. On January 11, a rally of 30,000-strong Christians gathered in the vicinity of the U.S. Embassy in a show of "pro-Americanism." The following week, the largest pro-U.S. rally ever of nearly 100,000 (according to organizers) gathered in Seoul supporting the U.S military presence in Korea, referring to Americans as "blood brothers," and equating support for the alliance with peace in Korea (rather than the association with war, as anti-American demonstrations had done). And on the weekend after the presidential inauguration in February, civic groups planned a rally of nearly one million in Seoul, including former prime ministers, university presidents, democracy civic groups and veterans affairs associations, in favor of the United States.[17] Polls in 2003, one year after the death of the two Korean schoolgirls, show a marked change in attitudes. While 78 percent of twenty-something Koreans in December 2002 had negative perceptions of the United States, in June 2003, this number had shrunk to 39 percent. Moreover, 48.5 percent of South Koreans in June 2003 supported the Bush administration's policies toward North Korea (see table 8.4 and 8.5).

Two key observations are worth noting from these events. First, anti-Americanism is a much more contested, and far less one-dimensional notion than popular perception gives it credit for. And second, views on the United States in Korea are far from zero–sum. Nowhere was this more apparent than in April 2003 when civic groups organized another anti-North Korean, pro-U.S. rally in front of Seoul's city hall; and

Table 8.4   South Korean attitudes toward the United States (June 2003)

	Negative *(20 year-olds)*	*Positive* *(20 year-olds)*	*Neutral*	*Comments*
June 2003	27.6 (39.0)	25.4 (21.1)	46.9	In December 2002, negative perceptions of the United States among 20 year-olds was 76 % (see table 8.3)

Source: *JoongAng Ilbo* (English Edition), July 26, 2003, p. 8.

Table 8.5   South Korean views of the Bush administration's policy toward North Korea

	Strongly *disapprove*	*Generally* *disapprove*	*Generally* *approve*	*Strongly* *approve*
June 2003	9.4	39.0	37.3	11.2

Source: *JoongAng Ilbo* (English Edition), July 26, 2003, p. 8.

Table 8.6   Attitudes on the withdrawal of U.S. forces from Korea

Age	*In favor of* *withdrawal*	*Opposed to* *withdrawal*	*Don't know/not* *applicable*
20s	47.2	42.4	10.4
50+	13.4	67.6	19.1
All	31.7	54.8	13.6

Source: *Gallup Korea* (December 2002).

only a few blocks away, another demonstration (near the Kyobo building in Gwanghwamun) protested the South Korean dispatch of troops to the Iraq war.[18] The point is that the reality of the situation in South Korea is that, as the "pro-American" demonstrations showed, one can strongly support the United States and its presence in Korea in spite of disagreeing with its policy toward North Korea. And as the "anti-American" demonstrations showed, one can oppose inequities in the alliance and demand revision of SOFA, but at the same time support the alliance. Civic group leaders who organized the demonstrations in December 2002 noted exactly this point. Indeed, polls at the height of anti-American sentiment in this month still showed a clear majority of respondents (55 percent) still supporting a U.S. troop presence (see table 8.6).[19]

If the U.S. role as "impeder" to Korean peace were truly permanent, then neither of these observations should be pertinent. In other words, one would expect that anti-Americanism would be an uncontested "truth" rather than a contested proposition. And views on the U.S. presence and alliance would be zero–sum and one-sided.

Kathy Moon has referred to this as the distinction between "banMi" anti-Americanism and "biMi" anti-Americanism.[20] The former term refers to a deeper ideological and hegemonic view of the United States. Had this been what was represented in Korea, then the U.S. role as "impeder" would be permanent. The latter term refers less to an ideological opposition to the United States and more to a critical, yet supportive view. Arguably, not only is this latter view less severe, but it is actually healthy for the alliance. "Bimi" anti-Americanism is arguably a product of the development and democratization of South Korea. The emergence of a young, affluent generation that is educated and views quality of life issues such as the environment, labor, and rule of law as critical to the national agenda. Sometimes referred to as part of the 3-8-6 generation (thirty-somethings, went to college in the 1980s and born in the 1960s), this generation's views naturally will tend to bump up against some of the more anachronistic aspects of a Cold War alliance that puts a major foreign military presence in the heart of the host nation's capitol city. In this sense, South Korean complaints represent growing pains within the alliance as the junior partner matures, rather than a permanent fissure in the relationship.

The backpedaling in the South Korean viewpoint on U.S. troops, evident particularly from March 2003, offers another lesson about how deep and zero–sum anti-American views may run. A number of prominent conservative American commentators filled the pages of major newspapers with op-eds criticizing the South Koreans as ungrateful allies and calling for the pullout of U.S. troops after the anti-American demonstrations at the end of 2002.[21] This was followed by explicit references in early March 2003 by Defense Secretary Donald Rumsfeld that "adjustments" in the U.S. presence on Korea were being considered, and a movement within the Pentagon and State Department bureaucracy toward serious study and plans for changing the presence on the peninsula.[22]

If the United States were viewed truly as an impediment to inter-Korean relations, one would expect the popular response to be somewhat welcoming of these steps. On the contrary, South Koreans from all walks of life, expressed vehement opposition to U.S. plans. In an unusual public plea, ROK Prime Minister Goh Kun, on behalf of the new Roh government, asked Ambassador Hubbard on March 6 that the United States not withdraw forces from Korea. Newly elected President Roh, who during the campaign called for a more equal relationship with the United States, and pointedly asked the top ROK military brass whether they had prepared for self-reliant defense, called for an end to anti-U.S. vigils in Seoul. As one observer noted, "The anti-American demonstrations here have suddenly gone poof. U.S. soldiers are walking the streets of Seoul again without looking over their shoulders. The official line from the South Korean government is: Yankees stay here."[23] If anything, a permanent U.S. "impeder" view should have given rise to at least conditional welcoming of the U.S. plans, but not the sort of unadulterated opposition that was evident.

Second, a permanent U.S. "impeder" role would suggest greater gaps in the Roh government's policies toward North Korea and that of the Bush administration. Most certainly, the campaign rhetoric gave the impression that the gaps would be quite wide, but in actuality, since Roh has taken office, the gaps have closed with a distinct moderating in the Roh government's attitudes toward both the North Korea issue and as alluded to earlier, the relationship with the United States. Just after the December election, Roh met with anti-American civic groups and called for moderation. Despite campaign statements that he would not meet with Americans purely for photo opportunities, Roh did just that on January 15, 2003 stating that in spite of this past position supporting a U.S. troop pullout as a human rights lawyer, Roh acknowledged that "US troops are necessary at present for peace and stability on the Korean peninsula and will be in the future as well."[24] After North Korea's three cruise missile tests in February–March 2003, the ROK president criticized such actions and stated that the prospect of a nuclear North Korea is unacceptable. In terms of critical foreign policy advisors, the president chose experience over ideology, and individuals with substantial understanding and interaction with the United States.[25] He supported publicly the U.S. war in Iraq and in a controversial decision, agreed to dispatch a contingent of noncombatant forces to the country. Despite explicit pledges to maintain a primary role for the South Koreans in "mediating" talks between the North and the United States, Roh not only acceded to being excluded from the U.S.–North Korea–China talks in Beijing (April 23–24, 2003), but also defended the format by saying that substance was more important than form. And in an extraordinary public admission in an interview with the *New York Times* during his first summit trip to the United States, Roh admitted that his signing of a declaration in his past activist days calling for the removal of U.S. forces from the Korean peninsula was a "mistake."[26]

Granted at the time of this writing, we are still early in the Roh government and things could change rapidly. But there is no denying that since December 2002, there has been substantial moderation in the position of the Roh leadership. Indeed expectations of the gaps to come in U.S.–South Korea relations in December 2002 have been replaced in April 2003 by new confidence in the relationship. When this author wrote an op-ed in the *Washington Post* the day after the South Korean election predicting such a moderation in policy of the new ROK government, few if any believed such a prediction.[27]

If the impeder role for the United States in inter-Korean relations were permanent, one would not expect this sort of outcome, particularly given the current government's ideological beliefs. Again, this assessment is greatly handicapped by the fact that the Roh government is only several months old; U.S.–ROK relations have yet to be fully tested by the North Korea crisis and bilateral meetings, but the question naturally arises as to why the moderation in Roh's position thus far has been so marked, contrary to what many experts had predicted.

There are a variety of factors that could explain this moderation. These range from the differentiation between campaign promises made by candidates and their actual policies, to the "politics meets reality" argument that new leaders taking office for the first time often find the policies they may have criticized are the way they are for a reason. But there are also three longer-term factors that deserve consideration.

First, and perhaps most important as a facilitating condition, is the fact that South Korea is a vibrant democracy. Roh Moo-hyun, as chief executive, contends with a very different support base than he did during the election campaign. In the most parsimonious terms, his policies need to represent the majority of the country rather than a more narrow local constituency. This basic dynamic is common to most liberal democracies and resonates with recent Korean political history. Many were deeply concerned in 1998 when Kim Dae-jung took office that his past views and beliefs would lead to extremely difficult policies with the United States. But Kim, as Roh has done, made appointments across the political aisle, moved more to the Center, and ended his presidency as pro-American as any other president in South Korea's modern political history. In this sense, the moderation of political maverick Roh is as much a function of the moderating impulses of the democratic system as much as they are the exigencies of political cycles.

Second, although political leaders change in South Korea, geography does not. Korea, whether divided or united, will remain a relatively smaller country in a region of great powers all contending for influence on the peninsula. Historically, Korea has contended with this geostrategic environment with one of two grand strategies. One of these has been a policy of isolation or neutrality (hence, the "hermit kingdom"), trying to remove itself from the region's power politics. This proved relatively unsuccessful (and arguably is still practiced in North Korea today). The other strategy has been to ally with one of the great powers. This strategy was fairly successful vis-à-vis China pre-twentieth century, and it was clearly a successful strategy in the postwar era turning the South into the most vibrant liberal-democracy in Asia and the fourth largest economy in Asia, twelfth largest in the world. In the future, it behooves Korea's interests to continue placing their "bets" on a relationship with the great power in the region that is the furthest away and shares the same political and market values, and regime-type as the United States. Detractors might argue for a different strategic choice, but this is largely a reactionary view that does not take account of the powerful, almost indisputable logic of the alliance with the United States. This geostrategic logic inclines toward moderation in the new president Roh's view on the alliance when compared with his past views. Nowhere was this more evident than in his admission in May 2003 that his past opposition to the alliance was misconceived.[28]

Third, Roh's moderation is intimately tied to economic development imperatives, particularly with regard to policies toward North Korea. At the beginning of 2003, it was clear that the crisis over North Korea was having a vastly negative effect on the South Korean economy. Roh's desires to continue South Korea's slow but steady recovery from the financial crisis of 1997–98 is perhaps his most important domestic objective (indeed voter exit polls named this to be the highest priority issue). Arguably, South Korea has made the most serious internationally recognized efforts at reforming the economy, yet much of the international confidence in these efforts were being undermined by North Korean agitations.

On February 11, Moodys downgraded South Korea's country outlook for the first time after successive years of positive assessments since the financial crisis some five years ago. The following week, Standard and Poor's (S&P) did not increase Korea's foreign currency and local corporation credit rating, and cut back expected growth outlook from 5.7 percent to 5 percent. What makes this fairly innocuous judgment significant is that S&P upgraded Korea's credit rating the year prior (to A-) and its general country outlook to stable, leading many experts to bank on further upgrades given improvements in South Korean credit fundamentals in the public and private sectors, and progress in corporate restructuring.

The primary reason for these sober assessments? S&P Director Takahira Ogawa could not have been more direct, stating "There is a risk from the North, which constrains the sovereign rating of South Korea." Those who think that an eternally optimistic South Korean government, committed to the peaceful status quo and engagement with North Korea, will be able to muddle through are sorely mistaken. All it took was one short-range missile test by Pyongyang into the Sea of Japan for the KOSPI (Korean Composite Stock Market Price Index) to tumble almost 4 percent (24 points) in one day despite a litany of parallel confidence-inducing events including Roh Moo-hyun's inauguration, the U.S. announcement of the resumption of food aid to the North, and Secretary Powell's statements in Seoul that the United States would eventually seek to dialogue with North Korea.

After North Korea's second short-range missile test last month, the Korean stock market dropped to its lowest level in 16 months; the Japanese Nikkei closed at its lowest level in 20 years, and the Korean won depreciated to a four-month low. Wall Street investment houses, including JP Morgan, Merrill Lynch, Goldman Sachs, and ABN AMRO, all issued reports in the first quarter of 2003 advising investors to shed Korean shares (despite acknowledging that these shares were undervalued).[29] Investment from the United States tumbled 72 percent during the January–March 2003 quarter and the Korean stock market dropped by 18.3 percent.[30] South Korean economic growth estimates are predicted to shrink to 1.4 percent from 6.2 percent in 2002.

The economics of the North Korean threat therefore suggest that gaps between the United States and South Korea may narrow. As has been frequently noted, Seoul and Washington may not share identical interests with regard to North Korean proliferation, but this does not rule out the possibility that they could care about the same thing for different reasons. Roh's presidency is five years according to the Korean constitution, but his immediate tenure is one year before the next general elections in 2004. And the primary issue for voters is continuing the slow but steady recovery of the economy since the 1997–98 financial crisis (according to voter exit polls at the presidential elections in December 2002). If North Korea continues to agitate in ways that hurt international investor confidence in South Korea and growth, then there is a limit to which the South Korean public and elite can continue to blame the United States as an impeder in inter-Korean relations, rather than blaming North Korea for the problems. Some might contend that these imperatives would push South Korea in the direction of appeasing the North to avert further destabilizing actions. But the opposite appears to be taking place. During Roh's May 2003 visit to the United States, he admitted that he was not naive about North Korea's record of ignoring agreements and that he "doesn't trust North Korea that much."[31] The point is not that this is the assured direction in which inter-Korean and U.S.–ROK relations are likely to go. Far from it. The point is that there is a strong counterargument laid out above for why the elite gaps between the United States and the ROK on North Korea may narrow. And initial evidence at the start of the Roh presidency offers some confirming evidence. The narrowing of such gaps lends credence to the view that the U.S. role as impeder between the two Koreas may be less permanent than many of the younger generation are led to believe.

Notes

1. This is loosely defined as the shift toward greater fluidity in dialogue around the peninsula that started with Soviet and Chinese recognition of the South in 1990 and 1992; the

beginnings of Japan and U.S. dialogue with the North, and of course, North–South dialogue culminating with the 2000 summit.

2. Peter Katzenstein and Nobuo Okawara, "Japan, Asia-Pacific Security, and the Case for Analytical Eclecticism," *International Security* 26: 3 (Winter 2001/02): 153–185.

3. For further discussions, see Victor Cha, *Alignment Despite Antagonism: The US–Korea–Japan Security Triangle* (Stanford, CA: Stanford University Press, 1999), ch. 4. Also see *FEER* July 1, 1974 ("America in Asia 1974," Kim Sam-o "Credibility Gap"); and *Korea Herald* March 12, 1972 ("Travel Ban Easing on North Korea Favored").

4. This section is based on American archival documents declassified from the Eisenhower administration. Although these archives have been available for some time, I believe this is the first analysis of the "restraint" aspect of the U.S.–ROK alliance that utilizes these materials about U.S. contingency plans on South Korean governments.

5. Operational command authority dates back to the outset of the Korean War when Syngman Rhee (July 14, 1950) transferred authority over Korean forces to the commander in chief of UN Forces. In the aftermath of a mutual defense treaty (October 1953), the two governments signed a memorandum of understanding giving operational control authority over ROK forces to the UN Command (November 1954). In 1961, this understanding was revised to pertain only to control authority over forces to defend against an external communist invasion.

6. NSC 5817 "Statement of U.S. Policy Toward Korea," August 11, 1958 in *FRUS, 1958–1960* Vol. XVIII, document 237, p. 485.

7. The provision regarding covert support of alternative leadership to Rhee (in the event he planned unilateral action) was first contained in a president-approved revision of an 1953 NSC policy document on Korea (NSC 170/1 Annex A). See NSC 170/1 "US Objectives and Courses of Action in Korea," November 20, 1953, in *FRUS 1952–1954*, pp. 1620–1624. The revision stated: "d. To select and encourage covertly the development of new South Korean leadership prepared to cooperate in maintaining the armistice, and if Rhee initiates or is about to initiate unilateral action, assist such new leadership to assume power, by means not involving overt U.S. participation until and unless U.S. overt support is necessary and promises to be decisive in firmly establishing such new leadership." This provision was considered extremely sensitive and circulated only to the Secretaries of State and Defense, Chairman of the Joint Chiefs of Staff, and Director of Central Intelligence. Subsequent NSC policy reviews on Korea made reference to the annex (later known as annex F) as regular practice, but the actual contents were kept separate. The internal instructions noted, "This revision is being disseminated only to [selected] addressees..., and it is requested that special security precautions be observed in the handling of this memorandum and that access to it be very strictly limited on an absolute need-to-know basis." ("Memorandum from the Acting Executive Secretary of the National Security Council (Gleason) to the Secretary of State, February 18, 1955," in *FRUS, 1955–1957*, Vol. XXII, document 21, pp. 37–38. The provision about U.S. unilateral abrogation of the treaty took place in the context of deliberations a couple of years later on revising NSC 5817, which was then standing policy on Korea (revised as NSC 5907). See NSC 5907 July 1, 1959 "Statement of U.S. Policy Toward Korea," *FRUS, 1958–1960*, document 279, pp. 571–579. Also see superceding policy document NSC 6018, November 28, 1960, which carried the same provisions (*FRUS 1958–1960*, Vol. 18, document 334, pp. 699–707).

8. On these two aspects of North–South competition, see Samuel Kim, "North Korea in 1999: Bringing the *Grand Chollima* March Back In," *Asian Survey* 40: 1 (January/February 2000): 151–163; and "North Korean Informal Politics," in *Informal Politics in East Asia*, ed. Lowell Dittmer, Haruhiro Fukui, and Peter N.S. Lee (New York: Cambridge University Press, 2000), pp. 237–268.

9. Fritz Heider, *The Psychology of Interpersonal Relations* (London: Lawrence Erlbaum Associates, 1958). Jones and Davis referred to this as correspondent inference theory. See

Edward E. Jones and Keith E. Davis, "From Acts to Dispositions: The Attribution Process in Person Perception," *Advances in Experimental Social Psychology 2*, ed. L Berkowitz (New York: Academic Press, 1965), pp. 219–266. Also see Edward E. Jones and Victor A. Harris, "The Attributes of Attitudes," *Journal of Experimental Psychology* 3 (January 1967): 1–24. Robert Jervis and Jonathan Mercer have applied these social psychology findings to international relations generally and to alliance theory specifically. Building on attribution error dynamics and the actor-observer bias, Mercer has argued that *between allies, we tend to interpret undesirable behavior by the other as dispositional and desirable behavior by the other as situational.* The reason, as Mercer argues, has largely to do with cognitive constraints we face in distinguishing between what motivates our actions versus what motivates other's actions. Robert Jervis, *Perception and Misperception in International Politics* (Princeton: Princeton University Press, 1976); and Jonathan Mercer, *Reputation and International Politics* (Ithaca, NY: Cornell University Press, 1996), pp. 48–53.

10. For the history, see Cha, *Alignment Despite Antagonism*; and Oberdorfer, *The Two Koreas.*
11. Leon Sigal, *Disarming Strangers* (Princeton: Princeton University Press, 1998) chapter 3. Source: CBS, 60 Minutes, aired February 8, 2003.
12. 60 Minutes, aired February 8, 2003.
13. For example, according to polls in early 2003, 58.7% of Koreans in their twenties and thirties viewed the Korean War as a proxy war between the United States and Soviet Union (versus a national average of 44.5%) rather than as the result of an illegitimate armed invasion by the North (24.2% versus a national average of 31.2%). See *Chosun Ilbo-Gallup* Korea polls, published January 1, 2003 at http://www.gallup.co.kr/News/2003/release004.html.
14. See MBC-Korea Research Center polls aired January 1, 2003.
15. Cited in Choong Nam Kim, "Changing Korean Perceptions of the Post-Cold War Era and the US-ROK Alliance," *East-West Center Analysis* 67 (April 2003): 5.
16. This was, of course, neither the only dimension of the 2002 presidential campaign, nor the demonstrations in Seoul at the time. In the case of the campaign, for voters the main priority affecting voter choice (according to exit polls) was not the United States or policy toward North Korea, but economic recovery from the financial crisis (followed by rooting corruption out of the government and society). The demonstrations also were more than an embodiment of anti-Americanism, as popularly portrayed in the media. Instead, they were seen by many scholars and public commentators in Asia as an expression of a new youthful Korean identity. The catalyst for this arguably was not the two Korean schoolgirls' death but rather the World Cup and the Korean national team's unexpected success. The outpouring of nationalism that accompanied this event became hard to differentiate from the "peace demonstrations" that soon followed the World Cup rallies in downtown Seoul. See Han Sang Jin and Koo Hagen, papers presented at the Hawaii Korean Centennial Conference, January 2003.
17. *Korea Herald*, February 26, 2003 (Kyung-Ho Kim, "Conservatives Push to Keep US Troops"); *UPI*, January 20, 2003 (Jong-Heon Lee, "Anti-U.S. Sentiment Cooling in South Korea"); *AP* January 11, 2003 (Sang-Hun Choe, "Tens of Thousands of South Korean Christians Rally to Support U.S. Military, Condemn North Korea"); *Agence France Press*, January 8, 2003 (Jae-Hwan Kim, "Pro-US Demonstrators Burn North Korean Flag Outside American Air Base").
18. *BBC*, April 19, 2003 ("South Korean Groups Hold Rallies Against North Korea, US War in Iraq").
19. *Hankook Ilbo*, December 28, 2002 ("NYT Editorial on US Troop Pullout Sparks Controversy"); and December 24, 2002 ("55% Of South Koreans Want US Troops to Stay").
20. Katherine Moon (Department of Political Science, Wellesley College), "Political Sociology of USFK-Korea Relations," unpublished paper presented at the Ilmin Institute, Korea University, November 7, 2002.

21. Richard Allen, "Seoul's Choice: The U.S. or the North," *New York Times*, January 16, 2003; William Safire, "Three-Ring Circus," *New York Times*, January 2, 2003; Buchanan & Press Show, *MSNBC* aired January 3, 2003, 2 PM EST; Meet the Press, NBC aired January 5, 2003, 10AM EST.

22. *Christian Science Monitor*, March 10, 2003 (Robert Marquand, "Rethinking US Troops in S. Korea").

23. *Washington Post*, March 14, 2003 (Doug Struck, "Anti-U.S. Sentiment Abates in South Korea; Change Follows Rumsfeld Suggestion of Troop Cut"); *New York Times*, March 7, 2003 (James Brooke, "Musing on an Exodus of G.I.'s, South Korea Hails US Presence"). Granted, part of this newfound opposition was due to fears that the United States might preemptively attack North Korea, but this argument made little sense. First, U.S. statements intimated a repositioning rather than withdrawal of U.S. forces, in which case, they would still be vulnerable to North Korean counter-attack. Second, a repositioning of some 17,000 U.S. troops away from the DMZ would not remove the deterrent to a U.S. preemptive attack as the entire American expatriate community (numbering some 20,000), not to mention South Koreans, would still be acutely vulnerable to North Korean artillery.

24. *Agence France Presse*, January 15, 2003 (Kwanwoo Jun, "South Korean President-Elect Roh Softens Anti-US Image").

25. The appointment of Sung-Joo Han as ambassador to the United States offers a small example of the change in thinking. At the time of then-president-elect Roh's special envoy delegation's trip to Washington, members of the delegation scoffed at the idea that someone identified as a more conservative, establishment-type might be chosen for this post, and yet only a few months later, this was exactly the president's choice.

26. *New York Times*, May 13, 2003 (David Sanger, "South Korean Leader Wants US Troops to Stay, for Now").

27. Victor D. Cha, "Stay Calm on Korea," *Washington Post*, December 20, 2002.

28. Interview with *New York Times*, May 13, 2003 (David Sanger, "South Korean Leader Wants U.S. Troops to Stay, for Now").

29. *Chosun Ilbo*, March 18, 2003 (Na Ji-hong, "Global Securities Firms Pessimistic on Korean Shares").

30. *AP*, April 4, 2003 ("Foreign Investment in South Korea Falls").

31. *New York Times*, May 13, 2003 (David Sanger, "South Korean Leader Wants US Troops to Stay, for Now").

THE LEGAL AND INSTITUTIONAL APPROACH TO INTER-KOREAN RELATIONS

Jeong-Ho Roh

Introduction

The year 2003 was notable for marking the fiftieth anniversary of the "end" of the Korean War. An end to war would generally imply the presence or creation of certain instruments or institutional mechanisms, formal or otherwise, which serve as the basis upon which to preserve a permanent state of peace following military conflict between belligerent parties. In the case of Korea, however, reliance on this assumption as the point of departure for analyzing inter-Korean relations raises more questions than it answers; not so much due to a lack of such mechanisms, but more so because of the tentative nature of the legal foundation upon which the state of peace has been preserved. In this instance, the 50-year old state of "peace" is for the most part based on a tenuous document known as the Military Armistice Agreement.[1] The purpose of this agreement was to achieve a *temporary* cessation of military hostilities until a permanent political agreement could be reached to formally end the war. Such a political agreement did not ever materialize. As a consequence, the year 2003 could more accurately be described as marking the fiftieth anniversary of the *continuation* of the temporary cease-fire on the Korean peninsula rather than of an end to the war. While there is no active state of war in Korea, by the same token, nor does there exist a recognized—an institutionalized and legal—state of peace between the two Koreas. Hence the often used phrase of describing the two Koreas to be "technically still at war"—an odd sort of fictional twilight zone of neither war nor peace, with the two Koreas having been locked in time for 50 years to an arrangement that had been intended to be of a temporary nature.

The divergent paths taken by the two Koreas after the end of the Korean War naturally raise questions of whether it is realistically possible to achieve enduring reconciliation—or even unification. The unprecedented brisk increase in inter-Korean exchanges and cooperation (family reunions, sports, and economic) following the landmark summit meeting in 2000 under the Sunshine Policy of engagement (changed to the Peace and Prosperity Policy under the Roh Moo-Hyun administration) is overshadowed by recurrent military clashes such as separate naval engagements in 1999 and 2002 across the Northern Limit Line on the West Sea and a North Korean submarine intrusion in 1996 on the East coast of South Korea resulting in the death of 24 North Korean commando troops and 11 South Koreans. Of greater implication to inter-Korean relations in 2003 was the unfolding of a new standoff over North Korea's nuclear program brought about by, among other things, North Korea's withdrawal from the NPT and reactivation of the nuclear reactor at Yongbyon. While these kinds of events underscore the highly volatile nature of relations on the Korean peninsula, they fall short of providing clarification on the actual makeup and extent of the transformation in relations between the two Koreas since signing of the Military Armistice Agreement.

Under this backdrop, the purpose of this chapter is to examine the nature of inter-Korean relations from the vantage point of the legal framework. Select inter-Korean accords, including the Military Armistice Agreement and the activities of KEDO under the Agreed Framework of 1994 will be used to track and explain the changes and continuities in inter-Korean relations. Particular focus will be on exploring the root causes behind obstacles to faithful implementation and performance of inter-Korean agreements. I argue that one of the core obstacles stems from the absence of a meaningful enforcement mechanism between the two Koreas that would ensure binding legal effect on both parties. As a consequence, inter-Korean agreements and bilateral relations rest on an illusory—or fictional—legal foundation. This illusory or fictional foundation of inter-Korean relations is a product of uncertainty surrounding the continued application of the 1953 Military Armistice Agreement vis-à-vis the two Koreas. Framing a workable formula that clarifies the nature of inter-Korean relations remains an important analytical stepping stone in order to explain a relationship that still exists in the context of a war that has yet to be formally ended. The second part of this chapter addresses North Korea's nuclear program and focuses on the work of KEDO and the 1994 Agreed Framework. This part attempts to highlight the progression of multilateralism as the means by which to address issues caused by the uncertain legal foundations of inter-Korean relations. Despite the shortcomings and questionable future of the arrangement originally envisioned under the 1994 Agreed Framework, the multilateral dimensions of KEDO embodied a structurally sound arrangement to use as a model for approaching inter-Korean relations. Of particular note is the perceivable attempt to characterize inter-Korean relations as one of *intra*-Korean relations detached from the exigencies of the multilateral nature of the geopolitical atmosphere of the immediate region.

Complexities of Defining the Nature of Inter-Korean Relations

Inter-Korean Agreements

One of the central conceptual difficulties of comprehending the nature of inter-Korean relations is the complexity involved in formulating a clear definition of the precise relationship between South and North Korea. Simply put, what is the foundation that supports the relation—friendly or hostile—between the two Koreas? On the one hand, as the direct belligerent parties to the Korean War, neither side officially recognizes the other as a sovereign state. For example, the territorial clause contained in Article 3 of the South Korean constitution provides that "the territory of the Republic of Korea shall extend to the Korean peninsula and its surrounding islands." The interpretation of this clause is that South Korea is the sole legitimate government of the Korean peninsula and that the area north of the DMZ is an un-reclaimed area illegally occupied by North Korea. Likewise, Article 1 of the North Korean constitution proclaims that "the Democratic People's Republic of Korea is an independent socialist state representing the interests of all the Korean people." However, in spite of the competing claims to sovereign control over the Korean peninsula, numerous declarations of peaceful reunification and mutual cooperation and exchange exist between the two Koreas. The South–North Joint Declaration of June 2000 between the leaders of the two Koreas declared a new era of cooperation and peaceful coexistence where "The South and North will pursue a balanced development of their national economies and build mutual trust by accelerating exchange in the social, cultural, sports, health and environmental sectors."[2] Even as far back as the 1972 South–North Joint Communiqué, both sides declared their intention to faithfully abide by an agreement to "stop military provocation which may lead to unintended armed conflicts, to cultivate an atmosphere of mutual trust between North and South by refraining from vilifying the other side" and to "restore the severed national lineage and promote mutual understanding by implementing multi-faceted North-South exchange of information." However, these agreements have carefully sidestepped directly addressing the fundamental threshold issue of defining the actual relationship between the two Koreas.

The 1991 Agreement on Reconciliation, Non-aggression, and Exchanges and Cooperation ("Basic Agreement") provides indirect guidance on this issue. The preamble to the Basic Agreement carefully articulates the peculiarities of "inter-Korean relations" by an ambiguous statement that inter-Korean relations "not being a relationship as between states, is a special one constituted temporarily in the process of unification." This point is further articulated in Article 1 which states that the two Koreas "shall recognize and respect the system of each other." The 1972 South–North Joint Communiqué also indirectly alludes to this problem by stating that "both parties must promote national unity as a united people over any differences of our ideological and political systems." The far-reaching implications, and hence the complexities, of defining with precision even the most conceptually basic aspect of a relationship in the Korean case become all too apparent when viewed from the context of legitimacy over the Korean peninsula. Consequently, defining the legal relationship as a temporary one pending unification and not as one between two sovereign states achieves the purpose of providing the basis for engaging in inter-Korean cooperation and exchange without having to address the question of which Korea has the rightful claim to the Korean peninsula. This artificially invented concept is not without its drawbacks. Without a true legal basis for relationship, relying on this legal fiction undermines the binding effect of the inter-Korean agreements that have so far served as the only written expression of South–North relations. The lack of a meaningful enforcement mechanism between the two Koreas results in a minimal avenue of recourse for frequent breaches of the numerous agreements beyond a symbolic expression of protest. For example, the January 2003 withdrawal from the NPT by North Korea and subsequent nuclear standoff precipitated by its nuclear program would constitute a direct violation of the Joint Declaration of the Denuclearization of the Korean Peninsula.[3] Nonetheless, the practical and legal consequences which ordinarily would attach to acts that would otherwise constitute a clear breach become in this instance obscured or conveniently diminished depending on the exigencies of the times.

Military Armistice Agreement and "Multilateralization" of Inter-Korean Relations
In order, therefore, to classify the true nature of South–North relations in the conventional sense, the Military Armistice Agreement that was signed on July 27, 1953 becomes the most relevant point of departure. In spite of its flaws, the Military Armistice Agreement provides the logical starting point for analyzing inter-Korean relations as it embodies the basic underpinnings upon which all formal and informal inter-Korean relations are based.[4] Another important aspect of the Military Armistice Agreement is the uneven and distinct manner in which it defines relations between the two Koreas and their respective relations with the United States, which to this day have not changed to a measurable degree. The Military Armistice Agreement was a temporary military measure whose objective was to put an end to active armed conflict. However, it did not formally end the war, leaving the two Koreas in a legal quandary of still technically being in a state of war. The Military Armistice Agreement was "purely military in character," and a *political* agreement had been envisioned as the next step in ensuring permanent settlement to an otherwise temporary *military* agreement.[5] This point is also underscored by the signatures of the top military commanders of the Korean War rather than political leaders: General Mark W. Clark, Commander-in-Chief of the United Nations Command, Marshall Kim Il Sung, Supreme Commander of the Korean People's Army and Peng Teh-Huai, Commander of the Chinese People's Volunteers. President Syngman Rhee's refusal to sign the Military Armistice Agreement left unresolved for five decades not only South Korea's standing vis-à-vis North Korea but also the practical consequences of inter-Korean relations resting on a temporary military accord that survived past its originally intended design. While unquestionably a direct party to the Korean War, South Korea was nonetheless not a signatory to the very instrument that has in retrospect been the basis for maintaining the status quo on the peninsula since 1953. In the ensuing 50 years since the breakdown of the Political Conference in Geneva in 1954, little meaningful progress—bilateral or multilateral—has been made in replacing the armistice with a "final peace settlement"—an agreement on the political level.

The 1991 Basic Agreement represented the first attempt since the South–North Joint Communiqué of July 4, 1972 for a bilateral resolution to the unsettled Korean question. The Basic Agreement was significant because for the first time since the Military Armistice Agreement it contained a clause calling for adherence by both South and North Korea to the Military Armistice Agreement and for the two Koreas to "together endeavor to transform the present state of armistice into a firm state of peace between the two sides."[6] In addition, it contained a nonaggression clause calling for an end to the use of force and armed aggression against each other and to "resolve peacefully, through dialogue and negotiation, any differences of views and disputes arising between them."[7] Optimism for a breakthrough in inter-Korean relations followed the simultaneous entry of the two Koreas to the United Nations and the signing of the Joint Declaration of Denuclearization of the Korean Peninsula in February 1992. Notwithstanding the seemingly positive progress in establishing what would have appeared to be a workable framework for inter-Korean relations, these efforts fell short of providing any meaningful impetus toward crafting the required permanent solution to the Korean question. Multilateral efforts during the

Four Party Talks of 1997–1999 essentially followed the same path of irrelevance in addressing this open question. As a consequence, despite its wishes to the contrary, South Korea's relationship with North Korea on the Korean question has by and large remained on the same continuum since 1953 of being intimately entwined with the interests of the United States in the region as opposed to being determined by inter-Korean interests. Paradoxically, the same may be true for North Korea's relations with South Korea but from a diametrically opposite position: as a party to the Military Armistice Agreement, North Korea, by design, equates the United States as its negotiating partner and as a proxy in its relations with South Korea regarding resolution of the Korean question while simultaneously approaching bilateral relations as an *intra*-Korean rather than an *inter*-Korean matter. The unintended role of the United States on the Korean peninsula as both the umpire and sheriff has inevitably institutionalized and reinforced the notion of the "multilateralization" of inter-Korean relations, making purely bilateral relations impracticable without reference to other powers in the region.[8]

The individual and collective interests of China, Russia, and Japan in resolving the Korean question and the impact of progress or digression in inter-Korean relations to those countries have begun to take on far greater relevance as components of the multilateral aspect of inter-Korean relations due in part to their geographic proximity to North Korea. This has been particularly true in the case of China, and to a lesser degree Russia, after normalization of relations with South Korea in the early 1990s. Early attempts to engineer a peace treaty through the Four Party Talks exemplify movement toward the extension of the multilateralization component of inter-Korean relations and at the same time can also be seen as an implicit recognition that North Korea may be left with no other option but to recognize South Korea as a legitimate counterpart in resolving the Korean question.[9] The April 2003 trilateral talks between the United States, North Korea, and China is significant in establishing the precedent of a multilateral approach to resolving the Korean question in the face of efforts by North Korea to portray its nuclear issue as a matter to be resolved bilaterally with the United States. While it is uncertain whether the talks will yield a swift 1994 Agreed Framework–style resolution to the North Korean nuclear problem, the subsequent expansion to a Six Party Talks format in 2004 by including the country most noticeably missing from the process—South Korea—and other interested parties—Japan and Russia—signifies the pivotal step favoring a diplomatic solution over use of the military option.[10] At the same time, attempts to ensure representation of the interests of Russia and Japan in this relationship foretell a new dimension to fashioning a multilateral resolution to the Korean question.

The "multilateralization" feature of inter-Korean relations suggests a relationship grounded not on conventional principles of international law and practice but on a set of historical turns unique to the Korean peninsula. The uncertain legal basis that formed the very foundation of inter-Korean relations has become, during the course of five decades, the *de facto* norm defining those relations. Viewed from this perspective, the Agreed Framework of 1994 and the formation of KEDO, as a multilateral organization, is an extension of and something that perpetuates the original legal fiction that formed the basis for inter-Korean relations in 1953. The indirect involvement of South Korea in negotiation and signing of the Agreed Framework between the United States and North Korea, compared to the "central" role that South Korea played in financing and implementing the nuclear project, lends support to the inevitable acquiescence, though unwillingly and not by design, of the multilateralized dimension of inter-Korean relations. While the future of KEDO and the Agreed Framework has been placed in a precarious state as a result of the standoff with North Korea since October 2002 over its suspected nuclear program, as a test case in evaluating the effectiveness of multilateral arrangements as the vehicle for improving relations at the inter-Korean level, the structure of KEDO suggests a workable paradigm to address the uncertain nature of inter-Korean relations precipitated by the Military Armistice Agreement. KEDO, however, is not by any measure without its own structural limitations and shortcomings. The legal status of KEDO vis-à-vis North Korea is less than clear under international norms and practices. Questions relevant to this line of inquiry are whether KEDO is an international organization recognized as such under international law and whether, related to the first question, acts of KEDO have legally binding effect vis-à-vis North Korea and on the Executive Board Member Countries (United States, South Korea, Japan, and the EU).

Reliance on a Legal Fiction

The ambiguity surrounding the precise legal status of KEDO follows from the uncertain nature of the Agreed Framework. A product more of the situational necessity than careful deliberation, it has been argued that the Agreed Framework is nothing more than a written understanding reached between the United States and North Korea with the objective of fulfilling an urgent need to diffuse a nuclear situation that had the potential of spiraling out of control. It has further been argued that as an instrument lacking U.S. congressional ratification, the Agreed Framework is neither a treaty in the formal sense nor can it be characterized as a *legally* binding international agreement between the United States and North Korea.[11] This point was made clear in the 1996 U.S. General Accounting Office report that characterized the Agreed Framework as "a non-binding political agreement" or "non-binding international agreement."[12] The characterization as a *political* agreement rather than a treaty permitted the Agreed Framework to be exempt from formal congressional scrutiny, which undoubtedly would have brought with it imposition of strict conditions that could well have jeopardized the nuclear deal reached with North Korea. Although this legal point is subject to debate and has not been clearly settled, it is important to note that North Korea has consistently viewed the 1994 Agreed Framework as a "binding legal document" with the United States.[13] While the formation of KEDO and the subsequent signing of the Supply Agreement with North Korea, the principal document outlining the specifics of implementation of the project, are based on a foundation that arguably lacks legal clarity, this point is of less importance since inter-Korean relations have not depended on legal clarity as a precedent condition. Thus, in a relationship characterized by the lack of a formal institutionalized framework, an argument could be made that clarity and formalism in the Korean case may tend to be an obstacle to the need to be responsive to a fluid and dynamic relationship.

In this sense, the Agreed Framework and KEDO's role in inter-Korean relations is the reverse situation of the circumstances surrounding the Military Armistice

Agreement of 1953. In both cases, the agreements addressed a particular need at the time by means of either a *military* agreement as in 1953 or a *political* agreement as in the case of 1994. On the other hand, whereas a *political* agreement failed to follow the military agreement in 1953, there was a lack of a *legally* binding basis to the political agreement made in 1994. This distinction is significant for two reasons. First, it creates a relationship based on an uncertain—fictional—legal basis and, second, this uncertain legal state paradoxically removes barriers to the creation of quasi-formal relations and a level of cooperation that otherwise would have been hampered by political and legal considerations. This has required KEDO to exhibit and seek balance to a dual personality: an entity dispassionate and detached from the geopolitical events on the Korean peninsula but at the same time recognizing the need to abide by and comply with the mandates and collective interests of its constituent executive board member countries (United States, South Korea, Japan, and the EU). For the opposite reasons behind the lack of a peace treaty freeing either Korea from accountability for military clashes and allowing either side to violate the Military Armistice Agreement with impunity,[14] this uncertain legal foundation allows KEDO in theory to be a politically neutral buffer entity less constrained by the politics surrounding relations between North Korea and the United States, South Korea, and Japan. Accordingly, by resorting to reliance on a legal fiction as the basis for its relationship due to the difficulties in formulating a single and simple workable characterization of inter-Korean relations, the "multilateralization" component has become an aspect of relations between the two Koreas that needs to be viewed as an alternative to conventional definitions.

North Korea's Nuclear Program as Redefining the
Nature of Inter-Korean Relations

North Korea's Withdrawals from the NPT
North Korea has the distinction of being the only country to have twice withdrawn from the NPT. Its first withdrawal on March 12, 1993 occurred less than one year after signing the Safeguards Agreement with the International Atomic Energy Agency (IAEA) as obligated under the NPT, a treaty to which it had acceded in December 1985. The declaration of its intent to withdraw had considerable implications to the NPT regime since, after the prescribed waiting period of 90 days pursuant to Article X of the NPT, this action would in effect remove the sole *legal* basis that had thus far barred North Korea from building nuclear weapons or otherwise diverting "nuclear energy from peaceful uses to nuclear weapons or other nuclear explosive devices."[15] Under the NPT, a signatory is permitted to withdraw from the treaty "if it decides that extraordinary events, related to the subject matter of this Treaty, have jeopardized the supreme interests of its country." In a statement outlining the reasons behind its intent to withdraw from the treaty, North Korea declared,

> The United States and the south Korean authorities have defiantly resumed the "Team Spirit" joint military exercises, a nuclear war rehearsal against the Democratic People's Republic of Korea (DPRK), and...following the lead of the United States had a

"resolution" adopted at the February 25 meeting of the IAEA Board of Governors, demanding a special inspection of our military sites unrelated to nuclear activities. This is an encroachment on the sovereignty of the DPRK, [interference] in its internal affairs and a hostile act aimed at stifling our socialism.[16]

Almost ten years later on January 10, 2003, North Korea again declared its intent to immediately withdraw from the NPT. In its statement it declared,

A particular mention should be made of the fact that the IAEA in the recent "resolution" kept mum about the U.S. which has grossly violated the NPT and the DPRK—U.S. Agreed Framework, but urged the DPRK, the victim, to unconditionally accept the U.S. demand for disarmament and forfeit its right to self-defense,... The U.S. went so far to instigate the IAEA to internationalize its moves to stifle the DPRK, putting its declaration of a war into practice. This has eliminated the last possibility of solving the nuclear issue of the Korean Peninsula in a peaceful and fair way... As it has become clear once again that the U.S. persistently seeks to stifle the DPRK at any cost and the IAEA is used as a tool for executing the U.S. hostile policy towards the DPRK, we can no longer remain bound to the NPT, allowing the country's security and the dignity of our nation to be infringed upon.[17]

The "supreme interests of the country" or, stated differently, the often invoked notion by North Korea of safeguarding its sovereignty has been its key *modus operandi* and central to many of the motives that drive its behavior and relations with the outside world. The standoff with the IAEA over verification of its non-proliferation obligations under the NPT, which ultimately culminated in its withdrawal from the NPT, underscores the obsessive extremity to which North Korea will go as a means of protecting any perceived infringement of its sovereign rights. At the same time, accession to the NPT by North Korea and signing of the Safeguards Agreement granted the IAEA an explicit right to carry out inspections, a core component of its monitoring and enforcement functions, for purposes of verifying a signatory's compliance with its non-proliferation obligations. The inability of the IAEA, in spite of repeated *ad hoc* inspections, to rectify inconsistencies contained in the initial report submitted by North Korea on May 2, 1992 and suspicions that North Korea may have extracted between 35 and 50 pounds of plutonium from its Yongbyon facility[18] caused the IAEA Board of Governors to declare North Korea to be in violation of its Safeguards Agreement and to take the extraordinary act of reporting its noncompliance to the UN Security Council on two separate occasions.[19]

The first nuclear crisis actually permitted a diplomatic breakthrough between the United States and North Korea through a series of bilateral meetings leading to an agreement on a set of principles that would ultimately lay the groundwork for attempts to resolve the nuclear issue. One day prior to the effective date of its first withdrawal from the NPT, in what would be the first of three joint statements with the United States that would precede signing of the Agreed Framework on October 21, 1994, North Korea agreed to unilaterally suspend withdrawal from the NPT.[20] Among the principles agreed to were a "nuclear-free Korean Peninsula, including impartial application of full-scope safeguards, mutual respect for each other's sovereignty, and non-interference in each other's internal affairs." So began the odd unfolding of events that set the stage for subsequent nuclear diplomacy involving a complicated matrix of players and interests that would ultimately lead to what is now known as the "Agreed Framework."[21] Conceptually, the Agreed Framework was nothing more than a carefully outlined but straightforward *quid pro quo* involving explicit mutual undertakings. First, North Korea would suspend its withdrawal from the NPT, freeze and dismantle its graphite-moderated reactors and "come into full compliance with its safeguards commitments under the NPT." In return, a U.S.-led international consortium, KEDO, would supply two proliferation-resistant light-water nuclear reactors by a target date of 2003 with a combined total generating capacity of approximately 2,000 megawatts of electrical power. North Korea would also be provided with interest free loans to finance the reactors, the repayment of which would not start until 20 years after completion of the first reactor, and 500,000 metric tons of heavy fuel oil annually until completion of the first light-water reactor to offset the energy that would otherwise have been produced by North Korea's graphite-moderated reactors. Second, and perhaps of greater importance to North Korea, was an agreement for both parties to "move toward full normalization of political and economic relations" and formal assurances by the United States "against the threat or use of nuclear weapons" against it. Under the terms of the Agreed Framework, both sides would reduce barriers to trade and investment within 3 months of the agreement and ultimately upgrade bilateral relations to the Ambassadorial level. While the Agreed Framework was conceived ambitiously as the vehicle by which an "overall resolution" to the nuclear issue would be reached, implementation of the Agreed Framework through KEDO, which in theory would function as an apolitical entity, has proven not to be immune from the ebb and tide of geopolitical circumstances on the Korean peninsula with proponents and opponents of the Agreed Framework and KEDO in both Washington and Seoul frequently at odds with each other regarding what shape the end game to this purported overall resolution would take.

Revisiting the Role of KEDO in the Context of Inter-Korean Relations

In March 2000 testimony before the Senate Foreign Relations Committee, Assistant Secretary of Defense for International Security Affairs, Franklin D. Kramer, echoed concerns relating to KEDO and the Agreed Framework by characterizing U.S. policy toward North Korea as one of a dilemma by stating "at present, the DPRK is too reprehensible to fully embrace but too dangerous to completely ignore."[22] The Agreed Framework has even been viewed as the "initial blackmail payment" made by the Clinton administration to North Korea as a payoff in return for closing down nuclear reactors capable of producing weapons-grade plutonium.[23] Placing North Korea along with Iran and Iraq as among the countries comprising the "Axis of Evil" revealed the fragile political foundation upon which the successful implementation of the light-water reactor project was based. On the other hand, Seoul's view of the light-water reactor project has tended to echo a familiar optimistic tone as one of ensuring peace and stability on the Korean peninsula and fostering a favorable atmosphere for reconciliation between North Korea and the outside world. The potential role of KEDO in accelerating inter-Korean relations and cooperation has been described as follows:

> The light-water reactor project is expected to be the largest construction effort on North Korean soil since the division of the Korean peninsula, combining South Korean

money and technology with efforts of South and North Korean workers for the next eight or nine years, and without a doubt will revive the spirit of national union and harmony that will bring a half-century of discord to a close. The reactor project will also be the largest single effort at inter-Korean cooperation, with KEPCO (the main contractor) and dozens of South Korean firms participating in the design, construction, and manufacture of parts; North Korea will provide for thousands of laborers, materiel, and other services necessary for the project.[24]

The dichotomy in perspectives between the United States and South Korea regarding the Agreed Framework and the KEDO project foreshadow possibilities of future policy disagreements in other areas with respect to North Korea. The focus by the United States on the non-proliferation dimensions as opposed to the South Korean focus on the inter-Korean reconciliation dimensions remain one of the core areas of disagreement that will necessitate a fundamental re-clarification of the original purpose and intent behind the Agreed Framework and reassessment of the end game originally envisioned by the KEDO process.[25] In light of the decision reached in late 2003 to formally *suspend* the KEDO project for a period of one year and the uncertain status of the Agreed Framework stemming from competing claims of breach by the United States and North Korea, continuation of the light water reactor project in one form or the other, or eventually termination, will depend to a significant degree on what processes and steps are taken to reach an ultimate resolution of the nuclear issue involving North Korea.

Death of Kim Il Sung and Birth of KEDO

The signing of the Agreed Framework between the United States and the DPRK on October 21, 1994 came on the heels of chaotic events following the sudden death of Kim Il Sung just three months earlier on July 8, 1994. Kim Il Sung's death came at a particularly inopportune time as it coincided with the third round of high-level talks between North Korea and the United States on the nuclear issue and, more significantly, came just a few weeks before the first-ever scheduled but aborted summit meeting between the then leaders of the two Koreas, Kim Young-Sam and Kim Il Sung. Kim Il Sung's sudden death was almost as much a surprise to South Korea as it was a shock to the North. However, it was clear that the summit meeting would be canceled, as it was politically unfeasible at the time for Kim Young-Sam to meet with his son, Kim Jong Il, because of doubts about how the political leadership would play out in the aftermath of Kim Il Sung's death. Inter-Korean relations reached one of the lowest points during this period as South Korea launched a massive vilification campaign against Kim Il Sung and Kim Jong Il and raised doubts about survivability of the regime.[26] In addition, the refusal of Kim Young-Sam to express condolence over the death of Kim Il Sung whom he had planned to meet just weeks later was in stark contrast to the United States, which paid a condolence call at the North Korean mission in Geneva. This particular act was perceived as an intentional insult by South Korea against the North and was met with furious condemnation.[27] The situation on the Korean peninsula had already been tense as a result of the nuclear standoff and earlier North Korean threats during a meeting at Panmunjom to turn Seoul "into a sea of fire."[28] The actions of South Korea and the failure to pay due respects to the death of the Great Leader only helped to exacerbate the already evident open hostilities on the Korean peninsula. A senior North Korean official expressed, "We consider South Korea's refusal to express condolence over President Kim Il Sung's death as an intention not to have a dialogue with us,"[29] and inter-Korean dialogue and relations accordingly came to a standstill.

While North Korea has always approached the nuclear issue as a bilateral matter to be resolved with the United States at the exclusion of South Korea, the nuclear deal that had been reached in principle in August 1994 and that finally culminated in the Agreed Framework in October would have been unworkable without South Korea's participation and funding. The hostile mood between the two Koreas during this period soon became evident, resulting in an impasse over the role that South Korea would play in the nuclear deal. South Korea's insistence that any nuclear reactor to be provided to the North be a "South Korean style light-water reactor" built with South Korean capital and technology had been made clear by President Kim Young-Sam.[30] Equally clear was North Korea's vehement objections over perceptions of a leading South Korean role in the process. Any reference to a South Korean model was simply unacceptable and threatened to derail the entire process.[31] Attempts to resolve this impasse had not been successful even leading up to the establishment of KEDO in March 1995 and consequently delayed the signing of the Supply Agreement, which was required to have been concluded within six months of the signing of the Agreed Framework. Neither South Korea nor North Korea was in a position, or willing, to make concessions on this pivotal issue—an issue having more to do with saving face than substance. The breakthrough came in a compromise reached during talks in Kuala Lumpur in which the nuclear reactors were described as being of "U.S.—origin, design, and technology" with no reference to the South Korean model. It was also announced that KEDO would select the prime contractor for the project. KEDO immediately announced selection of the Korean Standard model and KEPCO as its most probable prime contractor for the project. Although not readily apparent at the time, this example foreshadowed the usefulness of KEDO as an apolitical project-oriented entity that could very well prevail over exigencies of inter-Korean relations. More significant was the far-reaching implications of a multilateral organization that included South Korea, North Korea's arch enemy at the time, successfully resolving an issue consistent with the interests of South Korea while providing North Korea with a plausible face-saving rationale for agreement.

Linking KEDO to Inter-Korean Relations
With the impasse having being resolved, the KEDO project began to move forward in earnest. In August 1995, it sent a ten-member team to survey Sinpo, which was the proposed site for the light-water reactor project, and in October, North Korea received the second of three heavy fuel oil shipments for 1995. With conclusion of the Supply Agreement in December of that year, the legal basis for the project between KEDO and North Korea had been established. In spite of developments on the KEDO project, inter-Korean relations had not improved to a measurable degree, and there had been no resumption of inter-Korean dialogue. The North was not

about to let inter-Korean dialogue be a precondition to improvement in relations with Washington. A December 1995 editorial by the *Rodong Sinmun* claimed that the South was not an appropriate dialogue partner as it was responsible for failing to foster an appropriate environment for dialogue. It went on to say, "We will never have talks with the South because sitting with South Koreans will be construed as blasphemous dialogue and will make fools out of aspirations for national reunification.... The United States must not put the resumption of inter-Korean dialogue as a precondition for improvement in relations between Pyongyang and Washington if the United States really wants to improve relations with the North."[32]

Meanwhile, North Korea continued its military probes against South Korea. In April 1996, North Korea officially announced its unilateral withdrawal from the Military Armistice Agreement claiming that South Korea was transporting large numbers of troops and heavy weapons into the DMZ and began introducing heavily armed soldiers and vehicles into the Joint Security Area.[33] President Kim Young Sam convened an emergency National Security Council (NSC) meeting in accordance with Article 91 of the constitution. Such an NSC meeting had been only called on two prior occasions: the first in June 1994 during the North Korean nuclear crises and the second immediately after the death of Kim Il Sung.[34] In September 1996, in a series of two other submarine incursions that would follow, a nationwide manhunt went underway in South Korea after a disabled North Korean submarine was discovered off the east coast of Korea. In the ensuing battle, 24 infiltrators were killed and 11 South Korean military personnel and civilians were killed.[35]

South Korea immediately halted all work on the light-water project and demanded an apology for the incident from North Korea as a condition for resumption of the KEDO project.[36] The North Koreans responded by threatening to unfreeze their nuclear program if KEDO did not resume work on the light-water reactor project.[37] In a standoff that threatened to jeopardize the future of the KEDO project, South Korea repeated that "it would never engage in any talks with North Korea until after the North apologized for the submarine incursion." In an odd but telling tit for tat the North also issued a statement that it would not talk to South Korea before it apologized for failure to send a South Korean delegation to express condolences for the death of Kim Il Sung.[38] More than two years had passed since Kim Il Sung died but this was a reminder to the South that this incident was still relevant to inter-Korean relations. The test-firing of the Taepodong-I missile over Japanese airspace in 1998 was another case in point in which the future of the KEDO project remained very much linked to North Korea's behavior. In reaction to this incident, Japan suspended food aid and political normalization talks with North Korea as well as funding of its $1 billion contribution to KEDO for the light-water reactor project.[39] Although both incidents were resolved after considerable persuasion and diplomatic maneuvering by the parties not directly affected, ultimately, KEDO was also not immune from the ebb and flow of military and political events on the Korean peninsula. While KEDO served as a useful vehicle for multilateral engagement with North Korea, by the same token, it also served as a convenient method by which to communicate displeasure when the direct interest of a member country was at stake.

Unlinking KEDO from Inter-Korean Relations
North Korea has traditionally linked the Agreed Framework to economic cooperation with the United States and diplomatic recognition. The United States, on the other hand, has tended to link the Agreed Framework more to North Korea's nonproliferation obligations, ballistic missile program, and inter-Korean dialogue. In its most simplified form, the linkages represent a set of priorities, the fulfillment of which each party attaches importance to, as the incentive for implementing their respective obligations outlined under the Agreed Framework. Understandably, North Korea has criticized South Korea, Japan, and the United States for linking its missile program to the provision of the heavy fuel oil shipments and to the light-water reactor project and has claimed that there is no linkage between the two.[40] On the other hand, North Korea had also threatened to nullify the Agreed Framework unless the United States removed economic sanctions. A spokesman for the North Korean Foreign Ministry is quoted as saying the "U.S. move to link North Korea's missile development program to the provision of funds for KEDO is threatening the entire agreement."[41] The specific linkages that the United States and North Korea attach to the Agreed Framework will not change in a fundamental way. However, their importance as bargaining leverage, while crucial in the beginning stages, becomes less compelling during the course of implementation as the degree of commitment (or sunk cost) in the endeavor increases. As noted in the figures listed in table 9.1, the project was over 32 percent complete with total expenditures of over US$1.3 billion by South Korea, Japan, and the EU as of the end of August 2003.[42] The United States had also provided over US$370 million in heavy fuel oil prior to the decision to suspend shipments in late 2002.

North Korea's withdrawal from the NPT and the standoff over its nuclear program have raised a new debate over whether the KEDO project can be delinked or separated from inter-Korean relations in light of the resources and manpower expended in the project. Even as early as 1998, President Kim Dae Jung had begun to hint at a dual track approach to KEDO and inter-Korean relations. In a meeting with Secretary General Kofi Annan at UN Headquarters, President Kim indicated that the South Korean

Table 9.1 LWR construction status as of end of August 2003: Overall completion—32.85%

	Overall design	*Procurement purchase*				*Construction*	*Test run*	*Cumulative (%)*
		Reactor	*Turbine generator*	*Balance of plant*	*Subtotal*			
Unit rate of progress	58.45	65.73	40.44	20.27	40.65	21.22	0	—
Overall rate of progress	5.85	11.83	2.43	4.46	18.72	8.28	0	32.85

Source: Ministry of Unification, *Major Statistical Figures for the Light-Water Reactor Project as of August 2003* (*kyungsuro saup juyo tonggye*) (translated from Korean).

government is "adopting a two-pronged policy toward Pyongyang, under which it stands firm against the north's nuclear issue, while giving necessary assistance to the North, including the construction of nuclear light-water reactors."[43] This dual track approach to KEDO and inter-Korean relations became even more evident after the June 29, 2002 naval clash inside the Northern Limit Line where both sides accused each other of starting the hostilities that resulted in the sinking of one South Korean patrol boat and the death of four South Korean sailors. While this case may arguably be distinguishable from the 1996 submarine incursion episode due to an indication of regret by North Korea, the effects on KEDO in the aftermath was noticeably less significant. Shortly thereafter, a group of 25 North Koreans came to South Korea under the auspices of KEDO for nuclear safety training that would last approximately one month. In addition, the test flight for the first direct air route linking North Korea and South Korea to transport people and materials for the KEDO project was inaugurated. The significance of this change in perception of KEDO and inter-Korean relations cannot be viewed in the abstract and would be incomplete without reference to North Korea's outlook on the KEDO project. Nonetheless, as suggested by a South Korean official, "Pyongyang is responding positively. It tries to distinguish the reactor project as a deal with KEDO, not a part of inter-Korean relations."[44]

Conclusion

I have argued in this chapter that multilateralization of inter-Korean relations has become a *de facto* norm governing relations between the two Koreas despite the habitual contrary claims and denials of the two Koreas. Inter-Korean agreements are inherently limited by the absence of an "international law" nexus between South Korea and North Korea and the still unresolved legal state of the Korean War. On the other hand, much of the credit for initiating a new level of rapprochement in inter-Korean relations is rightly due to the activities of KEDO and its multilateral structure. Keeping inter-Korean politics and functional cooperation on a separate track has succeeded in insulating to a certain degree KEDO and its activities from the exigencies of the political relations between North Korea and the respective members of KEDO. While it is clear that such a separation of politics and functional cooperation did not occur immediately upon the founding of KEDO, or even many years thereafter as shown by intervening events such as the firing of Taepodong over Japan or the submarine incursions, the role of an organization like KEDO is illuminative in providing at least a model for a multilateral approach to inter-Korean relations.

Nonetheless, a multilateral approach to North Korea is in the final analysis merely today's answer to yesterday's problems. As a means of expressing the nature of institutional conflict management in inter-Korean relations, the possibilities of achieving an enduring resolution to the North Korean nuclear problem are less than clear. To suggest that multilateralism is a key component in this equation without acknowledging the underlying limitations brought on by the lack of a workable legal basis between the two Koreas as a result of the questionable resolution to the Korean War, ignores fundamentally the nature of relations between the two Koreas. Early attempts at the Four Party Talks in August 1999, the Three Party Talks in April 2003, and the Six Party Talks in 2003—illustrate the usefulness of multilateralism as a means of engaging North Korea but ultimately reveal the limitations of a multilateral setting brought on by the need to cater to the interests of each party and to North Korea's concern for security assurances from the United States.[45] While multilateralism may have taken an important place in the mode with which the international community approaches North Korea, what is less certain is how successful this process can be in the absence of a fundamental resolution to the uncertain nature— legal and otherwise—of relations between the two Koreas.

Notes

1. For a full text of the Military Armistice Agreement dated July 27, 1953, see http://news.findlaw.com/hdocs/docs/korea/kwarmagr072753.html (last visited August 2003).
2. Paragraph (4) of the June 2000 South North Accord.
3. The Joint Declaration of the Denuclearization of the Korean Peninsula provides that the South and the North shall not "test, manufacture, produce, receive, possess, store, deploy or use nuclear weapons . . . and shall use nuclear energy solely for peaceful purposes . . . and shall not possess nuclear reprocessing and uranium enrichment facilities."
4. Robert E. Bedeski, "Challenges to Peace on the Korean Peninsula" July 28, 1997, The Nautilus Institute for Security and Sustainable Development.
5. The Preamble to the Military Armistice Agreement states that the objective is to "ensure a complete cessation of hostilities and of all acts of armed force in Korea until a final peace settlement is achieved." Paragraph 62 also provides that the "Armistice Agreement shall remain in effect until expressly superseded either by mutually acceptable amendments and additions or by provision in an appropriate agreement for a peaceful settlement at a political level between both sides."
6. Article 5 of the Basic Agreement states, "South and North Korea shall together endeavor to transform the present state of armistice into a firm state of peace between the two sides and shall abide by the present Military Armistice Agreement until such a state of peace is realized." Article 11 goes on to provide that "The South-North demarcation line and the areas for non-aggression shall be identical with the Military Demarcation Line provided in the Military Armistice Agreement of July 27, 1953, and the areas that each side has exercised jurisdiction over until the present time."
7. See Article 10 of the Basic Agreement.
8. Bedeski, "Challenges to Peace on the Korean Peninsula."
9. "DPRK's Agreement to 4-Way Talks Seen as Acceptance of ROK as Partner in Replacing Armistice," *The Korea Herald* (Internet Version-WWW), October 14, 2000, FBIS-EAS-2000-1013.
10. "US, PRC 'Strategic Ambiguity,' DPRK 'Opposition' Seen to Obstruct Six-Way Security Forum," FBIS-EAS-2002-0827, August 28, 2002; see also "Seoul Opposed to Six Party Talks," *Korea Times*, September 2, 2002.
11. See also, Ralph A. Cossa, "The U.S.-DPRK Agreed Framework: Is it Still Viable? Is it Enough?" (Honolulu: Pacific Forum CSIS, April 1999), http://www.csis.org/pacfor/opUSDPRK.pdf, pp. 5–6.
12. See "Nuclear Nonproliferation-Implications of the U.S./North Korean Agreement on Nuclear Issues," GAO Report to the Chairman, Committee on Energy and Natural Resources, U.S. Senate, October 1996 (GAO/RCED/NSIAD-97-8).
13. "Further on DPRK Report on Delay in LWR Construction" (FBIS translated title), FBIS-EAS-2001-0517, May 16, 2001.
14. Steven Lee Myers, "It Takes One to Start a War, but Four to Make Peace," *New York Times*, August 10, 1997 at E5.
15. See Article III.1 of the NPT.

16. Statement of the Government of the Democratic People's Republic of Korea, reproduced as Annex 7 of INFCIRC/419, International Atomic Energy Agency, April 8, 1993.

17. "Statement of DPRK Government on its withdrawal from NPT," *KCNA* (January 10, 2003) available at http://www.korea-dpr.com/library/203.pdf.

18. Gus Constantine, *Washington Post*, March 12, 1993, p. A1.

19. *IAEA Press Release*, April 1, 1993 and February 12, 2003.

20. Joint Statement of the DPRK and the U.S.A., New York, June 11, 1993.

21. Agreed Framework between the United States of America and the Democratic People's Republic of Korea (1994) ("Agreed Framework"), IAEA INFCIRC/457, cite also http://www.kedo.org/Agreements/agreedframework.htm.

22. Testimony of Asistant Secretary of Defense for International Security Affairs, FRANKLIN D. KRAMER before the Senate Foreign Relations Committee March 21, 2000.

23. See, George Melloan, *What to Make of Kim Jong-Il's Unexpected Charm Offensive, Wall Street Journal*, A27 (October 31, 2000).

24. http://www.nis.go.kr/english/national/korea09.html. National Intelligence Service 2001

25. See Costa, pp. 7–8.

26. See, Leon V. Sigal, *Disarming Strangers: Nuclear Diplomacy with North Korea* (Princeton: Princeton University Press, 1999), pp. 172–176.

27. Sigal, Disarming Strangers, p. 175.

28. North Korea's "Sea of Fire" Threat Shakes Seoul, *Financial Times* [London], March 22, 1994, p. 6.

29. "North Rejection of Seoul Message 'Willful Act' " Seoul, *Yonhap*, August 9, 1994, FBIS-EAS-94-153.

30. *Reuters*, August 18, 1994.

31. Sigal, *Disarming Strangers*, p. 201.

32. Hwang Tu-hyung, "KEDO-N.K. Nuke Accord Fails to Bring Thaw to Inter-Korean Relations," *Yonhap*, December 19, 1995, FBIS-EAS-95-243.

33. Hsiang Tung "Korean Peninsula Takes on Tense Situation Again" Hong Kong TA KUNG PAO (in Chinese) April 6, 1996, FBIS-CHI-96-069.

34. "Kim Yong-sam Orders 'Iron-Tight' Posture Against DPRK" (translated title), Seoul *Yonhap*, April 6, 1996, FBIS-EAS-96-068.

35. For a list of DPRK provocations see Rinn S. Shinn, "North Korea: Chronology of Provocations, 1950–2000" (Washington, DC: Congressional Research Service, March 15, 2000). See also, http://www.koreascope.org/english/sub/2/nk10_7.htm (last visited August 2003).

36. "ROK Not To 'Proceed' With LWR Project Without DPRK Apology" (translated title), Seoul *Yonhap*, November 25, 1996, FBIS-TAC-97-001.

37. *Washington Times*, November 8, 1996, p. A16.

38. "DPRK Official Insists on Framework Agreement's Continuation" (translated title), *Yonhap*, October 31, 1996, FBIS-EAS-96-212.

39. "Angry Japan Sets Measures Against North Korea," *Reuters*, September 9, 1998; in NAPSNet Daily Report, http://www.nautilus.org, September 9, 1998. See also, Michiyo Nakamoto, *Financial Times* (London), September 4, 1998, p. 7.

40. "U.S. Stand on DPRK-U.S. Agreed Framework Flayed," *Korean Central News Agency* (Pyongyang), http://www.kcna.co.jp, May 31, 1999.

41. "North Korea calls for U.S. 'Good Faith' on KEDO," *Reuters*, July 27, 1999.

42. As of August 2003, South Korea had expended approximately US$955 million, Japan US$353 million, and the EU US$18 million.

43. "Kim DJ, UN's Annan Discuss DPRK, Nuclear Proliferation" (translated text) June 7, 1998, FBIS-EAS-98-158.

44. "DPRK's LWR Construction Reportedly To Progress Despite 29 June ROK-DPRK Sea Clash" *Seoul Yonhap*, July 14, 2002, FBIS-EAS-2002-0718.

45. "Keynote Speeches Made at Six-Way Talks," *Korean Central News Agency* (Pyongyang), http://www.kcna.co.jp, August 30, 2003.

Chapter Ten

International Organizations and the Inter-Korean Peace Process: Traditional Security Versus Nontraditional Security[1]

Shin-wha Lee

Introduction

During most of the Cold War period, inter-Korean relations were tainted by distrust and propaganda, fomenting the fear of confrontation and armed conflict between the two Koreas. Such confrontation not only affected the South and North's ability to cooperate and extend their dialogue, but also greatly affected the extent of their respective political and diplomatic engagements with the international community. Both Koreas were occupied in a war of diplomacy in order to promote ideological causes and obtain political legitimacy in the United Nations and other intergovernmental organizations (IGOs). For instance, the two Koreas had a long history of status competition in and out of the United Nations (UN), until September 1991 when both Koreas gained UN membership.

Just as the end of the Cold War—the dissolution of the Soviet Union being one cause—brought about a difference in the security paradigm, it also has given some room for reconsideration of the security issues relevant to the Korean peninsula. This has raised the necessity of the Korean question to be tackled from the perspectives of "comprehensive security" including economic and humanitarian dimensions, particularly since the manifestation of the North's food and refugee crisis. Yet, since North Korea's clandestine nuclear program was again raised in October 2002, "low politics" has been pushed to the back burner. Issues dealing with North Korea's economic reform plan and its defection problems, which caught the attention of international media and dominated much of the academic and policy debates in recent years, were largely replaced by a series of the North's provocative nuclear moves.

As an effort to resolve this new nuclear threat, a multilateral scheme in the form of six-party talks involving the United States, the two Koreas, Japan, China, and Russia was scheduled in August 2003. However, this scheme was not within the multilateral context of international or regional organizations but was instead established by the Northeast Asian countries on a bilateral basis with the United States.

In regard to this shift, the primary objective of this chapter is to take a critical look at the roles of international organizations (IOs) in general, and the United Nations in particular, in order to more effectively promote the inter-Korean peace process by enhancing comprehensive security in the Northeast Asian region. Although the role of the United Nations has been undermined in maintaining post–Cold War peace and security, especially in the aftermath of the campaign against Iraq, which was initiated by the United States without a UN Security Council resolution, it is too hasty to conclude that the United Nations has stopped serving its founding objective. It should be noted that the organization has a broader mandate and diverse day-to-day activities, which go beyond traditional boundaries in promoting international peace and security. In fact, UN activities in the area of peace and security broadly range from disarmament and the non-proliferation of weapons of mass destruction (WMD), to peacekeeping, humanitarian aid, electoral assistance, and the implementation of international laws through its different subsidiary organs and specialized agencies.[2] In this sense, just as the United Nations had a critical role during the Korean War, it now has to act to implement its primary *raison d'être* by facilitating peace and stability according to traditional and nontraditional terms. Economic incentives and humanitarian aid to the North, which are channeled through different UN programs and agencies, are key factors in not only ameliorating the living conditions within North Korea but also in improving inter-Korean relations and enhancing regional security.

In view of this, this chapter examines the role of IOs in engaging North Korea as a means of enhancing the inter-Korean peace process. It will be analyzed from the perspectives of both international IGOs and international nongovernmental organizations (INGOs) by exploring their achievements and dilemmas, with the United Nations in particular, when dealing with the North. This chapter discusses four separate but interrelated aspects of the relations between North Korea and IOs—diplomatic/political, military/security, economic, and humanitarian.

North Korea–IO Relations in Traditional Security Concerns

Diplomatic and Political Dimensions

While the ROK (South Korea) was founded under the auspices of the United Nations and largely benefited from UN support for its security and postwar reconstruction, the establishment of the DPRK (North Korea) lacked such official recognition and support from the United Nations. Furthermore, the relationship between the North and the United Nations was at times adversarial, particularly during the Korean War and its aftermath, as described in table 10.1. In May 1973, recognizing the importance of the UN's normative and institutional strength in international relations, North Korea became a full-fledged member state of the World Health Organization (WHO), a specialized agency of the UN system, through which it earned UN observer status the same year.[3] During the 1970s and 1980s, North Korea was very active in its diplomacy toward Third World countries, mainly in order to gain the support of nonaligned countries in the United Nations and thus win recognition and legitimacy from the United Nations.[4]

As South Korea was eager to prevail over its Northern counterpart in the UN System, and the General Assembly in particular, the UN appeared to be a forum for

Table 10.1 Chronology of North Korea–UN relations, 1947–91

October 30, 1947	UN Department of Political Affairs (DPA) approved of the dispatch of the UN Temporary Commission on Korea (UNTCOK) to Korea.
November 12, 1947	North Korea issued statements opposing the approval initiated by the DPA.
November 14, 1947	UN General Assembly adopted Korean resolution, which included the formation of the UNTCOK that would monitor national elections.
January 8, 1948	UNTCOK arrived in Seoul, South Korea.
January 9, 1948	North Korea rejected the request by UNTCOK to enter North Korea.
December 12, 1948	UN General Assembly recognized the Republic of Korea as the only legitimate state on the Korean peninsula.
January 19, 1949	South Korea applied for UN membership.
February 9, 1949	North Korea applied for UN membership.
October 1, 1949	UN General Assembly adopted South Korea's request for admission into the UN, while rejecting North Korea's application.
June 25, 1950	UN Security Council adopted a resolution enabling UN forces to participate in the Korean War.
June 27, 1950	North Korea issued a statement declaring the Security Council resolution was adopted without participation from the Soviet Union or China on June 25.
July 1, 1950	UN ground forces landed in Pusan, South Korea.
September 7, 1950	UN Security Council rejected the Soviet Union's proposal to withdraw UN forces out of Korea.
July 27, 1953	Armistice Agreement was signed between the United Nations and communist forces.
September 9, 1957	UN Security Council rejected the admission of South Korea to the United Nations due to the Soviet Union's veto.
December 4, 1964	North Korea emphasized the exclusion of the United Nations and the independent resolution of national reunification issues.
October 28, 1973	North Korea announced its "opposition to the South–North joint entry to the UN."
August 5, 1975	North Korea opposed the simultaneous entry of the two Koreas to the United Nations.
May 2, 1979	Kurt Waldheim, UN Secretary General, visited Pyongyang from May 2 to 3, and Seoul from May 4 to 8.
December 12, 1985	North Korea acceded to the Nuclear Non-Proliferation Treaty (NPT).
July 26, 1989	North Korea argued for North–South entry to the United Nations as a single Korean nation
April 7, 1991	South Korea's newly appointed UN Ambassador Chang Hee Roe informed the president of the Security Council that his government was determined to enter the United Nations, whether or not South Korea and North Korea became unified.

Table 10.1 Continued

July 8, 1991	North Korea submitted its application for entry to the United Nations to the UN Secretariat.
August 5, 1991	UN Security Council unanimously passed the bill to allow both South and North Korea to join the United Nations.
September 17, 1991	The two Koreas officially joined the United Nations as its one hundred and sixtieth and one hundred and sixty-first member states.

Source: Quoted from the Chronicles of Inter-Korean Relations at the English website of the Korean Ministry of Unification, at http://www.unikorea.go.kr (October 8, 2003).

South–North rivalry. Such rivalry was demonstrated in the debates over the two conflicting draft resolutions on the Korean question (a pro-South Korean resolution cosponsored by the United States, United Kingdom, and Japan versus a pro-North Korean resolution supported by the Soviet Union, China, and Algeria) in the General Assembly sessions in 1973 and 1975, respectively.[5] Indeed, the United Nations debated the Korean question every year from 1954 until 1976 when the two Koreas finally decided not to place the Korean question on the UN agenda anymore in order to avoid unnecessary confrontations through that forum.[6]

With respect to UN membership, North Korea had consistently opposed separate admission of the two Koreas and insisted that the two countries should be reunified and then join the United Nations as a single delegation. As a consequence, from 1949 South Korea applied for UN membership and failed five times due to vetoes by the Soviet Union and China, until it finally succeeded in September 1991.[7] Despite this, the South was still an active participant in affairs at various UN agencies. South Korea entered the WHO and the Food and Agriculture Organization (FAO) as a divided country in 1949 and established its UN observer mission in New York in 1951.[8] By 1988, when the Seoul Olympic Games were held with the participation of 160 countries including the Soviet Union and China, South Korea had joined 66 UN subsidiary organs, UN specialized agencies, and other IOs. To compare, North Korea had maintained membership in only 24 IOs by 1988 since it first established membership in the WHO in 1973.[9] The demise of the Cold War structure, the successful hosting of the Seoul Olympics, South Korea's impressive economic development, and the South Korean government's pursuit of *Nordpolitik*[10] contributed positively to the South's aspiration to become an official part of the UN. As South Korea's policy of "UN admission before unification," based on the political realities of the Korean peninsula, increasingly gained support from the UN member states since the end of the Cold War, North Korea also sought UN membership, as it did not want to be "left out."

Despite its initial reluctance to become a member state, North Korea, once it obtained official membership, utilized its permanent mission to the United Nations in New York as its main venue for bilateral and multilateral diplomacy and even as a mechanism for establishing new diplomatic ties. The United Nations has also served as a politically useful and convenient forum for the North to publicize its all-encompassing theory of *Juche* (self-reliance) to consolidate its national identity. In addition to these traditional political causes, North Korea also has found UN membership advantageous in addressing its domestic problems such as its economic difficulties and food and health-care crisis, by making requests for international assistance and by utilizing the capabilities of UN agencies.

As of the end of 2001, according to statistics provided by the Korean Ministry of Unification, North Korea had joined 38 other IOs, including UN agencies, while the South had 94 memberships including all the organizations that North Korea had joined (table 10.2).

Regardless of the contributions of the United Nations in the inter-Korean peace process, the North's official participation has laid an important legal foundation in defining the relationship between the North and the rest of the world. Given that all UN member states have international rights and obligations in maintaining global peace and security, as stated in Article 1 of the UN Charter, having a membership status in the UN itself is interpreted as North Korea's consent to abide by such rules. It is therefore important to explore ways and strategies to extend the North's participation in other IOs both at the global and the regional level.

As for the EU, it has strongly supported the inter-Korean peace process. The EU's efforts to engage with North Korea began in October 1995, when the European Commission Humanitarian Office (ECHO) provided humanitarian assistance to the North. In September 1997, the EU became a member of the executive board of the KEDO,[11] joining the three founding members, that is, the United States, Japan, and South Korea. In July 1999, the EU Council of Ministers adopted conclusions on the Korean peninsula, which set out a roadmap for future EU relations with North Korea. In response to the historic inter-Korean summit in June 2000, the Stockholm European Council of March 2001 declared increased support for the inter-Korean reconciliation process. In May 2001, a high-level EU delegation, including its head Göran Persson, visited Seoul and Pyongyang in support of the peace momentum generated by the inter-Korean summit and to establish diplomatic relations between North Korea and the EU. At present, among the 15 EU member states, all but France and Ireland have established diplomatic ties with Pyongyang.[12] During 1998–2002, five rounds of political dialogue took place between North Korea and the EU, allowing both parties to directly exchange views not only on the issues of peace and security but also on human rights and the economic and social development of North Korea.[13]

At the regional level, North Korea was admitted in July 2000, as the twenty-third member of the ARF, an official-level security forum for the Asia Pacific region.[14]

Table 10.2 South and North Korea's Membership in International Organizations, as of 2001, by number

	UN and affiliates	*UN special agencies*	*UN independent organizations*	*Other inter-governmental organizations*	*Total*
South Korea	5	16	3	70	94
North Korea	4	11	0	23	38

Source: Quoted from information of North Korea at the English website of the Korean Ministry of Unification, at http://www.unikorea.go.kr (October 8, 2003).

Given that the acceptance of ARF principles such as agreements on the non-proliferation of WMD and missile programs in the region as a prerequisite for ARF membership, North Korea's participation was welcomed as a sign of progress in the regional multilateral attempt to address peace and security issues. From Pyongyang's point of view, its inclusion in the ARF has enabled it to take advantage of the noncontroversial *modus operandi* of the ARF and thus increase engagement with member countries without experiencing a sense of threat to its sovereignty. In short, North Korea's participation is considered to be a win–win situation, facilitating Pyongyang's international socialization. ARF members had declared North Korea's admittance to the ARF to be the "beginning of the end of North Korea's isolation."[15]

However, the ARF, which has 23 member states and still lacks an organized mechanism for implementing concrete measures, has proved to be too large and loose an organization to deal with the Korean peninsula *problématique*. Moreover, the primary *raison d'être* of the ARF is to cope with China's challenge in the Southeast Asian and South China Seas settings, not Korea's security issues, although the annual ministerial meeting of the ARF since 2000 has provided a useful venue for North Korea's bilateral talks with South Korea, the United States, and Japan. Thus, it is recommended that a more narrowly and tightly constructed regional institution be established either by building a suborganization under the ARF or by creating a Northeast Asia–specific organization.

This suggestion could be supported by a recent finding of the State Failure Task Force, which has produced a list of 114 state-failure events between 1955 and 1998. According to this study, there is a strong negative correlation between membership in regional organizations and state failure. The greater the number of regional organizations to which a country belongs, the less likely it is to become a failed state. In the case of Muslim countries studied by the Task Force, all other conditions being equal, the countries with a below-average index level of memberships had a 70 percent higher possibility of failure than those with an above-average index level. This therefore highlights the importance of a country's political and diplomatic engagement with its neighboring countries.[16]

At the nongovernmental level, the Council for Security Cooperation in the Asia-Pacific (CSCAP), a multilateral, Track II security organization that analyzes security issues relevant to the Asia Pacific, provides support to the governmental level dialogues at the ARF. Since Track II provides the forums for informal mechanisms through which information and knowledge not readily identified or available to government policy-makers can be collected and interchanged, CSCAP facilitates dialogues among non-state actors including civilians, field workers, and academics—as well as among government officials participating in their private capacity—to generate consensual policy recommendations concerning security issues. As the only Track II mechanism in which North Korea participated with (since 1994), the CSCAP complements ARF efforts to encourage further progress in inter-Korean relations by facilitating opportunities for dialogue—particularly through issue-oriented working groups such as the CSCAP Nuclear Energy Experts Group and the Confidence and Security Building Measures and Comprehensive and Cooperative Security working groups.[17] Although not entirely free from government intervention, the CSCAP and the epistemic communities in East Asian countries carry the potential not only to assist in intergovernmental dialogues, but also to ultimately formulate coordinated mechanisms that can lead to cooperative security in East Asia.

Military and Security Dimensions

North Korea's nuclear development programs and ballistic missile capability, as well as its ongoing chemical and biological weapons programs, remain as some of the most prominent security concerns in the post–Cold War world. In December 1985, North Korea acceded to the Treaty on the Non-Proliferation of Nuclear Weapons (NPT), committing to halt the production of bombs and to open up its nuclear sites to the inspection teams of the International Atomic Energy Agency (IAEA), a specialized agency of the UN system. Signatory states are required to bring a safe-guard agreement with the IAEA into force within 18 months after accession, but the North complied with the agreement in April 1992, almost 5 years after the deadline. The North Korean government submitted its "Initial Report" on all nuclear materials subject to inspection, but the IAEA raised the suspicion that the North had produced more plutonium, a material critical in producing nuclear weapons, than it had actually reported. Also, the United States provided the IAEA with a high-resolution satellite photo, which showed two undeclared spent fuel sites at the Yongbyon nuclear complex, about 60 miles north of Pyongyang. By that time, the United States believed that the North had produced enough plutonium for one or two nuclear weapons. In March 1993, North Korea rejected the IAEA's demand for a special inspection of the suspected nuclear weapons facilities and declared its intention to withdraw from the NPT. The IAEA soon reported the North's violation of its NPT safeguards agreement to the Security Council, which issued a resolution (S/RES/825) by a vote of 13–0 with 2 abstentions (China and Pakistan), to call upon North Korea to comply with its obligations.[18] However, such action was of little avail in disciplining the North.

It was finally the United States that, on June 11, 1993, the day before the withdrawal of North Korea from the NPT was to take effect, successfully persuaded the North to suspend its withdrawal and accept IAEA inspection. However, North Korea continued to limit IAEA access until June 1994 when the IAEA decided to suspend all IAEA technical assistance to North Korea. This decision promptly led the North to give notice of its withdrawal from the IAEA. The United States requested that the Security Council impose sanctions on North Korea for violating its IAEA and NPT obligations but faced resistance and reluctance from the Council. North Korea claimed that such sanctions would be tantamount to a declaration of war, a position that it still maintains today.

In the midst of escalating tensions on the Korean peninsula, former U.S. President Jimmy Carter met with then-President Kim Il Sung in Pyongyang. This meeting was a turning point leading to the successful conclusion of U.S.–DPRK negotiations held in Geneva, culminating in the U.S.–DPRK Agreed Framework (hereafter the Agreed Framework) of October 1994. In November 1994, the IAEA resumed its inspection activities in North Korea at the request of the Security Council. Under the Agreed Framework, the North was obligated to suspend all nuclear activities in exchange for the construction of two light-water reactors (LWRs). In accordance with the Framework, North Korea apparently ceased plutonium production and allowed IAEA supervision of the facilities in Yongbyon. However, KEDO, established in March 1995, as an American-led consortium to help build the reactors, underwent a series of construction delays and disagreements over the time frame needed to bring the North into full compliance with safeguards required by the NPT/IAEA before suspending its activities in the wake of the DPRK's October 2002 nuclear revelations.[19]

Apart from the nuclear issue, the Agreed Framework seems to have failed in correcting North Korea's "bad behaviors" as evidenced by the Northern attempt to infiltrate the South by an armed submarine in September 1996, its test-firing of a two-stage ballistic missile over Japan in August 1998, and its continuous attempts to blackmail the rest of the world by threatening to take military actions. The UN General Assembly adopted a resolution in November 1998 and again in November 1999 urging the North to implement the Nuclear Safeguards Agreement.

Furthermore, while the Agreed Framework envisions gradual diplomatic and economic normalization between the United States and North Korea and improved inter-Korean relations through South–North dialogue, U.S.–North Korean relations have substantially deteriorated since the beginning of the current Bush administration. President George W. Bush has adopted a hawkish stance, labeling North Korea, together with Iraq and Iran, as an "axis of evil." In its agenda against terrorism, the United States has listed North Korea as one of seven terrorist-friendly governments that are allegedly "sponsors of terrorism."[20]

North Korea's revelation about its secret highly enriched uranium nuclear weapons program in October 2002—arguably a violation of the spirit if not the letter of the Agreed Framework—and its "nuclear steps" are once again posing a serious challenge to the security of Northeast Asia and the entire international community. The North increased the tension by reactivating the nuclear facilities that had been frozen under the 1994 nuclear agreement, expelling IAEA inspectors from the Yongbyon site in late December 2002, and subsequently declaring its withdrawal from the NPT on January 10, 2003.

It is believed that Pyongyang has once again started using the nuclear issue as a means of brinkmanship to seek a "big deal" with Washington, that is, to obtain a promise of a security guarantee, economic aid, and the normalization of diplomatic relations in the form of a bilateral nonaggression treaty. Yet, the current U.S. administration is less amenable to a deal than the previous one. In fact, it is argued that a series of radical fundamentalist (right-wing) shifts in America's strategic thinking and behaviors since the coming of the ABC (All But Clinton) administration in January 2001 has prompted Pyongyang's brinkmanship-breakdown-breakthrough tactics. President Bush has assumed a hard-line attitude against the North's challenge and has refused to give in to any demands from the North unless the latter shuts down its nuclear program and allows IAEA inspectors back. Contrary to Pyongyang's insistence on bilateral talks with the United States, Washington has emphasized a multilateral approach,[21] urging the IAEA to refer the North Korean issue to the UN Security Council. Accepting this suggestion, the IAEA unanimously voted to adopt such a resolution on February 12, 2003.[22] This prompted the North to announce that any sanctions from the United Nations would be treated as a declaration of war.[23]

While a negotiated bilateral agreement between North Korea and the United States may well be the most important factor in managing the current North Korean nuclear crisis, a multilateral mechanism can bring many countries and organizations to collectively call upon the North to comply with its agreements with the outside world. Relations with the international community are ever more important, considering that North Korea, despite its resistance, is becoming increasingly tied to and dependent upon the outside world. In this context, it is encouraging to note that in August 2003, North Korea finally agreed to hold six-party talks on the nuclear standoff, where China, South Korea, Japan, and Russia were included, along with the United States. Still, the most important factor is not whether the negotiations are bilateral or multilateral but the substance of the talks.[24] It remains uncertain whether multilateral negotiations will succeed in returning IAEA inspectors to North Korea or in scrapping the North's nuclear weapons program. Such an achievement would require a security guarantee for the Kim Jong Il regime from the United States and economic incentives for the North.

While multilateral dialogue to settle the North Korean nuclear problem has been initiated, the United States seems to be continuing to urge the UN Security Council to take action against the North. In a speech in Seoul in July 2003, U.S. Undersecretary of State John Bolton criticized the Council for not undertaking any action in the six months since the IAEA had referred the issue of North Korean nuclear violations to it. He asserted that action through the Security Council should complement action via the Proliferation Security Initiative (PSI, the U.S. efforts to curb the spread of WMD by countries such as North Korea),[25] as well as diplomatic efforts by the United States to resolve the nuclear standoff through multilateral talks.[26]

It is difficult for the United Nations to take timely and effective action not only because of limits on intervention in the internal issues of sovereign states but also because the United Nations cannot act, in principle, without the consent of its member states. For example, the United Nations was paralyzed by the squabbles of major powers, especially the permanent members of the Security Council, for much of its existence during the Cold War period. Vetoes were common, mainly used by the Soviet Union and the United States, during this ideologically divided period.[27] Although ideology is no longer a driving force in dividing the post–Cold War world, it was China that opposed Security Council involvement in North Korea's current nuclear issue, wishing to avoid the deterioration of its relations with the North, which is China's remaining ideological ally. At the meeting of April 9, 2003, the Security Council's first meeting since North Korea announced its withdrawal from the NPT, the IAEA referred to the Council the North's "noncompliance." This meeting could have launched a process that might have developed into sanctions against the North. However, faced with China's opposition, the Council failed to agree on any kind of statement or resolution. Furthermore, just as North Korea had rejected the IAEA's resolution in the first nuclear crisis in 1993, it announced on April 6, 2003 its refusal to respect any UN decision in relation to its nuclear issues, thus threatening the United Nations with the risk of losing legitimacy should it fail to oblige its member states to comply with the accords and resolutions adopted.

On the other hand, the United Nations is currently facing a dilemma given growing resistance to military actions or sanctions from the European countries in particular, especially in the aftermath of the U.S.-led attack on Iraq, which was not authorized by the Security Council. The end of the Cold War has brought about a "renaissance" in the security role of the United Nations, as seen in Operation Desert Storm, an offensive action against the forces of Iraq under the provisions of UN Security Council resolutions in 1991. However, it has become apparent that the end of the Cold War did not position the United Nations as the focal point for legitimizing the collective actions of member states in order to settle global problems, as the United Nations has faced a lack of systematic engagement by the United States. The uneasy relationship between the United Nations and the most powerful sovereign state in the post–Cold War world has often resulted from the unilateral attitude of the United States in deciding whether military intervention is necessary, even though the responsibility for maintaining global peace and security and issuing mandates for the use of force ostensibly belongs to the Security Council.

In fact, the United States has been more often criticized for doing too little in military (and humanitarian) intervention campaigns, as in the crises of Bosnia and Rwanda, rather than for doing too much.[28] Such inadequate UN action was largely attributed to the U.S. unwillingness to get involved in crisis zones where it has found little national interest. With the United States having bypassed the need for a Security Council resolution in the case of the war on Iraq in March 2003, the United Nations once again confronted the uncertainties of its role in safeguarding peace and security. This time it was not because of its failure to mandate the use of force but due to its failure to stop the United States from enjoying an exemption from legal accountability in regard to the use of force irreconcilable with the UN Charter and international law.[29] As for the current North Korean nuclear issue, the United States has called for the active role of the Security Council in forcing the North to give up its nuclear weapons ambitions. Confronted with a series of North Korean provocations in recent months, George W. Bush has indicated that if necessary, the United States would not hesitate to use preemptive measures as well as military force to solve this crisis.[30] Although most of the countries around the world have no opinion of the U.S. position on the North Korean issue, if the six-party talks were to break down and a military option were to be raised, it is doubtful that the Security Council members that perceive U.S. initiatives as no more than adding a legitimizing cover to Bush's runaway unilateralism in and out of the United Nations, would support an American claim to use force.

In short, on the issue of the current nuclear standoff, there still remain several thorny issues to be resolved on a bilateral basis with the United States, rather than through the United Nations, the ARF, or other multilateral frameworks. Therefore, the role the United Nations can play in addressing the Korean peninsula security issue is limited, with little substance to discuss or decide at this stage. Nonetheless, it is still important for the United Nations to ascertain that North Korea abides by its accords in order to preserve and increase its legitimacy, especially in the eyes of the United States.

Roles of International Organizations in North Korea's
Nontraditional Security Concerns

Development and Economic Dimensions
It is only in recent times that North Korea has ever so slightly opened its doors to seek aid from the outside world. This limited opening appears not to arise from an

eagerness to learn and gain from its membership in IOs but for the sake of the state's survival, which has been challenged by internal economic and political woes. Still, the international community has been trying to find ways to engage with North Korea not only to address traditional security concerns but also to expand into nontraditional security areas such as North Korea's development and humanitarian crises.

The Tumen River Area Development Programme (TRADP) is a good test case for exploring the outer possibilities and limitations of international aid in facilitating North Korea's development. Initiated by the UNDP in 1991, the TRADP, the first such multilateral economic cooperative mechanism in the Northeast Asian region, is an area development project in the Tumen River area, where the borders of the five adjacent states of the region (that is, South and North Korea, China, the Russian Federation, and Mongolia) meet. The UNDP vision was to transform the Tumen River delta into an international trade center. The contracting states have agreed to cooperate in many different capacities to develop the region's industry, commerce, trade and tourism and also to protect the environment.[31]

However, the UNDP's initial expectations during the first phase (1991–95), particularly concerning the investment and trade potential of the Tumen region, have proved unrealistic. Recognizing the need to restructure the TRADP, the UNDP transferred the Tumen Programme Management Office from New York to Beijing for a more practical developmental strategy based on the real needs of the different member countries, emphasizing the local level. In December 1995, three treaty agreements were signed by the five member states, which became the formal institutional arrangements for the Programme.[32] With the establishment of these intergovernmental agreements, technical cooperation with the Programme was broadened beyond the UNDP to other UN specialized agencies such as the UN Industrial Development Organization (UNIDO), the UN Conference on Trade and Development (UNCTAD), the UN Department of Economic and Social Affairs (UN/DESA), and the Global Environmental Facility (GEF).[33]

Unfortunately, neither the region's economic conditions (especially in the wake of the Asian economic crisis) nor political climate (e.g., inter-Korean confrontation) has been conducive to the development of the second phase of the TRADP (1996–2000). The failure by IOs and foreign investors to recognize and address such regional complexities has also contributed to a state where the existence and future direction of the Programme are in doubt.[34] Furthermore, support from the UNDP has decreased since mid-1998, as the UNDP and the Tumen Secretariat decided to cease funding for local area development activities of the TRADP and instead to focus on broader regional economic cooperation initiatives. In April 2001, the UNDP confirmed that funding would continue into the third phase of the TRADP (2001–03). Yet, the need for member states to increase the capacity of the TRADP has become a major task in order to secure continuous funding from the UNDP.[35]

Despite several difficulties and uncertainties, the TRADP has been considered a useful institutional structure to provide North Korea with special opportunities to engage in international cooperation. North Korea has been continually expressing its expectation of improved relations with other Northeast Asian states through the TRADP. Working under the Programme, North Korea established the Rajin-Sonbong Free Economic and Trade Zone (where ground taxes are maintained at a low rate in order to attract international investors) in December 1991 to stimulate international trade and investment in the area. To note, between 1971 and 2000 the FDI total for North Korea was only $88 million, compared to $576 million for Russia, $519 million for China, and $392 million for Mongolia.[36]

In recent years, North Korea has made a series of efforts to tackle the nation's economic crisis and build ties with the outside world to induce more investment and aid. For instance, Pyongyang established diplomatic relations with most of the EU member states during 2000–01. On July 1, 2002, North Korea announced its decision to abandon the food rationing system. As a means to facilitate the implementation of its economic reform policies of July 2002, North Korea designated the city of Sinuiju, on the Yalu River (Amnok-gang to Koreans) across from Dandong, China, as a Special Administrative Region (SAR) in September 2002. The Sinuiju SAR is unique from the Rajin-Sonbong Economic and Trade Zone in that the former is guaranteed independent legislative, judicial and administrative powers, while the latter is under the control of the central government. Despite growing tension in the aftermath of the North's acknowledgment of its nuclear program, the two Koreas have agreed to build an industrial complex in Kaesong, a western North Korean city, in December 2002 with a groundbreaking ceremony held in June 2003.

All these moves on the North's side suggest that Kim Jong Il seems to have no choice but to take the risk of acquiring outside aid and undertaking much-needed economic reforms because his country's famine and economic conditions have reached a catastrophic point. It is therefore important for the international community, both IOs and concerned countries, to ensure that the North does not undergo a sudden, chaotic collapse, referred to as a "hard landing." This would not only have negative consequences for the stability of the Korean peninsula and the region, but would also impose enormous economic burdens on the South. In order for North Korea to recover from its economic crisis, it is important not only to increase South–North economic cooperation but also to attract foreign investment. However, due to the poor conditions of investment at the private level, as well as the strained political climate on the Korean peninsula, North Korea should search for a way of obtaining international financial aid through IOs.

There are at least two compelling reasons for international financial organizations such as the International Monetary Fund (IMF), the International Bank for Reconstruction and Development (IBRD, hereafter the World Bank) and the Asian Development Bank (ADB) to become involved. First, by interaction with such organizations, North Korea could receive much-needed financial resources. Since the IMF requires a country to provide transparent economic data in the public domain prior to granting a loan, the substantial economic and financial inducements from the IMF could persuade the Kim Jong Il regime to release statistics of the nation's economy that have remained secret over the decades. Second, these international financial institutions can provide the North with expertise and supervision to run its economy, enabling North Koreans to better understand how market economies work and to reduce the likelihood of a chaotic regime collapse, particularly in post–Kim Jong Il North Korea.

Needless to say, in order to receive financial aid from the IMF and the World Bank, North Korea must first acquire official membership in these organizations.

North Korea officially applied for membership to the ADB in February 1997 and received inspectors from the IMF in September 1997 and the World Bank in February 1998. In fact, until the deterioration of U.S.–North Korean relations after the Bush administration came into office and the North Korean nuclear issue reemerged, relations between North Korea and the international financial organizations had been showing much progress. This is illustrated by the UNDP proposal to supervise a training program for North Korean government officials in Pyongyang.[37]

However, it remains uncertain when the North will be permitted to become a member of the IMF and the World Bank, given U.S. economic sanctions. Furthermore, rising tensions in the wake of North Korea's nuclear program will deter foreign investors from investing in the North for at least the foreseeable future. Thus, North Korea should first be removed from the U.S. list of "rogue states" since this labeling makes it impossible for the North to attain assistance from the World Bank, the IMF, or similar organizations.

Yet, there are still ways to receive financial aid before becoming a member, if certain conditions are met. Though it might not be in the form of official financial aid, it is possible for North Korea to receive noneconomic support such as technical support that would help the North to adapt to international society. Even if memberships in the IMF and World Bank are granted, it is first necessary to successfully meet negotiated policy measures with these institutions in order to receive financial aid. Thus, the only possible plan for the time being is to utilize the technical support given by such organizations. As a reference, Vietnam had actively utilized the technical support programs of such institutions before it was granted official membership into these institutions.[38] Participation in such programs would help states like North Korea to understand the mechanisms of the market economy.

While the initial aim is to promote economic reform and development in impoverished North Korea, there is a pronounced political, security subtext since more open trade will induce greater involvement of the North in the international community, which would be beyond the economic and development domains. In the long run, the participating states and IOs will reach agreement, conscious of the need to improve political relations and promote peace and stability on the Korean peninsula and in the region in general through international engagement with the North on economic and development issues.

Meanwhile, international NGOs can play a valuable role in addressing North Korea's development needs. This is particularly true when political and diplomatic tensions impede cooperative engagement with the North. NGOs not only share their developmental expertise, but they also pose less of a political threat to the North's regime, since their contacts with the North are issue-specific and usually focused on technical and pragmatic areas. For instance, the U.S.-based Nautilus Institute's wind power project, though small in scale, has been operating in North Korea since 1998. This project is designed to focus attention on the North's energy problems as a key factor in the country's food crisis, as well as to help prepare North Koreans to accept development aid, and demonstrate that cooperative engagement with North Korea is possible by serving as a case of cooperation between North Koreans and Americans.[39]

Humanitarian Dimension[40]
International Responses to North Korea's Food Crisis
The food crisis is currently the most immediate and severe humanitarian problem in North Korea. The famine plight is attributed to consecutive natural disasters, coupled with the collapse of the special trading relationships with China and the former Soviet-bloc countries, as well as the North Korean government's inability to handle the crisis.

In late 1995, the international community began to seriously acknowledge the problem of the North's food deficit, resulting in increased donor pledges. Between 1995 and 2001, a total of two million metric tons of food aid worth $500 million was given to the North by the World Food Program (WFP), mainly contributed by the United States, South Korea, Japan, and the EU.[41] UNICEF, the Office for the Coordination of Humanitarian Affairs (OCHA), and the WHO have also conducted coordinating efforts with regards to providing health care and famine relief. In an attempt to increase international aid donations, field research and fact-finding surveys have been conducted by the International Federation of the Red Cross and the WFP to reassure donors by providing reliable information about the quality of the relief operations.

Meanwhile, international collective action, both at the regional and nongovernmental levels, has been critical in meeting the needs of the North Korean people. For instance, the European Union's Council Conclusions on the Korean Peninsula (July 1999) and Council Conclusions of General Affairs (October 2000) outlined the EU's goals to be part of the international effort in addressing North Korea's humanitarian crisis by encouraging the North's economic reforms and non-proliferation, and promoting peace on the Korean peninsula.[42] These goals were strengthened by the Stockholm European Council of March 2001. Having established diplomatic relations with North Korea since 2000, EU countries bilaterally and collectively have been assisting the North in such areas as food aid and economic assistance in the form of technical and farming assistance, amounting to a total of €393 million.[43]

International NGOs have also been active in providing humanitarian aid to starving North Koreans, although in terms of quantity, NGO contributions constitute a relatively small percentage of the total international humanitarian aid. For example, the American Friends Service Committee (AFSC), which has been involved in building trust with Pyongyang officials since the 1970s, has helped bring delegations of agriculture experts and cardiologists to the United States to learn how to more effectively meet the needs of their people. The AFSC also has sent experts to North Korea to find new types of productive seeds and to experiment with new fertilizers.[44] Several European NGOs have also built relations of trust with the North Korean government, thus contributing a great deal to reducing the wide-scale food shortage in North Korea. In addition to the NGOs directly operating within North Korea, many NGOs outside the country have also been engaged in advocacy work, holding or participating in conferences, and making international community appeals for humanitarian assistance.

Yet, the food situation has hardly improved after years of aid and the FAO and the WFP announced that 13.2 million North Koreans are now malnourished.[45] On the whole, the international community's response to the North's food crisis has been in need of a broader and more systematic process of providing international support and cooperation. The North Korean government's continuing lack of transparency and abiding reluctance to open the whole country to on-the-spot monitoring and donors' consequent reluctance to provide aid explain the decline of international humanitarian assistance in recent years.

On-site monitoring of food distribution has also been controversial. Although international pressure has compelled the North to admit international relief agencies to monitor food distribution (at the end of 2002, the WFP had access to 163 of the 211 counties in the country),[46] the North Korean government has not yet admitted international delegations into certain areas such as border regions and areas with sensitive military installations. As a consequence, Médecins Sans Frontières (MSF) and OXFAM United Kingdom, both international humanitarian NGOs, protested against the many restrictions on field workers in the North and pulled out in September 1998 and December 1999, respectively. Action Contré a Faim (ACF, a French NGO), Action Against Hunger (AAH, a British aid agency), and Cooperative for American Relief Everywhere (CARE, a U.S. private relief group) announced their withdrawals from North Korea in March and April 2000, citing constraints imposed by the Pyongyang regime on their relief activities and attempts at effective monitoring.[47]

The shortfall of international donations can also be understood in the context of "donor fatigue"—a phenomenon prevalent worldwide in which international humanitarian action has been decreasing despite the continued life-threatening suffering of civilians in humanitarian disaster areas afflicted with famine, forced displacement, and civil wars. As a rule, many states remain passive toward the crises of other nations unless the crises threaten their own national interests and security. They are unwilling to take an initiative in providing aid or preventing the further deterioration of crises since such humanitarian actions cost money, energy, and time better served with regard to other national causes. Donor fatigue, or the lack of compassion and willingness, is not the only reason why donor nations are slow to respond to humanitarian emergencies or why millions of people still go hungry while there is an abundance of food in other parts of the world. It is closely related to the *realpolitik* of state actors in the international community. Government leaders hardly ever go through the trouble of sacrificing their political gains for a humanitarian cause. For instance, referring to the delay in food aid in 1995, the United States, South Korea, and Japan were questioned as to whether or not they used food aid as leverage to bring North Korea to the negotiating table for the Four Party Talks, while at the same time, the North Korean government politicized its famine situation and requested outside aid as a precondition to any talks.

In brief, although North Korea's leaders are primarily responsible for the country's famine, IOs and donor governments could play a role in decreasing the consequences of the humanitarian tragedy through early action. Despite all the frustrations and difficulties of providing and monitoring humanitarian aid, it is inhumane to withhold relief aid from North Korea and wait for the Kim Jong Il regime to undertake reforms or collapse. Cutting aid to the North not only fails to give any guarantee that the regime will collapse, but more importantly, it can be readily assumed that without food aid, additional resources will not be provided by the North Korean government to feed its people, resulting in the death and suffering of the common people.[48]

The long-term effects of the food crisis on the health of the population have proved to be immense. John Power, the WFP Regional Director for Asia, has said that a generation of North Koreans is at risk of death from malnutrition, as starving children and babies delivered by underfed mothers are subject to low birth weight, mental retardation, and short life spans.[49]

International response to North Korea's famine is also important for security and political considerations. Even the most unsuccessful famine relief efforts in North Korea have at least given the North Korean population an opportunity to increase contact with the outside world, which in turn provides contrast to the regime's propaganda about *juche* ideology and helps citizens recognize their reliance on so-called imperialist aid from the West. As documented by various NGO surveys and interviews with North Korean defectors, ordinary North Koreans, who have been indoctrinated to blindly follow the authority of their government and leaders without being allowed to express their own political opinion have begun to express grievances about the political and social conditions that have caused the famine. This change of perceptions among North Korean citizens appears to have arisen from increased contact with international relief organizations, as well as years of an inefficient communist system controlling the economy and agriculture, which expends enormous amounts of resources on the military at the cost of the civilian sector.

International Responses to the North Korean Refugee Crisis in China[50]
The deteriorating living conditions within North Korea have driven hunger-stricken North Koreans to flee the country. In June 2003, the UN High Commissioner for Refugees (UNHCR) estimated the number of North Korean defectors in China to be about 10,000, but according to unofficial estimates by NGOs, the number could be as high as 300,000.[51] Most of these escapees usually live in fear of arrest and forced repatriation by Chinese authorities. However, despite these sufferings, North Korean defectors have received little humanitarian protection or support from the international community, mainly due to the following reasons.

First, inconsistencies within the set of international rules and norms on refugees (e.g., the 1951 UN Convention Relating to the Status of Refugees and the 1967 Protocol) prevent North Koreans, who flee in search of food, from being recognized as refugees, because evidence of being forced to leave one's home state for political reasons is a prerequisite for refugee status. Second, with the surplus of cases concerning treaty-defined political refugees in the post–Cold War world, the UNHCR and the international community face increased difficulties in allocating time, personnel, and funds to deal with new displacements. As a result, the UNHCR would be placed in a difficult position; if it granted refugee status to North Korean escapees, it would face pressure to grant refugee status to nonpolitical asylum seekers from all over the world. Third, labeled as illegal aliens by the Chinese government, North Koreans are subject to forced repatriation. Although the UN High Commissioner for Refugees Ruud Lubbers reported in June 2003 that China has eased its tough policy of deporting North Korean defectors back home, China will not fundamentally change its policy on handling North Korean refugees.[52] As a consequence, North Korea's "food refugees" will remain in limbo. The only possible exception to this would be those escapees, who are involved in dramatic headline-grabbing incidents, such as the

Gil-Su Chang's family of seven that sought refuge at the UNHCR office in Beijing in June 2000 and the 25 defectors that sought asylum at the Spanish Embassy in Beijing in March 2001.

However, despite these impediments, there are reasons why hunger-stricken North Korean escapees must be granted international support and protection. First, a distinction has to be drawn between "simple" displacement, resulting from natural factors alone, and "complex" displacement, caused by combined effects of environmental disruption, economic deprivation, government incapability or repression, and armed conflict. The UNHCR rationalizes that the people at risk from environmental and natural disasters can usually rely, at least in part, on protection from their state, whereas genuine refugees have no choice but to turn to the international community for help. It should be noted that people of many underdeveloped countries have suffered from problems of complex displacement as their leaders are more interested in maintaining the regime than promoting the welfare of its citizens. The North Korean food crisis is such a case as it fundamentally results from structural problems such as a large proportion of the budget going to military expenditure and the existence of a closed, centrally planned economy. At present, North Korean food refugees may not be regarded as refugees by law, but the UNHCR and other IOs have set several precedents of protecting groups who have fled similar situations, such as the famine victims of Ethiopia in the mid-1980s. In this connection, the UNHCR and the governments concerned have the humanitarian obligations to at least help North Korean defectors survive, even if they are not able to grant the defectors asylum.[53]

Second, it should be noted that repatriated North Korean escapees suffer from political persecution.[54] Reports testify that a great number of the forcibly returned were sent to one of several North Korean concentration camps.[55] Those who avoid persecution are socially stigmatized or discriminated. The 1951 Refugee Convention states that no refugee should be forced back to his/her country of origin if his/her freedom or life is in danger. Though the North Korean "famine-refugees" would first need to gain proper refugee status in order for this convention to apply to their situation, the UNHCR released an additional resolution in 1977 that expanded upon the principle of *non-refoulement*—which prohibits the forcible return of refugees—by also applying it to people, who may be subjected to persecution if returned to their country of origin, irrespective of whether they have been granted formal recognition as refugees. Thus, China's forced repatriation of North Koreans is a clear violation of international law.

As of yet, few concrete steps have been taken to alleviate the refugee crisis. Nevertheless, it is positive to see the work of human rights activists and international human rights NGOs that have been very active in assisting North Korean escapees and attracting international attention to their situation. For instance, the Citizen's Alliance for North Korean Human Rights (CANKHR) has held several international conferences, the latest in Prague, where it tried to raise public awareness on the plight of North Korean escapees/defectors. In addition, CANKHR also publishes journals and newsletters and appeals for international protection of North Korean defectors.[56]

Amnesty International (AI), one of the best-known international human rights NGOs, has persistently helped North Korean refugees. AI has a wide range of research programs that uses its international networks to persuade and cajole governments and IGOs to take measures to protect the rights of refugees and asylum seekers. AI had played a contributing role in encouraging the UNHCR to protect the Gil-Su Chang family previously mentioned. Also, the potential problems created by the entry of 25 North Koreans into the Spanish Embassy and the successive waves of defections by North Koreans in China to various embassies were greatly relieved by the coordinated efforts of NGOs and activists operating both within and outside China.

Although the intent of these NGOs is commendable, there have been controversies over their tactics. In comparison with the total number of North Koreans roaming around China, relatively few have been able to receive aid, ironically because of the aggressive tactics of NGOs and human rights activists. Moreover, while international publicity on the North Korean refugee issue has raised greater public awareness, it has thus far been in many ways counterproductive, further endangering the North Korean escapees. For instance, if the wave of embassy invasions by North Korean defectors hoping to go to South Korea continues, China will most likely stop foreign NGO operations and close off its border with North Korea. As a result, conditions for people in the North would become much worse, and perhaps instigate further repression within North Korea, while tens of thousands of North Korean escapees would be subject to even greater danger in China.

Obviously, despite efforts of NGOs, greater cooperation involving states, IGOs, and NGOs is needed.[57] It is somewhat encouraging that the UNHCR has not only been directly addressing the problem, but has also been coordinating the efforts of national governments, other IGOs and NGOs to care for North Korean asylum seekers. In recent years, the UNHCR has been working more closely with the governments of China and North Korea respectively, to provide aid to North Korean refugees. For example, in May 2001, North Korean representatives met with the UNHCR to seek aid for victims of natural disasters and to study the international refugee convention and UNHCR activities. Consequently, a "memorandum of understanding" was signed with the UN body. The UNHCR is also actively involved in campaigning to governments for the protection of the rights of refugees. For instance, dealing with the "Spanish Embassy 25," the UNHCR visited the refugees and negotiated with the Spanish and Chinese governments to prevent the refugees from being sent back to the North. A UN spokesman made the strong case that the refugees would most certainly face persecution.[58]

In brief, the defection of a growing number of North Koreans to South Korea may prove to be a political burden for Pyongyang. As such, it is necessary for South Korea, in cooperation with the UNHCR and international relief NGOs, to pursue such possible alternatives as providing "temporary protection" to these defectors in their temporary host countries.

Conclusion

With respect to the inter-Korean peace process, the United Nations and other IOs have played a limited and indirect role. Yet, the two Koreas' interaction with the IOs has had some relevance to peace and security on the Korean peninsula. From a traditional security perspective, IOs, particularly UN bodies, have continually made efforts to exercise their influence so that North Korea would comply with international law, as demonstrated by the UN Security Council's and IAEA's statements and resolutions in the case of the previous and current North Korean nuclear threats. International organizations, both IGOs and INGOs, have been also instrumental in promoting nontraditional security matters by providing developmental and human-itarian assistance. In this sense, this chapter has discussed the role of IOs that complements traditional government-to-government diplomacy by engaging North Korea into international society. Such efforts are necessary not only to address current North Korean problems and facilitate the inter-Korean reconciliation process, but also to help prepare for a post–Kim Jong Il system.

In conclusion, North Korea's UN diplomacy seems to be increasingly important and relevant for both traditional and nontraditional causes because it can be used to strengthen the existing government. This will depend on whether the Kim Jong Il government can implement a new foreign policy of observing international laws and ethics, and promoting international cooperation, consequently moving out of its diplomatic isolation. The success of North Korea's UN diplomacy also relies on whether the North can utilize multilateral projects such as the UNDP-sponsored TRADP and humanitarian assistance from the WFP, the FAO, and other interna-tional relief organizations, in order to improve the economic and social conditions of its people. Such economic incentives and humanitarian aid can prove successful not only in stabilizing the domestic situation of North Korea but also in promoting a stable, peaceful, and mutually profitable interdependent situation between the two Koreas, and in further enhancing regional stability.

Notes

1. The author wishes to thank Prof. Samuel S. Kim for his valuable comments on the draft of this paper and Hyun Myoung Jae for her assistance in collecting materials.
2. United Nations General Assembly, "Role of the United Nations in Maintaining International Peace and Security," Global Agenda Forum in the Austrian Parliament, Vienna, April 7, 2003, at http:www.un.org/ga/president/57/pages/speeches/ (August 15, 2003).
3. Samuel S. Kim, "North Korea and the United Nations," *International Journal of Korean Studies* 1: 1 (Spring 1997). To compare, South Korea established a UN observer mission in New York in 1951.
4. Young Whan Kihl, "North Korea and the United Nations," in *North Korean Foreign Relations in the Post-Cold War Era*, ed. Samuel S. Kim (Hong Kong, Oxford, and New York: Oxford University Press, 1998).
5. Ibid.
6. Chi Young Pak, *Korea and the United Nations* (The Hague/London/Boston: Kluwer Law International, 2000).
7. The five Security Council permanent members—the United States, the Soviet Union, France, Britain, and China—must approve any application in order to obtain the UN membership.
8. Kim, "North Korea and the United Nations."
9. Chi Young Pak, *Korea and the United Nations*.
10. The term "Nordpolitik" refers to the Roh Tae Woo administration's diplomatic strategy to initiate rapprochement with North Korea and to establish economic and diplomatic ties with China and other communist countries.
11. KEDO was established by the United States, Japan, and South Korea in New York, in March 1995 to replace the North's existing nuclear facilities with safer light-water reac-tors, under the supervision of the International Atomic Energy Agency.

12. This does not include the ten new member states that were admitted to the EU on May 1, 2004.

13. European Union External Relations, "The EU Relations with the Democratic People's Republic of Korea-DPRK (North Korea)," November 2002 at http://europa.eu.int/comm/externalrelations/north_korea/intro/ (August 15, 2003).

14. The ARF was launched in July 1994 with the aim of enhancing dialogue and cooperation for peace and stability in the Asia Pacific region.

15. Mahesh Uniyal, "South-East Asia: Regional Meeting Thaws North Korea's Isolation," *World News*, July 27, 2000, at http://www.oneworld.org/ips2/july00/18_07_062.html (February 11, 2003).

16. Jack A. Goldstone et al., *State Failure Task Force Report: Phase III Findings*, September 30, 2003 at http://www.cidcm.umd.edu/inscr/stfail/ (August 14, 2003).

17. For instance, the Nuclear Energy Experts Group has been holding regular meetings to seek ways of enhancing transparency and public understanding of regional nuclear energy, see http://www.cscap.org/groups.htm (May 18, 2003).

18. UN Security Council Resolution (S/RES/825), May 11, 1993, at http://daccess-ods.un.org/doc/UNDOC/GEN/N93/280/49/IMG/N9328049.pdf?OpenElement (March 4, 2003).

19. Mitchell B. Reiss, "KEDO: Which Way from Here?" *Asian Perspective* 26: 1 (2002).

20. White House, Office of the Press Secretary, National Strategy for Combating Terrorism, February 2003 at http://www.state.gov/s/ct/rls/rm/2003/17798.htm (March 4, 2003).

21. Some argue that the United States, preoccupied with Iraq at the moment, wishes to buy time by having many countries and parties involved in the North Korean issue.

22. Judy Aita, "North Korean Nuclear Issue sent to UN Security Council," Office of International Information Programs, U.S. Department of State, February 12, 2003, at http://usinfo.gov/regional/ea/easecnorthkoreaaita.htm (May 18, 2003).

23. Reuters, "United Nations Delays Action on North Korea," *The New York Times*, February 20, 2003.

24. David Kang, "Guarantee North Korea's Security," *International Herald Tribune*, August 7, 2003 at http://www.iht.com/cgi-bin/ (August 14, 2003).

25. The PSI is aimed at intercepting ships and planes suspected of carrying nuclear, chemical, and biological weapons. South Korea does not belong to the 11 PSI nations. "US wants to Discuss PSI with Korea, Envoy Says," *The Korea Times*, July 29, 2003, at http://times.hankooki.com/lpage/nation/200307/kt2003072923094710510.htm (August 15, 2003).

26. John R. Bolton, "A Dictatorship at the Crossroads," speech delivered at the Seoul Hilton, Seoul, sponsored by the East Asia Institute, July 31, 2003.

27. "Vetoes were common during the Cold War, with the United States and the Soviet Union casting the majority of negative votes. There have been 251 public vetoes since the Security Council's inception in 1946, 238 of which occurred between 1946 and 1990. Of those Cold War vetoes, the United States and the U.S.S.R. accounted for 185 of the total." Quoted from Brendan I. Koerner, "Can You Bypass a U.N. Security Council Veto?" *Slate*, March 12, 2003, at http://politics.slate.msn.com/ (August 16, 2003).

28. Richard Falk, "War Prevention and the UN: After Iraq is There a Future for the Charter System?" Counterpunch, July 2, 2003, at http://www.counterpunch.org/falk07022003.html (August 15, 2003).

29. Ibid.

30. Statement by Defense Secretary Donald H. Rumsfeld, Howard W. French, "Tensions Remind U.S. Troops in South Korea of Their Mission," *The New York Times*, February 23, 2003; "U.S. to protest midair challenge by MiGs," March 5, 2003, at http://joongangdaily.joins.com/200303/05/200303050312293539900090309031.html (May 18, 2003).

31. Antti Rautavaara, "Tumen Programme: Forum and Institution to Promote Regional Cooperation in Northeast Asia," UNDP International Conference on Regional

Cooperation in Northeast Asia: Appraisals and Prospects, at http://210.90.217.5/ bdi/final/prg/VII2-01/htm; and http://www.tumenprogramme.org/tumen/programme (February 17, 2003).

32. The three agreements include: (1) Agreement on the Establishment of the Consultative Commission for the Development of the Tumen River Economic Development Area (TREDA) and Northeast Asia (NEA); (2) Agreement on the establishment of the Tumen River Area Development Coordination Committee; and (3) Memorandum of Understanding on Environmental Principles Governing the TREDA and NEA.

33. Ian Davies, Regional Cooperation in Northeast Asia, The Tumen River Area Development Program, 1999–2000: In Search of a Model for Regional Economic Co-operation in Northeast Asia, North Pacific Policy Papers 4, The Institute of Asian Research, University of British Columbia, 2000.

34. Ibid.

35. Rautavaara, "Tumen Programme."

36. Samuel S. Kim and Tai Hwan Lee, eds., *North Korea and Northeast Asia*, 2002 [table 1.6], (Lanham, MD: Rowman & Littlefield, 2002) p. 16.

37. Sangman Lee, "Status and Prospect of South-North Economic Cooperation," (in Korean), at http://61.74.68.188/minjoo21/04.html (March 8, 2003).

38. Ibid.

39. Timothy Savage and Nautilus Team, "NGO Engagement with North Korea: Dilemmas and Lessons Learned," *Asian Perspectives* 26 (November 2002).

40. The role of the South and North Korean National Red Cross in holding reunions of separated families should be acknowledged as an important feature of IOs in the humanitarian context of the inter-Korean reconciliation process. However, due to the broad range of issues that this chapter deals with, this subject will not be discussed.

41. WFP, 2002, "Food Security: Overview," Country Brief—Korea (DPR) at http://www.wfp.org/country_brief/indexcountry.asp?country408.

42. See the Council conclusions of July 19, 1999 and October 9, 2000, at http://www.fes.or.kr?K_Unification?GAC-Oct2000.htm; and http://www.ceip.org/files/projects/npp/resources/EUKoreapolicy.htm (April 18, 2003).

43. European Union External Relations, "The EU Relations with the Democratic People's Republic of Korea."

44. Burke Josslin, "American NGOs Quietly Building Trust with North Korea," *The Korea Herald*, April 7, 2002, at http://www.koreaherald.co.kr/SITE/data/html_dir/2001/04/27/200104270007.asp (April 18, 2003).

45. WFP, 2003, "World Hunger—Korea (DPR)," at http://www.wfp.org/country_brief/index.asp?continent=2 (June 17, 2003).

46. WFP, "World Hunger—Korea (DPR)," at http://www.wfp.org/country_brief/index.asp?region=5 (August 17, 2003).

47. Korean Ministry of Unification, *The Chronicles of Inter-Korean Relations* at the English website of the Korean Ministry of Unification, at http://www.unikorea.go.kr (August 15, 2003).

48. Timothy Savage and Nautilus Team, "NGO Engagement with North Korea; Dilemmas and Lessons Learned," *Asian Perspectives* 26 (November 1, 2002).

49. "A Generation at Risk in the DPRK," *The Choong Ang Ilbo English Edition*, May 8, 2002, p. 1.

50. Portions of this section were drawn from the author's previous works.

51. Korean Ministry of Unification, *The Chronicles of Inter-Korean Relations* at the English website of the Korean Ministry of Unification, at http://www.unikorea.go.kr (August 15, 2003).

52. AFP, "UNHCR Sees China Ease Policy on North Korean Refugees," June 16, 2003, at http://quickstart.clari.net/qs_se/webnews/wed/ak/Qunhcr-nkorea-chi (August 15, 2003).

53. Shin-wha Lee, "Preventing Refugee Crisis: A Challenge to Human Security," *Asian Perspective* 23: 1 (March 1999): 133–154.
54. Article 86 of the former North Korean Constitution requires repatriated North Koreans to be punished on a charge of treason against the nation and people. Despite the revision of the North Korean Constitution in 1998, where the "treason" clause of the Article 86 was deleted, the Article 47 of the 1987 Criminal Code, which stipulates "a citizen of the Republic who defects to a foreign country . . . shall be committed to reform institution for not less than seven years . . ." is still valid.
55. In a Paris conference in January 2000, and again in August 2000, French intellectual and civil group members claimed that the North Korean famine crisis and concentration camps were holocaust-like conditions; also see the Amnesty International Report 2002, Korea (Democratic People's Republic of), at http://web.amnesty.org/ web/ar2002.nsf/ asa/democratic+people's+republic+of+korea!Open (April 18, 2003).
56. Citizen's alliance for North Korean Human Rights homepage at http://nhkoreanhumanright. or.kr (May 13, 2003).
57. Samuel S. Kim and Abraham Kim, "Conflict Management," in *Encyclopedia of Government and Politics*, 2nd ed., ed. Mary Hawkesworth and Maurice Kogan (London and New York: Routledge, 2004), pp. 980–993.
58. Elisabeth Rosenthal, "UN group backs North Korea asylum seekers in China," *The New York Times*, March 15, 2002, at http://query.nytimes.com/search/abstract?res= F40D10FC355D0C768DDDAA0894DA404482 (March 18, 2003).

CHAPTER ELEVEN
THE CHALLENGES OF PEACEFULLY REUNIFYING THE KOREAN PENINSULA

Abraham Kim

There are few issues more politically charged and more hotly debated than the issue of the reunification of the two Koreas. During the last decade in both the ROK and the West, two polar perspectives have dominated the discourse. On one side of the debate, "liberal" circles, led by prominent figures such as former South Korean President Kim Dae Jung and the current President Roh Moo Hyun, argue that the key to a peaceful Korean reunification is by promoting South–North Korea bilateral cooperation and exchange at all levels of the two societies. Their rationale is that as the two countries reap the benefits of economic, cultural, and social collaborations over time, these factors will build the desire and the foundation for more ambitious forms of political cooperation, ultimately leading to a stage of mutual development where reunification can occur—a negotiated merger of equals.[1]

Opposing this view is a more skeptical group of "conservative" Korea watchers that questions whether any substantive political and economic change can occur in the DPRK. Pointing to the Kim Jong Il regime's dependence on sustaining the *Juche*-based political system to maintain its legitimacy and the North Korean leadership's unbending desire to dominate the Korean peninsula, advocates believe that no amount of goodwill, engagement, or cooperation can bridge the ideological and systemic disparities that separate the two Koreas and bring the reconciliation that liberal circles envision.[2] Therefore, if any peaceful reunification is to be achieved, these analysts have argued that it can only be actualized through the "collapse" of the North Korean *Juche*-based regime-state and a subsequent German-style absorption of the DPRK into South Korea.[3]

Although volumes have been written on both sides of the debate, analytically rigorous works offering a balanced explanation on what would cause the two Korean states to reunify peacefully are few. Much of the literature is prescriptive in nature or only offers descriptive discussions of plausible scenarios for the two Koreas' future. Though important in helping us to consider the myriad of possibilities for Korea's reunification, these works do not address the fundamental questions of how and to what degree are the wide range of domestic, dyadic, and international variables important to the Korean reunification process and what factors would ultimately compel the two Korean governments to relinquish their sovereignty.

This chapter attempts to address this conceptual gap by analyzing the prospect of peaceful reunification based on recent work done on intra-state/civil war termination.

Linking the Korean reunification question and the termination of intra-state (more specifically, ideological) wars offers a fitting comparison. For one, both events share the common challenge of compelling political elites and their supporters to work together toward managing a divided sociopolitical national community and building a single government. Second, the characteristics of intra-state wars—such as the high level of distrust, the competitive dynamics, the clashing interests of power elites and the willingness to go to great lengths among the belligerents to dominate the country—provide a closer representation of the past and current contentious nature of inter-Korean relations than the apolitical and almost genial depiction of reunification offered by the present South Korean administration and its liberal supporters.

Admittedly, there are notable differences between intra-state wars and reunification. High levels of armed violence are a major component of civil wars, but have not been characteristic of North–South Korean relations since 1953. Instead of conflict on the battlefield, the ROK–DPRK struggle of the past fifty plus years has taken place on the political and diplomatic front. Rhetorical attacks, economic competition, military threats, political posturing, and other much less violent or nonviolent measures have been the weapons of choice. Although the "weapons" are different, the goals of reunification and ideological civil war are similar: to delegitimate and destabilize a counterpart, hoping that the effort will tip the legitimacy competition in one's own favor to the point that the newly integrated state will consolidate around one's authority.[4] The proposition of this chapter is that by exploring the factors that facilitate political actors to accept a negotiated political settlement in the most extreme condition of an intra-state war, we can begin to understand the possibilities and the limitations that policy-makers will face as they seek to reunite a divided Korea.[5] The aim here is not to create a theory or a "Rosetta stone" for the two Koreas' reunification that will elucidate all the causal forces that are at work, but the attempt is a more modest effort to highlight some underlying causal factors that are at play when considering the challenge of political integration.

The framework used in this analysis to examine the Korean reunification question is a three-step bargaining process developed by civil war analysts who use incentive-based (or strategic bargaining) approaches to study how intra-state wars end:[6] (1) the "negotiation phase"; (2) the "settlement phase"; (3) the "implementation phase."[7] This multiphase approach assumes that in order to understand why competing elites settle we must consider separately and collectively the factors that would cause political actors: (1) to discuss a compromise settlement seriously, (2) to accept a final peace agreement and a new post-conflict order, and (3) to finally carry out the political agreement. This approach allows us to study national integration not as a mono-causal or single point event but more realistically as a multidimensional and dynamic process with different causal forces coming into play at different stages of political development. Viewing the Korean reunification issue through these insights, three interlinked arguments are presented: (1) the two Koreas will not seriously consider a negotiated reunification as a viable policy option unless both countries face immense pressures that make maintaining the status quo division unsustainable. (2) unless there is significant political transformation within the current North Korean regime that makes establishing a democratic government a nonthreatening prospect, a peaceful reunification is unlikely. Without this condition, the crisis that would create the first condition may trigger severe instability rather than facilitate integration. (3) the involvement of the United States or some other credible international actor will be critical for both integration processes to be eventually completed.

To substantiate my argument, this chapter proceeds in the following manner: in the next section, I expound on the different phases of civil war termination and the unique forces that must come into play to facilitate a peaceful settlement. Based on this discussion, I explain what implications they may have for the Korean reunification question. Finally, as a conclusion, I explore what the argument of this chapter suggests will be the likelihood of three different future scenarios for the two Koreas' reunification: (1) negotiated union; (2) perpetual division; (3) war.

The Logic of Civil Wars and the Korean Reunification Question

Civil wars are high-stake internal conflicts that, compared to interstate wars, tend to be bloodier, more protracted, and more likely to be settled with one side winning than through a negotiated solution.[8] An important reason for these distinctive features is that in order for peace to materialize belligerents are expected not only to stop fighting but also to live and govern together with violent adversaries in a common state.[9] For most political elites, such a prospect is too costly and risky to accept. Strategic-minded leaders are more inclined to fight to the end and try to win the war than to compromise and share power with their enemies.

Although the two Koreas have not engaged in a full-scale war since the early 1950s, the highly competitive and often contentious bargaining process over the question of what shape the future reunified Korea should take resonates with a similar dynamic as civil war. With the reunification question also involving the political future and ultimately the survival of governing elites, leaders are interested in controlling all the authority in the post-union state rather than engaging in a troublesome power-sharing arrangement. In place of warfare, Pyongyang and Seoul have used various political, economic, diplomatic, and ideological "weapons" to weaken the power of their opponent while simultaneously strengthening their own authority.[10] Even with the monumental June 15, 2000 summit meeting and the subsequent announcements by both Pyongyang and Seoul on the need for better cooperation, a closer look below the rhetoric reveals that a compromise solution and cooperating toward political integration is not in the interest of either government. Instead, both sides prefer to subdue the other and dominate the reunification process.[11] For example, President Roh Moo Hyun's promise to restore "peace and prosperity on the peninsula" is, in essence, a policy to transpose the ROK's capitalist democratic system on North Korea and to eliminate the DPRK's totalitarian dictatorship.[12] Alternatively, Pyongyang's vision of the future, although now preoccupied with survival, sees reunification as based on the great despotic leadership of Kim Jong Il, "the sun of the 21st century, and lodestar of the fatherland's reunification."[13] With the vast disparities between these two states and the unwillingness on either side to compromise its authority or principles to negotiate a reunification, is there any hope for reaching a negotiated end for this nationalist goal?

The literature on civil war termination provides some clues. Recent works on civil war resolution maintain that when understanding why some conflicts end successfully implementing a peace settlement while others do not, this cooperative endeavor must be viewed as a three-step process: (1) "negotiation phase" during which combatants decide whether to open discussions with their enemies; (2) "settlement phase" during which the disputants determine whether to reach a final agreement; (3) "implementation phase" during which they decide whether to carry out the peace settlement. The implication of this multistage approach for the reunification question is that in order to understand the complex forces that will bring about a negotiated reunification we must also consider separately the different dimensions of the reunification bargaining process: (1) the conditions that will bring the two Koreas to the negotiating table to discuss seriously a reunified state (negotiation phase); (2) the factors that will induce these two governments to finally reach a concrete agreement to integrate their political systems (settlement phase); and (3) factors that will firmly commit the two leaderships to fully execute the settlement (implementation phase).

Within each of these stages, certain conditions must be present in order for the bargaining process to progress forward. This analysis highlights three factors that must be present: (1) a severe crisis must make the existing status quo condition unsustainable in the negotiation phase; (2) disputed stakes must be divisible in the settlement phase in order for the competing elites to reach an agreement; (3) and finally, a credible outside force must be willing to involve itself to ensure that the groups comply during the implementation phase. Below, I discuss in detail these factors as well as explore what these conditions mean to our understanding of how the two Koreas can achieve a negotiated reunification.

Negotiation Phase: Bringing Competing Leaders to the Table
Warring groups begin the negotiation process for a settlement for a number of reasons. Some leaders, for example, may come together under the pretext of peace but, in reality, have no intention to seek a compromise solution. Their intention may instead be to test the resolve of their opponents; to reiterate demands for surrender; or to seek a moratorium in the fighting so that their forces can regroup and continue the fight later.

Others come to talk because they genuinely seek peace and are willing to pursue some form of negotiated settlement. One important condition that often pressures leaders to seek genuine peace is when the two sides are confronted by compounding costs of war—human casualties, collateral property damage, and the economic resources spent on fighting the war—diminishing hope of winning and gaining any benefits from continuing the fight. In other words, the cost of sustaining the status quo (i.e., the war) becomes unbearable, and the expected utility of a compromise peace settlement becomes higher than continuing the war.[14] William Zartman calls this condition a "hurting stalemate."[15] The critical factor is that this situational condition must be jointly felt by the warring parties. If not, the stronger and more resilient disputant would prefer to fight in hopes that their weaker opponent would capitulate, rather than settle for a compromise deal.[16]

Conversely, if the material pressures of war are mutually diminished, then the likelihood of reaching a peace settlement will also be lessened. For example, if a friendly third party state intervenes with economic and military assistance or if a cease-fire is signed and combatants are inadvertently given the opportunity to regroup before considering a full peace treaty, the likelihood of warring groups to settle may seriously diminish.[17]

This discussion on the important linkage between a mutually felt "hurting stalemate" condition and the belligerents' genuineness in seeking a settlement provides insight into a critical element that has been missing not only in the historical experience of the two Koreas, but also from the debate on the Korean reunification. While "liberal" circles argue that the benefits of reunification are a motivating force, this analysis shifts the focus to a more balanced consideration of costs and benefits in both the current status quo and in terms of reunification. According to this analysis, South Korean policy leaders have mistakenly argued that given the dire economic condition of North Korea, peaceful negotiated reunification is not possible because the fundamental concern of Pyongyang is not reunification, but survival.[18] The notion that only during a period in which both the ROK and the DPRK are both economically and politically stable will the two sides be capable of and willing to pursue a negotiated peace and reconciliation is a fantasy. Instead, a negotiated settlement is less likely during periods of stability. The highest priority of strategic-minded leaders in Seoul and Pyongyang would be "victory" or complete domination over the reunification process and control of the newly reunified state rather than engaging in a costly negotiated settlement that only promises a future of compromise, exposure to political vulnerabilities and political fighting as the two societies struggle to integrate. A negotiated reunification for the two Koreas, at best, would be the third option behind total control and continued division.

This hierarchy of priorities appears to correspond to the true preferences of Seoul and Pyongyang. For example, despite the insistence by the former Kim Dae Jung administration and the current Roh administration that they have no intention to absorb North Korea, a closer look at their reunification policy suggests the opposite. In fact, Seoul has repeatedly expressed its intention to both politically and economically reform the North Korean system by integrating the DPRK into the international community and expanding ties between the two Koreas before the two countries merge.[19] President Kim Dae Jung's three stages of reunification plan states: "the newly unified Korea will be founded on democracy and an open market economy"— implying that the establishment of a market democracy in North Korea is a key prerequisite before any integration is possible between the two Koreas.[20] From Pyongyang's perspective where the legitimacy and authority of Kim Jong Il's regime is tied to the persistence of the Juche ideology and the current political system, South Korea's reunification plan is a threatening prospect. Because of the ROK's demographic and economic predominance as well as experience in democratic politics, any democratic governing structure would likely result in the dominance of the South.

Growing sentiments in both the ROK and the DPRK to support a "peaceful" status quo (division) also suggest that the current preference for the status quo division outweighs the desire for negotiated reunification. The idea of reunification has lost its appeal among mainstream South Korean citizens especially after the painful 1997 financial crisis. One lesson from the German reunification that many IR analysts and policy-makers have learned is that there are enormous financial costs associated with reunifying two sovereign countries and socioeconomic stresses that reunification can impose on governments. Some economists have estimated that reunifying the bankrupt communist North Korea and capitalist South Korea would cost at a minimum $300 billion; other estimates have put the cost as high as three trillion dollars. The discouraging factor is that South Korean citizens will most likely have to bear most, if not all of this cost, which would, according to some estimates, set back the South more than ten years in its economic development.[21] Faced with this reality, many southerners have resorted to a two-faced approach to reunification as Ambassador Kim Kyung Won, former ambassador to the United States and president of Social Science Institute in Seoul explains: "There is a lot of romantic nonsense about wanting unification but when you come right down to it, people don't want to pay the bills. If they want unification, they want it in the future—the more distant, the better."[22]

This outlook appears to be shared even among governing leaders. Then-President Kim Dae Jung stated on CNN, "Unification is only a matter of time. But for now, there are more negatives than positives because we are currently not capable of economically supporting North Korea."[23] A few months later, during the historic 2000 summit meeting, President Kim announced that he did not expect to see reunification in his lifetime. In the DPRK, the North Korean Worker's Party newspaper, *Nodong Shinmun*, expressed that the DPRK too supported the persistence of the status quo when it proclaimed a few days after the summit that "the issue of unifying the differing systems in the north and the south is one that may be left to posterity to settle slowly in the future."[24] From the highest levels of government down to the grassroot levels, there is an overwhelming sense that reunification is an important nationalist objective but not an immediate priority worth pursuing.

As mentioned earlier, in the case of civil wars, the accumulating loss of life, collateral damage and other war-related costs serve as a powerful force to push leaders to reconsider their priorities. The challenge for reunification is speculating what would create a crisis so severe that both Koreas would face pressure to resolve their differences, adjust their priorities, and reach an agreement expeditiously. High defense spending related to the constant security threats on the divided peninsula is a possible factor to consider in calculating the costliness of sustaining the status quo. In South Korea, almost US$12.5 billion or 2.8 percent of GDP in 2000 went to support its national defense, while in North Korea, US$2.05 billion or an overwhelming 13.9 percent of GDP went to support its more than one million troop army.[25] In the case of the DPRK, these official and unreliable statistics may be underestimating the true level of spending on maintaining the fifth largest military in the world. Defense spending is no doubt exacerbating the country's economic troubles.[26] Yet, unlike fighting an actual war, the cost of the current noncombative struggle between the two Koreas is not acute and exorbitant. From what limited information we have, it appears sustainable at least for the immediate future.

Although economic stagnation, severe food shortage, and massive starvation still inflict the country, recent developments offer some cautionary optimism. The situation on the ground may be improving and for the immediate future, the government will continue to "muddle through." South Korea and the international community continue to give economic and humanitarian handouts and Pyongyang is still tinkering with its crippled socialist economic system.[27] Based on Bank of Korea calculations, between 1990 and 1998, the North Korean economy contracted by almost

50 percent, but recently, the trend has shifted back to growth with North Korea's GDP growing by 6.2 percent in 1999 and in 2000, 2001, and 2002 the economy expanding by 1.3 percent, 3.7 percent, and 1.2 percent respectively.[28] Equally significant are signs that the North Korean government may be gradually changing the way it manages its economy by instituting piecemeal market reforms. Some recent developments include: (1) the 1998 constitutional change that permitted private property in North Korea; (2) implementation of a more decentralized accounting system for industrial production and the institution of price reforms on consumer and food products in July 2002; (3) the promotion of "district markets" to sell food and consumer goods and the establishment of special economic zones in such areas as Kaesong and Rajin-Sonbong;[29] and (4) aggressive promotion of the expansion of commerce with South Korea and other capitalist developed countries.[30] It is too early to determine how far these new endeavors to build the DPRK into a "great power nation" (kangsong taeguk) will progress and what positive results, if any, will emerge. However, thus far, there is no acute pressure on either North Korea or South Korea that reunification is a critical issue to be decided upon immediately. In short, the current status quo in the civil war parlance resembles an "extended cease-fire" which provides no overwhelming pressure to move from the two Koreas' "equilibrium" of division.

At the same time, conditions in North Korea can change catastrophically, creating a circumstance in which the status quo is no longer sustainable. Although the North Korean regime remains standing, one fallout from its decade long economic crisis—besides the untold deaths—has been the steady flow of refugees into China and through China to third countries.[31] One possible scenario is that North Korea can become so destabilized that the outflow of refugees into South Korea and neighboring states will be explosive creating an overwhelming pressure for Seoul to consider immediate reunification as a means to control the chaotic situation. Such a scenario is not unprecedented. The massive East German defection and emigration during 1989–90 not only exacerbated the economic and political situation in the German Democratic Republic, but equally significant, made the crisis in East Germany a crisis for West Germany as well. This example empirically illustrates how the status quo became unbearably costly for both the West Germans and East Germans. Bonn feared that unless they took direct action to address the East German crisis, West Germany would be flooded with refugees, and the economy would be completely destabilized.[32] Based on recent scholarship on German reunification, it was not until the Berlin Wall came down that the Kohl administration began to consider seriously developing a plan for the two Germanys to merge and to the formation of his Ten Point Program that made unification an actual policy of Bonn. Before this turning point event, the West Germans were concerned about the developments unfolding in East Germany but were reluctant to take any action for the fear of further destabilizing the German Democratic Republic and creating an unnecessary crisis that they would have to pay for.[33]

In the case of Korea, it is clear that the refugee problem is not at crisis levels, although some reports estimate that as many as 300,000 refugees are hiding in China alone, while thousands more are captured each month and are being sent back to North Korea.[34] Although some speculate that this trickle maybe the beginning of a flood of North Koreans trying to escape oppression and hunger, current conditions are still far from comparable to the enormous outpouring that took place in East Germany. According to the ROK's Office of North Korean Defectors, 148 North Koreans came to the South in 1999, 312 in 2000, and approximately a thousand in 2001—far short of the 343,854 refugees and migrants that crossed into West Germany from the East in 1989 alone.[35] In addition, China, aware of the potential negative effect that a massive flood of North Korean refugees could wreak on its own stability and security, is also unlikely to throw open its borders to refugees as Hungary did for East German escapees who were interested in immigrating to the West.

This discussion regarding the balance between the value of the status quo and pursuing reunification highlights two important implications. The first implication is that there is an important trade-off between pursuing a policy of promoting immediate stability on the Korean peninsula and the long-term prospect for reunification. Pursuing a policy of economic assistance, humanitarian aid, trade, and investment may contribute to building goodwill and perhaps dismantle the Cold War environment on the Korean peninsula, but concomitantly, these efforts may diminish the cost of maintaining the status quo, thereby reducing the pressure for the two governments to make any binding commitment for reunification. Like most governments, the governing leaders in Seoul and Pyongyang value their political power. Voluntarily relinquishing their authority would be a difficult challenge. In addition, as long as reunification does not provide any tangible benefits to their basic interest in securing their power, they will delay any decision because they can afford to do so.

In a related vein, this discussion also highlights one important way in which outside powers like China impede reunification from occurring. In light of the "hurting stalemate" condition, China's policy of peace and stability on the Korean peninsula may be viewed as a counter-policy to reunification. In an attempt to ensure that North Korea sustains its system, the PRC has actively traded with and donated to the DPRK economic products and food goods to defray the chronic shortages of this country. China is by far the largest export and import market for North Korean goods. In 2001, while trade with other countries such as Japan declined, China's trade with North Korea grew by 51.6 percent, making the PRC account for 32.6 percent of DPRK's trade (up from 24.7 percent in 2000) for a total of $740 million.[36] Like much of its trade activities with other countries, North Korea is running an enormous deficit with China. But, many analysts agree that the Chinese economy has contributed far more food, consumer goods, and hard currencies to the North Korea's ailing economy than is reflected in these official statistics.[37] By providing economic life support, Beijing has not only successfully contributed to the extension of Kim Jong Il regime's life span but also provided a less threatening and generous alternative source of economic assistance than going to Seoul begging for concessions and potentially jeopardizing its legitimacy in the eyes of North Koreans and its leverage vis-à-vis South Korea.

The Settlement Phase: Divisibility of Stakes
Once disputants are at the bargaining table, the second step to consider is how easily the issues on the table can be divided in a way that is mutually acceptable to all parties.[38] When dealing with the issue of negotiating the possibility of a new shared

government, at a minimum, the principal interests of both belligerents must not require the annihilation of their opponents, must permit the idea of power sharing with an opposition group, and must be willing to resolve their differences in the future through governing institutions. Furthermore, both disputants must believe that the settlement will not "leave them permanently excluded from political power and expose them to continued abuse in the future."[39]

The problem with many civil wars is that the demands of competing groups are usually "absolute" goals that are indivisible. For example, in ideological conflicts, goals of warring groups often include the elimination of their rivals or the overthrow of the government. Ideological wars are particularly difficult to resolve because in order to reach a negotiated settlement, both enemies must forego claims to be the only legitimate authority of the national community and must agree to live under a common political system, even if the adopted system is not necessarily consonant with either of the group's ideological disposition.[40] The problem with such a compromise is that warring groups often tie their legitimacy as well as their raison d'être closely to the adherence and promotion of a certain political ideology. Therefore, living under the governing rules of another system is equivalent to de facto capitulation and would thereby undercut their own legitimacy and chance of survival. In such cases, reaching an agreement for a new reintegrated state does not provide a better option for leaders than maintaining the status quo (i.e., continuing the war) where they still have a fighting chance of survival.[41]

This issue of "divisibility of stakes" is arguably one of the principal impediments hindering the two Koreas from making any progress toward reaching a reunification settlement. The one-man dictatorship of Chairman Kim Jong Il and the market democracy of the ROK as two political and ideological systems are incompatible. Even if some political arrangement is possible, South Korea—with its clear economic, political, and demographic dominance—will likely have the upper hand in any bargaining situation and will likely push to institute a liberal democratic and capitalist system. For the Kim Jong Il dictatorship, accepting these terms would be equivalent to political death. Thus, in order for North Korea to consider a negotiated reunification when faced with a severe crisis, Pyongyang must see merging with South Korea not as a menacing alternative, but as a viable option. However, for this heroic perceptual transformation to take place, an important precondition for negotiated reunification is political liberalization and reform in North Korea, more specifically, democratization. Domestic political change must occur either prior or concomitant with events that are pressuring the two Koreas closer to reunification in order for an actual merger of the two states to materialize.

The events that led up to both the 1990 Yemeni reunification and the 1990 German reunification suggest, at least empirically, that there is some merit to this argument. In Yemen, for example, both the Marxist South Yemeni state and the authoritarian Arab North Yemeni government began to liberalize their political systems and economies prior to reunification. While political conditions in South Yemen were rapidly worsening, both leaderships, albeit reluctantly at times, agreed that an electoral democracy and a market economy would be the governing systems for their new unity government.[42] On the European continent, the East German communist party and autocratic government that had resisted the idea of reunification with the powerful West German government, had essentially collapsed by December 1989, leaving an interim government under the direction of Prime Minister Hans Modrow to manage the deteriorating state. Modrow's interim government agreed to establish a multiparty system and promised that the new East German parliamentary government would be reestablished by democratic elections. Rather than establishing a new government, the elections became a referendum for the unreserved adoption of the West's political and economic system and the immediate reunification of the two Germanys.[43]

In North Korea, the prospect of Kim Jong Il's regime closing the political gap between the two Koreas is unlikely to occur any time soon. Although Pyongyang has been working toward easing control over the economy, there is no comparable loosening in the political frontier. In fact, as Charles Armstrong points out, the poor economic performance of North Korea during the past decade have intensified the ideological rhetoric and bolstered political efforts by Pyongyang to control its population since it has few other options to maintain societal order until the economy begins to improve significantly.[44] In addition, the move to promote the military apparatus above the party (military-first politics) and firmly entrenching the military leadership into the central ruling circle may make any significant change toward pluralism less likely.[45] It gives the military a stake in the survival of the current regime and an interest to step in any time to obstruct any reforms process that will undermine national security and institutional interests or to crush any opposition group that seeks to threaten the regime. Moreover, civil society that normally serves as a counterbalance to the government and ultimately determines the rate and scope of opening and reforms in autocratic societies are virtually nonexistent in the DPRK. Civic groups or mass organizations that do exist are tools of the regime and serve more as means for control than autonomous space where counter-hegemonic ideas and leadership can develop to mobilize opposition against the state.[46]

The discussion, thus far, regarding the divisibility of stakes shows the potential danger of arguments among some hawkish pundits to "hasten" North Korea's demise.[47] In the case of intra-state wars, if leaders anticipate losing a war and expect severe political punishment for failing to win, then it is likely that leaders will risk the chance to keep fighting, hoping that some unforeseen event (e.g., intervention of foreign powers) will change the course of the conflict to their advantage or until they are conquered. Either way, the fate of leaders is equivalent, but by fighting, there is a chance of survival.[48] The implication for Korean reunification is slightly different. If faced with the likelihood that a negotiated reunification will ultimately lead to the subversion of the Kim Jong Il leadership, the DPRK is more likely to choose not to reunify. However, if the status quo division is unsustainable, then Chairman Kim Jong Il and his lieutenants, as Victor Cha recently points out, may find it rational to instigate some form of limited military option or even pursue a preventive or preemptive war option as a survival strategy.[49] The test launching of the Taepodong I ballistic missile over Japan, the June 2002 naval clash off the coast of Inchon, the incident of North Korean fighter jets tailing a U.S. reconnaissance plane over the East Sea, and the recent threats to use nuclear weapons against U.S. forces and the neighboring countries that host them are all reminders of the potential disruption that North Korea can wreak if it is faced with a destabilizing status quo situation.

Recognizing the unlikely prospect of bridging the enormous political, economic, and ideological gap between the DPRK and the ROK, recent discussions have turned to the idea of confederation as an interim solution, if not a compromise final solution to a complete reunification. Although the concept of confederation has long been discussed by leaders on both sides of the DMZ, it attracted new public attention during the June 2000 summit when the two heads of state acknowledged that the North Korean and South Korean plans for reunification had common factors. Recently, Selig Harrison makes the case that the two Koreas adopting a confederation system would significantly change the political and security environment of the Korean peninsula for the better. A confederation and a commitment to the coexistence of two political systems would "reduce the fear of North Korea that the South is trying to absorb them. And for the South, a confederation would not only keep alive the dream of eventual reunification but also provide a rationale for postponing formal integration until congruent economic systems evolve."[50]

However, a closer look at the characteristics of confederations and ideological conflicts make this quasi-reunification arrangement in lieu of a true convergence of North–South Korean political system and ideology a dangerous prospect.[51] In confederation arrangements, the power structure is organized so that states, rather than relinquishing complete sovereign authority, selectively delegate certain decisions to a supranational governing body.[52] The inherent weakness in this governing structure is that because the constituent states retain much of the administrative authority, constituent governments can secede from the confederacy if they choose to do so.[53] As Fredrick Lister points out, confederations function more as "a far-reaching alliance...a combination of sovereign states having a common purpose or several common purposes rather than as a single sovereign state."[54] Unless the states are similar in interest, beliefs, and size, disagreements and tensions in the relationship are inevitable. With tenuous institutional links to hold them together, the confederacy will be in constant danger of falling apart.[55]

Coupled with this weak governing structure are the inherent dangers of linking two political societies that function on opposing political values and principles. The nature of ideological competition makes the existence of two antithetical regime types side-by-side inherently unstable, especially during turbulent times. Ideological conflicts are about the hearts and minds of people; loyalties to ideologies are mutable, unpredictable, and can dramatically change over short periods.[56] The critical factor for discontent among the masses to translate into erosion of support for an incumbent regime or any political organization is the availability of preferable alternatives.[57] Adam Pzeworski writes: "[A]s long as no collective alternatives are available, individual attitudes toward the regime matter little for its stability. What is threatening to authoritarian regimes is not the breakdown of legitimacy, but the organization of counter hegemony: collective projects for an alternative future."[58] Without options even illegitimate governments can sustain their power and manage disgruntled citizens through coercion or selective incentives.[59] The unique predicament that the two Korean governments face is that an alternative model is constantly available just across the border for its citizens to compare their living conditions. In times of social and economic downturn, the juxtaposition of two antithetical political systems can be destabilizing within a common national community, if not fatal for the declining state. Disgruntled citizens may protest against the troubled regional regime or worse yet, vote with their feet and begin pouring into the more stable and prosperous state. The situation, ultimately, may create a situation where the weakened state (like the DPRK) fearing for its political security and stability may attempt to pull out of the confederation creating immense disruption and the possibility of war.[60]

Implementation Stage: International Commitment
The final and critical aspect that will determine whether a peace settlement will be realized following an intra-state war is the likelihood that the agreements will be fully enforced. Peace agreements "provide a framework for ending hostilities and a guide to the initial stages of post-conflict reform," but they do not provide "the conditions under which deep cleavages that produced the war are automatically surmounted."[61] During the post–civil war transition period when new governing institutions and new legal infrastructures are being established, there are few domestic mechanisms to manage groups with conflicting interests and to prevent different parties from cheating and exploiting their opponents.[62] This transition period is often so hazardous that, as Roy Licklider points out, approximately 50 percent of the negotiated settlements of civil wars collapse within the first five years.[63] To address this problem, analysts argue that the most effective way to address this underlying "commitment problem" is for a credible third party international enforcer to monitor and supervise the compliance of the peace settlement and to step in militarily when discontented participants try to disrupt the process.[64]

The implication for reunification is that even after the two Koreas have decided to reunify, if there is no international power committed to the settlement, political integration of the two Koreas may fail. For many Korean nationalists, this may be a hard reality to face. After all, the first article of the joint declaration issued at the June 2000 summit spells out that the Koreans are the master of their own destiny and would achieve reunification independent of foreign influence. However, looking beyond the rhetoric, there are some indications that both North and South Korea see international involvement critical in facilitating reunification when the time comes.

The emphasis on international involvement speaks directly to the controversial issue regarding the future of American military presence on the Korean peninsula. Presently, the United States may be the best suited to play the leading international role in the Korean peninsula's merger because: (1) 37,000 American soldiers are already stationed on the peninsula; (2) as the sole superpower, the United States is perhaps the only state that can provide the economic wherewithal and military power to serve this function; (3) as a democratic country, the United States can ensure that a liberal market democracy will develop in the newly reunified Korea. Both American and South Korean policy leaders including President Roh have expressed the importance of the continued presence of American troops during and even after the reunification of the two Koreas to serve as a "stabilizing force in the Northeast Asia region."[65]

International involvement in reunification may be critical given the current "unprepared" state of South Korea's liberal democracy and market economy to the coming challenges of reunification.[66] Although South Korea stands as one of the proud examples of democratic development in the East Asia region, it still falls short from being a consolidated democracy. Although many of the formal democratic institutions and procedures exist in South Korea, the underlying civil and political norms and values as well as informal institutions that buttress democratic systems remain underdeveloped.[67] If South Korea's current presidential impeachment crisis, regional cleavages, gridlock politics, party boss competition, and the general "confrontational" and "uncompromising" relationship between the main and oppositional parties are any indication of what the political environment may be in the future transition, outside assistance to facilitate the transition and to ensure participating groups committed to peaceful integration process may be imperative.[68] Moreover, the example of the Yemeni reunification based on a weak foundation of democratic institutions and the subsequent breakdown of this political integration effort a few years later illustrates the potential dangers that the two Koreas could face without outside support and a solid democratic infrastructure to mediate and sustain the state through the struggles of integration.[69]

Nevertheless, maintaining American involvement in the Korean peninsula may prove to be a challenge on both the domestic and regional fronts. Voices in the ROK and the United States calling for the immediate pullout of American troops from the Korean peninsula were a minority up to a few years ago, but recently, negative sentiments regarding American troops on Korean soil and the overbearing role of the United States in the U.S.–ROK security relations have touched a nerve in mainstream South Korea.[70] Many have attributed this growing resentment as a natural sentiment emerging from South Korea's growing sense of confidence as it grows in international prowess. Unfortunately, the intensity of these feelings have only been aggravated with increasing numbers of high-profile incidents, such as the death of two local teenagers after being struck by an American armored vehicle in a small rural Korean town; the 2002 Winter Olympic debacle where a South Korean skater was disqualified because of American skater Ohno; environmental abuses by U.S. Forces in Korea (USFK) bases. In addition, many South Koreans view the Americans' hard-line position toward North Korea, especially after President Bush's Axis of Evil speech, as a major obstacle to furthering South–North Korea relations and as the source of unnecessary instability on the peninsula that could ignite another Korean War.[71] The U.S.–ROK relationship still remains strong, but as inter-Korean relations improve, the perceived importance of U.S. troops may decrease, and the pressure on the ROK government to negotiate the permanent removal of troops from the peninsula will increase.[72]

In the United States as well, changes in North Korea would also make the withdrawal of U.S. forces a compelling issue. As Robert Manning and James Przystup point out: "In Washington, the end of North Korea will undermine the rationale for maintaining 37,000 troops in Korea. It will be an unenviable task for any administration official to explain to Congress why the US should continue subsidizing Korea's security…financial concerns and the lack of clear mission will lead, at a minimum, to major force reductions."[73] Already, plans for American troop reduction in South Korea have been made even though North Korea remains a significant threat. Recently, Lt. General Charles Campbell, commander of the U.S. Eighth Army, confirmed that the number of U.S. forces in Korea will be cut by an unspecified amount as part of efforts to relocate the 18,000 American troops deployed along and near the DMZ as well as to move the U.S. Forces Korea headquarters in Seoul to a central region in the ROK.[74] With the U.S. government's changing strategic priorities in light of the Global War on Terrorism and the conflicts in Afghanistan and Iraq, this force restructuring effort may mark the beginning of a gradual but growing momentum toward removing U.S. forces completely from the Korean peninsula.

On the regional front, policy leaders and scholars have widely recognized that the affairs of the Korean peninsula in general and reunification specifically are far too important to the security and stability of the region for the major powers to ignore or to remain as passive actors.[75] Although all regional powers have expressed the desire for peace and stability on the Korean peninsula, there is also a shared trepidation regarding a single power dominating over the affairs of the entire peninsula. China in particular would challenge any arrangement allowing the United States to dominate on the peninsula. The increasing role of the United States would signify the expansion of American hegemony, and seriously undermine China's leverage and influence regionally and globally, especially vis-à-vis the United States. Moreover, with the elimination of North Korea as a buffer zone, if the U.S. presence in Korea persists, it would put them on the Chinese border creating a serious security threat to the heartland of the PRC.[76] The alternative to the United States taking a leading role is a multilateral organization monitoring the affairs of the Korean peninsula. But, unlike the European continent, there is no NATO or EU equivalent in Northeast Asia to facilitate cooperation among states and deal with regional security and economic challenges. With the exception of the ASEAN Regional Forum, no current Asia Pacific organization has all four major powers as members to deal with region-wide issues. In the current regional order, bilateral relations are still the dominant form of interaction. Although the regional powers share common interests for peace on the Korean peninsula, the legacy of historical distrust, fundamentally different visions for the regional order and competing self-interests hinder close cooperation to support the reunification process.[77] Given these dynamics, not only will finding an international power to commit to the stability and security of the Korean peninsula present a challenge, but also having regional forces agree on the proper power to serve this role may be a serious issue as well.

Conclusion: Speculating about the Future?

Examining the Korean reunification question through the three-step sequential framework used by intra-state war analysts highlights three important points regarding what factors will compel Seoul and Pyongyang to achieve a negotiated political merger. First, negotiated reunification does not occur during periods of stability and prosperity, but rather during periods when both states are faced with crisis conditions that make the status quo division too costly to maintain. Both governments recognize the extreme economic costliness, the political perils of merging with their counterpart, and the wide disparity between the two political-economic systems. Thus, to give up their sovereignty and their autonomy to pursue a power-sharing arrangement that only assures years of political gridlock, infighting, and uncertainty would be irrational. In short, political actors seriously pursue a negotiated reunification not because they want to but because remaining as a divided nation no longer is a viable option.

Second, the divisibility of stakes is another important dimension in the pursuit of a political settlement. In reunification terms, this means that the power elites in both Seoul and Pyongyang must perceive that they can, at a minimum, survive in the new post-reunification political community. Without this expectation, any pressure that would make the status quo division unsustainable and force the governments to take action may lead to war rather than a peace process. Because engaging in a peace settlement does not provide a viable option, threatened elites in Pyongyang, for example, may choose armed violence as a survival strategy. But, in order for stakes to be divisible in this bargaining process to build a reunified political system, both the DPRK and the ROK must share a common political ideology and perception of what the "rules of the game" are. This means the DPRK must undergo some form of democratic change before reunification can take place.

Finally, participants in the peace process must perceive that the settlement will be enforced. In most cases, this constitutes the involvement of an international force to monitor and supervise the peace process once the two disputants agree on a plan for the new post-division order and are ready to implement it. State building is not a win–win situation for all involved members, but is frequently turbulent and faces constant danger of unraveling. Without credible outside support, the reunification of the two Koreas may collapse midstream, if begun at all, because of fears by political elites that the agreement will not be fully enforced.

Based on these three points and the perspective presented in this analysis, we can speculate about the possibilities of three future reunification scenarios: (1) negotiated reunification; (2) status quo division (a peaceful coexistence à la two Germanys in the 1980s before reunification in 1990); (3) reunification by force (Vietnam model).

Negotiated Reunification Versus Status Quo Division

Examining current conditions in and around the peninsula, it appears that the two Koreas will not be engaging in a negotiated reunification any time soon. A number of factors point to this conclusion. First, the two Koreas currently do not face any situational or structural pressures to reunify. It is true that the DPRK still stands on precarious economic ground, but at least, presently, no blatant signs point to an overwhelming crisis situation that would compel the two Koreas to take decisive action to change the status quo. Moreover, Seoul, Pyongyang, and the international community are aware of the immense costs and potential disruptions associated with reunification of the Korean peninsula. North Korea's position of weakness relative to South Korea instills fear in Pyongyang that reunifying now would be at the cost of their survival. Seoul and the neighboring powers, fearing the potential catastrophic consequence of allowing an autocratic DPRK armed with WMD including nuclear weapons and possessing a 1.2 million standing army to collapse, have funneled humanitarian aid and economic resources into the country to prop up the ailing regime, thereby staving off a situation where the status quo is unsustainable.

Second, both South and North Korea appear to have no interest in sacrificing its political system and adapting to the ideological order of its counterpart—consequently, making the idea of power sharing a virtually impossible task. In the DPRK, there are no signs of political reforms or democratization. There are no opposition forces within the government or society or other forms of pressure for such reforms. Such an endeavor is unlikely to be pursued by the current Pyongyang regime in the near future because allowing such internal division and opposition voice would be too destabilizing to the Kim Jong Il regime and would be equivalent to political suicide. Finally, even if conditions did exist for a negotiated reunification, the current regional environment is so divided regarding the future of the Korean peninsula that it is not clear whether any country would be able to step in to provide enforcement support without creating a region-wide disruption in the process. In sum, the situational pressures and the divisibility of stakes presently do not exist and the international factor is uncertain; thus, the probability of the status quo division of the Korean peninsula remaining into the immediate and medium-term future is quite high.

Reunification by Force

Of the three scenarios, reunification by force is perhaps the least desirable form. But, if the status quo division becomes unsustainable, war would be the more likely outcome than a negotiated reunification under current conditions. The irreconcilable difference between the two Koreas' political systems and the likelihood of a more powerful South Korea to dominate any peaceful reunification process would dispose strategic-minded and desperate Pyongyang to resort to taking military action against South Korea, Japan, or American troops located in these countries. With the overwhelming military dominance of the United States and South Korea, it is almost certain that any war with North Korea would be won, but such a triumphal reunification by force would only be a Pyrrhic victory. For example, with Seoul located less than 50 miles south of the DMZ and within range of North Korea's long-range artillery guns and missiles potentially armed with chemical, biological, and/or nuclear warheads, the city would most likely be devastated with its 12 million population during the first few days of a large-scale conflict.[78]

Unfortunately, events since the October 2002 revelation of North Korea's clandestine nuclear program suggests that we may be moving toward a situation where Pyongyang may perceive the status quo to be no longer sustainable. North Korea's move to reactivate its nuclear reactor frozen under the 1994 Agreed Framework, its claim of having nuclear weapons, and the intention to build more for its security and for export have created an extremely tense situation on the Korean peninsula.[79] In response, the United States has taken a firm position to penalize Pyongyang for its irresponsible behavior. Although the United States has not threatened to take military action or to oust the regime, Washington has not ruled it out as an option.[80] The Bush administration has taken action to slowly squeeze what little economic activity remains in the DPRK by (1) suspending oil shipments to North Korea promised under the Agreed Framework agreement, (2) actively lobbying regional countries including China to support economic sanctions against Pyongyang to halt its nuclear arms program, and (3) making plans to interdict any North Korean cargo ships suspected of carrying arms or illicit drugs.[81] The United States have further heightened the anxiety of the North Koreans by promising the already technologically advanced ROK military an additional $11 billion over the next three years to upgrade military intelligence, missile systems, and battlefield hardware.[82] With the recent U.S. actions against Iraq fresh in the minds of the North Korean leadership and with the country slowly deteriorating and being ostracized for its nuclear belligerence, Pyongyang may be put in a situation in which a preemptive military action may be its only viable option.

Viewing the Korean reunification question through civil war termination literature provides a sobering yet balanced account of the possible forces that may come into play in the highly political and difficult process of political integrating two competing states. The aim of this analysis has been to suggest a systematic way to study what different factors cause sovereign states to engage in reunification by linking insights derived from recent research on civil war termination. Although there is still much more work to be done to make Korean reunification research more rigorous, the objective of this analysis is to take the first step toward this end.

Notes

1. See e.g.: Ministry of Unification, Republic of Korea, *Sunshine Policy for Peace and Cooperation* (Seoul, Korea: Ministry of Unification, 2002); Soon-young Hong, "Thawing Korea's Cold War: The Path to Peace on the Korean Peninsula," *Foreign Affairs* 78: 3 (May/June 1999); Chung-in Moon, "Understanding the DJ Doctrine: The Sunshine Policy and the Korean Peninsula," in *Kim Dae-jung Government and Sunshine Policy: Promises and Challenges*, ed. Chung-in Moon and David Steinberg (Seoul, Korea: Yonsei University Press), pp. 35–56.; Ki-Jung Kim and Deok Ryong Yoon, "Beyond Mt. Kumkang: Social and Economic Implications," in *Kim Dae-jung Government and Sunshine Policy: Promises and Challenges*, ed. Chung-in Moon and Steinberg, pp. 105–134.
2. Lee Dong Bok, "Dealing with North Korea: Reality versus Fiction," *New Asia* 9:2 (Summer 2002): 23; Nicholas Eberstadt, "If North Korea Were really 'Reforming,' How Could We Tell—And What Would We Be Able to See?" *Korea and World Affairs* 26 (Spring 2002): 20–46; Chuck Downs, "Discerning North Korea's Intentions," in *Korea's Future and the Great Powers*, ed. Nicholas Eberstadt and Richard J. Ellings (Seattle: University of Washington Press, 2001), pp. 88–106.
3. For example, Aidan Foster-Carter argues in 1994 that the collapsist scenario was the most plausible end for North Korea because of its persistence to maintain its rigid political and economic system. He predicted that the North Korean regime will be overthrown. As in Germany, there will be "a strong demand for immediate integration. . . . Some version of the German scenario seems likely." Aidan Foster-Carter, "Korea: Sociopolitical Realities of Reuniting a Divided Nation," in *One Korea? Challenges and Prospects for Reunification*, ed. Thomas Henriksen and Kyongsoo Lho (Stanford: Hoover Institution Press, 1994), pp. 32–33; Nicholas Eberstadt, *The End of North Korea* (Washington, DC: AEI, 1999); Nicholas Eberstadt, "Hastening Korean Unification," *Foreign Affairs* 76: 2 (March/April 1997): 77–92.
4. See Nicholas Eberstadt, "North Korea's Unification Policy: 1948–1996," in *North Korean Foreign Relations in the Post-Cold War Era*, ed. Samuel Kim (Hong Kong: Oxford University Press, 1999).
5. Chaim Kaufman, "Intervention in Ethnic and Ideological Civil Wars: Why One Can't Be Done and The Other Can't," *Security Studies* 6: 1 (Autumn 1996): 65.
6. Barbara Walter, *Committing to Peace* (Princeton: Princeton University Press, 2002); Another author that uses this three phase process is: Fen Osler Hampson, *Nurturing Peace: Why Peace Settlements Succeed or Fail* (Washington, D.C.: US Institute of Peace Press, 1996).
7. There is some debate in the literature on which of these phases and what factors play a greater role in contributing to ending civil wars. Here, I offer a few of those positions in a coherent framework.

8. See Chaim Kaufman, "Intervention in Ethnic and Ideological Civil Wars: Why one Can't Be Done And The Other Can't," *Security Studies* 6:1 (Autum 1996) for insightful discussion on the difference between ethnic and ideological conflicts. See also Michael Brown, "The Causes of Internal Conflict: An Overview," in *Nationalism and Ethnic Conflict*, ed. Michael Brown and et al. (Cambridge: MIT Press, 1997).

9. Roy Licklider, "Obstacles to Peace Settlement," in *Turbulent Peace: The Challenges of Managing International Conflict*, ed. Chester A. Crocker (Washington, DC: US Institute of Peace, 2001): 697–718; Barbara Walter, "Critical Barrier to Civil War," *International Organization* 51: 3 (1997): 335–364.

10. See Nicholas Eberstadt, "North Korea's Unification Policy: 1948–1996," in *North Korean Foreign Relations in the Post-Cold War Era*, ed. Samuel Kim (Hong Kong: Oxford University Press, 1999).

11. For example, see: "Inter-Korean Ministerial Talks Pave for Improvement of Ties," *Yonhap News Agency*, April 3, 2003; "North Korean Party Organs Call for Patriotic National Cooperation with South," *Korean Central News Agency*, April 28, 2003; "North Korean Radio Urges National Cooperation Against US War Fever," *Pyongyang Broadcasting Station*, May 1, 2003; "North Korea Marks Anniversary of Joint Declaration with South," *Korean Central News Agency*, June 15, 2003.

12. See Ministry of Unification, *The Policy for Peace and Prosperity* (Seoul, Korea: Ministry of Unification, 2003); Ministry of Unification, *White Paper* (Seoul, Korea: Ministry of Unification, 2002). A copy of each of these booklets can be acquired at the ROK Ministry of Unification website: http://www.unikorea.go.kr

13. Cited in BBC Monitoring Asia Pacific Report, "North Korean Party Official Praises the Late Leader's Work on Reunification" [North Korea] *Central Broadcasting Station*, August 19, 2002.

14. David Mason and Patrick Fetts, "How Civil Wars End: A Rational Choice Approach," *Journal of Conflict Resolution* 40: 4 (December 1996): 22; Donald Wittman, "How Wars End: A Rational Choice Model," *Journal of Conflict Resolution* 23: 4 (1979).

15. William Zartman, ed., *Elusive Peace: Negotiating an End to Civil Wars* (Washington: Brookings Institution, 1995).

16. William Zartman, "The Unfinished Agenda," in *Stopping the Killing*, ed. Roy Licklider (New York: NYU Press, 1993), pp. 24–27.

17. Stephen Stedman writes that increasing the consequences and pain for continued conflict played a critical role in most of the civil war settlements in the 1980s and 1990s. With the exception of Cambodia, none of the negotiated civil war settlements were reached while a cease-fire was in place. In Angola, El Salvador, Mozambique, Nicaragua, and Zimbabwe, fighting continued while the parties negotiated. See Stephen Stedman, "Negotiations and Mediation in Internal Conflicts," in *The International Dimensions of Internal Conflict*, ed. Michael Brown (Cambridge, MA: MIT Press, 1996), pp. 351–356.

18. Soon-young Hong, "Thawing Korea's Cold War: The Path to Peace on the Korean Peninsula," in *Kim Dae-jung Government and Sunshine Policy: Promiss and Challenges* ed. Chung-in Moon and Steinberg, (Seoul, Korea: Yonsei University Press) p. 27; Hong Yung Lee, "Kim Dae Jung's Sunshine Policy and Breakthrough on the Korean Peninsula," in *Korea: Dynamics of Diplomacy and Unification*, ed. Byung Chul Koh (Claremont, CA: Keck Center for International and Strategic Studies, 2001), pp. 102–103.

19. President Roh Moo-Hyun recently stated at a seminar sponsored by the Heritage Foundation and the Korean Institute for Defense Analysis that he neither wanted "war nor the collapse of North Korea" but he added that "there are no alternatives than to reform and open up [North Korea]." "Roh Wants Neither War North Collapse of NK," *Chosun Ilbo*, February 21, 2003. For a good summary of President Dae Jung's North Korea and reunification policies, see Chung-Moon, "Understanding the DJ Doctrine: The Sunshine Policy and the Korean Peninsula," in *Kim Dae-jung Government and*

Sunshine Policy, ed. Chung-in Moon and David Steinberg (Seoul Korea: Yonsei University Press, 1999).

20. Chung-in Moon, "Understanding the DJ Doctrine: The Sunshine Policy and the Korean Peninsula," in *Kim Dal-jung Government and Sunshine Policy*, ed. Chung-in Moon and Steinberg pp. 45–46.

21. Soogil Young et al., "Preparing for the Economic Integration of Two Koreas: Policy Challenges to South Korea," in *Economic Integration of the Korean Peninsula*, ed. Marcus Noland (Washington: IIE, 1998), chap. 14.; Marcus Noland, "Economic Strategies for Reunification," in *Korea's Future and the Great Powers*, ed. Eberstadt and Ellings (Seattle: University of Washington Press, 2001) chap. 7.

22. "Not All for One; The South's Younger Generations are Indifferent or Even Hostile to the Notion of Reunification with the Impoverished North," *Los Angeles Times*, October 14, 2002.

23. Kim Dae Jung interview by *Cable News Network*, January 2, 2000. Cited in Harrison, 99.

24. Cited in Samuel Kim, "Surviving through High Hopes of Summit Diplomacy," *Asian Survey* 41: 1 (January/February 2001): 16.

25. International Institute for Strategic Studies, *The Military Balance 2001–2002* (London: Oxford University Press, 2001), p. 301.

26. Marcus Noland, *Avoiding the Apocalypse: The Future of the Two Koreas* (Washington: Institute for International Economics, 2000), pp. 71–72; Nicholas Eberstadt and Judith Bannister, "North Korea: A Statistical Glimpse into a Closed Society," *Journal of Korean Reunification* 2 (March 1993): 54; Selig Harrison, *The Korean Endgame* (Princeton: Princeton University Press, 2002):39.

27. Chung-in Moon and Yongho Kim, "The Future of the North Korean System," in *The North Korean System in the Post-Cold War Era*, ed. Samuel S. Kim (New York: Palgrave, 2001), chap. 10.

28. Economist Intelligence Unit, *Country Report: North Korea* 2002–2003, August 2002.

29. "Communist State Pushes Free Enterprise," *Los Angeles Times*, June 19, 2003.

30. Kang, Chol Hwan, "North Korea Undergoing Economic Reforms," *Chosun Ilbo*, July 25, 2002; Republic of Korea Ministry of Unification, "Changes in North Korea after Inter-Korean Summit," *North Korean Report*, August 14, 2001. Found in: www.unikorea.go.kr/eng/library/library2_view.php?db＋Tab_3&boardno.html. (accessed on July 6, 2002); Economist Intelligence Unit, "Is Change In the Air?" *EIU Viewswire*, August 6, 2002 (Accessed September 1, 2002).

31. Andrew Natsios, *The Great North Korean Famine* (Washington: United States Institute of Peace, 2001), pp. 227–231.

32. The flow of people from the East to the West was a common occurrence since the division of Germany, but with the rapid deterioration of the East European Communist government and the opening of the Berlin Wall, the numbers jumped to 343,854 in 1989. Within the first week after the opening of the Berlin Wall, according to one estimate, 4.3 million East Germans (one-fourth of the population) traveled to the West. With the borders open, Bonn feared if something was not done to address the economic problem in the East, then the West would be flooded with East Germans seeking a better life. See Albert Hirschman, "Exit, Voice and the Fate of the German Democratic Republic: An Essay in Conceptual History," *World Politics* 45: 2 (January 1993): 173–202.

33. Kristina Spohr, "German Unification: Between Official History, Academic Scholarship, and Political Memoirs," *The Historical Journal* 43: 3 (2000): 873–875.

34. Noland, *Avoiding the Apocalypse*, p. 189.

35. *Korea Times*, September 24, 2002; Hirschman, 176.

36. David Shambaugh, "China and the Korean Peninsula: Playing for the Long Term," *Washington Quarterly* 26: 2 (Spring 2003).

37. These official trade statistics do not fully capture the myriad of other ways that the PRC has involved itself in DPRK's "politics of survival." As Samuel Kim argues, through government humanitarian assistance, private barter transactions, unreported border trade between northeast China and North Korea, and other forms of economic activities provide additional flow of much-needed food, consumer goods, and hard currencies to the DPRK populace. Although the exact amount is uncertain, some analysts estimate that one-quarter to one-third of China's foreign assistance flow through the porous border shared by the two countries. See Samuel Kim, "China, Japan and Russia in Inter-Korean Relations" in *Korea Briefing 2000–2001*, eds. Kongdan Ho and Ralph Hassig (Armonk: M.E. Sharpe, 2002): p. 125.

38. Paul Pillar, *Negotiating Peace: War Termination as a Bargaining Process* (Princeton: Princeton University Press, 1983), p. 24.; See also Fred Ikle, *Every War Must End*, 2nd Ed. (New York: Columbia University, 1991), p. 95.; Harrison Wagner, "The Causes of Peace," in *Stopping the Killing: How Civil Wars End*, ed. Stephen Stedman (New York: New York University Press, 1993).

39. Walter, *Committing to Peace*, p. 27.

40. Licklider, pp. 706–709; According to many CM scholars, the most suited political system for post–civil war reconciliation is a democratic system. Although there is some debate regarding how soon after the peace settlement a democratic political system should be established and how the institutions should be structured (e.g., federalism vs. unitary government; parliamentarianism vs. presidentialism), most CM scholars agree that there is no viable alternative to democracy as "a system of just and stable conflict management."

41. See H.E. Goemens, *War and Punishment: The Causes of War Termination and the First World War* (Princeton: Princeton University Press, 2000).

42. Joseph Kostiner, *Yemen: The Tortuous Quest for Unity, 1990–1994* (London: The Royal Institute of International Affairs, 1996), pp. 22–27.

43. Philip Zelikow and Condoleeza Rice, *Germany Unified and Europe Transformed* (Cambridge: Cambridge University Press, 1995), pp. 199–205, 230–232.

44. Charles Armstrong, "'A Socialism of Our Style': North Korean Ideology in a Post-Communist Era," in *North Korean Foreign Relations in the Post-Cold War Era*, ed. Samuel Kim (Hong Kong: Oxford University Press, 1998), p. 46.

45. Dae-Sook Suh, "New Political Leadership," in *The North Korean System in the Post Cold War Era*, ed. Samuel Kim, p. 78–82.

46. Kyung-ae Park, "The Status of Civil Society in North Korea and Its Ramifications for Inter-Korean Integration," *Joint U.S.-Korea Academic Studies* 12 (2002): 207–210.

47. See Nicholas Eberstadt, *The End of North Korea* (Washington: AEI Press, 1999).

48. Goemens, chap.1.

49. See Victor Cha, "Hawk Engagement and Preventive Defense on the Korean Peninsula," *International Security* 27: 1 (June 2002).

50. Selig Harrison, 100.

51. Confederation as a feasible option has drawn some skepticism as well. Most recently, Kongdan Oh and Ralph Hassig ask the critical question that many analysts and policy-makers have failed to address: "President Kim's pursuit of reconciliation without reunification is promising in principle but problematic in practice: can the two Korean peoples live side by side in separate societies, the one capitalism democratic and the other communist authoritarian?" See Kongdan Oh and Ralph Hassig, "Introduction" in *Korea Briefing 2000–2001*, eds. Ralph Hassig and Kongdan Oh (Armonk: M.E. Sharpe, 2002): 5.

52. Recent discussions regarding the confederation option for the two Koreas envision that the issues delegated to the confederated government would begin with the management of nonintrusive issues such as foreign relations, postal service, and cultural affairs, while critical decisions would still be made by the member states. Laws are still made and enforced with approval of the regional governments. Selig Harrison, 76–101.; Chung-in Moon, "Sustaining Inter-Korean Reconciliation: North-South Korea Cooperation," in

The Challenges of Reconciliation and Reform in Korea (Washington: Korean Economic Institution of America, 2001), pp. 229–231.

53. Fredrick Lister, *The Later Security Confederations: The American, "New" Swiss, and German Unions* (Westport, Conn: Greenwood Press, 2001): chap.1.

54. Ibid., 2.

55. Ibid., chap. 1.

56. Kaufman, 65–67.; Timothy Sisk, "Democratization and Peacebuilding: Perils and Promise," in *Turbulent Peace: The Challenge of Managing International Conflict*, eds. Chester A. Crocker et al. (Washington: United States Institute of Peace, 2001): 786.

57. Juan Linz and Alfred Stepan, *Problems of Democratic Transitions and Consolidation* (Baltimore: Johns Hopkins University Press, 1996), pp. 79–81.

58. Adam Przeworski, *Democracy and the Market: Political and Economic Reforms in Eastern Europe and Latin America* (Cambridge: Cambridge University Press, 1991), p. 54, 55.

59. This point is illustrated by the different experience of the Netherlands and Germany during the economic turmoil of the interwar period. Despite the serious depression in the Netherlands, the democratic system did not collapse, while in Germany where conditions were slightly better, the democratic government collapsed in the face of political mobilization of the National Socialist Party. In both Germany and Austria, leftists and rightist parties were advocating an alternative system of rule. See Linz and Stepan, 80.

60. This is arguably what occurred in Yemen in 1994 when civil war broke out between the former northern Yemeni forces and members of the former southern Yemen state that sought to secede from the new union government. Although the unified Yemen was a unitary state and not a confederation, it illustrates the immense disruption and fallout that occurs when reunification fails.

61. Nicole Ball, "The Challenge of Rebuilding War Torn Societies," in Chester A. Crocker *Turbulent Peace: The Challenge of Managing International Conflict*, eds. Chester A. Crocker et al.: (Washington: United States Institute of Peace, 2001), pp. 608, 619.

62. According to Barbara Walter, these inherent uncertainties and dangers are particularly acute when groups must demobilize and disarm their separate militaries and surrender them to a central administration that is not necessarily under their control. The conundrum is that during periods when monitoring and verification is most needed (e.g., the demobilization of the military) against potential cheaters is when the participants are least capable to ensure that all the groups are adhering to the peace settlement and penalize those leaders who fail to meet obligations. Thus, if a deal spoiler decides to capture the new state, victims are vulnerable. See Walter, *Committing to Peace*, pp. 26–27.

63. Roy Licklider, "The Consequences of Negotiated Settlement in Civil Wars, 1945–1993," *American Political Science Review* 89 (1995): 686.

64. See Duane Bratt, " Explaining Peacekeeping Performance: The UN in Internal Conflicts," *International Peacekeeping* 4 (1997): 45–70.; Donald Rothschild and David A. Lake, "Containing Fear: The Management of Transnational Ethnic Conflict," in *The International Spread of Ethnic Conflict: Fear, Diffusion, and Escalation*, ed. David A. Lake and Donald Rothschild (Princeton, NJ: Princeton University Press, 1998): 203–226; Barbara Walter, *Committing to Peace: The Successful Settlement of Civil Wars* (Princeton, NJ: Princeton University Press, 2002).

65. "President Kim's Thanks the People in Farewell Speech," *Yonhap News Agency*, February 24, 2003; "ROK President-Elect No Stresses Need for USFK Presence in Korea During CFC Visit," *Yonhap News Agency*, January 15, 2003. What is most interesting but has recently left open to much skepticism are early Korean news reports of Pyongyang's alleged admission to the need for American military presence on the peninsula before the dramatic deterioration of U.S.–DPRK relations since the beginning of the Bush administration. Based on news reports regarding the conversations between the heads of states at the 2000 summit, Chairman Kim Jong Il agreed to President Kim Dae Jung's three-part view on the necessity of American forces to remain on the Korean peninsula: (1) a deterrent force

against war on the peninsula; (2) a strategic stabilizer in the region; (3) a peacekeeper even after reunification. Chairman Kim was even reported saying: "American forces can prevent you from invading the North," *Joongang Ilbo*, June 20, 2000. Cited in Chung-in Moon, "Sustaining Inter-Korean Reconciliation: North-South Korea Cooperation," *Joint U.S.-Korea Academic Studies* 12 (2002): 228.

66. Scott Snyder is correct in arguing that much will depend upon the strength of the ROK's political system to stabilize the turbulent and hazardous process of reunification: "South Korean social institutions, economic transparency and political commitment to democratic institutions must be strong enough to be the 'tugboat' that tows the North into the world by enabling the state to also accept greater transparency and political openness its own system; otherwise, the entire project of national integration and eventual reunification will be fated to crumble in failure on the rocks of bitter internal conflict, division, and virtually inevitable failure." See Scott Snyder, "The End of History, the Rise of Ideology and the Pursuit of Inter-Korean Reconciliation," in Kongdan Oh and Ralph C. Hassig, *Korea Briefing 2000–2001* (Armonk, NY: M.E. Sharpe, 2002): 12–13.

67. See Samuel Kim, *Korea's Democratization* (Cambridge: Cambridge University Press, 2003).

68. Sunhyuk Kim, "Party Politics in South Korea," in Chung-in Moon and David Steinberg, *Korea in Transition: Three Years Under the Kim Dae Jung Government* (Seoul: Yonsei University Press, 2002), pp. 58–62.

69. See Joseph Kostiner, *Yemen: The Tortuous Quest for Unity, 1990–1994* (London: The Royal Institute of International Affairs, 1996); Sheila Carapico, *Civil Society in Yemen* (Ithaca, NY: Cornell University Press, 2001).

70. A South Korean newspaper poll in February 2003 showed that 57% of South Koreans favored a reduction or total withdrawal of U.S. troops from South Korea. Cited in Larry Niksch, "Korea: U.S.-Korean Relations—Issues for Congress," *Issue Brief for Congress*, March 17, 2003, p. 14.

71. "Rising Anti-American Sentiment in Context of ROK's DPRK Policy, NGOs Role," *Joongang Ilbo*, June 7, 2002.

72. Seung Hwan Kim, "Anti-Americanism in Korea," *Washington Quarterly* 26: 1 (Winter 2002–03): 115–116.

73. Robert A. Manning and James J. Pryzystup, "Asia's Transition Diplomacy: Hedging Against Futureshock," *Survival* 41: 3 (Autumn 1999): 57.

74. "United States to Pull Back Frontline Troops is S. Korea," *Reuters*, June 5, 2003.

75. See Samuel Kim, "China, Japan and Russia in Inter-Korean Relations," in *Korea Briefing 2000–2001*, eds. Kongdan Oh and Hassig, pp. 108–149; Eberstadt and Ellings, eds., *Korea's Future and the Great Powers* (Seattle: University of Washington, 2001).

76. Samuel Kim, "The Making of China's Korea Policy in the Era of Reform," in *The Making of Chinese Foreign and Security Policy in the Era of Reform, 1978–2000* (Stanford: Stanford University Press, 2001), p. 401.

77. Samuel Kim, "China, Japan and Russia," 148.

78. Paul Chamberlin and Bill Taylor, "North Korea Wake-Up Call," *Washington Times*, July 22, 2003.

79. Larry Niksch, "North Korea's Nuclear Weapons Program," *CRS Issue Brief of Congress*, June 9, 2003, p. 2; "North Korea Deploys More Missiles," *Reuters*, July 19, 2003.

80. Thom Shanker and David Sanger, "North Korea Hides New Nuclear Site, Evidence Suggests," *New York Times*, July 19, 2003.

81. Larry Niksch, "North Korea's Nuclear Weapons Program," pp. 4–5; Barbara Slavin, "Eleven Nations Join Plan to Stop N. Korean Ships U.S. Hopes to Put Squeeze on Kim," *USA Today*, July 23, 2003.

82. Robert Manguard, "In Korea, A Quiet US Weapons Buildup," *Christian Science Monitor*, July 1, 2003.

Index

Abduction, 104–105
Afanasiev, Evgennii, 121
Afghanistan, 210
Agreed Framework (1994), 40, 45–46,
    49–50, 102, 104, 106, 124, 114, 143,
    144, 145, 160, 164, 166–168, 171,
    181, 182, 212
Agreement on Reconciliation,
    Non-aggression and Exchanges and
    Cooperation (1991) ("Basic
    Agreement"), 4, 10, 12, 24, 41, 68,
    101, 161, 162
Albright, Madeleine, 31
American Friends Service Committee
    (AFSC), 188
Amnesty International, 191
Angell, Norman, 59
Annan, Kofi, 171
Anti-Ballistic Missile (ABM) Treaty, 31, 133
ASEAN Plus Three (APT), 18
Asian Development Bank (ADB), 16,
    186–187
Asian Financial Crisis (AFC), 57, 65
ASEAN Regional Forum (ARF), 14, 18, 47,
    109–110, 115, 179–180, 210

Bargaining theory, 171, 198, 200, 211
Basic Agreement (1991) *see* Agreement on
    Reconciliation, Non-aggression,
    Exchanges and Cooperation
Berlin agreement (1999), 103
Berlin Declaration (2000), 71–72
Boehmer, Charles, 75
Bush Administration, 31, 85, 104–105, 109,
    125, 139, 146, 148–149, 182, 187,
    212; "axis-of-evil" speech, 31–32, 49,
    146–147, 148; *see also* United States

Carter, Jimmy, 44, 106, 181
Chang Myon, 43
China: xiv–xv, 2–4, 9, 13, 17, 43, 45, 48,
    59, 81–96, 116, 189, 203, 204, 210,
    212; alliance, 84–85; conflict
    management, 82–83; economic
    relations, 87–88; Korean War, 94;
    Kosovo crisis, 83; Nixon's visit to, 145;
    North Korean asylum seekers, 88–89;
    Korean unification, 90–92; ROK-PRC
    relations, 89, 163; Security Council
    membership, 183
Choi Sung Hong, 122
Chun Doo Hwan, 23, 44, 63, 141
Chung Ju Young, 25
Chung Se Hyon, 33
Citizen's Alliance for North Korean Human
    Rights (CANKHR), 191
Clinton Administration, 27, 31, 51, 103,
    109, 145, 167
Conflict management, 3, 6–9,
    62–63, 84
Comprehensive security, 175
Constructivism, 111, 115; *see also* national
    identity
Council for Security Cooperation in the
    Asia-Pacific (CSCAP), 180

Defensive realism, 98, 111, 113, 116
Demilitarized Zone (DMZ), 39
Democratic People's Republic of Korea
    (DPRK) *see* North Korea
Donor fatigue, 189
Doosung Industrial Company, 57

Eberstadt, Nicholas, 63
Eckstein, Harry, 73

Economic sanctions *see* Sanctions
European Union (EU), 74, 179

Fadeyev, Gennadyi, 129
Family reunions, 11, 40, 76, 159
Four Party Talks (1997–1999), 2, 18, 102, 163, 172, 189
Foreign direct investment, 167, 186, 187
Free Economic and Trade Zones (FETZ), 74, 185, 203
Funabashi Yoichi, 106
Functionalism, 60–62, 77–78

Gartzke, Erik, 75
German reunification, 1, 197, 203, 204, 205, 206
Globalization, 6
Gong Ro-myong, 144
Gorbachev, Mikhail, 24, 118–119, 122

Hallstein Doctrine, 43
Han Sung-joo, 144
Harrison, Selig, 56
Henderson, Gregory, 1
Highly enriched uranium (HEU) program, xv, 39, 106, 126
Hirschman, Albert, 60, 62
Hu Jintao, 81, 126
Hwang Jang Yop, 88
Hyundai, 26, 33, 40, 49, 57, 74, 76

Inter-Korean agreements, 69–71, 74
Inter-Korean investment, 72–76
Inter-Korean social and cultural exchanges, 76–77
Inter-Korean Summit (June 2000), xiii–xiv, 2, 4, 21, 28–31, 34, 42, 46–47, 65, 68–71, 139, 146, 147, 148, 161, 179, 200, 208
Inter-Korean trade, 57–58, 63–72
International Atomic Energy Agency (IAEA), 50, 114, 119, 165–166, 181–183
International Monetary Fund (IMF), 16, 186–187
International Organizations, 15–16, 18
Iraq War (March 2003), 152, 176, 183–184, 210, 212

"Iron Silk Road," 74, 86–88
Ivanov, Igor, 121, 126, 128

Japan: xiv–xv, 2, 4, 5, 13–14, 17, 39, 49, 59, 74, 97–116, 163, 170; abduction, 104–105; Agreed Framework, 104, 106, 114; KEDO, 109–110, 115; Koizumi-Kim summit, 110; Korean unification, 98, 100, 110–112; Obuchi Keizo, 103, 107–108; national identity, 111; Self-Defense Forces (SDFs), 107, 111, 114; Taepodong missile launch, 103, 107; TCOG, 102–105; threater missile defense (TMD) system, 107, 114; US–Japan alliance, 100, 105, 116; weapons of mass destruction (WMD), 9; Yasukuni Shrine, 108
Jiang Zemin, 81, 83, 85, 90, 126
Jo Myung Rok, 31, 51
Joint Communiqué (1972), 10, 41, 43–44, 68, 140, 141, 142, 161, 162
Joint Declaration of the Denuclearization of the Korean Peninsula, 4, 10–12, 45, 101, 161–162
Juche, 73, 178, 189, 197, 201 *see also* North Korea

Kaesong Industrial Complex (KIC), 11, 40, 50, 72, 74–75, 186, 203
Kangsong taeguk, 46
Kant, Immanuel, 59
Kelly, James, 50
Kim Dae Jung, xiii–xiv, 2, 5, 9, 21–33, 49, 53, 67–68, 71, 73, 103, 121, 124–125, 128, 146, 153, 171, 197, 201, 202; *see also* Sunshine Policy
Kim Hyun Hee, 1, 23
Kim Il Sung: 2, 47, 119, 122, 141, 144, 162, 181; death of, 12, 46, 168–169, 170
Kim Jong Il: xiii, 2, 10, 21, 30, 39, 44, 46–47, 49, 56, 104, 121–122, 127, 132, 197, 204, 205, 206; leadership of, 200
Kim Kyoung Won, 202
Kim Yong Nam, 83, 119
Kim Yong-sik, 141

Kim Young Sam, 2, 24, 120, 143, 144, 145, 168, 170

Kissinger, Henry, 43

Koizumi Junichiro, 39, 49, 104–105, 110

Korean Military Armistrice (1953), 84

Korean Peninsula Energy Development Organization (KEDO), 11, 13–14, 17–18, 66, 71, 83, 103, 109–110, 115, 124, 160, 163–165, 167–171, 179, 182; *see also* Light-water reactors

Korean People's Army (KPA), 91–92

Korean War (1950–1953): 1, 94, 98, 142, 146, 159, 177; armistice agreement, 4, 142, 159–160, 162, 165, 170; South Korean veterans, 149

Korean Workers' Party (KWP), xiii, 46

Korean unification, xv, 1–2, 23, 25, 29, 39–41, 43–45, 52, 62, 90–91, 110–112, 141–142, 148, 159, 198, 201, 202, 207, 211

Kunadze, Georgy, 132

Lee Hoi-chang, 28–29, 149

Legitimacy, 4, 9–10

Li Peng, 120

Li, Quan, 75

Light-water reactors (LWRs), 123, 167, 169, 170, 182

Lim Dong Won, 32, 49

Losyukov, Aleksandr, 117, 127

Mao Zedong, 82

Maretzki, Hans, 52, 56

Missile proliferation *see* Taepodong I missile

Mitrany, David, 60–62

Montesquieu, 59

Moscow declaration (2001), 121

Mt. Kumgang tourism, 11, 26–27, 40, 49, 66, 74, 76

Muddling through scenario, 202

Nakasone Yasuhiro, 113

National Defense Commission, 46

National identity, 7, 111; *see also* constructivism

National Security Law, 29

Nautilus Institute, 187

Naval clashes, 27, 33, 56

Nixon, Richard, 43

Noland, Marcus, 67, 72

Non-governmental organizations (NGOs), 16, 32

Non-Proliferation Treaty (NPT), 12, 122, 125–126, 160, 161, 165–167, 171, 177, 181, 182

Non-transactional trade, 11, 66–67

Nordpolitik, 9, 23, 119, 178

Northern Limit Line, 27, 172

North Korea: civil society, 206; collapse of, 2, 168, 186, 189; concentration camps, 191; constitution (1998), 73, 161; conventional military forces, 202, 211; democratic reform, 211; economic crisis, 179, 186; economic reform/openness policies, 10, 48, 73, 187; famine, 46, 186, 189, 191; food crisis, 179, 188–190; legitimacy, 39–41, 53; national identity, 49, 178; nuclear revelation (October 2002), xv, 182; nuclear weapons program, 143, 152, 160, 181, 186, 187, 211, 212; refugees, 189–192, 203, 204; terrorism, 44, 56; unification, 39–41, 43–45, 52; *see also* Juche

Obuchi Keizo, 103, 107–108

Offensive realism, 111

Oneal, John, 59

Paek Nam Sun, 110

Pak Hon-yong, 42

Pak Pong Ju, 66

Park Chung Hee, 15, 23, 43–44, 141, 142, 145

Perry, William, 27, 113

People's Republic of China (PRC) *see* China

Powell, Colin, 49

Pritchard, Jack L., 49

Processing-on-commission (POC) trade, 11, 65–66

Proliferation Security Initiative (PSI), 183

Pulikovskii, Konstantin, 122

Putin, Vladimir, 117, 121, 125, 127, 133

Rajin-Sonbong Free Economic and Trade Zone, 74, 185, 203; *see also* Free Economic and Trade Zones
Rangoon bombing, 44
Red Cross, 188
Rhee, Syngman, 15, 42, 54, 141, 142, 162
Roh Moo Hyun: 10, 15, 25, 33–35, 40, 50, 104–105, 125, 147–148, 151–154, 159, 197, 200, 208; election (December 2002), 140, 147, 152
Roh Tae Woo, 23, 57, 119, 144
Rumiantsev, Aleksandr, 127
Russett, Bruce, 59
Russia: xiv–xv, 2, 4, 11, 13–14, 17, 45, 74, 117–138, 163; arms sales, 125; as a mediator, 117–118; Korean unification, 120, 131–132; light-water reactors (LWRs), 123; non-proliferation treaty (NPT), 125–126; nuclear proliferation, 125–126; Russia–North Korean military relations, 125; Russian Far East, 126; sanctions, 123, 132; *see also* USSR

Samsung, 57
Sanctions, 132, 171, 181, 182
Seoul Olympic Games (1988), 1, 119, 178
Shevardnadze, Eduard, 119
Sinuiju Special Administrative Region (SAR), 10, 74, 87, 186
Six-Party Talks (August 2003), 163, 172, 175, 183, 184
South Korea: anti-Americanism, 144, 149; constitution, 154, 160; democratization, 142, 151, 152–153; economic growth of, 151; ideological cleavages, 21, 25–28, 32, 34; national identity, 22–25; North Korea's perception of, 22–25; perceptions of North Korean legitimacy, 23, 25, 29
South–North Joint Communique (1972)
South–North Joint Declaration (2000), 28, 42, 65, 68, 74
Soviet Union *see* USSR

Spanish embassy refugees, 191–192
State Failure Task Force, 180
Submarine incursions (1996), 12, 26, 159, 170, 172, 182
Sunshine Policy, 9, 18, 21, 28–34, 53, 67, 72–73, 147, 159; *see also* Kim Dae Jung

Taepodong-I missile lauch, 26, 57, 70, 103, 107, 171, 182, 206
Tang Jiaxuan, 83
Theatre missile defense (TMD) system, 107, 114
Three Party Talks (April 2003), 152, 163, 172
Trilateral Coordination and Oversight Group (TCOG), 14, 102–103, 105
Tumen River Area Development Programme (TRADP), 14, 87, 127, 129–130, 185

Unification *see* Korean unification
United States: xiv–xv, 2, 4–5, 13, 15, 17, 27, 54, 139–157, 162, 168, 171, 181, 183, 184, 208, 209; U.S.–DPRK bilateral talks, 143, 163, 164, 175; U.S. Forces Korea (USFK), 151, 209; U.S.–ROK alliance, 142, 144, 145
United Nations: 3, 9, 18, 98, 175–178, 185; command of Korean War forces, 142; General Assembly, 176, 177; membership in, 162, 175–6, 179; Security Council, 126, 177–178, 183; United Nations Children's Fund (UNICEF), 188; United Nations Conference on Trade and Development (UNCTAD), 185; United Nations Development Program (UNDP), 129–130, 185, 187; United Nations High Commission on Refugees (UNHCR), 189–192; United Nations Temporary Commission on Korea (UNTCOK), 177; World Food Programme (WFP), 188; World Health Organization (WHO), 176, 188
USS *Pueblo*, 43

USSR, 9, 98, 101; dissolution/collapse of, 1, 23; Security Council membership, 177, 183; *see also* Russia

Vietnam, 287

War on Terrorism, 210

Weapons of Mass Destruction (WMD), 99
World Bank, 16, 18, 186–187

Yang Bin, 48, 87
Yeltsen, Boris, 117, 120
Yemeni reunification, 205, 209